Florida Keys
& Key West

D0483365

Page 1: Pelicans on a dock in Islamorada

Page 2 (top left): Lighthouse in Key West; (top right): Street in Key West; (bottom): Fort Jefferson's arches leading to the ocean at Dry Tortugas National Park

Page 3 (top): A beach sunset in the Florida Keys; (bottom left): Coastal Fort Jefferson, Dry Tortugas National Park; (bottom right, upper): Crabcakes with smokey avocado corn relish served al fresco style on the Keys; (bottom right, lower): Hogfish on the Spiegel Grove in the waters off Key Largo

Page 4 (top): Mileage signpost in Key West; (bottom): Sunrise in Islamorada

INSIDERS' GUIDE® TO
FLORIDA KEYS & KEY WEST

HELP US KEEP THIS GUIDE UP TO DATE

We would love to hear from you concerning your experiences with this guide and how you feel it could be improved and kept up to date. Please send your comments and suggestions to:

editorial@GlobePequot.com

Thanks for your input, and happy travels!

INSIDERS' GUIDE® TO

FLORIDA KEYS & KEY WEST

SIXTEENTH EDITION

JULIET DYAL GRAY

INSIDERS' GUIDE

GUILFORD, CONNECTICUT
AN IMPRINT OF GLOBE PEQUOT PRESS

All the information in this guidebook is subject to change. We recommend that you call ahead to obtain current information before traveling.

INSIDERS' GUIDE ®

Editor: Kevin Sirois
Project Editors: Heather Santiago and Lauren Brancato
Layout: Joanna Beyer
Text Design: Sheryl Kober
Maps: Design Maps Inc. © Morris Book Publishing, LLC

ISSN 1529-174X
ISBN 978-0-7627-7320-6

Printed in the United States of America
10 9 8 7 6 5 4 3 2 1

CONTENTS

CONTENTS

Directory of Maps

ABOUT THE AUTHOR

Juliet Dyal Gray is a native Floridian who writes about the Florida Keys for many national publications including *Delta Sky* magazine. Her writing career has taken her on many journeys, including snorkeling around the islands of the Galapagos and on safari in South Africa. In addition to writing, Juliet produces and directs theater with the Performing Arts Project and the Red Barn Theatre in Key West. Juliet writes from her home in Key West, Florida.

ACKNOWLEDGMENTS

I am extremely grateful to the amazing people in the Florida Keys who tolerated and answered my many questions during the research of this book. My eternal thanks also to my family and close friends, including my parents, Jake and Kay Dyal, and my husband, Christian Gray, for all their support. I am especially grateful for the wisdom of the late Nancy Toppino, without whom this book would not have been possible. As I continue to live and work in the Florida Keys, I am also truly thankful to be a permanent *Insider* in paradise.

—JDG

Florida Keys

Upper Keys

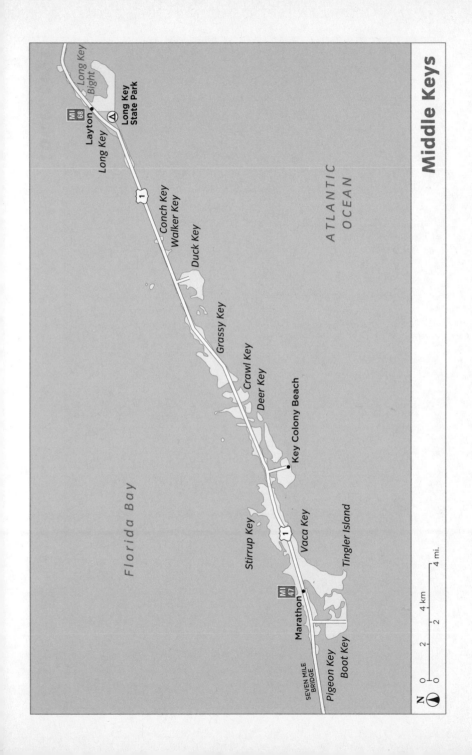

Middle Keys

Long Key Bight

Long Key

Layton

MI 68

Long Key State Park

1

Conch Key

Walker Key

Duck Key

Grassy Key

Crawl Key

Deer Key

Key Colony Beach

ATLANTIC OCEAN

Florida Bay

Stirrup Key

1

Vaca Key

Tingler Island

MI 47

Marathon

SEVEN MILE BRIDGE

Pigeon Key

Boot Key

N

0   2   4 km
0   2   4 mi.

Lower Keys

Key West

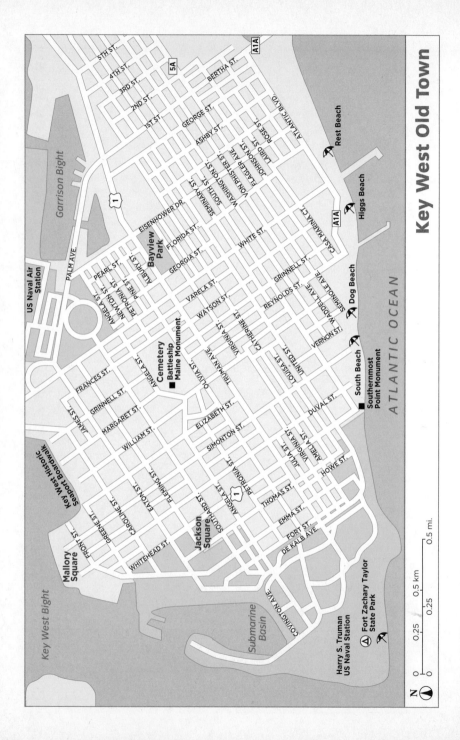

Key West Old Town

INTRODUCTION

Forget the black-and-white world you leave behind. When you arrive in the Florida Keys, life suddenly turns into Technicolor, and it doesn't take a twister to lead you to the lush Emerald City of Oz. Settle yourself in. Take Toto along, too.

Nowhere else on earth is there an Eden such as ours, where all are admitted freely and via so many varied means. Ours is the land of dreamers, doers, and do-si-doers, of train makers, treasure trovers, and time-honored tranquility. There are no Munchkins along the yellow brick road that unites each of our magical isles and then appends us to the mainland. In the Florida Keys everyone and everything is larger than life.

Look closely, and the enigmatic view from afar becomes as lucid as the crystalline waters of the Atlantic Ocean and the Gulf of Mexico that envelop us. From coconut palms to cormorants, you'll see that we are more than the Duval Street party scene in Key West. We are angelfish and anemones, gorgonians and groupers, lobsters and lizardfish, sponges and stone crabs. We're a thriving city of marine creatures commuting daily from North America's only barrier reef, approximately 6 miles offshore, to sweeping underwater meadows of turtle grass near shore where we forage and feed.

By day we are the golden sun that rises over the ocean, glows brightly, and then, in ardent shades of red, dips ever-so-gently beneath the gulf horizon. As darkness enfolds the Florida Keys, we are the cornucopia of stars that seem to gleam more brilliantly here in our endless skies than anywhere else.

We are a necklace of tiny pearl islands tenuously strung together by 42 majestic bridges and the dream of one man, Henry Morrison Flagler. We're divers and diesel mechanics, anglers and archaeologists, sailors and salvagers, cruisers and commercial fishermen, boaters and bartenders, gunkholers and guides, restaurateurs and real estate agents, hoteliers and hostesses. And our heart is in the sea.

We are hardwood hammocks, tropical pinelands, and mangrove islets. Unique in the universe, we are diminutive key deer, sour key limes, and endangered Key Largo wood rats. We are nesting great white herons, communal white pelicans, and showy roseate spoonbills. Creatures great and small, we are bonefish and billfish, sharks and stingrays, sea turtles, manatees, and dolphins. And because we vigilantly guard our copious treasures, we are the Florida Keys Wild Bird Center, Reef Relief, the Turtle Hospital, the Nature Conservancy, and the Reef Environmental Education Foundation. At last we have a brain.

Whether you mistakenly believe that you lack a heart . . . a brain . . . the nerve . . . you're sure to unearth it all, along with a deeply enriched spirit, on your journey through the mysteries, rich history, and legends of the Florida Keys. Experience all the marvels of this awe-inspiring Oz. You'll never want to click your ruby slippers, sandals, or bare feet—or board a plane, boat, or automobile—heading for home. One visit is, after all, what led so very many of us to become Insiders. Welcome to this side of the rainbow. We are the Florida Keys.

HOW TO USE THIS BOOK

Here at the southernmost tip of the continental US, the serpentine Overseas Highway fuses many of our 800-plus islands with ligaments of vaulted bridges and concrete connective tissue.

Ours is a marriage of land and sea. To merely introduce you to the topside society of the Florida Keys would neglect the flamboyant and fascinating communities living below. This guide lifts the curtain, bringing the many facets of our watery stage to life. We treat you to our unique geology and colorful history. We introduce you to the flora and fauna of the habitats of our tropical ecosystem. And we take you where you may have never been before—fishing, diving, and boating in our waters.

We'll help you sate your appetite with listings of restaurants, seafood markets, and specialty food shops. We'll show you where the action is with the rundown on attractions, recreation sites, festivals and special events, and nightlife of the Keys. We'll offer myriad alternatives for you to rest your weary head: hotels, motels, inns, guesthouses, and condos; campgrounds; even resort marinas and anchoring-out spots for your motor or sailing yacht. Landlubber or seafarer, everything you need to know is in the *Insiders' Guide to Florida Keys & Key West*.

To navigate this book, begin with the assumption you are traveling "down the Keys," that is, from Key Largo to Key West. We have organized our information alphabetically traveling down from the Upper Keys through to Key West. Most addresses are indicated by mile marker. Mile markers are those small green signs with white numbers you'll see posted at the sides of the Overseas Highway (US 1). We have designated mile-marker addresses as either oceanside (on your left as you travel down the Keys) or bayside (on your right as you go toward Key West). At Key West, which is MM 0, locations are stated using street names.

Most chapters have several parts. A general preface to the subject matter acquaints you with aspects of the topics common to all areas of the Florida Keys. This is followed by specifics for the Upper Keys (MM 106 on Key Largo to MM 70 on Long Key), Middle Keys (MM 70 to MM 39 on Ohio Key), Lower Keys (MM 39 to Stock Island), and finally Key West, the entrance to which is actually about MM 5 on Stock Island, although mile-marker appellations are not used in Key West.

Throughout all the chapters we have sprinkled **Insiders' Tips** (indicated by an **i**), extracted from those in the know (with a little arm-twisting). You'll find enlightening **Close-ups** chock-full of information on everything from where to find the best food festivals to details about our amazing and rich history. And just so you will be sure to understand the language, we have included a glossary of Keys-speak.

You'll also find listings accompanied by the ✳ symbol—these are our top picks for attractions, restaurants, accommodations, and everything in between that you shouldn't miss while you're in the area. You want the best this region has to offer? Go with our **Insiders' Choice.**

Moving to the Florida Keys or already live here? Be sure to check out the blue-tabbed pages at the back of the book, where you will find the **Living Here** appendix that offers sections on relocation, real estate, retirement, education, health care, and media.

You hold in your hand a passport to the Florida Keys. We help you hit the road, explore the sea, and speak the language of the natives. Locals call this Paradise. Judge for yourself.

HISTORY

The saga of the Keys, like the livelihoods of its inhabitants, tethers itself first, foremost, and forever to the sea. Our fragile strand of coral beads, which arcs southwest from the US mainland to within 100 miles of Cuba, has been for eons at the mercy of the elements. Nature determined, more than humans ever did, the course of our history. That is, until one man accomplished what natural forces could not: He connected the islands to each other and to the mainland US.

We will chronicle the Florida Keys, therefore, as a man-made triptych, highlighting the eras before, during, and after Henry Flagler's Florida East Coast Railroad Extension refashioned the subsequent history of the region.

PROLOGUE

Native Americans & the Spanish

The earliest recorded evidence of a Native American population in the Keys is estimated to be around AD 800, when maritime Indians populated the islands. Archaeologists believe that although ancient villages may have existed thousands of years before this time, the rising sea level has buried these settlements beneath the ocean.

Historians cannot agree on which tribes of Native Americans inhabited the Florida Keys in the ensuing centuries. The Tequestas, Calusas, Matecumbes, Caribbean Island tribes, and Seminoles from the mainland are all mentioned, although no archaeological evidence is conclusive. Widely accepted, however, is the notion that the Native Americans were seafarers by necessity and initially friendly to the white explorers they encountered.

Ponce de León garnered the credit for naming the Florida Keys "Los Martires" in 1513 during his exploration of the Gulf of Mexico. Legend maintains that the string of rock islands looked to him like suffering martyrs from his vantage point at sea. The Spanish took interest in the Native Americans of Los Martires in the centuries that followed but had no desire to seize their rocky islands. Priests from Havana attempted to convert the Native Americans to Catholicism. Some say this was an attempt not to save their souls but to teach them to be friendly to the crews of the Spanish ships and to hate the French and English, Spain's enemies who also were attempting to explore the New World. Spain's overriding interest in the Florida Keys at this time simply was to protect their fleet of treasure ships voyaging past its shores en route from Mexico and Cuba to the mother country.

The Gulf Stream: Treasure Highway

Long before the Overseas Highway became the main road of the Florida Keys, another highway controlled the islands' destiny: the great, blue river-in-the-Atlantic—the Gulf Stream. (The warm water of the Gulf Stream, the temperature of which varies greatly from surrounding waters, flows in a northerly direction between the Keys and Cuba, up the northeast coast of the US, and then turns toward the east where it crosses the Atlantic Ocean to the European continent.) Conquistadores, explorers, and adventurers capitalized on the pulsing clockwise current (2 to 4 knots) to carry them swiftly back to Europe, where they unloaded the harvested riches of the New World at the feet of greedy monarchs.

The Spanish were the first to send their treasure-laden ships on this precarious route past our island chain, which is protected from the ocean's fury by a barrier coral reef (see the Diving & Snorkeling chapter). The Gulf Stream, which is not a definitive channel, winds an uneven course about 45 miles wide just outside the reef. Bad weather or bad judgment dashed the hopes, dreams, and cargo of hundreds of ships against this unforgiving coral graveyard.

It was the Native Americans who initially took advantage of this unexpected shipwrecked bounty, but salvaging became big business in the Keys with the arrival of the Bahamian Conchs. The passing ships inspired piracy from many nations, particularly the English, who lurked in the cuts and channels between the islands waiting to raid the ships' caches of gold and silver.

The Native Americans learned the ways of the Europeans, trading with the Spanish in Havana by means of large ocean-going canoes, pirating English ships, and free-diving to salvage the cargo of their wrecked vessels. The white man's diseases, however, greatly reduced Native American numbers. In 1763 Spain gave Florida to England in exchange for Cuba. At this time the last of the indigenous Native American families fled to Havana, fearing retribution for the cruelty they had heaped upon the British sailors found dashed upon the reef and stranded.

Key West

A time-honored story persists that warring tribes of mainland Seminoles and island Calusas had one final battle on the southernmost island of our chain of keys. Spanish conquistadores purportedly found the island strewn with bleached bones of the Native Americans and called the key Cayo Hueso (pronounced KY-o WAY-so), or "island of bones." Bahamian settlers pronounced the Spanish name as Key West.

Settled long before the other keys in the chain, Key West was very much a maritime frontier town by the 1820s, booming with sea-driven industries. Ships sailing out of Key West Harbor set across the Florida Straits to Havana, their holds filled with the fish, sea turtles, and sponges harvested along the length of the Keys. A lively fishing trade with Cuba continued into the 1870s. The melting pot of Key West included seamen from many cultures: African-American Bahamians, West Indian African Americans, Spanish Cubans, and white Bahamians of English descent.

Key West was incorporated in 1828. Within 10 years it was the largest and wealthiest city in the territory of Florida, even though it could be reached only by ship, a geographic fact of life that continued until Henry Flagler's Florida East Coast Railroad Extension was finished in 1912. But it was the very waters isolating Key West from the rest of the world that contributed to its wealth.

Piracy

When the US gained possession of Florida and the Florida Keys in 1821, the island of Key West took on a strategic importance as a US naval base. Lieutenant Matthew Perry, who was assigned to secure the island for the US, deemed Key West a safe, convenient, and extensive harbor. It became the base of operations to fight the piracy that ravaged the trading vessels traveling the Gulf Stream superhighway and those heading through the Gulf of Mexico to New Orleans. English, French, and Dutch buccaneers had threatened the Spanish treasure galleons in the 18th century. In the early days of the 1800s, Spanish pirates, based mainly in Cuba, hid among the islands of the Keys and preyed on all nations, especially the US. Using schooners with centerboards that drew only 4 to 5 feet of water, the pirate ships dipped in and out of the shallow cuts and channels to avoid capture.

i In 1898 the battleship USS *Maine* sailed from Key West Harbor to Havana Harbor in Cuba, where the ship exploded and sank. The ship's gun sight hood is located at the Florida Keys Historical Military Memorial at Mallory Square in Key West. Crewmen from the disaster are buried in the Key West Cemetery, and the investigation took place in the Key West Custom House.

In 1830 Commander David Porter was sent to Key West to head up an antipiracy fleet and wipe out the sea jacking from the region. Commandeering barge-style vessels equipped with oars, Porter and his crews

were able to follow the sea dogs into the shallow waters and overtake them. After 1830 the area was safe from banditry once again.

The Wrecking Industry

Whereas the Gulf Stream was once the sea highway carrying Spanish treasure galleons back to Europe, in the 18th and 19th centuries the route was traversed in the opposite direction. Trading vessels sailed from New England ports to the French and British islands of the West Indies and the Antilles, hugging the shoreward edge of the Gulf Stream so as not to have to run against its strong northerly currents. They often ran aground on the reef, giving birth to a lucrative wrecking industry that salvaged silks, satins, lace, leather, crystal, china, silver, furniture, wine, whiskey, and more.

After the US took possession of Florida in 1821, Key West became an official wrecking and salvage station for the federal government, which sought to regulate and cash in on the lucrative trade that until this time was going to Nassau or Havana. Salvage masters had to get a license from a district court judge, proving that they and their salvage vessels were free of fraud. By 1854 wrecking was a widely practiced profession in the Keys. Fleets of schooners patrolled the Keys from Biscayne to the Dry Tortugas. First they would assist the shipwrecked sailors, then try to save the ship (there was no Coast Guard in those days).

Unlike early unregulated times, the wreckers couldn't just lay claim to the ship's cargo for themselves. They were paid off in shares of the bounty. During peak wrecking years, 1850 to 1860, nearly one ship per week hit the reefs, some with cargo valued in the millions of dollars.

Although by 1826 some of the reefs along the length of the Keys were marked by lighthouses or lightships, most remained treacherous and claimed many cargoes, particularly in the Upper Keys where the Gulf Stream meanders close to the reef. Stories have endured throughout the years that some of the more enterprising and unscrupulous wreckers even changed or removed navigational markers or flashed lights in imitation of a lightship to lure an unsuspecting vessel to its demise on a shallow shoal so they could salvage the cargo. The construction of additional lighthouses along the reef in the mid-1800s improved navigation to the point that the wrecking industry gradually faded away by the end of the 19th century.

Sponging

Sponging developed quickly in the Keys after the area became part of the US, maturing into a commercially important industry by 1850.

Sponge harvesting initially was accomplished from a dinghy: One man sculled while the other looked through a glass-bottomed bucket. The spotter held a long pole with a small, three-pronged rake on one end used to impale the sponge and bring it into the boat. On shore the sponges were laid on the ground to dry in the sun so that the living animal within would dehydrate and die. The sponges then were soaked for a week and pounded on a rock or beaten with a stick to remove a blackish covering. Cleaned of weeds, washed, and hung to dry in bunches, the sponges were displayed for sale.

Cubans, Greeks, and Conchs harvested the sponges as fast and furiously as they could, with little regard for how the supply would be maintained, and it inevitably

began to diminish. The Greeks began diving into deeper waters for the sponges, much in demand on the world market by 1900, and eventually moved to Florida's west coast at Tarpon Springs, where the sponging was more bountiful.

By 1940 a blight had wiped out all but about 10 percent of the Keys' sponge population. Although sponges again grow in our waters, commercial sponging is no longer a viable industry as synthetic sponges have absorbed the market.

i The colorful history of the Flórida Keys comes alive at palmm.fcla .edu/mile/about.shtml in a marvelous virtual road trip. Learn about the people, places, and history of the Keys through photos and postcards. This fascinating presentation of history and legend comes courtesy of the Monroe County Public Library, Florida International University, the Florida Center for Library Automation, and the Historic Florida Keys Foundation.

Cubans & the Cigar Industry

Cuba, closer to Key West than Miami is, has always played a role in the historical evolution of the Keys. Cuban fishermen long frequented the bountiful Keys waters, and in the 19th century Cuban émigrés brought new life and new industry to Key West. William H. Wall built a small cigar factory in the 1830s on Key West's Front Street, but it was not until a year after the Cuban Revolution of 1868, when a prominent Cuban by the name of Señor Vicente Martínez Ybor moved his cigar-making factory to Key West from Havana, that the new era of cigar manufacturing began in earnest.

E. H. Gato and a dozen or so other cigar-making companies followed Martínez Ybor, and an influx of Cuban immigrant cigar workers "washed ashore," joining the melting pot in Key West. Tobacco arrived in bales from Havana, and production grew until factories numbered 161, catapulting Key West to the rank of cigar-making capital of the US. Though the manufacturers moved their businesses to Key West to escape Cuban tariffs and the cigar-makers' union, the unions reestablished themselves in Key West by 1879, and troubles began anew.

The industry continued to flourish in Key West until its peak in 1890, when the city of Tampa offered the cigar manufacturers lower taxes if they would move to the Gulf Coast swamplands, an area now called Ybor City. With this incentive, the cigar-making industry left the Keys, but many of the Cuban people stayed, creating a steady Latin influence on Key West that has endured to this day.

The Salt Industry

Early settlers of Key West and Duck Key manufactured sea salt beginning in the 1830s, using natural salt-pond basins on both islands. Salt was essential for preserving food in those days because there was no refrigeration. Cut off from tidal circulation except during storms, the salt ponds were flooded with seawater and then allowed to evaporate. The resulting salt crystals were harvested.

Capricious weather often flooded the salt ponds with freshwater, ruining the salty "crop." By 1876 the salt industry no longer existed in the Keys. The destructive forces of repeated hurricanes made the industry economically unfeasible.

Homesteading the Keys

Bahamians also homesteaded in the keys in the early 19th century, settling in small family groups to farm the thin soil. Familiar with cultivating the unique land of limestone islands, the Bahamians worked at farming pineapples, key limes, and sapodillas, called "sours and dillies."

Many believe Indian Key was the first real settlement in the Upper Keys. By 1834 it had docks, a post office, shops, and a mansion belonging to the island's owner, Jacob Housman. It became the governmental seat of Dade County for a time, but attacks from mainland Native Americans proved an insurmountable problem for this little key. Through the ensuing decades, Bahamian farmers homesteaded on Key Vaca, Upper Matecumbe, Newport (Key Largo), Tavernier, and Planter. By 1891 the area that is now Harry Harris Park in Key Largo had a post office, school, church, and five farms (see the Recreation chapter).

The census on any of these keys varied widely over the course of the century, and little is known as to why. For instance, Key Vaca had 200 settlers in 1840, according to Dr. Perrine of Indian Key, but by 1866 a US census revealed an unexplained population of zero for Key Vaca.

> **i** Key West was once the largest manufacturer of cigars in the US. In 1915 Key West had 29 cigar factories, employing 2,100 workers, who hand-rolled 62,415,000 stogies from imported Cuban tobacco.

FLAGLER'S FOLLY: THE FLORIDA EAST COAST RAILROAD EXTENSION

The dream of one man changed the isolation of the Florida Keys for all time. Native New Yorker Henry Flagler, born in 1830 and educated only to the eighth grade, established the Standard Oil Company with John D. Rockefeller in 1870 and became a wealthy, well-respected businessman. In 1885 he purchased a short-line railroad between Jacksonville and St. Augustine and began extending the rails southward toward Miami, then only a small settlement.

Flagler's vision of his railroad project went beyond Miami, however. He wanted to connect the mainland with the deep port of Key West, a booming city of more than 10,000 people, in anticipation of the growing shipping commerce he thought would be generated by the opening of the Panama Canal in the early years of the 20th century. He may even have set his sights on eventually connecting Key West with Cuba.

i In 1885 a trolley line, the Key West Street Car Association, was established in Key West. The open-sided wooden cars had four benches and were pulled by two mules. In 1898 the Key West Electric Company bought the line and ran 10-bench cars that operated on existing broad-gauge tracks using power from a double-wired overhead system.

By 1904 the railroad extended to Homestead, at the gateway to the Keys. The year 1905 saw the commencement of what many perceived as an old man's folly: a railroad constructed across 128 miles of rock islands and open water, under the most nonidyllic conditions imaginable, by men and materials that had to be imported from throughout the world. Steamships brought fabricated steel from Pennsylvania, and cement from Germany and Belgium was used to create concrete supports below the waterline. Cement for above-water concrete came from New York State, sand and gravel from the Chesapeake, crushed rock from the Hudson Valley, timbers and pilings from Florida and Georgia, and provisions from Chicago. Barges carried freshwater from Miami to the construction sites. Nothing was indigenous to the Keys except the mosquitoes and the sand flies.

By 1908 the first segment, from Homestead to Marathon, was completed, and Marathon became a boomtown. Ships brought their cargoes of Cuban pineapples and limes here, where they were loaded onto railway cars and sent north. (The railroad turnaround was at the current site of Knight's Key campground.) Railroad workers used Pigeon Key as a base for further railway construction.

The 7-mile "water gap" between Marathon and Bahia Honda took some engineering prowess to overcome, and the completion of the project was severely hampered by several devastating hurricanes in 1909 and 1910. But on January 22, 1912, Henry Flagler—by then age 82—finally rode his dream from Homestead to Key West. He traveled across 42 stretches of sea, more than 17 miles of concrete viaducts and concrete-and-steel bridges, and more than 20 miles of filled causeways, ultimately traversing 128 miles from island to island to the fruition of his vision. He entered Key West that day a hero. He died the following year, probably never knowing that his flight of fancy changed the course of the Florida Keys forever.

Flagler's railroad, called the Key West Extension, made Key West America's largest deepwater port on the Atlantic Coast south of Norfolk, Virginia. Trade with the Caribbean increased, and Key West flourished for 23 years, recovering from the loss of the sponge and cigar industries. The Florida East Coast Railroad Company completed construction of Key West's first official tourist hotel, the Casa Marina, in 1921. La Concha was built in 1928.

In 1923 Monroe County appropriated funds to construct a road paralleling the railroad. The bumpy rock road crossed Card Sound with a long area of fill and a wooden bridge. A half-dozen humpback bridges crossed the creeks and cuts on Key Largo. Extending the length of Key Largo, the road continued across Plantation Key, Windley Key, and Upper Matecumbe. At the southern end of our island chain, a narrow, 32-mile road connected Key West with No Name Key off Big Pine Key. By 1930 a car ferry service provided the waterway link between the two sections of roadway, which traversed what we now call the Upper and Lower Keys.

By 1934 the failing economy prompted the Federal Emergency Relief Administration to step in, and it commenced development and promotion of Key West as a magnet for increased tourism in the Keys.

To that end, developers began building bridges to connect the Middle Keys to each other and to the two sections of finished roadway. A "bonus army" of World War I veterans was employed to accomplish this momentous task. However, in 1935 Mother Nature reasserted her authority and once again charted the destiny of our islands. On Labor Day what today we would call a Category Five hurricane hit the Upper and Middle Keys, destroying much of Flagler's

railroad. Hundreds of lives were lost when the 17-foot storm surge hit the crew working on a bridge at Islamorada.

Because of mismanagement and lack of foreign freight heading northward from Cuban and Caribbean ports, the railroad was already in receivership. The railroad chose not to rebuild, citing financial difficulties. By this time it had become cheaper to haul cargo by truck than by train. The county's Overseas Road and Toll Commission purchased the right-of-way from the Florida East Coast Railroad and converted the single-track railway trestles, which remained intact after the hurricane, into two-lane bridges for automobiles. The highway from Homestead to Key West opened for traffic in 1938.

The 100th anniversary of Henry Flagler's railroad was celebrated in 2012. The website flaglerkeys100.com offers a historical time line, photos, and videos about the ill-fated Florida Keys Over-Sea Railroad.

Missiles of Key West

It was in 1962, in the salt ponds near the Key West International Airport, the Casa Marina Hotel, White Street Pier, and Smathers Beach, that the US Army poised Hawk missiles 6 inches above sea level. They were aimed at Cuba following the threat of nuclear war with Russia. Once the threat was removed from Cuba, the sites were abandoned in 1979. Traces of old bunkers, buildings, and towers still exist. Go to missilesofkeywest .com for more on this scary event in recent American history.

EPILOGUE

In the late 1930s the US Navy, stationed in Key West, began construction of an 18-inch pipeline that carried freshwater from wells in Homestead to Key West. The naval presence in Key West grew with the beginning of World War II, when antisubmarine patrols began surveillance of surrounding waters. The navy also improved the highway to better accommodate the transfer of supplies for its military installation. The Card Sound Road was bypassed. The new road, which followed the old railroad bed, now is known as the "Stretch." By 1942 the Keys enjoyed freshwater and electricity service, and the Overseas Highway (US 1) officially opened in 1944, ushering in a new era of development that continues to this day.

After World War II the Florida Keys became more and more popular as a sportfishing destination, and fishing camps dotted the shores from the Upper Keys to Key West. Still a rather remote, primitive spot to visit, the Keys nevertheless continued to evolve into a desirable tourist terminus, and Key West burgeoned as a port of call. Also contributing to Key West's rebirth was the discovery of pink gold: shrimp. Fishermen who had caught a shark in the waters between Key West and the Dry Tortugas found the fish's stomach filled with large pink shrimp. This led to the discovery of a bountiful shrimping area off the Tortugas, and the Key West "pinks" shrimping industry was spawned in the Florida Keys. It is still a viable occupation as far up the Keys as Marathon.

From 1978 to 1983 the old rail-bed conversion bridges were retired. Modern concrete structures, some four lanes wide, now span our waters. Most mind-boggling as an engineering feat is the seemingly endless Seven Mile Bridge, which connects the once insurmountable watery gap between Marathon and Bahia Honda Key. Many of the old bridges have been recycled as fishing piers, but others still stand, abandoned and obsolete alongside their successors, crumbling reminders of the Keys' not-so-distant past.

By the 1980s the Florida Keys had emerged as a tourist-driven economy. Tourism remains the major industry of the Keys today, with the water-based attractions of Key West topping the list of popular agendas.

Of growing concern is the effect the influx of visitors will ultimately have on the delicate balance of habitats within the tropical ecosystem of the Florida Keys (see the Area Overview chapter). The jury is still out. Will humans or Mother Nature determine the postscript for Paradise?

AREA OVERVIEW

Make no mistake, the sea is in charge here and always has been. Throughout the ages the fluctuation of the sea has determined the fate of the coral islands we call the Florida Keys and will dictate its future as well. Put into simple perspective, sea level has been rising for the past 15,000 years, and the rate appears to be increasing due to the long-range effects of global warming. Just imagine: A 6-foot rise in sea level would eliminate all of the Lower and Middle Keys except Key West. The Upper Keys, being somewhat higher, would escape extinction for a time. But if sea level increases by 15 feet, the string of islands known as the Florida Keys will be reduced to a couple of tiny islets, and the majority of Paradise will be lost once again to the sea.

To be in the Florida Keys is to become one with nature, for the Keys offer unparalleled opportunities to be in direct daily contact with her substantial bounty. You'll know what we mean the moment you crest the first of the 42 bridges now spanning our islands and feel the vast power of the surrounding seas. Gaze down on our string of coral pearls from the air and you'll see that the Keys look insignificant juxtaposed against the encompassing Atlantic Ocean and Gulf of Mexico.

Insiders' Guides to other locales will introduce you to the lay of the land. But to gain an understanding of our world, which we reverently refer to as "Paradise," you must be forearmed with the scope of our waters, for all things revolve around the sea here. We will acquaint you with our climate, weather, and the multiple interrelated habitats of our tropical ecosystem—the only such ecosystem in the continental US.

HABITATS OF THE FLORIDA KEYS

The word *tropical* generally refers to plants and animals living in the latitudes between the Tropic of Cancer in the Northern Hemisphere and the Tropic of Capricorn in the Southern Hemisphere. The Florida Keys are somewhat north of the Tropic of Cancer, but the warming influence of the nearby Gulf Stream assures us the benefits of a tropical climate.

Our natural flora grows nowhere else in North America, and the combination of our eight interrelated habitats and the creatures dwelling therein is truly unique.

The Land

Hardwood Hammocks
When the coral reef emerged from the sea eons ago and calcified into limestone bedrock, floating debris accumulated on it, decomposed, and gradually evolved into a thin layer of soil. Seeds from the hardwood

forests of the Yucatan, Honduras, Nicaragua, South America, and the Caribbean Islands were carried to the Florida Keys by the winds of hurricanes, the currents of the Gulf Stream, migrating birds, and eventually even humans. Thus, the vegetation of the Florida Keys is more common to the tropical Caribbean Basin than to the adjoining temperate areas of mainland Florida.

Found throughout the Keys, these West Indian tropical hardwood hammocks nurture highly diverse communities of rare flora and fauna—more than 200 species—some found nowhere else in the US. The hammocks (originally an Indian word meaning "shady place") also shelter a variety of endangered species.

Most of the hardwood hammocks of the Keys were cleared years ago to supply the wood for shipbuilding and home building and to clear the land for planting pineapples or citrus as a commercial venture. But several good examples of West Indian hardwood hammocks still flourish in the Keys. The largest contiguous hammock in the continental US is on North Key Largo. Known as the Key Largo Hammock State Botanical Site, it encompasses 2,700 acres. A dense understory of plants, shrubs, and vines adapts to the shady conditions on the hammock floor. Wildflowers must reach for the sky under the shady foliage top hat of the hammock, often turning into creeping vines.

The Key Largo wood rat, an endangered species that looks more like a big-eared Disney mouse than a London sewer rat, joins the key raccoon, the Key Largo cotton mouse, opossums, gray squirrels, and an assortment of migratory birds amid the flora of the hammocks. The 16-inch-long rodent, found only in the hammocks of North Key Largo, has been dubbed a "pack rat" because

it likes to collect empty shells, aluminum pop-top tabs, and the colorful rings from plastic milk bottles.

i With 42 bridges connecting the Florida Keys, 15 percent of travel time is spent on bridges. The longest bridge is Seven Mile Bridge and the shortest is Harris Gap Bridge, a mere 37 feet long.

The Pinelands
Pinelands in the Lower Florida Keys differ from the vast forests you may have seen in other areas of the US. Adapting to growing conditions with limited freshwater, the tall, spindly trees are small in girth and sparsely foliated. Primarily found on Big Pine Key, these South Florida slash pines mingle with an understory of silver palms and brittle thatch palms, both of which are rare outside the Keys and protected under the Preservation of the Native Flora of Florida Act. Among the 7,500 protected acres in the Lower Keys, other pinelands grace No Name Key, Little Pine Key, Cudjoe Key, Sugarloaf Key, and Summerland Key.

The most famous pineland resident in the Lower Keys is undoubtedly the key deer, a subspecies of the Virginia white-tailed deer, found nowhere else in the world. These tiny deer, each about the size of a large dog, attempt to coexist with human inhabitants who have taken over much of the unpreserved woodlands of the Lower Keys. However, the diminutive animals frequently venture out of the woods and onto the Overseas Highway, where they are often struck and killed by vehicles. For that reason, speed limits through Big Pine Key are reduced (45 mph daylight, 35 mph nighttime) and strictly enforced by law enforcement officials.

In 1957 the National Key Deer Refuge was established in Big Pine Key to ensure a sheltered natural habitat for the endangered species. About 800 key deer exist in the Lower Keys today. The key deer feed on red and black mangroves, thatch palms, and a variety of native berries. While they can tolerate small quantities of salt in brackish water, freshwater is essential to their survival. No official records document the origin of the key deer in the Florida Keys, but it is widely believed they migrated from the mainland as white-tailed deer when the seas receded. When sea level rose again during the current interglacial epoch, the deer were trapped in their pineland habitat. Over time their diminutive stature evolved as an adaptation to their sparsely vegetated environment.

The Shoreline

Mangrove Habitats

Called the island builders, mangroves comprise the predominant shoreline plant community of the Florida Keys, protecting the landmass from erosion. Able to establish itself on the coral underwater bedrock or in the sand, the mangrove's root structure traps, holds, and stabilizes sediments. Over time the infant mangrove habitats establish small islets such as those you'll see peppering Florida Bay and the oceanside nearshore waters. Mangrove habitats bordering the Keys filter upland runoff, maintaining the water quality of our seas.

The leaf litter that falls from the red mangroves decomposes in the tangle of its prop roots, forming a critical base in the food chain that supports the myriad species of the marine community inhabiting shoreline waters. Important as a breeding ground and nursery for juvenile spiny lobster, pink shrimp, snook, mullet, tarpon, and mangrove snappers, the mangroves also shelter these sea creatures from their predators. (See the Diving & Snorkeling and Fishing chapters for more on the fascinating underwater creatures living here.) Great rookeries of wading birds and shorebirds roost and nest on the canopy of broad leaves of the mangrove habitats, creating a virtual aviary in every uninhabited islet.

Three kinds of mangroves thrive in the Florida Keys. The distinctive high-arching prop roots of the red mangrove enable the plants to exchange gases and absorb oxygen from the seawater. Long, pencil-like seedpods, called propagules, develop during the summer and drop off the mangroves in the autumn, floating upright hither and yon with the tides. Eventually snagged on a branch or caught against a rock, the seedling establishes itself by growing prop roots, and a key is born.

The black mangrove, with dark, scaly bark, grows in the high-tide zone. The white mangrove, smallest of the three species, looks like a shrub with broad, flat, oval leaves and grows above the high-tide line along with stands of buttonwood trees.

> **i** Cuba is closer to Key West than Miami is. Cuba sits roughly 90 miles off the southern tip of Key West, while Miami is 130 miles north of "the Rock."

Sand Beach Habitats

Most of the islands of the Florida Keys have a limestone rock shoreline, but Long Key, Bahia Honda Key, and small portions of the shoreline of Lower Matecumbe have beaches of sand consisting not of quartz but of tiny fossils. These minuscule remains of calcareous, lime-secreting marine plants and animals are broken down by wave action upon the sea bottom. Only keys that have a break in the offshore reef line or are near a deep tidal channel receive enough sediment to build a natural beach. Fronted in most cases by beds of sea grass, the Keys' beaches always have a "weed line" on shore made up of remnants of turtle grass, manatee grass, or sargassum weed washed up with the tide.

Sunset Views

Mallory Square in Key West isn't the only public place to view our world-famous sunsets. Many oceangoing vessels offer sunset cruises, and if you are a land lover, head up the Keys. On Big Pine Key, Bahia Honda State Park on the beach offers an unobstructed scenic view. Head on up to Marathon and stop at the entrance to the old Seven Mile Bridge for the nightly celebration where gazers can see the Florida Straits and the Atlantic Ocean.

The natural beaches of the Keys don't have sand dunes but rather more bermlike mounds. Sea oats grow in the sand, helping to hold the particles together. State law mandates that you may not pick sea oats at any time.

The Sea

Sea-Grass Habitats

In the shallow nearshore waters of the ocean and Florida Bay, sediments build up on the limestone bedrock sea bottom, supporting a variety of sea grasses that perform an integral function in our tropical ecosystem.

Sea grasses grow entirely underwater, one of the few flowering plants to do so. Most prevalent of the sea grasses in the Florida Keys are the sweeping meadows of turtle grass, which have interlocking root systems that burrow as deep as 5 feet into the sediment. The wide, flat blades, often more than 12 inches long, break the force of the waves and slow current velocity.

The turtle grass traps marine sediments and silt carried in and out on the tides, allowing them to settle to the bottom. This natural filtration system clarifies the water and enhances coral growth in the nearby reef habitat. The sunken pastures of turtle grass and the less abundant shoal grass and manatee grass, which have rounded leaves and weaker root systems, become very dense, providing food and shelter for marine life at all levels of the food chain (see the Fishing chapter for more on the species dwelling within).

More than 80 species of resident and migratory coastal birds forage the sea grasses, feeding on fish and invertebrates of the habitat.

Hardbottom Habitats

Wave action and tidal currents sweep the limestone bedrock of the nearshore sea-bottom habitats nearly clean, permitting no sediment buildup. Algae, sponges, gorgonian corals, and stony corals attach themselves directly to the bedrock. Snapping shrimp often make their homes within the sponges; they make a popping sound with their large snapping claw to repel predators. More seaward of the nearshore waters, colonies of soft corals dominate the underwater hardbottom landscape. A feathery fairyland blooms like a backstage theater costume room.

Tentacled anemones also call the hardbottom habitat home and peacefully coexist with conchs and tulip snails, the spiral-striped, spindle-shaped mollusks. The much-sought-after stone crabs and juvenile spiny lobsters try to stay out of sight here (see the Diving & Snorkeling chapter). Boat wakes, anchor damage, and collection of sea creatures by divers and snorkelers threaten the hardbottom habitats.

Coral Reef

Extending 200 miles, from Fowey Rocks near Miami to the Dry Tortugas, our living coral reef habitat—the only one in the continental US—is a national treasure. The reef, composed of the limestone remains of colonies of individual animals called polyps, plays host to an unbelievable assortment of marine creatures, fish, and vegetation (see the Diving & Snorkeling and Fishing chapters). The coral reef habitat, together with the mangrove and sea-grass habitats, is the breeding ground for 70 percent of the commercial fishing industry's catch.

This wave-resistant barrier, which protects the sea-grass meadows from erosion and heavy sedimentation, is particularly beautiful off the Upper Keys. The landmass of Key Largo shields the coral habitat from changing water temperatures and sediments that emanate from Florida Bay through the tidal channels of the Middle and Lower Keys. Though it rigidly protects the shoreline of the Florida Keys from tropical storms, the coral reef itself is a fragile habitat. Field studies since 1984 have indicated some coral die-off and the sometimes fatal bleaching or discoloration of the corals in select areas of the Keys' barrier reef. Excessive nutrients in the water due to land-based pollution will degrade water quality and foster the growth of algal blooms, which screen the sunlight, robbing the coral of the oxygen that is necessary for healthy development.

Humans constitute one of the reef's most destructive threats. Anchor damage, boat groundings, and snorkelers and divers touching, collecting, or stepping on the delicate organisms can cause injury and certain death to the reef. See Protectors of Paradise in this chapter for more information on how you can help preserve and protect our reefs while still enjoying them.

Bare-Mud & Bare-Sand Bottom Habitats

Along the barrier reef, skeletons of reef plants and animals form areas of open, bare-sand sea bottom, inhabited by species of algae, sea urchins, snails, clams, and worms that serve as the food train for visiting starfish, conch, and finfish. Similar belts or patches of bare-mud bottom habitats, both oceanside and in Florida Bay, support a like assemblage of marine creatures. Joining this group are burrowing shrimp, whose tunneled dwellings leave telltale mounds in the mud.

Our Wildlife

Rachel Carson may have said it all in *The Edge of the Sea:* "I doubt that anyone can travel the length of the Florida Keys without having communicated to his mind a sense of the uniqueness of this land of sky and water and scattered mangrove-covered islands."

Nowhere will you be more aware of our quintessence than when you are experiencing the Florida Keys in a small dinghy, canoe, sea kayak, or shallow-draft skiff equipped with a push pole and tranquilly gliding through our shallow, mangrove-lined inshore waters in search of sightings of indigenous birds and aquatic creatures.

Though the dedication to spotting feathered friends may be referred to as "birding" or "bird-watching" in some areas of the country, here in the Keys another arena of fascinating marine creatures presents itself in the shallow waters of our flats. You can easily explore on your own without a guide, or you can sign up for a guided ecotour (see the Recreation chapter).

Hundreds of virgin mangrove islets sprinkle the inshore waters of the inhabited Keys, often serving as giant rookeries for shorebirds and wading birds that are attracted to the abundant chow wagon beneath the surface of the water. Look to our Recreation chapter for information on renting a kayak, canoe, or small skiff. See the Attractions chapter for descriptions of the wildlife refuges of the Florida Keys, many of which encompass myriad outlands. Read on for a primer of the most frequently encountered species in our tropical ecosystem.

Nature's Aviary
When exploring around the mangrove islets in search of wild birdlife, be sensitive to the presence of nesting birds. Do not anchor within 200 feet of an island, and keep noise to a minimum so as not to frighten the birds. If you do happen to flush a bird from its nest, move away from the nest area so that the bird will swiftly return to guard its young. Here are several species you can expect to spot:

- **Brown Pelican:** Some say the brown pelican's mouth can hold more than its stomach can, but this common resident of the Florida Keys will push this theory to the limit given half a chance. The brown pelican will dive from 20 to 30 feet above the sea, entering the water like a competing Olympian and scoring with freshly caught fish every time. You'll see these cute, personality-packed fish-beggars everywhere, especially hanging out at fishing marinas. Look for them on their favorite gravity-defying perches atop mangroves or feathery Australian pines.

- **American White Pelican:** With a wingspan of 10 feet, the white pelican is more than a bird of a different color. These winter visitors to the Florida Keys (they are frequently spotted in Montana in the summer months) live a much different lifestyle than their brown cousins. Completely white except for black-tipped wings and long yellow beaks, white pelicans live together in flocks in the uninhabited wild of the backcountry keys. The white pelicans, far from the panhandling ways of the browns, are cooperative feeders, congregating as a team on the water's surface and herding fish into an ever-narrowing circle where the group will dine. Look for white pelicans at Little Arsnicker or Sandy Keys in the Upper Keys backcountry.

- **Cormorant:** Cormorants by the thousands inhabit rookeries in the mangroves of the unpeopled islands. These large-bodied, hook-billed black birds, consummate fish-catchers all, will launch themselves in attempted flight at the first inkling of an approaching gunkholer, often hitting the water in a brief belly flop before gaining momentum to become airborne. Like the lesser-seen anhinga, or water turkey (more prevalent in the Everglades), the cormorant's plumage becomes waterlogged, which facilitates diving and swimming skills in its endless search for fish. You'll often see the birds perched on poles and buoy markers, wings outstretched in a drying maneuver. Cormorants swim with only their necks and heads visible above the water.

- **Snowy Egret & Great Egret:** Plume hunters nearly eradicated the egret population at the turn of the 20th century, for the birds' magnificent snow-white aigrettes were high fashion in the millinery industry. The egrets achieve their feathery plumage only in breeding season, so it was easy for the hunters to kill the birds in their nests. Both snowy and great egrets thrive once again in the Florida Keys. Distinguished from their cousins the great white herons, which also grace the shorelines of the Keys, the white egrets have black legs with yellow feet and black bills. Though both egrets display magnificent white plumage, the snowy egret is about half the size of the great egret.

- **Great White Heron:** Formerly considered a separate species from the great blue heron encountered in many parts of the US, what we commonly call the great white heron is actually the white "morph," or color phase, of the great blue. Found only in the tropical ecosystem, this large white heron, more than 4 feet tall, is not as fearful of humans as other species, and is often seen in backyards and other inhabited areas. You'll be able to tell a great white heron from a great egret because the heron has long yellow legs and a yellow beak. The heron still-hunts for its food: Standing stiffly at full alert, the heron stalks a prey of fish, frogs, or lizards; it then stabs the prey with its beak, flips the prize whole into its narrow throat, and swallows it in one long neck-expanding gulp. Herons and egrets build

their lofty stick nests atop the mangroves of remote rookery keys.

- **Roseate Spoonbill:** A rare sighting in the Florida Keys, the roseate spoonbill, or pink curlew, is more common in the upper Florida Bay near Flamingo in Everglades National Park. Like the great white heron and egret, it also was slaughtered to near extinction in the early 1900s for its brilliant pink plumage, which was used for ladies' hats. The roseate spoonbill moves its large spatulate bill from side to side underwater in the shallows, searching for minnows and small aquatic creatures. This distinctive bird is costumed like a vaudeville dancer—pink body accented by an orange tail, a bare greenish head, bright red shoulder and chest patches, and a black-ringed neck.

- **White Ibis:** Common in the Florida Keys, the white-plumed ibis bears black-tipped wings, most apparent when spread in flight, a distinctive scarlet, down-curved bill, and red legs. You'll often see young ibises, which are brown, in a flock of their white brethren, searching for aquatic insects, crabs, shrimp, and small snakes. The ibis was once worshipped in Egypt as a bird-headed god, and the pharaohs were buried alongside a mummified ibis. Killing an ibis for any other purpose was an offense punishable by death.

- **Osprey:** The high platform-topped poles you may see along the Overseas Highway have been erected for the osprey, which builds its bulky nest atop, laying three eggs out of harm's way each breeding season. Look up when trying to spot these fish-eating birds in the wild as well, for their nests will be constructed on the very pinnacles of the trees. Resembling a bald eagle, the osprey can be distinguished by a black streak behind each eye.

- **Magnificent Frigatebird:** The graceful, effortless flight of the frigatebird, or man-o'-war bird, often heralds fish below, for this coastal forager is constantly on the lookout for finned pleasures. Often known to harass other seabirds until they drop their catch, the piratical frigatebird catches the spoils midair. Having a wingspan greater than 7 feet, the frigatebird inflates its throat sac and floats on air currents, its deeply forked, scissorlike tail a distinctive sight.
- **American Bald Eagle:** Once endangered nearly to the point of extinction, American bald eagles have made a recovery all across the US due to preservation efforts. Look for the bald eagle's distinctive white head and tail high in the mangroves of uninhabited keys in Florida Bay, where they build their nests. Fish dominate their diet, and it is not uncommon for the bald eagle to steal the catch of a neighboring osprey.

Nature's Aquarium

As you pass through the shallow sea-grass, mud, sand, and hardbottom habitats surrounding mangrove areas of our uninhabited keys, you may observe life below the surface of the water. Be sure to wear polarized sunglasses and proceed in a shallow-draft craft.

- **Starfish:** Commonly adorning the sandy bottom areas or sea-grass meadows of the shallow waters are cushion sea stars, often referred to as "starfish." These heavy-bodied, orange-brown creatures with five thick, starlike arms don't look alive, but they are.

- **Loggerhead Sponge:** The most common sponge you will see from your small skiff or while snorkeling in these waters is the loggerhead sponge, a barrel-shape sponge easily identified by the dark holes in its upper surface.
- **Stingray:** This unusual creature, shaped like a diamond or disk, often lies motionless on the ocean bottom, partially buried in the sand. The ray has eyes and breathing holes on its topside, with its mouth positioned on the underside to feed off the seafloor. When frightened, the stingray will swim away, its huge, winglike fins flapping in gentle undulation.
- **Horseshoe Crab:** You'll quickly spot the distinctive spikelike tail and smooth, horseshoe-shaped body shell of this 300-million-year-old species as the crab forages the sea-grass habitat for algal organisms.
- **Sea Turtle:** Keep a close lookout for the small head of the giant sea turtle as it pops out of the water for a breath of air. Loggerheads can remain submerged for as long as three hours. Green turtles, once commonplace here but overharvested for use in soup, for steaks, in cosmetic oils, and for leather, are rarely encountered today. The sea turtles' front appendages have evolved into flippers.
- **Manatee:** On a lucky day, you may catch a rare glimpse of the timid West Indian manatee, or sea cow, a docile aquatic mammal that likes to graze on the turtle-grass flats. The brownish gray manatee has armlike flippers; a broad, spoonlike tail; and an adorable wrinkled face. It can grow to 15 feet long, weighing in at nearly a ton. Protected as an endangered species, the manatee often rolls on the

water's surface for air and cannot swim rapidly enough to avoid collision with oncoming boaters, a constant source of peril (see the Boating chapter for regulatory information).

- **Bottlenose Dolphin:** A more frequent sight on any water-based excursion is that of bottlenose dolphins, which you probably remember as the "Flipper" performers of marine parks. Seen in free-swimming pods in open waters, the graceful dolphins undulate through the waves with rhythmic regularity, and they are sometimes curious enough to approach your boat.
- **Fish of the Flats**: Alert attention to underwater movements in the sea grass of the flats may net you a sighting of a baby black-tip or bonnethead shark, a nurse shark, barracuda, bonefish, and more. See The Flats section of the Fishing chapter for descriptions of the finned treasures lurking beneath the shallows.

WEATHER & CLIMATE

The mild tropical climate of the Florida Keys has no equal in the US. In fact, neither frost, nor ice, nor sleet, nor snow visits our islands.

Temperature

The proximity of the Keys to the Gulf Stream in the Straits of Florida and the tempering effects of the Gulf of Mexico dictate that average winter temperatures vary little more than 14 degrees from those of the summer months. Average year-round temperature is about 75 degrees. Cold, dry air moving down from the north in the winter is greatly modified by the gulf waters over which it passes. And southeasterly trade winds and fresh sea breezes keep summer temperatures from

ever reaching the triple-digit inferno experienced by the Florida mainland. The water and land heat and cool at different rates, creating thermal currents that air-condition the Keys.

Rainfall

The Florida Keys experience two seasons: wet and dry. From November through April, the sun shines abundantly and less than 25 percent of the year's precipitation falls, usually associated with a cold front in the dead of winter. May through October is the rainy season, when nearly three-quarters of our annual rainfall occurs during brief daily showers or thunderstorms. But these percentages are deceiving; our climate is really quite dry. Average rainfall in the winter is less than 2 inches a month; summer months see closer to 4 to 5 inches of rain.

i The long blue line that divides part of the new Stretch from Florida City to Key Largo is not just any "blue line." Famed artist Wyland (a resident of Islamorada; see the Arts & Culture chapter) was asked by the Florida Department of Transportation to choose a color for this otherwise dull 3-foot-high line of concrete. He chose "Belize Blue" from his personal color book, and explained that it represented the color of the Florida Keys.

Hurricanes

The piper must be paid for this idyllic climate, and hurricanes have always been a key ingredient in our tropical mix. The potentially deadly weather systems move westerly off the African coast during hurricane season (officially June 1 to November 30 but most prevalent in August and September) and generally turn north near the Lesser Antilles, often heading our way.

Hurricanes have been harassing visitors to our shores for centuries. In 1622 at least five ships of the Spanish Tierra Firma Fleet wrecked as a result of a hurricane west of the Dry Tortugas. One of the most famous of these ships, the *Atocha*, was discovered and salvaged in 1985 by Mel Fisher (see Mel Fisher Maritime Heritage Society and Museum in the Attractions chapter). The New Spain Armada suffered a fatal blow by a hurricane in 1733, when 17 of 21 galleons struck the reefs of the Upper Keys, spewing treasure cargo amid the coral.

Key West suffered a devastating hurricane in 1835, but the hurricane of 1846 is considered the city's most severe. Key West residents pluckily rebuilt after these hurricanes and through the repeated hammerings of 1909, 1910, 1914, and 1919. On Labor Day 1935, a Category Five hurricane tore through the Upper Keys and Lower Matecumbe, totally destroying the area, including Flagler's Florida East Coast Railroad Extension. Five hundred people lost their lives in the high winds and 7-foot tidal surge in Lower Matecumbe alone. Experts estimate that the Labor Day hurricane packed winds of between 200 and 250 miles per hour. In comparison, Hurricane Katrina's winds, which devastated much of Mississippi and Louisiana in 2005, hit 140 miles per hour at landfall.

On August 29, 1960, an African storm caused an airplane crash near Dakar, Senegal, Africa, killing 63 people. Three days later this storm system was officially named Donna by the National Hurricane Center, which was formed in 1955 in Miami. By September 9, Donna's eye, which stretched 21 miles wide, passed over the region, bringing horrendous winds that effectively leveled the area from Marathon to Lower Matecumbe. Tides in Marathon were more than 9 feet high, and the surge in Upper Matecumbe topped 13 feet. Tea Table Bridge washed out, the freshwater pipeline broke in six places, and electricity was out. Donna ranks among the most destructive storms in US history.

Three hurricanes have hammered the Florida Keys in recent years. Hurricane Georges, a strong Category Two hurricane with sustained winds of 105 mph, wreaked havoc from the Middle Keys to Key West on September 25, 1998. The massive cleanup and repair effort took residents nearly a year, but courtesy of La Niña, a wet summer in 1999 restored most of the lost foliage to its former glory. Then on October 15, 1999, Hurricane Irene battered the Keys with 75-mph winds and dumped 10 to 20 inches of rain on the still-recovering islands. And on October 24, 2005, the Lower Keys had an uninvited tourist by the name of Wilma. This Category Five hurricane, with winds of 125 mph, inundated a large portion of the Lower Keys. An accompanying storm surge of 10 feet from the Gulf of Mexico flooded and destroyed everything in its path.

Visitors to the Florida Keys during hurricane season should heed official warnings to evacuate our islands in the event of a potential hurricane. Because we have only one main artery linking our islands to the mainland (the Overseas Highway), it takes 22 to 26 hours of crawling, bumper-to-bumper traffic to clear residents and visitors out of the Florida Keys. Officials warn that storm-watching during a hurricane is not a diversion to be considered here. A sizable hurricane will cut off all services in the Keys and communications to the outside world.

PROTECTORS OF PARADISE

The natural wonders that make up the Florida Keys have good friends in the following organizations, which oversee efforts to protect the region's environment as best they can.

National Marine Sanctuary

In 1990 President George H. W. Bush signed into law the Florida Keys National Marine Sanctuary and Protection Act, designed to protect our spectacular marine ecosystem. The resulting Florida Keys National Marine Sanctuary encompasses 2,800 square nautical miles, incorporating within its boundaries the previously formed Key Largo National Marine Sanctuary (1975) and the Looe Key National Marine Sanctuary (1981). The Florida Keys National Marine Sanctuary engulfs all of the Florida Keys, including the Marquesas Keys and the Dry Tortugas, and surrounding waters. In an effort to provide a secure habitat for the marine flora and fauna that make the Florida Keys so special, the protection act immediately prohibited oil drilling within the sanctuary and created an "area to be avoided" (ATBA) for large ships in our waters.

Ecologists hope that the access restrictions and activity regulations in select areas of the Florida Keys National Marine Sanctuary will help protect sensitive areas of the ecosystem. Furthermore, professionals feel that, with minimal human contact, areas of high ecological importance will evolve naturally and those areas representing a variety of habitats will be sustained. This zoning program is monitored for revision every five years (see the Boating chapter for more information on specific regulations and restrictions). For more information, call the Florida Keys National Marine Sanctuary Headquarters at (305) 809-4700 or visit floridakeys.noaa.gov.

The Nature Conservancy

The Nature Conservancy established a Florida Keys program in 1987 to protect the health and extraordinary diversity of our tropical ecosystem. This nonprofit conservation group states its mission as "preserving plants, animals, and natural communities that represent the diversity of life on Earth by protecting the lands and waters they need to survive." The conservancy's work includes monitoring, management, and stewardship actions in the water and on the land; advocacy efforts; and support for volunteer programs. The conservancy established the Florida Reef Resilience Program to develop strategies to improve the health of our fragile coral reefs. This program includes a coral restoration project, which, in addition to research, establishes underwater nurseries to help grow coral. As of this writing, eight in-water coral nurseries exist, with more on the way in the coming years. For more information about the Nature Conservancy, please visit nature.org.

Reef Relief

Reef Relief, a Key West–based nonprofit group of volunteers founded in 1987, works toward the preservation and protection of the coral reef habitat of the Florida Keys. The group's first project was to install more than 100 mooring buoys, which, when used properly, eliminate anchor damage at the reef. The Florida Keys National Marine Sanctuary maintains the mooring buoys.

Another part of Reef Relief's mission is public awareness and education regarding

Close-up

Sunrise, Sunset

In the Florida Keys we justifiably lay claim to the most spectacular sun awakenings and finales in the universe. Anglers rise early enough to witness the brilliant fireball burn its way out of the ocean, its igneous shafts dramatically piercing the clouds overhead. Divers relish the midday sun's intense rays, which light up the ocean waters like a torch, illuminating the colorful corals below. Sunbathers lie prone on pool decks and man-made beaches, soaking in the solar rays, storing up some much-needed vitamin D.

But our sunsets take center stage in the twilight hours. Both visitors and residents jockey for an unobstructed vantage point from which to watch the smoldering orange ball ooze into the sea like a sphere of molten lava. Flotillas of small boats drift anchorless in the gulf waters . . . waiting. Travelers pull their autos off the Overseas Highway and stand at the water's edge, their awestruck attention riveted on the setting sun. Key West even has a daily sunset celebration ceremony at Mallory Square, complete with fire-eaters, jugglers, and Keys buskers of every shape and description.

If you are vigilant, you may see the green flash, a brilliant emerald-colored spark of light that occasionally appears just as the sun melts into the sea. The rare sighting lasts only a second or less and has inspired legends the world over. According to the *Boston Globe,* "The green color results from the refraction, or bending, that sunlight undergoes as it passes through the thick layers of atmosphere near the horizon. Blue and green wavelengths of light are refracted the most, just like in a prism, so the setting sun appears to have a very thin blue-green fringe on its top edge. This fringe is hidden by the glare from the rest of the sun until all but the last of the sun's rim is blocked by the horizon."

In the Florida Keys the sun sets over the Gulf of Mexico. The day must be clear, and the sun must meet the horizon through a cloudless sky to reveal the green flash. Although sighting a green flash is a singular phenomenon akin to spotting a comet or a shooting star, every sunset is reason for celebration in the Florida Keys.

the living coral reef habitat. To this end, each year the organization sponsors a cleanup campaign that attracts hundreds of volunteers. They comb shorelines and out-islands and dive the reef, collecting trash and storm-driven debris. For more information, contact Reef Relief Environmental Center and Headquarters, 631 Greene St., Key West; (305) 294-3100; reefrelief.org.

Turtle Hospital

Located near MM 48.5 Bayside, in Marathon is the famed Turtle Hospital, a turtle rapid-care center and recovery room run as a labor of love by Ritchie Moretti since 1986. In the winter of 2009–10, the Turtle Hospital took in more than 200 sea turtles at one time, which were ailing due to the unseasonably cold weather. Local veterinarians volunteer their time, often performing complicated turtle surgery on fibro-papilloma tumors, impactions, and shell fractures caused by hit-and-run boating injuries. After surgery, the turtles are moved to the recovery room, some in outdoor tanks and the rest in the property's original saltwater pool.

More than 5,000 schoolchildren visit the Turtle Hospital every year, learning about the fascinating reptilian order *Chelonia*. The general public visits, too. The Turtle Hospital offers a 45-minute guided educational experience three times daily. The tour requires reservations and, since this is a working hospital, cancellations occur due to turtle emergencies and/or weather. For more information, visit turtlehospital.org or call (305) 743-2552.

GETTING HERE, GETTING AROUND

You are headed for the Florida Keys. Whether you travel by land, by sea, or by air, you must conform to some strict, uncompromising standards that your travel agent may have neglected to tell you.

First, remove your socks. You won't need them here. Don your shorts. They are *de rigueur*. Slip on those shades. How else can you see? And reset your watch. The pace is slower here—you're on Keys time now.

Things really are different here. Our single main street stretches 126 miles—from Florida City to Key West—and dead-ends at the sea. Our 42 bridges span the kissing waters of the Atlantic Ocean and the Gulf of Mexico, from Key Largo to Key West. And our Keys communities resound as distinctively as the ivories of a piano. So come on down. We're playing your song.

BY AIR

Commercial Flights

KEY WEST INTERNATIONAL AIRPORT
3491 S. Roosevelt Blvd., Key West
(305) 296-5439
keywestinternationalairport.com
The facility doubled in size to 50,000 square feet in 2009 following an extensive renovation garnering a $31 million price tag. The airport can now accommodate many more passengers traveling in and out of the southernmost city. Although Key West is the Florida destination of choice for thousands of visitors each year, do not expect to arrive here via commercial jetliner. Air service to this island in the sun is of the commuter variety. The planes are small and flights are often overbooked during peak seasons, especially in January and February, so be sure to arrive early to check in for your flight.

The Conch Flyer restaurant/lounge has propellers from actual airplanes hanging out of the wall. In back of the massive cocktail bar are loads of pictures and memorabilia of Key West history. The bar stools are designed with propellers as legs to support the seats. The food is really great, too.

If you are meeting a flight, short-term metered parking is available. You may also park in the long-term lot. Weekly rates are available.

Avis, Budget, Dollar, and Hertz rental cars are available at the airport terminal; Alamo and Enterprise are just a courtesy call away (see listings in our Rental Cars section in this chapter). Whenever possible, make reservations for your vehicle in advance. Taxis stand by in front of the airport awaiting each

Directions to the Keys

Directions from Miami International Airport via Florida's Turnpike: Take LeJeune Road south to Highway 836 West. As you approach the ramp, get in the right-hand lane. Be aware, however, that a frontage-road access just before the sign and arrow often lures confused first-timers into turning too soon. The ramp is actually just after the sign and arrow. Follow Highway 836 West to Florida's Turnpike South, Homestead. Continue on Florida's Turnpike until it ends in Florida City at US 1. Continue south on US 1 to the Keys.

flight, and many hotels offer complimentary shuttle service.

Flights into and out of Key West are provided by the following airlines:

- **Air Tran Airways,** (800) 247-8726; airtran airways.com
- **American Airlines,** (800) 433-7300; aa .com
- **Cape Air,** (305) 293-0603, (800) 352-0714; flycapeair.com; provides scheduled service between Key West and Fort Myers
- **Continental Airlines,** (800) 523-3273; continental.com
- **Delta Air Lines,** (800) 221-1212; delta .com
- **SeaCoast Airlines,** (866) 302-6278; seacoastairlines.com; provides scheduled service between Key West and St. Petersburg/Clearwater
- **US Airways,** (800) 428-4322; usair.com

MIAMI INTERNATIONAL AIRPORT
4200 NW 21st St., Miami
(305) 876-7000
miami-airport.com
An international airport offering flights on most major airline carriers, Miami International Airport is accessible from either I-95 or Florida's Turnpike via Highway 836 and LeJeune Road. You can rent a car (see the

listing in this chapter for contact information) and drive the distance to the Keys. Miami to Key Largo is approximately 60 miles; to Islamorada, 80 miles; to Marathon, 115 miles; to Big Pine, 130 miles; to Key West, 160 miles.

i A Russian-made 1972 Antonov AN-24 Air Cubana was hijacked from Havana in 2003 and flown to Key West by architect Adermis Wilson Gonzalez with 32 passengers aboard. Purchased by someone at auction, then left in airport storage for years, the plane is now used as a permanent training tool for airport emergency crews.

FORT LAUDERDALE–HOLLYWOOD INTERNATIONAL AIRPORT
100 Terminal Dr., Fort Lauderdale
(866) 435-9355
fortlauderdaleinternationalairport.com
Smaller than Miami International, this airport off I-595 offers fewer flight options but is hassle-free when compared to Miami. To drive to the Keys from Fort Lauderdale–Hollywood International Airport, follow signs to Florida's Turnpike via I-595. Driving from Fort Lauderdale–Hollywood International Airport will add about 45 more minutes to your total trip.

Private & Charter Aircraft

AIR KEY WEST

3491 S. Roosevelt Blvd.
(at Key West International Airport)
(305) 923-4033
airkeywest.com

Fully certified, licensed, bonded, and insured as an FAA air carrier, Air Key West can take you away to other US cities, the Bahamas, or the Caribbean. This aircraft charter service offers affordable rates and professional, reliable service.

MARATHON JET CENTER

MM 52 Bayside, Marathon
(305) 743-1995
marathonjetcenter.com

Located at the west end of Florida Keys Marathon Airport, Marathon Jet Center is a flight-based operation that caters to general aviation and light aircraft. It offers a maintenance facility on the premises and sells 100 low-lead (LL) and Jet A fuel. Tie-down fees are charged per overnight or per month. Marathon Jet Center offers aircraft charter for rent in and out of the Florida Keys.

SEACOAST AIRLINES

3491 S. Roosevelt Blvd.
(at Key West International Airport)
(866) 302-6278
seacoastairlines.com

Enjoy flightseeing trips in a relaxed atmosphere on SeaCoast Airlines from Key West to St. Petersburg/Clearwater. SeaCoast Airlines also offers charters to other Florida cities.

BY SEA

Visit the Florida Keys as the pirates and buccaneers did before you: by sea. Revel in the beauty of these sea pearls, strung together by the wisp of the Overseas Highway. Your perspective of the Keys will be different when viewed from our waters. Navigate your motor or sailing craft through the Intracoastal Waterway, which extends from Miami through Card Sound and Barnes Sound and down the length of the Keys in the Florida Bay/Gulf of Mexico. Or parallel the oceanside shores following Hawk Channel, a well-marked route protected by the reef.

Long a bustling port, Key West Harbor is still busy—full of commercial traffic, tourist-filled tour boats, and visiting cruise ships. If you choose to navigate your motor or sailing craft to Key West from the Atlantic, come in through the Main Ship Channel, which is marked the Southeast Channel on the charts. From the gulf take the Northwest Channel until it intersects with the Main Ship Channel. You can anchor out in protected areas of the harbor or put into one of the comprehensive Key West marinas.

For complete information on arriving and vacationing on your pleasure craft, see our Cruising chapter.

KEY WEST EXPRESS

100 Grinnell St.
(888) 539-2628
seakeywestexpress.com

Key West Express is a fun alternative for traveling to and from Key West for visits to Ft. Myers and Marco Island. Operating four vessels daily and offering the only high-speed ferry service to these points, you can stay for a few hours or a couple of days in these locations. Two vessels are docked in Ft. Myers under the San Carlos Sky Bridge, at Fishermen's Wharf. The 140-foot *Atlanticat Catamaran* has two enclosed, climate-controlled cabins, sundeck, satellite TV, full galley, and bar. The 170-foot *Key West Express*, with full state-of-the-art electronics and amenities, alternates trips but shares the same schedule as the *Atlanticat Catamaran*. Departures and arrivals vary per season. Only in season, the 130-foot *Whale Watcher* is docked at the Marco River Marina, on Marco Island, with five jet-drive motors, two climate-controlled enclosed cabins, sundeck, full galley, and bar. Departures and arrivals vary according to season. There is a full galley and bar that is cash only aboard all of these vessels.

BY LAND

The Overseas Highway tethers our islands to the mainland like one long anchor line. Addresses along this common main street are issued by mile markers, designated as MM. Commencing with MM 127 in Florida City and culminating with MM 0 in Key West, small green markers with white numbers are posted every mile.

The Overseas Highway actually curves and drifts toward the southwest, rendering it all but impossible to refer to directions as "north to here" or "south to there." Here in the Keys everything is grounded by a mile marker, and you'll note that we orient most of the addresses we give in this book by mile marker.

As you head toward Key West, mile marker numbers descend in order. Anyplace on the right side of the road bordering Florida Bay or the Gulf of Mexico is referred to as bayside. The opposite side of the road, bordering the Atlantic Ocean, is therefore called oceanside. So addresses on the Overseas Highway will usually be referred to by both mile marker number and a bayside or oceanside distinction.

The old saying "All roads lead to the sea" could very well have been written about the Keys. The occasional side street you might encounter on one of our wider islands—such as Key Largo, Marathon, or Big Pine Key—will terminate at the bay, the gulf, or the ocean after only a few blocks.

Key West, the southernmost point in the continental US, slumbers closer to Havana than it does to Miami—when it sleeps, that is, which is not all that often. In Keys-speak, this is where the action is.

Although nearly 28,000 people make Key West their home, this island still retains a small-town charm. The quaint Old Town area remains essentially a charming, foliage-canopied grid of streets lined with gingerbread-trimmed frame structures that evoke a succession of bygone eras and a cache of simmering secrets. This area, by the way, boasts the largest collection of frame structures in a National Register historic district of any city in Florida—nearly 3,000—and some architectural elements that are found nowhere else in the world.

The Mid Town area is predominantly residential. New Town takes in the shopping centers and fast-food and hotel chains along N. Roosevelt Boulevard on the gulf side and across the island to the airport and beaches along S. Roosevelt Boulevard on the Atlantic side.

Old Town, destination of choice for most visitors to Key West, is accessed from the Overseas Highway by either N. Roosevelt Boulevard (US 1) to Truman Avenue or S. Roosevelt Boulevard (A1A) along the beach to White Street. From White Street, Southard Street runs one way toward the heart of Old Town. Fleming Street is one way leading the opposite direction.

Close-up

Keys-Speak Glossary

backcountry: shallow sea-grass meadows and mangrove islet waters of Florida Bay.

bayside: anything on the opposite coast from the Atlantic; for instance, Florida Bay in the Upper Keys, the Gulf of Mexico in the Middle and Lower Keys.

bight: a body of water bounded by a bend or curve in the shore; several are found in Key West.

blue water: deep, offshore waters of the Atlantic Ocean.

bubba: slang for best friend, buddy.

chickee: an open-sided, thatched-roof hut commonly found near the water's edge that is used as shelter from the sun.

coconut telegraph: local gossip about any subject, person, place, or thing.

Conch (pronounced "konk"): a descendant of the original Bahamians who settled the Keys; a person born in the Florida Keys.

conch: meat of a marine mollusk used in chowder and fritters; once a staple in the diet of early Conchs and Keys-dwelling Native Americans, now an endangered species that may not be harvested in the Keys.

conch cruiser: a bicycle that is painted and decorated with outrageous artwork and embellishments.

con leche: this is the fuel that keeps the locals humming: hot coffee with steamed milk and sugar.

Duval crawl: the notorious bar-hopping Key West scene from one end of Duval Street to the other.

Old Town is anchored by Duval Street, which has been dubbed "the longest street in the world" because it runs from the Atlantic to the Gulf of Mexico. It is actually only a little more than a mile long. Although finding your way around Key West is not difficult, the narrow, often one-way streets—combined with a proliferation of tourist-driven rental cars and scooters in peak seasons—can make driving around this island both frustrating and time-consuming. Old Town is best explored on foot or by bicycle.

Key West provides public bus service and several other unique modes of transportation, which we describe in this chapter.

Rental Cars

Public transportation in the Keys is practically nil. You really need a car to get around, unless you are staying strictly in Key West.

Fat Albert: two large, white blimps tethered on Cudjoe Key (MM 23) that the US government uses to track aircraft, boat traffic (especially for drug enforcement), and weather by radar. Fat Albert is also used to broadcast TV Marti—a TV station targeted toward audiences in Cuba.

flats: shallow, nearshore waters of the Atlantic.

freshwater Conch: a person who has lived in the Florida Keys for at least seven years.

hammock: an elevated piece of bedrock covered with a hardwood tropical forest; also a woven lounger strung between two palm trees.

Keys disease: the party life in the Keys has a tendency to have a lengthy duration; starting early in the day to late at night, drinks and other vices can be a 24/7 lifestyle.

mile marker, or MM: the green-and-white signs along US 1 that mark miles, in descending order, from Florida City (MM 127) to Key West (MM 0).

no-see-ums: tiny, biting flies with a hot, painful stinging bite.

oceanside: anything on the Atlantic coast of the Keys.

Paradise: the Florida Keys.

puddle jumpers: small commercial planes that fly in and out of the Key West airport and carry passengers to major airport hubs.

the Rock: slang for the Florida Keys, usually uttered by locals heading for the mainland: "I need to get off the Rock."

the Stretch: this is not an aerobics move but the "stretch" of highway (US 1) that leads into and out of the Keys, from MM 123 near Florida City to MM 105 in Key Largo.

Most rental car agencies are at the airports in Fort Lauderdale, Miami, or Key West. Some pick up and deliver vehicles. Reserve your automobile before you arrive in the Keys—availability in peak seasons is often limited—at one of the following agencies:

ALAMO RENT A CAR
2516 N. Roosevelt Blvd.
(888) 826-6893
alamo.com

AVIS RENT A CAR
3491 S. Roosevelt Blvd.
(at Key West International Airport)
(305) 296-8744 or (800) 831-2847
avis.com

BUDGET CAR & TRUCK RENTAL
3491 S. Roosevelt Blvd.
(at Key West International Airport)
(305) 294-8868 or (800) 527-0700
budget.com

DOLLAR RENT A CAR
3491 S. Roosevelt Blvd.
(at Key West International Airport)
(305) 296-9921 or (800) 800-4000
dollar.com

ENTERPRISE RENT-A-CAR
2516 N. Roosevelt Blvd.
(305) 292-0220 or (800) 736-8222
enterprise.com

HERTZ RENT A CAR
3491 S. Roosevelt Blvd.
(at Key West International Airport)
(305) 294-1039 or (800) 654-3131
hertz.com

THRIFTY CAR RENTAL
3491 S. Roosevelt Blvd.
(at Key West International Airport)
(305) 294-8644 or (877) 283-0898
thrifty.com

TROPICAL RENTALS
1300 Duval St.
(305) 294-8136
tropicalrentacar.com

Taxi Service

If you don't have your own automobile or haven't rented a car for the duration of your visit, you may find yourself in need of ground transportation within the Keys. Be aware that the fare could get pricey (sometimes approaching the cost of a daily rental vehicle), especially if you are traveling any distance. But if you need a lift, try one of these:

Upper Keys
- **Key Largo Cabs,** (305) 451-9700 or (305) 852-8888
- **Mom's Taxi,** (305) 852-7999 or (305) 453-4049

Middle Keys (Marathon)
- **Action Taxi,** (305) 743-0077
- **On Time Taxi,** (305) 289-5656
- **Friendly Cab Company,** (305) 289-5454

Lower Keys
- **Sugarloaf Key Taxi,** (305) 745-2319
- **Sunset Taxi,** (305) 872-4233

Other Key West Taxis
- **A Airport Cab Company,** (305) 292-1111
- **Five 6's Cab Company,** who have "gone green" with hybrids, (305) 296-6666, keywesttaxi.com
- **Friendly Cab Company,** (305) 295-5555

i Everyone has heard of the Blue Ridge Parkway, Route 66, and the Las Vegas Strip. They have each been designated as one of America's Byways, according to the National Scenic Byways Program—there are 150 such roads in 46 states. Now, US 1 has officially become one of America's Byways. Visit byways.org for more information.

Airport Limousine & Shuttle Service

In the event you are stranded without transportation to either of the mainland airports, alternative transport is available. These companies offer a variety of services, often also catering to private groups and functions. The following are dependable options in the Florida Keys: **Keys Shuttle** (305-289-9997 or 888-765-9997; keysshuttle.com) and **Sea the Keys** (305-896-7013; keywestdaytrip.com).

Bus Service

CITY OF KEY WEST DEPARTMENT OF TRANSPORTATION
627 Palm Ave.
(305) 293-6426
keywestcity.com

Public-transport city buses circle the island of Key West several times a day along color-coded routes. Signs at all of the bus stops sport colored dots to indicate the routes they serve. Remember that this is an island where the buses traverse in a great big circle. You simply cannot get lost if you stay on a particular bus, since it will eventually return to the stop where you boarded it. For more information, call the Key West Department of Transportation (KWDOT).

On weekdays, bus service starts as early as 5:30 a.m. and continues until 11:30 p.m.; on weekends and holidays, the hours may be shorter and the stops less frequent, depending on the route. A complete timetable and route map is available from KWDOT. "BOB" is the Bikes on Buses program. This allows customers to take their bicycles on the bus at no additional cost by securing them onto a bike rack attached to the front of the bus.

GREYHOUND BUS LINES
Miami International Airport, Miami
Key West International Airport, Key West
(800) 231-2222
greyhound.com

Greyhound bridges the gap in mass ground transit from Key West to Miami and beyond. Buses depart Miami International Airport for the Key West depot, which is housed in the Adam Arnold Annex at the airport, usually twice a day, 7 days a week. The trip will take 4 hours, 30 minutes from Key West to Miami International. Fares to and from Miami International Airport depend on embarking and disembarking sites. Greyhound schedules and fares are subject to change. Be sure to confirm your specific travel arrangements when purchasing tickets.

DADE-MONROE EXPRESS
(305) 770-3131
miamidade.gov/transit

Miami-Dade Transit (MDT) provides bus service from Florida City to the city of Marathon at MM 50. The route designation is #301. Stops are Key Largo MM 98, Tavernier MM 90, and Islamorada MM 74.

LOWER KEYS SHUTTLE
(305) 809-3910
monroecounty-fl.gov

Lower Keys Shuttle operates between Key West and Marathon, connecting with the Dade-Monroe Express in the City of Marathon at MM 50. This provides the link between Key West and Florida City. Scheduled stops are Key West MM 3, Boca Chia MM 8, Big Coppitt MM 10, Bay Point MM 15, Sugarloaf MM 17, Cudjoe Key MM 22.5, Summerland MM 25, and Big Pine MM 30. The fare for each one-way trip is $4, and exact fare is required.

Alternative Key West Transportation

CITYVIEW TROLLEY
330 Elizabeth St.
(305) 294-0644
cityviewtrolleys.com

Experience Key West and learn about its rich history from the comfortable seating of this new hop-on/hop-off open-air trolley service. There are 9 stops on the route, including Mallory Square, La Concha, the White Street Pier, the Southernmost Point, and the Hemingway Home. The first tour begins at 9:30 a.m., with the last reboard at 4:30 p.m., and trolleys run at a 30-minute frequency. Tickets for adults are $19 and children (4–12) are $9. Children under 4 ride free.

*CONCH TOUR TRAIN
303 Front St.
(305) 294-5161 or (800) 868-7482
conchtourtrain.com

Take a train ride around Key West and travel through time as you learn about this historic city. Enjoy open-air seating with a personal narrative from the driver of the train. Departing every 30 minutes, the tour lasts 1.5 hours and there is only one stop toward the end of the ride. Adult tickets are $29; kids 12 and under ride free. Buying tickets online will save you about 10 percent. *Note:* The Conch Trains that you see chugging around town are bona-fide touring vehicles; you cannot get on and off a Conch Train at will. See our Attractions chapter for further information on this and other tours.

OLD TOWN TROLLEY TOURS OF KEY WEST
3840 N. Roosevelt Blvd.
(305) 395-4958 or (800) 213-2474
historictours.com/keywest

Listen to a narrative of historic Key West on this continuous loop tour, learning as you go. Although this transportation option is promoted and sold as a 90-minute tour, with over 100 points of interest, you can hop on and off the trolley as many times per day as you wish. It's one hassle-free way to shop, dine, or take in the myriad attractions Key West has to offer.

You can park your car for free at the Key West Welcome Center (3840 N. Roosevelt Blvd.; 800-284-4482; keywestwelcomecenter.com), where you can also buy tickets and board the trolley. Day-trippers will find the welcome center readily accessible upon entry into Key West. Bear right and follow the signs for US 1. The welcome center is on the left side of the road. Park your car, then grab a trolley and let your conductor spirit you around Key West. You can also pick up the trolley at Mallory Square beginning at 9 a.m. daily. The trolley disembarks at 12 different stops, including Mallory Square, Historic Key West Seaport, Crowne Plaza La Concha, and the Southernmost Point. Trolleys stop at each location every 30 minutes.

Cost of the trolley tour is $29 per day for adults and teens; children age 12 and younger ride free. Buying tickets online will save you about 10 percent.

> **i** The Florida Keys have sights fit for a queen! In 1991 Queen Elizabeth II and Prince Philip spent a weekend cruising the Florida Keys on board their ship the HMY *Britannia*. In Key West they toured Fort Jefferson National Monument at the Dry Tortugas.

Mopeds, Scooters & Electric Cars

Key West is the perfect place to explore by moped or electric car, although we wouldn't recommend riding in the Mallory Square/lower Duval Street area or along N. Roosevelt Boulevard, which are heavily congested with people, automobiles, and delivery trucks. The egg-shaped electric cars are eerily quiet and understandably slow. They seat two or four, have no doors, and top out at 25 mph, making them ideal for an island where the speed limits never go above 35. Many places rent a choice of mopeds, electric cars, or bicycles by the hour, day, overnight, or week (see our Recreation chapter for information on bicycle rentals).

Some companies consider a daily rental to be 24 hours; others cap the day at 8 hours. Inquire when you call. Some rental agencies even have double scooters that seat two; it is illegal to carry a passenger on any other kind. The following Key West companies rent a full range of vehicles:

- **A & M Rentals,** 523 Truman Ave., (305) 294-8888
- **Adventure Scooter & Bicycle Rentals,** 611 Front St., (305) 293-9955
- **Moped Hospital,** 601 Truman Ave., (305) 296-3344
- **Pirate Scooter Rentals,** 401 Southard St., (305) 295-0000
- **Randall J's Scooter Rentals,** 505 Greene St., (305) 296-0208
- **Sunshine Rentals,** 1910 N. Roosevelt Blvd., (305) 294-9990
- **Tropical Rentals,** 1300 Duval St., (305) 294-8136

✳**PARADISE PEDICAB**
401 Southard St.
(305) 292-0077
Take a tour of Key West the slow-and-easy way in a velotaxi, better known as a pedicab. These bicycle-powered vehicles are a great way to feel the warm breeze on your face and breathe in the tropical air as your cyclist narrates the sights. A most unique mode of transportation in this most unique town. Just make sure you agree on the price before you start your journey.

Foot Power

Strolling Key West is a great way to work off the pounds you'll be packing on by grazing the tempting kiosks, juice bars, ice-cream shops, restaurants, and, of course, bars of Key West. The sidewalk-lined streets in Old Town often front little-known lanes where unusual

Are We Almost There?

Driving in the Keys takes time and patience. Speed limits are strictly enforced and in some areas, 45 mph is as fast as the law allows. Here are approximate drive times from various locations (please note that times may vary due to weather and road conditions):

Miami to Big
Pine Key . . . . 2.5 hours
Key West to West
Palm Beach. . . . . 5 hours
Key West to Miami. . . . 3.5 hours
Marathon to Orlando . . . 7 hours
Key West to Fort
Lauderdale . . . . 4 hours
Key West to Naples . . . 5.5 hours
For you road warriors:
Key West to Anchorage,
Alaska (4,020 miles) . . 81 hours

shops or galleries hide beneath ancient foliage. You'll miss these—and much of the mystery and charm of this southernmost city—if you don't get out of your car and walk a bit.

Key West Parking

Parking is plentiful and free of charge in the Keys, until you visit Key West. Ask any Key West local if there's a downside to living in Paradise, and he or she will almost always complain about parking. There are simply too many cars in Old Town Key West and too few places to put them. And because the permanent population of this tiny island keeps growing and most visitors either arrive by car or rent a vehicle when they get here, the parking problem isn't going away anytime soon.

Patrons of the shops and restaurants in Duval Square (1075 Duval St.) will find free parking available in an adjacent lot accessed from Simonton Street. Free parking for patrons of some Duval Street restaurants, shops, and bars may also be available in designated lots off either Whitehead or Simonton Streets, both of which run parallel to Duval. Metered curbside parking is, of course, available on several downtown streets, including Duval, Whitehead, and Simonton, as well as along most of the streets that intersect them. Special curbside parking areas are designated for scooters and mopeds; do not leave vehicles on the sidewalk.

In the past, tourists who wanted to avoid feeding meters and didn't mind a little extra walk could simply secure a free curbside parking spot in the many residential Old Town neighborhoods several blocks off Duval. No more. In an effort to appease Key West residents who complained about having to park several blocks from their homes because tourists had taken their curbside spots, the city of Key West has a resident parking program.

Here's how parking in residential Old Town works: Curbside spots along many Old Town streets have been ruled off with white paint and marked with the large white letters spelling out RESIDENTIAL PARKING. In order to park your vehicle in one of these spots, your car must display either a Monroe County license plate or a residential parking permit (available from the City of Key West with proof of residence).

If you park in one of the residential parking spaces and your car does not show

the proper proof of residence, you may return to find it gone. Your illegally parked vehicle will likely have been towed to the city's impound lot on Stock Island. If you want to be right in the thick of things, you will either have to feed a meter or pay to park in a lot. The city is now equipped with machines on parts of Duval and Southard Streets that allow you to pay for hours at a time via credit card and place the receipt on your dashboard, thus eliminating the need for coins. The traditional meters still exist as well. Meter maids (and men) regularly patrol the streets of Key West at all hours, and tickets are liberally distributed. All-day parking is available for more reasonable prices at several privately owned lots on either side of Duval Street; watch for the lot attendants holding cardboard signs. You might also consider one of the convenient parking facilities described below.

In 1931 travelers on the Overseas Highway (US 1) would drive to No Name Key, then ferry to Key Vacas and on to US 1 to Grassy Key. A ferry would then go to Lower Matecumbe Key and on to Card Sound Road to the mainland.

KEY WEST BIGHT PARKING LOT
Corner of Caroline and Margaret Streets
(305) 809-3864
Located adjacent to the attractions at Key West Historic Seaport, this open-air lot offers full-day parking for a maximum of $16.25. If you just need to run a quick errand, you can park here for an hourly charge. The fully automated lot is accessible 24 hours to cars, motorcycles, and scooters only; no RVs, trailers, or buses permitted.

MALLORY SQUARE PARKING LOT
Corner of Wall and Front Streets
(305) 292-8158
keywestcity.com
This parking lot abuts the cruise-ship dock off Wall Street in the Mallory Square area and is convenient to all the west-end attractions and the sunset celebration. Through the years, however, it has been reduced in size to accommodate the enlarged and improved Mallory Square, so parking space is limited. Rates run $4 per hour, day and night, or $32 for 24 hours. The lot is open from 8 a.m. until midnight. Cars, motorcycles, small trucks, and vans are welcome; campers, RVs, buses, and trailers are not.

OLD TOWN PARKING GARAGE
Key West Park N' Ride
300 Grinnell St.
(305) 293-6426
keywestcity.com
The Old Town Parking Garage offers you the chance to find one of 250 covered parking spaces at a reasonable rate anytime, day or night. Cars, small trucks, and motorcycles are welcome here. For $2 an hour ($13 maximum), you can park and then ride one of the shuttles to the downtown area several blocks away. Don't misplace your ticket, though, or you will incur a $20 fee. There is no extra charge for the shuttle when you show your ticket; a shuttle ride will cost 50 cents per person without the ticket. If your stay will be long-term, choose the monthly rate of $99 plus tax.

ACCOMMODATIONS

From luxury resorts to little-known hideaways, the Florida Keys' myriad accommodations suit every vacation fantasy and budget. What began in the 1930s as a small assortment of fishing camps experienced a renaissance after World War II ended. Henry Flagler's railroad and the creation of the Overseas Highway had made our islands more accessible, but residents still relied on cisterns for freshwater until water lines were installed to service the Key West naval base during World War II. The availability of freshwater made our region a more civilized and desirable vacation destination, and in the 1950s and 1960s, when motoring became a popular means of travel, hotels and motels sprang up throughout our islands.

OVERVIEW

In this chapter we escort you through some of the Florida Keys' more outstanding facilities. Our selections are based on attributes of rooms, service, location, property, and overall ambience.

Location & Amenities

Like our Conchs (those of us born in the Keys) and Keys characters (those of us who were not), accommodations in the Florida Keys are highly individualistic. Most are situated on the Florida Bay, the Gulf of Mexico, or the Atlantic Ocean. We commonly refer to the Atlantic as "oceanside." For simplicity's sake in this chapter, we refer to the bayside and gulfside as "bayside."

Oceanside accommodations offer exotic sunrises and proximity to dive sites, oceanside flats, and blue-water locations for sportfishing. Water access is generally deeper on the oceanside than in the bay, affording boaters and sailors more options. Bayside lodgings can boast of our spectacular Keys sunsets, which sink into the placid skinny waters of the gulf like a meltdown of molten lava. Some hotels, motels, resorts, and inns sit alongside inland canals or marina basins, and many of our waterfront facilities are accessible by boat.

Many of our small mom-and-pop lodgings you will see lining the Overseas Highway were primarily built in the 1950s and 1960s as fishing camps. These facilities offer basic, affordable rooms and efficiencies, some with screened patios. Mom-and-pop motels often draw cost-conscious families, last-minute travelers, anglers, and scuba divers—those active, outdoorsy types seeking nothing more than a bed and a shower. These motels have a high return rate.

Our large comprehensive resorts offer all the amenities of a mom-and-pop facility and then some. From fitness and child-care centers to concierge and room service, these hotels cater to families and honeymooners, business travelers and sports enthusiasts, power players and movie stars. You'll find tennis courts and water sports, fishing charters and dive excursions. Some offer optional conference rooms or a variety of travel/sport packages. Couples often opt for romantic weddings and honeymoons amid our tropical breezes, lush foliage, crystalline seas, and magnificent sunsets.

Ecotourism in the Keys

Ecotourism is on everyone's mind. More and more companies are "going green" worldwide, and this includes properties in the Florida Keys. Meeting the criteria means purchasing renewable energy, recycling, installation of low-flow shower heads, energy-efficient lighting, energy-efficient appliances, upgrading air-conditioning filters, using environmentally friendly cleaning products, and in the case of the Hyatt, using natural woods for room furnishings. In addition to the entire Southernmost Hotel Collection, over 600 resorts in Florida have completed the Florida Department of Environmental Protection's Certified Green Lodging Program and are designated as such. For a complete list of designated properties in the Keys, visit floridagreen lodging.org. To learn more about companies that are going green in the Keys, visit keysglee.com.

Whether the accommodations are large, small, or somewhere in between, all of our guest properties exude a casual, barefoot ambience. To one degree or another, all

bestow the uninterrupted escape for which the Florida Keys have always been known.

Rate Information

Rate structures for Keys lodgings vary nearly as much as the accommodations themselves, but you can draw a few generalizations. Rates fluctuate by season and depend largely upon the size of the accommodation and its proximity to the water.

High season (December through April) supports the highest rates. High-season rates usually prevail during sport lobster season at the end of July (a near holiday in the Keys; see the Diving & Snorkeling chapter), Fantasy Fest in October (our southernmost decadent version of Mardi Gras; see our Annual Events chapter), and most national holiday weekends. You must make reservations well in advance of your visit during any of these times. Many facilities fully book available accommodations one year in advance for the high season and the holidays.

A second season commences in May and continues through the summer months, attracting vacationers seeking to escape the steamy heat of the rest of Florida and the Deep South. Rates during this period are generally slightly less than high season.

Low season is September, bringing a savings of about 20 percent off high-season rates. Just keep in mind that a lot of the local businesses and restaurants close in the month of September for vacation.

In all cases, rates are quoted for the high season. Prices are figured on a double-occupancy average rate per night. Villas, efficiencies, and condominium units, which generally establish rates per unit rather than per person, will be quoted as such. And even though these units traditionally are rented by the week, we have computed our code on an average daily rate so that you can compare apples with apples.

It is not uncommon to find accommodations that run the gamut of several price-code categories all at the same place. The code will indicate if you can expect a range of space and pocketbook possibilities.

Price Code

Price codes are high-season rates figured without additional fees, such as room service and parking, and without the 12.5 percent room tax.

$............... **Less than $120**
$$ .... **$120 to $200**
$$$ .... **$200 to $300**
$$$$ ....**$300 and higher**

ACCOMMODATIONS

Barnacle Bed & Breakfast, Big Pine Key, 58

Best Western Hibiscus Motel, Key West, 59

Best Western Key Ambassador Resort Inn, Key West, 61

The Blackfin Resort and Marina, Marathon, 51

Blue Marlin Resort Motel, Key West, 59

Blue Parrot Inn, Key West, 69

Blue Waters Resort Motel, Marathon, 51

Bonefish Resort, Grassy Key, 52

Crystal Bay Resort, Marathon, 53

Deer Run Bed & Breakfast, Big Pine Key, 58

Fairfield Inn & Suites by Marriott Key West, Key West, 60

The Frances Street Bottle Inn, Key West, 72

Jules' Undersea Lodge, Key Largo, 45

La Siesta Resort & Marina, Islamorada, 46

Largo Lodge, Key Largo, 46

Old Wooden Bridge Guest Cottages and Marina, Big Pine Key, 58

The Palms Hotel, Key West, 74

Parmer's Resort, Little Torch Key, 59

Pegasus International Hotel, Key West, 61

The Pelican Key Largo Cottages on the Bay, Key Largo, 49

Quality Inn at Key West, Key West, 60

The Reef Resort, Marathon, 55

Sea Isle Condominiums, Key Colony Beach, 55

Sombrero Resort and Lighthouse Marina, Marathon, 56

Sunset Cove Beach Resort, Key Largo, 49

Westwinds Inn, Key West, 77

White Sands Inn, Grassy Key, 57

$–$$$
Breezy Palms Resort, Islamorada, 42

La Casa de Luces, Key West, 70

$
Key Colony Beach Motel, Key Colony Beach, 54

THE FLORIDA KEYS

Upper Keys

At the top of the Keys, **Key Largo,** home of John Pennekamp Coral Reef State Park, bustles with an energetic crowd of divers and snorkelers in all seasons. The orientation here is definitely geared toward the underwater treasures of the coral reef that lies just 4 miles offshore. Many motels and resorts in this area offer diving and snorkeling packages.

The settlement of **Tavernier** snuggles between Key Largo and Islamorada. This quiet area is known for its historic qualities. Dubbed the Sportfishing Capital of the World, **Islamorada** stretches from **Plantation Key** at mile marker 90 to **Lower Matecumbe Key** at mile marker 73. This village of islands, incorporated in 1998, is renowned for its contingent of talented game-fishing guides (see the Fishing chapter) and prestigious fishing tournaments.

The Upper Keys pulsates with tiki bars and watering holes as well as an array of fine restaurants (see the Restaurants and Nightlife chapters) and activities for families and sports enthusiasts alike (see the Attractions chapter).

AMY SLATE'S AMORAY DIVE
RESORT $$
MM 104.2 Bayside, Key Largo
(305) 451-3595 or (800) 426-6729
amoray.com
An eclectic collection of plantation-style villas springs to life daily as scuba enthusiasts rustle about, eager to embark on the resort's 45-foot *Amoray Diver* for the half-hour ride to John Pennekamp Coral Reef State Park (see the Diving & Snorkeling chapter). Varying in size, amenities, and price, the rooms range from the standard motel variety to small apartments with full kitchens. Some accommodations afford partial water views. A pool and hot tub front Florida Bay, and a bayfront sundeck and small sandy area at the water's edge sport a picnic table, barbecue grill, and hammock, allowing for swimming and snorkeling. Wi-Fi is included in the room rate.

ATLANTIC BAY RESORT $$$
MM 92.5 Bayside, 160 Sterling Rd.,
Tavernier
(305) 852-5248 or (866) 937-5650
atlanticbayresort.com
Atlantic Bay Resort enjoys 3 acres of prime bayfront property, planted with palms and bougainvillea, and featuring a large beach area peppered with chaise lounges and barbecue grills, Adirondack beach chairs, and hammocks. Unique to this property is a special feature of Florida Bay called the "deep hole," where depths drop dramatically to 20 feet right offshore. A coral rock ledge shelters lobsters, starfish, sergeant major fish, mangrove snappers, and parrotfish. This assortment of marine life, as well as a sunken Haitian raft, makes for dynamic snorkeling. The Atlantic Bay Resort offers 19 efficiencies, cottages, or suites for up to 4 people, all with full kitchens and free Wi-Fi. Boat

dockage and use of the boat ramp are available to guests at no extra charge. Guests also enjoy complimentary use of rowboats and paddleboats.

AZUL DEL MAR $$$–$$$$
MM 104.3 Bayside, Key Largo
(305) 451-0337
azulhotels.us
The sprawling lawn that flows to the private beach that rolls into the Gulf of Mexico sets the mood at this adults-only property. Rooms feature soft beds with down comforters; sleek kitchens with microwaves, fridges, mini-dishwashers, and coffeemakers; and TVs, CD players, and DVD players to watch movies from their in-house library. Aveda products are located in the bath, and pastries, yogurt, and coffee packets are offered to guests in the mornings. There is no formal dining area at Azul, but gas grills are available for guests, and there are many fine restaurants in the vicinity.

BAYSIDE INN KEY LARGO $$–$$$
MM 99.5 Bayside, Key Largo
(305) 451-4450 or (800) 242-5229
baysidekeylargo.com
Located on beautiful Florida Bay in the heart of Key Largo, this location is an ideal getaway. Fifty-six bright, tropical-themed guest rooms with 2 double beds overlook the bay. One-bedroom Waterfront Suites feature a full kitchen, living room with a king-size Murphy bed, dining room, private bathroom, bedroom with a king-size bed, pull-out queen couch, and a private balcony overlooking the pool, beach, and sunsets. Bay View Rooms offer a full waterfront view, surrounded by tropical gardens and palm trees. Each room has a king-size bed with beach, waterfront, and sunset views and

small refrigerator and microwave. In addition to the rooms, there is also a fitness center and a fabulous sushi restaurant called Sushi Nami, which is open for lunch and dinner.

BREEZY PALMS RESORT $-$$$
MM 80 Oceanside, Islamorada
(305) 664-2361 or (877) 412-7339
breezypalms.com

Quaint coral buildings with turquoise doors, trim, shake roofs, and screened porches mark Breezy Palms Resort, a cozy place nestled on 320 feet of oceanfront. The brightly wallpapered motel rooms, efficiencies, apartments, and cottages are clean, spacious, and well appointed, featuring rattan furniture and colorful island floral prints. Chickees and copious coconut palms pepper the property, which sits directly on the Atlantic Ocean and sports a sandy beach as well as a swimming pool. A brick barbecue, picnic table, and volleyball net add to the amenities; dockage is available for an additional fee. No straight inboards or personal watercraft, such as Jet Skis or WaveRunners, are permitted. Breezy Palms is accessible by boat. Children younger than age 13 stay free.

CALOOSA COVE RESORT $$$
MM 73.8 Oceanside, Lower Matecumbe Key
(888) 297-3208
caloosacove.com

An irregularly shaped condominium complex set apart from civilization on a 10-acre parcel of prime oceanfront property, Caloosa Cove offers 30 spacious, light, and bright efficiencies and one-bedroom suites. All are decorated with tropical rattans and pastels. A covered deck that looks directly at the Atlantic fronts every unit. Caloosa Cove's large irregularly shaped pool, surrounded by extensive decking and thatched-palm chickees, sits directly on the ocean's edge, affording endless vistas of the beyond. The grounds encompassing the coral-laden exterior of Caloosa Cove burgeon with mature tropical plantings. Activities and amenities on condo premises include shuffleboard and basketball courts, a barbecue area, lighted tennis courts, a full-service marina, fishing charters, and boat and bicycle rentals. The nearby Safari Lounge serves your choice of cocktails.

CASA MORADA $$$-$$$$
MM 82.2 Bayside, 136 Madeira Rd., Islamorada
(305) 664-0044 or (888) 881-3030
casamorada.com

Tucked on the shores of Florida Bay, out of the fray of US 1 on a residential street, this all-suites hotel exudes the charm of a Mediterranean villa. The 16 suites, each unique, have private terraces or semiprivate gardens overlooking the water and are decorated with a mixture of wrought-iron and mahogany furniture, which was exclusively created for Casa Morada. Unusual memorabilia from throughout the world accent the rooms. Cross a small, circa-1950 bridge to a private island and you'll find a sandy playground with a pool, secluded cabana, and terrace with breakfast, lunch, and beverage service. Continental breakfast is complimentary as are yoga classes held at 8:30 a.m. Thurs through Sun.

*CHEECA LODGE & SPA $$$$
MM 82 Oceanside, Islamorada
(305) 664-4651 or (800) 327-2888
cheeca.com

Majestically sprawling amid 27 manicured, tropical acres with more than 1,100 feet of beachfront, Cheeca Lodge & Spa creates a vacation enclave with all 203 spacious guest rooms and suites sporting tropical themes and colors. Many rooms have balconies that overlook the ocean or across the grounds of the resort, and some units have screened porches. There is also a 5,700-square-foot luxury spa on-site and an overflowing cache of recreational options: A saltwater lagoon is stocked with tropical fish for easy on-site snorkeling. A fishing pier juts out into the ocean, where guests can dock boats or just drop a line and try their luck. There are 2 heated adults-only pools, 2 Jacuzzis, 6 Har-Tru tennis courts, nature trails, water sports, and envirotours of the Everglades, as well as kayaking and windsurfing.

CHESAPEAKE BEACH
RESORT $$$-$$$$
MM 83.4 Oceanside, Islamorada
(305) 664-4662 or (800) 338-3395
chesapeake-resort.com

The elegant Chesapeake Beach Resort hugs the Atlantic on 6.5 acres of lushly landscaped grounds. This pristine 3-story, 65-unit resort is home to 13 villas, 44 guest rooms, and 8 suites. The Chesapeake sports 2 heated pools, a hot tub, tennis courts, on-site laundry facilities, and an outdoor gym, as well as a 700-foot sunning beach and a saltwater lagoon used for parking boats. A boat ramp and boat dockage are provided. Suites and villas offer full kitchens and have balconies or screened porches. Fishing, snorkeling, diving, and parasailing excursions, as well as sunset cruises, can be booked nearby. Use of kayaks and paddleboats are included in your stay. Chesapeake provides a playground for children, who can stay for free if they are younger than age 13.

CORAL BAY RESORT $$$$
MM 75.6 Bayside, Islamorada
(305) 664-5568
thecoralbayresort.com

Coral Bay Resort's 3 motel rooms, 11 efficiencies, and 2 villa suites are secreted away in white-trimmed, pastel pink, air-conditioned Conch-style cottages, each with a lazy-days front porch. A painted icon distinguishes each unit, creating a virtual school of tropical fish. The fresh interiors sparkle with light furniture, pastel fabrics, and tile floors. You'll enjoy Coral Bay's heated pool as well as the sandy beach on the Gulf of Mexico. Fishing and snorkeling in the 14-foot-deep saltwater tidal pool are excellent. The pier itself has built-in seating and a fish-cleaning station. Guests can dock their own vessels for free or use the resort's paddleboat for exploration. Waters beyond the dock are illuminated at night, so the seaside fun doesn't have to end at sunset.

COURTYARD KEY LARGO $$$
MM 99.7 Oceanside, Key Largo
(305) 451-3939 or (800) 272-6232
ramadakeylargo.com

Sister hotel to the Holiday Inn and Marina Del Mar Resort and Marina, the Ramada exudes a quieter, more laid-back ambience. Reciprocal privileges exist among the three facilities, so guests may enjoy dining at or room service from Bogie's Cafe and Coconuts, as well as the Tiki Bar. The Courtyard's 88 rooms and 5 king Jacuzzi suites have all the amenities you would expect. The spacious rooms have king-size beds or 2 queen beds, a private balcony, coffeemaker, fridge, cable TV/HBO, hair dryers, and iron and ironing boards. The king suites also have a queen pullout sofa, and all rooms open onto a private patio or balcony. Certain packages include a daily continental breakfast. The hotel wraps around a small, private kidney-shaped swimming pool.

DOVE CREEK LODGE $$$
MM 95 Oceanside, Key Largo
(305) 852-6200 or (800) 401-0057
dovecreeklodge.com

The Dove Creek Lodge was established to create an atmosphere for the serious fishing person. Any type of Florida Keys fishing obsession is met here with enthusiasm because they can handle any request, place you on the water with a guide, and even suggest the correct tackle to turn that passion into reality. The lodge also houses a full tackle shop to outfit you with all the proper gear. The property sits right next door to one of the best seafood establishments in the Keys, Snapper's Waterfront Restaurant (see Restaurant and Nightlife chapters), where they say: "Our seafood is so fresh we have to change the menu daily 'cause we don't know what's coming in off the boats." You can arrive by land or sea for your stay. Dove Creek Lodge offers family and wedding packages and group rates. No pets or smoking allowed.

HAMPTON INN & SUITES
ISLAMORADA $$$
MM 80 Oceanside, Islamorada
(305) 664-0073 or (800) 426-7866
hamptoninn.com

Situated directly at ocean's edge, the Hampton Inn offers 59 suites, 16 standard rooms, and 4 wheelchair-accessible rooms with vistas of our endless sparkling sea. The common lobby area of the hotel sports a fishing theme with giant mounted dolphin, wahoo, and tarpon. Tables and comfy chairs flank a keystone fireplace, which is more decorative than functional, given the balmy

Keys weather. A complimentary continental breakfast buffet is served here daily. Outside, guests enjoy a heated pool and spa, a tiki bar, and a palm-laden, sandy sunning area. You'll also find a complete selection of water sports on the premises, including snorkeling and diving excursions, parasailing, and fishing charters. The popular Outback Steak House (305-664-3344) also is on-site.

HAMPTON INN KEY LARGO $$$
MM 102 Bayside, Key Largo
(305) 451-1400
hilton.com

Not far from John Pennekamp Coral Reef State Park, Dolphin Cove, Theater of the Sea, Florida City Outlet Mall, and Everglades National Park, you will discover Key Largo's Hampton Inn. There are 100 rooms, newly decorated with a quiet tropical coolness, each offering flat-screen TVs, free Wi-Fi, a refrigerator, microwave, coffeemaker, and wet bar. Each guest room has either a private balcony or patio that opens directly to the heated pool, beach, or surrounding tropical gardens. Pets are welcome at the Hampton Inn.

HILTON KEY LARGO RESORT $$$
MM 97 Bayside, Key Largo
(305) 852-5553 or (800) 871-3437
keylargoresort.com

This luxury resort lounges on 12.5 acres in a lush hardwood forest along the Gulf of Mexico. Accommodations are comfortable for both business and leisure travel, with nature trails, a private beach, exciting water sports, sportfishing, 2 heated pools (family and adult), fitness/sauna/whirlpool facilities, 2 outdoor lighted tennis courts, 3 restaurants, a 10,000-square-foot meeting/event space, and for guests arriving by boat, a 21-slip docking facility at the marina. All 190 rooms and suites have modern tropical decor. The on-site Splashes Pool Bar has grab-and-go food for lunch and dinner, Treetops Bar & Grille offers dining with a Mediterranean and Caribbean twist for breakfast and dinner, and the Waves Beach Bar is the best place to enjoy lunch or an afternoon cocktail.

HOLIDAY INN KEY LARGO RESORT AND MARINA $$$
MM 99.7 Oceanside, Key Largo
(305) 451-2121 or (800) 843-5397
holidayinnkeylargo.com
This Holiday Inn is situated on a busy boat basin, which bustles with activity from dawn until dark. Rooms at the Holiday Inn face lush tropical gardens or the harbor, and the colorful accents in each room reflect the flora that flourishes outside. Palm trees, frangipani, and bougainvillea weave a foliage trail between the hot tub and 2 heated pools, one of which is embellished with a tropical waterfall. There is a fitness center on-site as well as a Jacuzzi for your post-workout recovery. Bogie's Cafe offers breakfast, lunch, and dinner, and the Tiki Bar serves light fare all day while live music percolates poolside on most weekend evenings.

JULES' UNDERSEA LODGE $$
MM 103.2 Oceanside, 51 Shoreline Dr., Key Largo
(305) 451-2353
jul.com
For a unique experience that is one to write home about, Jules' Undersea Lodge has to be near the top of the list. You actually dive 21 feet beneath the surface of the sea to enter the lodge. This only underwater hotel in the world is under the surface of a tropical mangrove in the Emerald Lagoon. The cottage-size building has hot showers, a well-stocked kitchen (with refrigerator and microwave), books, music, and video movies. As you snuggle in your bed, you can view the sea life that appears at the windows of this aquatic habitat. Dive certification is offered at the facility, and individuals must meet the requirements of the Professional Association of Diving Instructors (PADI) and Discover Dive in order to stay in the lodge.

KONA KAI RESORT $$$$
MM 97.8 Bayside, Key Largo
(305) 852-7200 or (800) 365-7829
konakairesort.com
Toward the southern end of Key Largo sits this adults-only gem with 11 intimate, cottage-style suites and guest rooms. Feel free to help yourself to some of the tropical fruits in season, such as the guava and star fruit that grow near the tennis courts, as you wander throughout the gardens of this 2-acre property. There is a heated swimming pool and a hot tub accented by a magnificent circular staircase and paver-stone deck; a glass-block wall shelters a saltwater pond with a waterfall. Lounge chairs, picnic tables, and barbecue grills sit close to Kona Kai's white-sand beach, which is guarded by a stone alligator. You'll be able to snorkel, swim, or fish off a platform at the end of a dock, and a paddleboat, kayak, and other water "toys" are available free of charge.

KON-TIKI RESORT $$–$$$
MM 81.2 Bayside, Islamorada
(305) 664-4702
kontiki-resort.com
Kon-Tiki's pebbled walkways, private patios, and cottages consistently attract anglers and families alike. The resort's quiet, U-shaped property boasts a shuffleboard court,

chickee, pier, private beach on Florida Bay, park benches, and a brick barbecue. The primary attraction here, though, is the saltwater pond stocked with all sorts of tropical fish. Guests are invited to don snorkel and mask and take an underwater looksee. Accommodations feature bright, clean, and comfortable motel units, fully equipped efficiencies, and one-bedroom apartments, most of which have private patios or screened porches. Two-bedroom, two-bath apartments and three-bedroom, three-bath villas, priced according to size, accommodate as many as six. Kon-Tiki offers a heated pool and a boat ramp and dockage for vessels up to 24 feet long at no extra charge.

✴LA SIESTA RESORT & MARINA $$
MM 80.2 Oceanside, Islamorada
(305) 664-2132 or (877) 278-0369
lasiestaresort.com

Tucked away amid the palm trees and the tropical foliage, you'll find La Siesta Resort & Marina. There are a few options for lodging on the property, including one-, two-, and three-bedroom cottages and suites. The Insider tip here is to request cottage 101. It has been newly renovated with a navy-and-white nautical theme replete with white wainscoting and framed photos of fishing expeditions from yesteryear hanging on the walls. Cottage 101 also has a flat-screen TV, a king-size bed, a Mitchell Gold sleeper sofa, and a personal patio with a view of the marina and ocean beyond. And then there is the best amenity of all: your own personal hammock under the palm trees. Sure, there are water sports and a heated pool on-site as well, but the hammock beckons. How can you resist?

LARGO LODGE $$
MM 101.7 Bayside, Key Largo
(305) 451-0424
largolodge.com

At Largo Lodge, a collection of 6 cottages, 1 efficiency, 1 bay unit, and 1 garden unit resides among 3 acres of lush, tropical gardens overflowing with bromeliads, orchids, and trickling water fountains. A quiet and spacious sandy pier faces the waters of Florida Bay, where you can relax and read, swim, picnic, or simply worship the sun. Each of the cottages features a living room, a bedroom with 2 queen beds, and a combination kitchen/dining area. All units are located in the garden, a short distance from the sandy beach and waterfront. Boat dockage is available, but the lush tropical plantings make it difficult to maneuver a trailer. Guests must be over age 16, and no pets are allowed.

LOOKOUT LODGE RESORT $$$
MM 87.7 Bayside, Islamorada
(305) 852-9915 or (800) 870-1772
lookoutlodge.com

Situated next to Marker 88, one of the Upper Keys' most distinguished restaurants (see the Restaurants chapter), Lookout Lodge is a clean, modestly priced motel of Spanish-influenced architecture. The resort's 9 basic rooms feature decidedly 1960s decor and amenities. All suites have kitchenettes, tile floors and baths, and ceiling fans. A limited number of pet-friendly rooms (small pets only) are available. Steps lead from the resort's raised man-made beach to the bay for swimming and snorkeling. The property features gas grills, picnic tables, and lounge chairs, but no swimming pool. Dock space, available for an additional fee, is limited and must be reserved in advance. Two weeks' advance cancellation is required.

MARINA DEL MAR RESORT AND MARINA $$$
MM 100 Oceanside, 527 Caribbean Dr., Key Largo
(305) 451-4107
marinadelmarkeylargo.com

The Marina Del Mar Resort and Marina, on a quiet, dead-end street along an ocean-fed canal and boat basin, draws an active boating, fishing, and diving crowd. The 76 rooms are bright and modern, with tile floors, ceiling fans, white wicker furnishings, and bold tropical accents, and feature king-size beds or 2 double beds. A complimentary continental breakfast is offered daily, and restaurants and attractions are nearby. The hotel also maintains 2 tennis courts and a small fitness room with Nautilus equipment. Overlooking the heated swimming pool, complete with brick sundeck and hot tub, is Coconuts, a casual indoor-outdoor restaurant (see the Restaurants and Nightlife chapters). This is a pet-friendly resort.

MARINER'S RESORT VILLAS AND MARINA $$$
MM 98 Oceanside, Key Largo
(305) 853-5000
keyscaribbean.com

This gated resort on 16 lush acres brimming with coconut palms, bougainvillea, and mangrove trees amid the beautiful town-homes and villas, allows guests the comforts of a private residence with all the amenities of a resort. Classic Caribbean color schemes, along with a 43-slip marina, give you a feeling of being on an island. Nearby is the famous John Pennekamp Coral Reef State Park (see the Recreation chapter), or ask the "Adventure Concierge" to plan an outing of diving, fishing, snorkeling, ecotouring, para-sailing, or jet skiing. On the premises are 2

pools—one of which is a 7,800-square-foot, oceanfront lagoon-styled pool that has 2 zero-entries—a Jacuzzi, clubhouse, fitness center, 2 tennis courts, a professional dive shop, and just about any kind of water sport you can imagine.

MARRIOTT KEY LARGO BAY BEACH RESORT $$$
MM 103.8 Bayside, Key Largo
(305) 453-0000 or (888) 236-2427
marriottkeylargo.com

Bayside sunset views and a prime location near John Pennekamp Coral Reef State Park are only two of a multitude of pluses at the Marriott Key Largo Bay Beach Resort. The 153 hotel rooms of this Key West–style resort vary in view, and all but 30 rooms have patios or balconies. The resort offers on-site dining and bar options in addition to 2 fitness centers and a day spa that has treatments indoors as well as private, open-air tiki huts for outdoor massage options. Pirate Island Divers provides on-premises water-sports ranging from diving, snorkeling, parasailing, and glass-bottomed boat excursions to boat and personal watercraft rentals. Fishing charters can be booked through the hotel as well. Boat dockage is available for guests' vessels at no extra charge.

*THE MOORINGS VILLAGE RESORT $$$$
MM 81.5 Oceanside, 123 Beach Rd., Islamorada
(305) 664-4708
themooringsvillage.com

Eighteen cottages and homes are sprinkled among 18 acres of this former ocean-front coconut plantation. Hammocks laze between majestic palms; winding, floral-draped trails emit the essence of gardenia;

and canoes and skiffs dot the 1,100-foot white-sand beach. Cottages range from 1 to 3 bedrooms with 1 to 3.5 baths. All are painted white with Bahamian shutters and trimmed in bright Caribbean colors. Most units have plantation-style porches as well as washers and dryers. Only 4 cottages can be rented by the night (2-night minimum); the rest require a 1-week minimum stay. Guests enjoy use of sailboards and kayaks, a lap pool, and a tennis court. Citrus trees are scattered about the lush bougainvillea-bedecked grounds. Pristine and private, the Moorings Village rates as one of the best-kept secrets in the Keys.

OCEAN DAWN SUITES $$$
MM 82.9 Oceanside, Islamorada
(305) 664-4844 or (866) 540-5520
oceandawnsuites.com

Nothing looks like a million dollars in decorating until you have spent a million dollars! The owners of Ocean Dawn Suites started out just giving this property a facelift, but when the zeros started adding up, this once 8-room lodge reopened after a complete renovation with style and pizzazz, containing marble bathrooms, porcelain floors, custom furniture, and 40-inch flat-screen TVs. Outdoors, guests will enjoy a new clay tennis court, pool, croquet lawn, and a man-made beach, just yards from the Atlantic Ocean. It's ideal for intimate wedding parties, offering a bridal suite that features a private balcony, kitchen, and Jacuzzi.

OCEAN POINTE SUITES $$$
MM 92.5 Oceanside, 500 Burton Dr.,
Tavernier
(305) 853-3000 or (800) 882-9464
opsuites.com

Directly on the Atlantic Ocean, this tropical, contemporary, 3-story, all-suite stilt condominium complex offers 160 units with gingerbread-trimmed balconies with either ocean or mangrove views. Suites at Ocean Pointe are individually owned and decorated, but, for the most part, expect to find tropical prints with wicker and rattan furnishings. Just outside your door are nature walks, a private beach, a large heated swimming pool, barbecue grills, picnic areas, beach volleyball courts, and lighted tennis courts. The 60-acre property also has a playground, a boat ramp capable of handling watercrafts up to 28 feet, and a marina. If you feel like a bite, head for the Waterfront Cafe for breakfast, lunch, an afternoon snack, or a light dinner. Kayak and canoe rentals also are available.

PELICAN COVE RESORT AND MARINA $$$
MM 84.5 Oceanside, Islamorada
(305) 664-4435 or (800) 445-4690
pcove.com

Perched beside the Atlantic Ocean, Pelican Cove Resort—constructed in concrete with a tin roof and Bahamian shutters—ensures a balcony and ocean view from almost every one of its 63 rooms. Behind the resort, steps connect the raised man-made beach to the ocean, where dredging for a once-used quarry has caused waters to run 30 feet deep. A swimming pool with sundeck, outdoor cabana bar and cafe, poolside hot tub, volleyball net, and water-sports concession all front the beach. Complimentary coffee and juice are offered in Pelican Cove's office 24 hours a day. Children younger than age 17 stay free at Pelican Cove. Limited boat dockage is available to guests for an additional fee.

THE PELICAN KEY LARGO COTTAGES ON THE BAY $$
MM 99.34 Bayside, Key Largo
(305) 451-3576 or (877) 451-3576
hungrypelican.com

Murals of manatees, pelicans, roseate spoonbills, and egrets decorate the outside walls of the 1-story "old Keys" buildings at the Pelican, which are linked by masses of bougainvillea. Each of the 23 rooms is air-conditioned and has a small refrigerator, TV and DVD player, private bathroom with a shower, tile floors, and Internet access. Some also have kitchens, and there is a coin-operated laundry facility available as well. You'll be able to swim or snorkel between the Pelican's 2 fishing piers, but the facility does not have a swimming pool. You may launch your boat from the Pelican's boat ramp, and dockage for small boats is free for guests. Use of paddleboats, canoes, and kayaks is complimentary. The property sports a large chickee for lounging, and barbecue pits are scattered about.

SUNSET COVE BEACH RESORT $$
MM 99.3 Bayside, Key Largo
(305) 451-0705 or (877) 451-0705
sunsetcovebeachresort.com

Concrete camels, elephants, lions, tigers, and leopards lurk on the grounds of the Sunset Cove Motel, incongruously poised among cottages and waterfront suites. Don't worry, they are only life-size painted statues of the African beasts, remnants of a former owner's travels and hobbies. All the pet-friendly units at Sunset Cove are individually decorated, most still sporting 1950s and 1960s decor and furnishings. The cottages also have full kitchens. Each unit showcases wall murals of exotic flora and fauna, painted by area artists. Down at the waterfront, you'll enjoy free use

of paddleboats and canoes. Maid service is available with fresh towels supplied to rooms daily. Sunset Cove does not have a swimming pool, but there is beach access. Guests enjoy a free continental breakfast.

TARPON FLATS INN $$$
MM 103.5 Oceanside, Key Largo
(305) 453-1313 or (866) 546-0000
tarponflats.com

Standing on the banks of Largo Sound, this 3-story sunshine yellow B&B offers modern accommodations with a Caribbean flair. A fishing camp in the 1960s and '70s, the resort comes complete with its own beach! British Colonial mahogany furniture is the decor in suites and rooms. The verandas off the rooms frame fabulous views of Largo Sound and the John Pennekamp Coral Reef State Park (see the Campgrounds and Cruising chapters). Tarpon Flats Inn's marina can accommodate your boat or charter one for some of the best fishing and fun in the Keys. Fishing not your thing? The inn can arrange snorkel and dive trips, or you can just go along for the ride and take some dazzling photos to show folks back home.

TOPSIDER RESORT $$$
MM 75.5 Bayside, Islamorada
(305) 664-8031 or (800) 262-9874
topsiderresort.com

The 20 octagonal, elevated time-share villas at Topsider Resort flank a wood boardwalk that marches from the secluded parking lot to the crystalline waters of the Gulf of Mexico. Units are identical in layout. Each features 2 bedrooms, 2 baths, a dining area, living room, full kitchen, and a washer and dryer. The units are updated on a rotating basis. Be sure to inquire as to when your unit was last renovated before booking. Guests at Topsider Resort enjoy an elevated heated pool and spa, a tennis court, children's swings and slides, grills, picnic tables, and bayfront wood lounges for sunning on the sandy lagoonside beach. Free boat dockage is available on Topsider's long pier. Minimum stay here is 3 nights, but most guests opt for a week's sabbatical.

i The Monroe County Tourist Development Council can help you find the perfect spot to rest your head as well as help you plan your entire Florida Keys vacation. Call them toll-free at (800) 352-5397 or visit fla-keys.com.

WHITE GATE COURT $$–$$$
MM 76 Bayside, Islamorada
(305) 664-4136 or (800) 645-4283
whitegatecourt.com
The 7 private 1940s-era restored villas and bungalows at White Gate Court are situated on 3 acres abutting the placid Gulf of Mexico. Spacious interiors feature fully equipped, stylistically European white kitchens and sparkling modern bathrooms. Beds are covered with exquisite individualized quilts. All units have covered porches and outdoor tables and chairs, and some even feature rope hammocks. White iron gates front a long, narrow driveway lined with palm trees, oleanders, and white coach lamps. Lounge chairs pepper a 200-foot white-sand beach where guests enjoy swimming and snorkeling in the sandy-bottom gulf. White Gate Court does not have a pool. A finger dock stretches into the water for fishing, and tiki torches and barbecue grills are available for an evening cookout. A guest laundry also is provided. Pets and children are welcome.

Middle Keys

The Middle Keys, known locally as the "heart of the Keys," stretch from the Long Key Bridge to the Seven Mile Bridge. **Long, Conch, Duck,** and **Grassy Keys** lead the way to the string of bridge-connected islands known as the incorporated city of **Marathon.**

Basing your accommodations in the Middle Keys offers some distinct advantages. The barrier reef sheltering the prolific fishing waters of the Atlantic supports a plethora of marine life and harbors a number of primo shipwrecks for divers (see the Diving & Snorkeling chapter). Fishing in the Middle Keys rivals that of the famed Islamorada, a well-kept secret. From flats to backcountry, blue water to bridges, you won't hear too many tales of the "one that got away" here (see the Fishing chapter).

Marathon currently offers one golf course, the nine-hole Key Colony Beach public course.

The Dolphin Research Center on Grassy Key is a must-do regardless of where your accommodations might be. And in Marathon, Crane Point Museum and Nature Center will captivate the whole family, as will historic Pigeon Key, at the end of a length of the old Seven Mile Bridge accessed at mile marker 47 (see the Attractions chapter). Sombrero Beach in Marathon, a very nice man-made public beach, provides endless ocean vistas to all.

Like the rest of the Keys, this whole area is packed with recreational water options from party fishing boats and glass-bottomed reef excursions to personal watercraft and sea kayak rentals (see the Recreation chapter).

The pace is less tiki-bar frenetic here than in the Upper Keys. The sidewalk rolls up at a relatively early hour. But this area will appeal to families with children as well as serious anglers and divers who, after a day on or under the water, relish a relaxing dinner at one of the many top-notch restaurants and then a nocturnal refueling of energy for whatever tomorrow may bring.

BANANA BAY RESORT & MARINA $$$
MM 49.5 Bayside, Marathon
(305) 743-3500 or (866) 689-4217
bananabay.com
This dazzling 10-acre plantation-style resort on Florida Bay is a popular Marathon destination. The grounds are ancient: gnarled trunks of massive royal poinciana trees, 20-foot traveler's palms, and mature bird-of-paradise plants. And don't miss the bananas, 15 varieties tucked between towering scheffleras and gumbo-limbos, papayas, and staggering banyan trees. Don't let this quiet island charm fool you. There is plenty to do besides loll by the L-shaped swimming pool or soak in the hot tub. Banana Bay offers an on-premises playland: tennis, parasailing, sea kayaking, sailboarding, or rentals of personal watercraft, sailboats, and more from Fish-n-Fun Boat and Watersport Rentals. Banana Bay offers popular island wedding packages, including a choice of romantic settings for the ceremony.

BAY VIEW INN MOTEL AND
**   MARINA $$$**
MM 63 Bayside, Conch Key
(305) 289-1525 or (800) 289-2055
bayviewinn.com
Located in the heart of Conch Key, with views of the Gulf of Mexico, the brightly colored Bay View Inn Motel and Marina is a quiet retreat from the busy crowds of larger resorts. The inn offers free Wi-Fi, free boat dockage, a swimming pool, and a variety of rooms, efficiencies, and family suites. Some

of the efficiencies and rooms are situated at the waterfront on the marina and have individual grills for that daily catch or late-night dining. Regular rooms come with a refrigerator, cable TV, and 2 queen-size beds. The efficiencies, which also sleep 4, come with kitchenettes to support family-style vacations. The Bay View can arrange for Jet Ski, kayak, and boat rentals so you are sure to enjoy the great outdoors during your stay.

THE BLACKFIN RESORT AND
**   MARINA $$**
MM 49.5 Bayside, Marathon
(305) 743-2393 or (800) 548-5397
blackfinresort.com
The 35-unit Blackfin Resort and Marina sits on 4.5 acres abutting the Gulf of Mexico. The grounds are peppered with poinciana, gumbo-limbo, strangler fig trees, and curving coconut palms. Stone paths wind through gardens of tropical flora. On a remote point of land at the end of the marina marked by a miniature lighthouse, guests enjoy a 600-foot, man-made, sandy beach sprinkled with lounge chairs, picnic tables, barbecue grills, and a thatched chickee. A freshwater pool overlooks the gulf. The placid waters of the gulf shelter a potpourri of tropical fish, a virtual aquarium for anglers and snorkelers. Personal watercraft and kayak rentals are available on-site. Also on the premises are the Hurricane Grille restaurant and a jazz/blues bar with live entertainment.

BLUE WATERS RESORT MOTEL $$
MM 48.5 Bayside, Marathon
(305) 743-4832 or (800) 222-4832
bluewatersresortmotel.com
You'll enjoy a Mediterranean feeling here at Blue Waters Resort Motel, for the white stucco buildings, gray tile roofs, and bright,

turquoise-blue doors evoke visions of Greece. Two banks of motel units, some with efficiency kitchens, flank the parking lot. The rooms feature 2 double beds or a king-size bed. For a real getaway, try renting an Island Home. This is a 1,400-square-foot house floating on the water! It has 2 bedrooms with queen beds, 2.5 baths, and a fully appointed kitchen. A raised swimming pool affords a view of a small boat basin on the gulf where guests may dock their boats for a small additional charge per day.

BONEFISH RESORT $$
MM 58 Oceanside, Grassy Key
(305) 743-7107 or (800) 274-9949
bonefishresort.com
Family owned and operated, Bonefish Resort is one of those little gems reflecting old Florida Keys. This true motel is a "happy camper" resting among coconut palms, banana trees, hibiscus flowers, and tropical gardens. Open the hand-painted door to your efficiency or room and step into a bright, fun space. The deluxe efficiency has a full kitchen, private deck/patio, and barbecue grill, while the efficiency offers a full kitchen and outdoor area. Guest rooms have a double bed and furnishings to suit. Walk the white-sand beach and come back for a swim in the pool or enjoy the picnic area. Rent a tandem kayak or pedal boat, then take a stroll and retire to a hammock or an old-fashioned swing. Truly a Keys kind of day!

COCOPLUM BEACH AND
TENNIS CLUB $$$$
MM 54.5 Oceanside, 109 Coco Plum Dr.,
Marathon
(305) 743-0240 or (800) 228-1587
cocoplum.com

Hidden among 53 varieties of palm trees and other tropical plantings, this pod of 20 art deco–colored 3-story "mushrooms" bestows a true island ambience. Cocoplum Beach and Tennis Club has planted a fruit-and-spice park that sports banana trees, citrus, and key lime trees. Guests are invited to freely pick any of the ripe fruit and enjoy the tastes of the tropics. Loll by the illusion-edge swimming pool, or pop into one of the blue cabanas sprinkled about the sandy beach area. The hot tub awaits your tired muscles after a few hours of spirited tennis or beach volleyball. Or just fold yourself into one of the many secluded hammocks and take a snooze. Reservations for 7 nights are preferred, but 3- to 6-night stays are available, space permitting.

CONCH KEY COTTAGES $$$
MM 62.3 Oceanside, Walker's Island
(305) 289-1377 or (800) 330-1577
conchkeycottages.com
The pastel, gingerbread-trimmed Conch Key Cottages—like an upended basket of Easter eggs—are as unique as the conch shells for which they're named. A small swimming pool sits amid towering palms, and several varieties of bananas hang at the ready for guest consumption. Plantings reflect the owners' philosophy of growing old-fashioned vegetation that attracts birds and butterflies. Conch Key Cottages maintains a boat ramp and marina that can accommodate an 8-foot draft. Guests may dock their vessels at no extra charge. So you are sure to bring those freshly caught snappers to the table, there is a fish-cleaning station complete with water and electricity.

CONTINENTAL INN $$$
MM 53.8 Oceanside, 1121 W. Ocean Dr.,
Key Colony Beach
(305) 289-0101 or (800) 443-7352
marathonresort.com

Don your mask, fins, and snorkel, because a small, rocky formation at the edge of Continental Inn's beach supports an aquarium of marine life. Located on the coveted sandy stretch of Key Colony Beach, this condominium resort, with its white-stone balustrade, looks faintly Mediterranean. Gulls and terns dart about the oceanfront chickees as guests drink in the limitless vistas of the Atlantic. These individually owned, simply decorated, one-bedroom efficiencies flank a large, heated swimming pool. You can play the links at the nearby public golf course, head for the tennis courts, or take your kids to a nice playground (see the Recreation chapter). No boats or trailers are allowed.

CORAL LAGOON RESORT AND
   MARINA $$$
MM 53.5 Oceanside, Marathon
(866) 904-1234
corallagoonresort.com

These 25 Key West–style villas and detached marina homes with white picket fences and wood shutters sit on 6 acres next to the Boat House Marina (see the Boating chapter). The 2-story homes offer an open floor plan with 3 bedrooms, 2.5 baths, and luxury interiors with peaceful tropical colors and tasteful decorations. You'll enjoy the full gourmet kitchens, washers and dryers, Wi-Fi, cable, a film library for your viewing pleasure, housekeeping services, and wonderful water views from the first- and second-floor private porches. The resort rents these homes daily, weekly, or monthly and allows easy access to the Atlantic Ocean for excellent blue-water

offshore fishing and the Gulf of Mexico for thrilling backcountry wreck fishing and boating.

CRYSTAL BAY RESORT $$
MM 49 Bayside, Marathon
(305) 289-8089 or (888) 289-8089
crystalbayresort.com

Situated on the Gulf of Mexico and dotted with hammocks, coach lights, and a gazebo, Crystal Bay Resort offers reasonably priced lodging in its 26 Conch-style bungalows. Children enjoy the extensive sandbox play yard; adults like the picnic area, which is peppered with brick barbecue grills; and everyone loves the free-form swimming pool and waterfall. Equipped with fiber-optic lighting, the waters change colors in the evening, creating a kaleidoscopic effect that carries on where the spectacular sunset left off. Chaise lounges and chickees are sprinkled about the water's edge, and a small marina basin allows easy access to explore surrounding waters. Guests may launch their boats here; dockage is an extra fee. A fishing pier, complete with cleaning station, juts offshore.

GULF VIEW WATERFRONT RESORT $$$
MM 58.7 Bayside, Grassy Key
(305) 289-1414 or (877) 289-0111
gulfviewwaterfrontresort.com

This small, private resort hosts 11-unit accommodations that include guest rooms with refrigerators and microwaves as well as one- and two-bedroom apartments with full-size kitchens. Clean, bright furnishings make this a wonderful Middle Keys location for families, and they also welcome your pet. On the property is a lovely freshwater heated pool, boat ramp, dock, and even a putting green for the land lovers. Swing low in a hammock or sit under one of the tiki huts and gaze out over hundreds of palm trees surrounded by beautiful tropical vegetation. For the more active guest, bikes are available for rent, and complimentary kayaks, canoes, and paddleboats are just begging to be used in the clear blue Keys waters.

THE HAMMOCKS AT MARATHON $$$
MM 48.2 Bayside, Marathon
(305) 743-9009 or (800) 456-0009
bluegreenrentals.com

Perched in lush tropical foliage, the Hammocks at Marathon offers you an escape. Wildlife of parrotfish, tarpon, and lobster are in the clear waters of the lagoon, and egrets, pelicans, and herons populate the mangroves. Palm trees and tiki huts dot the landscape, which also features a pool and hot tub. Lodging options include studio rooms (without kitchens); 1 bedroom, 1 bath, and kitchen; or 2 bedrooms, 1.5 baths, and kitchen. On the property, Barnacle Barney's Tiki Bar & Grill overlooks the marina, with a full bar and menu to satisfy. Barney's also celebrates the famous Florida Keys sunsets with the firing of a cannon as the sun sizzles into the cool gulf waters. Water sports and fishing abound to keep your appetite humming.

HAWK'S CAY RESORT AND
   MARINA $$$$
MM 61 Oceanside, Duck Key
(305) 743-7000 or (888) 395-5539
hawkscay.com

Hawk's Cay's rambling 60-acre Caribbean-style resort resides on one of the five islands of Duck Key. Accommodations in the main building offer West Indies elegance offset by local art and photography. Unique to this Keys property is the saltwater lagoon, belted by a man-made, sandy beach. Get your sun in at the lagoon or the family or adults-only pools, or visit the Calm Waters Spa, where services vary daily. You can also observe the ongoing dolphin discovery program at the Dolphin Connection (see the Attractions chapter); sign up for fishing, parasailing, sailing, or sea kayaking; play tennis; or work out at the Indies Club recreation and fitness center. There are also two popular restaurants on the premises to ensure that however you spend your day, you can follow it up with a great meal.

INDIGO REEF RESORT & MARINA $$$
MM 53 Bayside, Marathon
(305) 396-3002 or (866) 643-5397
indigoreefresort.com

Built on 15 acres in the heart of Marathon, this waterfront enclave offers classic Florida Keys architecture and lush tropical landscaping. Sixty-seven "homes" are casually themed with 3 bedrooms, 2.5 baths, gourmet kitchens, and Wi-Fi, with first- and second-level porches for maximum water views. On the property is a waterfront swimming pool, and full-service private spa services can be arranged by appointment in your villa. The marina was built with anglers and boaters in mind, with easy access to the Gulf of Mexico and tropical reefs, private boat slips just steps away from each home, and an on-site dock master. Guests can also avail themselves of the services of the Adventure Concierge Program for personalized dive, snorkel, boat, and fishing trips.

KEY COLONY BEACH MOTEL $
MM 54 Oceanside, 441 E. Ocean Dr., Key
Colony Beach
(305) 289-0411

Sitting proudly beside the ocean in Key Colony Beach—often called "condo row"—the modest Key Colony Beach Motel provides simply furnished rooms, each featuring 2 double beds, a refrigerator, and an excellent location. A lovely, palm-lined, sandy beach fronts this 2-story white motel, which also has a heated swimming pool. All you need here is a towel, some sunscreen, and a good book.

LIME TREE BAY RESORT $$$
MM 68.5 Oceanside, Long Key
(305) 664-4740 or (800) 723-4519
limetreebayresort.com
Located on the "island" of Long Key among 100 palm trees, the Lime Tree Bay Resort is a true gem. In addition to the idyllic location, the property also contains a pool that sits right on the water's edge, and tiki huts, hammocks, and barbecue areas all dot the property. Take a swim in one of the 2 pools, snorkel right off the beach, or take out a complimentary sea kayak. Each of the rooms and suites features free Wi-Fi and handsome tropical furnishings, like Mexican-tile flooring and paddle ceiling fans. This beautiful resort has received a Superior Small Lodging Award and offers different packages throughout the year, so be sure to ask if they are running any specials.

RAINBOW BEND RESORT $$$
MM 58 Oceanside, Grassy Key
(305) 289-1505 or (888) 929-1505
rainbowbend.com
Stretched across 2.5 acres of palm-speckled oceanfront beach, Rainbow Bend presents a mixed bag of sleeping rooms, efficiencies, and suites, and each day of your stay entitles you to 4 free boating hours. Use of canoes, kayaks, and paddleboats is also complimentary. Small pets under 40 pounds are allowed for an additional fee. Relax on the beach, or if

freshwater appeals to you, dip into the large pool and hot tub that edge the property. A long, wooden pier extends into the shallow ocean waters for fishing or docking your own small watercraft for the duration of your stay. The Hideaway Cafe, which overlooks the beach, offers lunch and dinner (see our Restaurants chapter). A complimentary breakfast is served here each morning.

THE REEF RESORT $$
MM 50.5 Bayside, Marathon
(305) 743-7900
thereefatmarathon.com
As you drive through Marathon, you may spot what looks like a cluster of beige spaceships hugging Florida Bay. No, the aliens have not landed. These 22 octagonal villas, suspended on "landing" shaft stilts, actually provide a luxurious Keys getaway. Lushly landscaped grounds on 6 acres, surrounding the 2 tennis courts, belie the fact that the Reef Resort borders the Overseas Highway. Bicycles, canoes, paddleboats, and rowboats are available at no extra charge for guests who can tear themselves away from the swimming pool. Picnic tables, grills, and chickees on the waterfront inspire a cookout at sunset. The Reef Resort's marina offers dockage for your boat of 25 feet or less (5-foot draft at low tide). Rentals are available for the week or the month.

SEA ISLE CONDOMINIUMS $$
MM 53.8 Oceanside, 1101 W. Ocean Dr.,
Key Colony Beach
(305) 743-0173 or (877) 743-0173
seaislecondos.com
The sandy beach and ocean views distinguish this 24-unit condo resort. Three tri-level white buildings, one behind the other, line Sea Isle's narrow strip of Key Colony

Beach. Built in the late 1960s and individually owned and decorated, the furnishings of these spacious two-bedroom, two-bath apartments swing widely among styles of ensuing decades. Nevertheless, all necessities for a sun-filled, fun-filled vacation are provided: a heated swimming pool, gas grills, picnic tables, lounge chairs, and chickees. Stroll down Key Colony's "condo row" to the public golf course and tennis courts or head into Marathon for a selection of boating, fishing, and diving activities (see the chapters devoted to those subjects). Reservations require a 1-week minimum stay.

SOMBRERO RESORT AND LIGHTHOUSE MARINA $$
MM 50 Oceanside, 19 Sombrero Blvd., Marathon
(305) 289-7662 or (800) 433-8660
sombreroresortmarina.com

The Sombrero Resort flanks Boot Key Harbor and an adjoining inland canal, and offers efficiencies and condominium accommodations with all the amenities of a resort. Though not on the ocean, this destination resort allows you to be within steps of all the action, yet bathed in a laid-back and relaxing atmosphere. The 93 suites and efficiencies are situated in a pair of 3-story white buildings with covered parking beneath. A keystone deck surrounds the large swimming pool, complete with a tiki bar and poolside game room with billiards, table soccer, and arcade games. You'll be able to improve your tennis on one of the 4 courts, get your daily workouts in the exercise room, and pamper yourself in the salon and spa.

TRANQUILITY BAY BEACHFRONT HOTEL & RESORT $$$$
MM 48.5 Bayside, Marathon
(305) 289-0888 or (866) 643-5397
tranquilitybay.com

Built on 12 acres overlooking the aquamarine Gulf of Mexico, Tranquility Bay is your own little "private island." Magnificent palm trees shade the sand dunes, where sea oats sway in warm breezes and a 2.5-acre white-sand beach sparkles in the sunlight. The beach houses are decorated with tropical cottage flair, offering a choice of 2 or 3 bedrooms. Twenty-four-hour room service and daily maid service are available. Part of your stay should include their Island Spice Private Spa, which offers in-home treatments. And be sure and catch a sunset or two at TJ's Tiki Bar, which is perched on the beach. Tranquility Bay also has a supervised children's program called Keys Kids Adventure Camp.

TROPICAL COTTAGES $$$
MM 50.5 Bayside, Marathon
(305) 743-6048
tropicalcottages.net

Built in 1952, this enchanting hideaway caters to honeymooners, weddings, reunions, and small groups (adults only; no one under the age of 18). Tropical Cottages is adjacent to the Florida Keys Land and Sea Trust, which offers kayak trails that make for quiet exploring of backcountry and calm waters. (Don't forget to put snorkeling on your list as well.) Daily housekeeping (upon request) and complimentary use of the resort's bikes, rowboats, canoes, and sea kayaks are all included in your stay. Also, one of their special touches is a treasure map to help you uncover natural bathing beaches, scenic bike paths, and picnic spots, with a bonus of restaurant and shopping tips.

WHITE SANDS INN $$
MM 57.6 Oceanside, Grassy Key
(305) 743-5285
whitesandsinn.com

Hugging a prime piece of direct ocean frontage on Grassy Key, the pale-pink-and-white White Sands Inn houses 7 one-room units, a Tree Top Terrace suite, and the Sunrise Beach House, a 3-unit house at ocean's edge that enjoys sweeping vistas of the Atlantic and a heated swimming pool. The inn rests amid towering coconut palms at water's edge, where sparkling white imported sand forms a beach. Grills are available, and a large picnic table rests under a thatched chickee. A long, curved pier stretches out into the ocean, where kayaks, a rowboat, and a paddleboat are docked for free usage by guests. At low tide the nearshore waters abutting the inn recede, forming a natural sandy beach that you can walk along for miles.

YELLOWTAIL INN $$$
MM 58 Oceanside, Grassy Key
(305) 743-8400 or (800) 605-7475
yellowtailinn.com

The quaint Yellowtail Inn is charming, and its ocean-view efficiencies, cottages, and private oceanfront suites are reminiscent of old Keys style. All of the accommodations are decorated in Keys tropical-casual, with the light and airy colors of carefree sunny days. On the lovely grounds, located on unspoiled Grassy Key, you will find a small heated swimming pool, fishing pier, small private beach, and barbecue grills. Kayaks, pedal boats, fishing and snorkeling gear, and bicycles are all available for rent on the property. There is also a coin laundry facility on the grounds. Nearby attractions include the Dolphin Research Center, Pigeon Key, fishing charters, and sunset sails.

i If you are not staying at one of the large resort properties in the Keys, no big deal! Their restaurants and bars still offer an excellent atmosphere for socializing. Typically, establishments have casual eats at an outside bar, and in many cases reservations are not necessary.

Lower Keys

The Lower Keys, sleepier and less densely populated than the Middle or Upper Keys, distinguish themselves with acres and acres of shallow-water turtle-grass flats and copious uninhabited mangrove out-islands. The Lower Keys are surrounded by the **Great White Heron National Wildlife Refuge,** a large area in the Gulf of Mexico encompassing tiny keys from East Bahia Honda Key to the Content Keys to Cayo Agua and the Bay Keys. **Big Pine Key** is the home of the **National Key Deer Refuge,** a preserved area of wilderness sheltering our diminutive key deer.

Fishing is outstanding here, though ocean access is more limited. The Lower Keys can also boast of the **Looe Key National Marine Sanctuary,** one of the best snorkeling and diving reefs in the world. (See the Area Overview and Diving & Snorkeling chapters for details.)

Accommodations are scattered all throughout the Lower Keys, where campgrounds tend to dominate. (See the Campgrounds chapter if you'd like to camp in the area.) Most of the accommodations here started as fishing camps decades ago and have been updated to varying degrees. Several wonderful bed-and-breakfast inns are tucked away on a little-known oceanfront road, offering seclusion, privacy, and limitless vistas of the sea.

Crowning the assets of Lower Keys accommodations is **Little Palm Island,** a premier resort that rules in a class by itself. Whatever your lodging choice in the sanctuaries of the Lower Keys, your proximity to Key West more than makes up for any tourist attractions or nightlife that may be lacking here.

BARNACLE BED & BREAKFAST $$
1557 Long Beach Dr., Big Pine Key
(305) 872-3298 or (800) 465-9100
thebarnacle.net
Barnacle Bed & Breakfast resides on a serene stretch of beach that extends out into the Atlantic. Constructed as 3 rotated, star-shaped levels, the Barnacle houses a foliage-filled atrium that serves as the location for the complimentary breakfast buffet. Comfortably furnished with ceiling fans, a sofa, television, table, and chairs, the atrium also serves as a common room. Guests enjoy use of kayaks, bicycles, snorkeling gear, and barbecue grills. Children younger than age 16 are not permitted. Finding Long Beach Road is a little tricky: Turn left at Big Pine Fishing Lodge, mile marker 33, oceanside, and proceed about 2 miles.

DEER RUN BED & BREAKFAST $$
MM 33 Oceanside, Long Beach Dr., Big Pine Key
(305) 872-2015
deerrunfloridabb.com
The diminutive key deer really do have the run of this bed-and-breakfast, as they stroll the grounds like boarded guests. Staying at Deer Run is akin to vacationing in a nature preserve, and the care for animals is not limited to the outdoors. The food at Deer Run is vegan and is prepared without the use of any animal products or by-products.

In addition, all products at Deer Run are cruelty-free, without any animal ingredients or animal testing. Deer Run's Florida Cracker–style home overlooks a peaceful beach, only 50 feet beyond a raised hot tub that fronts a productive bonefish flat. Deer Run caters to adults; children under the age of 18 are not permitted.

LITTLE PALM ISLAND RESORT & SPA $$$$
MM 28.5 Oceanside, Little Torch Key
(305) 515-4004 or (800) 343-8567
littlepalmisland.com
An exquisite resort encapsulated on its own island, 3 miles offshore from Little Torch Key, Little Palm is the centerpiece of the jeweled necklace of the Florida Keys. Television sets, telephones, and alarm clocks are banned, and the unhurried pace encourages serious lounging beside the free-form pool, atop the crystal sand beach, enveloped in a two-person hammock, or in the meditative Zen garden secreted away deep within the 5.5 acres of island. If you are looking for a more active vacation, complimentary surf bikes, day sailers, kayaks, canoes, a Hobie Cat, and snorkeling and fishing equipment are available. Meals are taken in the outstanding gourmet dining room (see the Restaurants chapter), and all-inclusive packages are available. Children younger than age 16 are not permitted.

OLD WOODEN BRIDGE GUEST COTTAGES AND MARINA $$
MM 30.5 Bayside, 1791 Bogie Dr., Big Pine Key
(305) 872-2241
oldwoodenbridge.com
In operation since the 1950s, the Old Wooden is tucked away at the foot of the

bridge that connects Big Pine Key to No Name Key. (The bridge was wooden when the camp was built, but it has since been replaced with a concrete structure.) The Old Wooden Bridge Guest Cottages and Marina sits on Bogie Channel, where you can access both the Gulf of Mexico and the Atlantic Ocean. There is nothing fancy or pretentious about this place. There are 14 one- and two-bedroom cottages, as well as campsites and picnic and barbecue areas where key deer roam free. The full-service marina supplies folks with gas, tackle, bait, and rental boats. They also have a family-size swimming pool, along with a store, boat launch, marina, and fuel dock.

PARMER'S RESORT $$
MM 28.5 Bayside, 565 Barry Ave., Little Torch Key
(305) 872-2157
parmersplace.com
Originally a fishing camp in the 1930s, Parmer's Resort offers 43 units in 13 buildings sprinkled over the 5-acre property in a homey 1960s style that differ widely in both size and amenities. Small, medium, and large motel rooms; standard and small efficiencies; cottages; and one- and two-bedroom apartments are all clean and simple. Fronting Big Pine Channel, Parmer's offers boat dockage at a small additional fee, but there is no beach. A free-form swimming pool anchors the center of the property. You'll need to pick up after yourself or pay a fee for maid service. But you can always stoke up the barbie, because Parmer's loans small gas grills to cook your catch of the day. A complimentary continental breakfast is served daily.

KEY WEST

This diverse, charming, historic city is considered one of the nation's top travel destinations. Key West's accommodations range from the comfort of a standard motel room to the luxury of a private suite in a historic inn. In this section we escort you through a variety of facilities. Our selections are based on attributes of rooms, service, location, and overall ambience. All facilities have air-conditioning, cable television, and telephones unless stated otherwise.

Motels

BEST WESTERN HIBISCUS MOTEL $$
1313 Simonton St.
(305) 294-3763 or (800) 780-7234
bestwestern.com
As Best Westerns go, this independently owned affiliate is small and understated. It is also one of only a few chains or franchises within Key West's historic Old Town. Of concrete-block construction, the Hibiscus has 61 units, including standard rooms and 5 one-bedroom efficiencies. Standard rooms are relatively large, with 2 queen-size beds, while efficiencies offer separate bedrooms and kitchens. Decor is bright and clean and features wood furnishings, carpeting, and coordinating wallpaper and bedspread patterns. All units overlook either the motel's heated swimming pool and hot tub or the street and a variety of palms. Four people can share a room at the given rate. Breakfast is included.

BLUE MARLIN RESORT MOTEL $$
1320 Simonton St.
(305) 294-2585 or (800) 523-1698
bluemarlinmotel.com

ACCOMMODATIONS

With its reasonable rates, heated swimming pool, and off-street parking, the Blue Marlin is a good choice for families who want to be near the action but don't want to pay dearly for the privilege. This 2-story, cement-block structure is not luxurious, but the 57 rooms—all of which overlook the pool—are clean, bright, and spacious. The best thing about the Blue Marlin, perhaps, is its location. It's tucked just a block off Duval Street on the Atlantic side of the island, and the Southernmost Point and South Beach are about 3 blocks away. There's no restaurant on the premises, but several reasonably priced eateries and a convenience store are located nearby.

COURTYARD KEY WEST WATERFRONT MARRIOTT $$$
3031-41 N. Roosevelt Blvd.
(305) 296-6595 or (888) 869-7066
marriott.com
This property faces the Gulf of Mexico side of Key West in "New Town," just 10 minutes away from all the downtown activity. On-site is a junior Olympic pool, Jacuzzi, and tiki bar (serving lunch and cocktails). Laze on a sunbathing beach or walk along a 300-foot observation boardwalk. Check into your room with king- or queen-size beds, all with patios or balconies. Family suites are available with a microwave, fridge, and pull-out queen sofa. Courtyard Key West has a meeting room that can seat up to 35 people, ideal for small gatherings, and offers free Wi-Fi. A complimentary shuttle runs to and from downtown from 8 a.m. to 11 p.m. There is a strict nonsmoking policy at the Courtyard.

FAIRFIELD INN & SUITES BY MARRIOTT KEY WEST $$
2400 N. Roosevelt Blvd.
(305) 296-5700 or (800) 228-2800
fairfieldinnkeywest.com
Fairfield Inn's easygoing prices and comfortable, well-kept facilities make this one of Key West's popular choices with vacationers. The motel offers 106 standard rooms and 26 suites throughout a trio of 2-story buildings, remodeled at a price tag of $7.5 million. Standard rooms primarily are furnished with 2 double beds, each with a comfortable pillow-top mattress; suites with varying amenities, including kitchens or kitchenettes and king-size beds, are other options. Fairfield Inn offers an oversize outdoor swimming pool, gas grills, a tiki bar, volleyball court, and guest laundry facilities. A separate concessionaire offers on-premises scooter rentals. Complimentary continental breakfast is offered daily, and covered parking spaces are available.

QUALITY INN AT KEY WEST $$
3824 N. Roosevelt Blvd.
(305) 294-3773 or (877) 424-6423
comfortinn.com
Guests at the Quality Inn have a choice of 100 rooms housed in 3 buildings. Options include rooms with 2 double beds or a few larger rooms with king-size beds. They are all carpeted and have comfortable furnishings; rollaways are provided upon request to a limited number of rooms. The rooms face either the pool or the parking lot, and all have free Wi-Fi. The motel offers complimentary continental breakfast and maintains a large outdoor swimming pool surrounded by concrete decking. Complimentary hot and cold beverages are served in the lobby

throughout the day. The motel is less than 0.5 mile from the Stock Island Bridge.

Hotels

BEST WESTERN KEY AMBASSADOR RESORT INN $$
3755 S. Roosevelt Blvd.
(305) 296-3500 or (800) 432-4315
keyambassador.com
The Key Ambassador Resort Inn consists of a cluster of 2-story buildings scattered across 7 acres of profuse tropical gardens punctuated by palm trees and hibiscus across the road from the Atlantic Ocean. Every room has a private balcony, and all 100 units have pleasant views of the garden, the harbor, the pool, or the ocean. Central to Best Western Key Ambassador and overlooking the ocean is a (heated in winter) swimming pool with a sundeck. A small bar and grill sits beside it. For do-it-yourselfers, a cookout area offers barbecue grills and outdoor tables and chairs. Other amenities include guest laundry facilities and a daily complimentary continental breakfast. From the Key Ambassador, it's a 10-minute walk to Smathers Beach and 2 miles to historic Old Town.

CROWNE PLAZA KEY WEST LA CONCHA $$$$
430 Duval St.
(305) 296-2991 or (877) 270-1393
laconchakeywest.com
Not only is La Concha the tallest building on the island of Key West, but it's also situated in the center of busy Duval Street. Originally opened in 1926, La Concha has weathered many changes and undergone numerous face-lifts. Today, its 150 guest rooms and 10 suites are furnished with a mix of vintage design and modern touches. The spacious pool, set amid lush island foliage, features a multilevel sundeck and a tiki bar. Jack's Seafood Shack serves breakfast buffet, lunch, and dinner. and the Top, a seventh-floor wraparound observation deck, not only offers a bird's-eye perspective on downtown Key West, but is also one of the best places in town to view the sunset. A full bar at the Top is open limited hours around sunset each evening and serves cocktails and appetizers.

THE INN AT KEY WEST $$$
3420 N. Roosevelt Blvd.
(305) 294-5541 or (800) 330-5541
theinnatkeywest.com
The Inn at Key West is located along N. Roosevelt Boulevard just 3 miles from Duval Street. With 106 rooms, this complex can accommodate a getaway for 2 or a family reunion for 20. All rooms are decorated in Tommy Bahama furnishings, and some offer private balconies where you can take in a wandering tropical breeze from the Gulf of Mexico. On the premises is the largest tropical freshwater pool in Key West. Creatively landscaped foliage and vegetation surround a lively full-service tiki bar. The Inn at Key West houses the casual open-air Cafe at the Inn, which is under the umbrella next to the bar. You can enjoy a breakfast buffet and lunch till early afternoon or Sunday brunch. Concierge services are also available for booking everything from sightseeing tours to sports activities.

PEGASUS INTERNATIONAL HOTEL $$
501 Southard St. (corner of Duval)
(305) 294-9323 or (800) 397-8148
pegasuskeywest.com
Located on a busy corner in the heart of downtown Key West, Pegasus International Hotel offers 30 rooms with various bedding

combinations, including 2 double beds, a queen-size bed, or a king-size bed. The rooms are tastefully appointed in tropical decor. Rates are reasonable, especially considering the hotel's prime location, which is within easy walking distance of Mallory Square and the restaurants and bars on lower Duval Street, plus the fact that parking is free. Amenities here include a rooftop swimming pool, hot tub, and sundeck, all located on the second floor and all overlooking bustling Duval Street. Aside from the complimentary continental breakfast, there are no on-premises food outlets at Pegasus; however, several restaurants are conveniently located within a block or two.

PELICAN LANDING RESORT & MARINA $$$$
915 Eisenhower Dr.
(305) 296-0500
pelicanlandingkeywest.com
The inconspicuous gulfside Pelican Landing is a 16-unit condominium and marina complex on Garrison Bight. Guests are offered a choice of standard rooms with 2 double beds or one-, two-, or three-bedroom suites. All accommodations are decorated according to the taste of their individual owners; suites have balconies overlooking the marina, and all have washer-dryers. Pelican Landing's heated swimming pool is surrounded by a sundeck, and gas barbecue grills and a fish-cleaning station are available for guests. The facility is boat accessible by powerboat only, because a fixed bridge offers only an 18-foot clearance. The marina offers 15 boat slips accommodating vessels up to 35 feet with a 12-foot beam. All guests have off-street parking. Charter fishing boats are just across the dock. Pets are welcome.

SOUTHERNMOST HOTEL $$$
1319 Duval St.
(305) 296-6577 or (800) 354-4455
southernmostresorts.com
Gingerbread architectural detail and native flora come together at Southernmost Hotel, reminding visitors that they have reached an eclectic city on an island. Situated just across from Southernmost on the Beach, Southernmost Hotel's 6 buildings with 124 rooms available are surrounded by ample parking and are trimmed with exotic plants, flowers, and trees. One of the hotel's 2 swimming pools sits in the center of the parking lot, concealed by lush greenery and a wall. The courtyard features the main pool, surrounded by decking, and a hot tub. Each pool has its own outdoor tiki bar. Scooter and bicycle rentals and concierge services are available. The tiki bars serve light bites for breakfast and lunch.

SOUTHERNMOST ON THE BEACH $$$$
508 South St.
(305) 296-6577 or (800) 354-4455
southernmostresorts.com
So you want to stay at a gorgeous property right on the beach? Then book your reservation at the Southernmost on the Beach. This 80-room lodging was built in 2009, and its location and perks will pamper you and everyone in your party. All the suites at the Southernmost are 400 square feet; 13 of them are oceanfront and 48 are oceanview rooms. In addition to a private beach, there is also a private pier and a pool with pool bar on-site. Have lunch or wine and dine at the Southernmost Beach Cafe. Duval Street is just a block away, but once at this lovely resort, you will think you are on a deserted island.

TRUMAN HOTEL $$$
611 Truman Ave.
(305) 296-6700 or (866) 487-8626
trumanhotel.com

If you like the convenience of your hotel being within walking distance to all the major attractions, including Duval Street, then book your stay at the newly expanded Truman Hotel. Twenty-one rooms, including a cottage that sleeps 8, have all been redone. The spectacular baths contain glass-tile walls, mahogany vanities, and glass sinks that "float" atop marble surfaces and flow perfectly with the cool blues, browns, and creams in the rooms. An open courtyard with tables and chairs for reading or sunning is very inviting. The pool, replete with relaxing underwater jets, is surrounded by palm trees and lounge chairs and is the perfect place to unwind before cocktail hour. This is a nonsmoking hotel. Harry and Bess would approve!

Full-Service Resorts

BEACHSIDE MARRIOTT $$$$
3841 N. Roosevelt Blvd.
(305) 296-8100 or (866) 679-5490
beachsidekeywest.com

Proudly standing sentinel at the entrance to Key West on Roosevelt Boulevard is the Beachside Marriott. Elegance abounds here, but still with a Key West charm about the property. The 5,600-square-foot ballroom can handle any event, and if you wish to impress your best friends and family, they can land at the helicopter pad on the lobby roof. There is a heated pool on the grounds flanked by lush tropical foliage, rooftop sundecks, and a small beach for midnight strolls. Head to the Blue Bar by the pool for casual afternoon refreshments. Then in the evening, glide indoors to the swank Tavern N

Town restaurant set with white tablecloths, for classic dishes of foie gras and grilled duck. You get the picture!

CASA MARINA RESORT AND
BEACH CLUB $$$$
1500 Reynolds St.
(305) 296-3535 or (888) 679-5490
casamarinaresort.com

This beautiful property is a Florida Keys fairy tale, a legend that has hosted the likes of baseball great Lou Gehrig, actress Rita Hayworth, and president Harry Truman. Sleek guest rooms, suites, and public areas; 2 new pools; private cabanas; new landscaping; and a private water walkway to the Atlantic Ocean await guests. The Sun-Sun Beach Bar and Grill is located between the beach and pool area for a romantic breakfast, lunch, or dinner. The Rambler Lounge is a full bar with nightly entertainment, and room service is available. All that combined with the Casa Marina's location on the largest private beach in Key West, minutes from Old Town and Duval Street and 3 minutes from Key West International Airport, makes this laid-back, elegant hotel an ideal choice.

DOUBLETREE GRAND KEY RESORT $$$
3990 S. Roosevelt Blvd.
(305) 293-1818 or (800) 222-8733
doubletreekeywest.com

Grand Key Resort, located near the airport on the north side of the island, offers 216 guest rooms in a variety of configurations. The upper floors have a pretty decent view of the Atlantic Ocean and Smathers Beach in the distance. A focal point in the lobby is the 25,000-gallon aquarium that stretches from floor to ceiling and is filled with the kind of colorful fish you would likely see on a trip to the reef. The Palm Haven Restaurant, which overlooks the pool at the far end of the lobby, serves island fare. Snacks and tropical libations are available at an open-air bar positioned poolside. A large deck and plenty of blue cushioned chairs beckon sun worshipers. An on-premises gift shop, meeting facilities, and concierge services are also available.

HYATT KEY WEST RESORT AND SPA $$$$
601 Front St.
(305) 809-1234 or (888) 591-1234
keywest.hyatt.com
Fronting the Gulf of Mexico, the 5-story Hyatt Key West is a 3-building, 118-unit complex of luxurious rooms that overlook the city, pool, or Gulf of Mexico. The Hyatt has an outdoor swimming pool and hot tub, 2 dive boats, a charter fishing boat, and a 68-foot sailing yacht for afternoon snorkeling and early-evening sunset sails. There is also the Jala Spa to soothe and pamper guests in addition to an on-site fitness center. Water sports and scooter and bike rentals are available, and the hotel has a small private beach. A 3-tier sundeck overlooks the beach, and the resort's own SHOR American Seafood Grill (see the Restaurants chapter) is a great place to enjoy the sunset.

OCEAN KEY RESORT AND SPA $$$$
Zero Duval St.
(305) 296-7701 or (800) 328-9815
oceankey.com
Ocean Key is a 100-unit resort with an intimate flavor. From their rooms and balconies, Ocean Key guests can see the ocean, our famous sunsets, and the offbeat Mallory Square entertainers. On the premises are the Sunset Pier, which has a full bar, waterfront dining, and live entertainment nightly; the

Hot Tin Roof restaurant (see our Restaurant chapter); the poolside Liquid Lounge bar, only open to resort guests; and a marina with fishing, snorkeling, dive charter boats, and a glass-bottomed tour boat. Ocean Key offers its tranquil SpaTerre for its guests. This serene escape is a 2,550-square-foot Indonesian-inspired spa. The theme of this facility originated at the sister property, famed Little Palm Island Resort & Spa (see listing in this chapter) located on Little Torch Key.

ORCHID KEY INN $$$
1004 Duval St.
(305) 296-9915 or (800) 845-8384
orchidkey.com
Built in the 1950s and tucked between old Conch houses and storefronts, the owners (they also own the Almond Tree Inn; see listing in this chapter) have brought this 24-room property back to life in a big way. After massive renovations made while maintaining the original footprint, the Orchid Inn is open and warmly greets guests. The pool has a dramatic sunning shelf, and the hot tub features a tiled wall with a purple orchid mosaic and a rain waterfall. Near the pool is a bar where guests are served drinks in the afternoon and evening and a continental breakfast in the morning. This property is centrally located for all activities in Old Town Key West, so you can walk or ride bikes to restaurants, shops, and activities.

PARROT KEY HOTEL & RESORT $$$
2801 N. Roosevelt Blvd.
(305) 809-2200 or (888) 665-6368
parrotkeyresort.com
This newcomer to Key West has 118 rooms, 4 pools, and a sunning beach. It is a few minutes from downtown Old Town and is on the

Gulf of Mexico. Owned by the Singh Company (which owns Tranquility Bay Beachfront Hotel & Resort; see listing in this chapter), each room in the Parrot Key is decorated in a seaside cottage motif with original Florida Keys art for accents, fine linens, and king beds. Tropical landscaping hides you away, with lush gardens and sunbathing terraces surrounding two sides of the resort. There is a full conference center on the property, and a casual dining facility steps from the pool.

PIER HOUSE RESORT AND CARIBBEAN SPA $$$$
1 Duval St.
(305) 296-4600 or (800) 723-2791
pierhouse.com
For more than 40 years, the Pier House has offered luxury lodging in Key West with views of the Gulf of Mexico, the swimming pool, or the city. Rooms facing the water may look out on the beautiful Key West Harbor or on sunbathers along a portion of the resort's private beach. Lush tropical foliage and brick paving surround the swimming pool and outdoor hot tub. The Pier House is also host to the Caribbean Spa, a full-service spa that offers fitness facilities, facials, massages, a hair salon, and manicures and pedicures. Room service is available, and a concierge will arrange for additional needs. The hotel also features a restaurant called HarbourView Cafe and the Chart Room Bar (see the Nightlife chapter). Off-street parking is abundant.

THE REACH RESORT $$$$
1435 Simonton St.
(888) 318-4316
reachresort.com
The Reach Resort offers miles of ocean water to view and a glistening white-sand beach with sounds of rolling waves. All 150

guest rooms and suites are furnished with sunny lemon-colored walls and terra-cotta-tiled floors with Caribbean artistic touches and private balconies. The resort has an outdoor swimming pool, hot tub, and full water-sports concession for rafts, parasailing, personal watercraft rentals, and more right on the beach. The Strip House restaurant, known for its amazing steak dinners (see our Restaurants chapter), sits on the first floor with stunning ocean views and dining inside and out. Room service, valet laundry service, and concierge services are available, along with complimentary transportation to and from Key West International Airport.

For information about accommodations in Key West—whether you're looking for a quaint guesthouse or a full-service resort—contact the Accommodation Center, accommodations keywest.com; Rent Key West, rentkeywest.com; or the Innkeepers Association, keywestinns.com.

SHERATON SUITES KEY WEST $$$$
2001 S. Roosevelt Blvd.
(305) 292-9800 or (800) 325-3535
sheratonkeywest.com
Situated across from Smathers Beach, the brightly colored 3-story, 180-unit Sheraton is a luxurious all-suite facility built around an expansive concrete sundeck and a swimming pool. The roomy suites (550 square feet) are decorated in relaxing tropical colors and furnished in colorful wicker. The Coral Crab Cafe offers breakfast, lunch, and dinner. Sheraton Suites offers guests complimentary shuttle service to and from the airport as well as transportation to Mallory Square (see the Attractions chapter). The staff at the guest activities desk will assist you in

planning fishing and diving excursions, restaurant bookings, and more. On the premises are a hot tub, fitness center, off-street parking, and a gift shop. The Sheraton Suites is a pet-friendly resort, as animals weighing less than 40 pounds are welcome.

SUNSET KEY GUEST COTTAGES $$$$
245 Front St.
(305) 292-5300
sunsetkeyisland.com

The guest cottages at Sunset Key are an extension of the Westin Key West Resort and Marina (see listing in this chapter) and are tucked away on a private island directly across the harbor from the main hotel. Access is strictly by private launch, which operates throughout the day and night between Sunset Key and the Westin marina. Located amid swaying palms and lush flowering hibiscus, the cottages offer beachfront, ocean, or garden views. In addition to a white-sand beach, the island features a freshwater pool, hot tub, 2 tennis courts, a health club, and a full-service gourmet restaurant and bar, Latitudes (see the Restaurants chapter), which is the perfect place to view the sunset. No cars are permitted on Sunset Key; however, parking is available in the Westin garage.

THE WESTIN KEY WEST RESORT
AND MARINA $$$$
245 Front St.
(305) 294-4000 or (866) 716-8108
westinkeywestresort.com

The bayfront Westin was designed so that all rooms provide views of the pool, the bay, or the marina and its surrounding waters. Guests here also are provided launch service to a relatively secluded beach at Sunset Key (see this chapter's Sunset Key Guest Cottages listing). The 2 buildings that make up the Westin have 178 rooms. The 3-story building overlooks the marina; the other, a 4-story structure, sits adjacent to Mallory Square. Situated in historic Old Town near the old Custom House, the Westin and its grounds are surrounded by brick walkways. On the premises are a swimming pool, hot tub, and sundeck area; fitness facilities; a restaurant offering indoor and outdoor dining; and a sunset deck and lounge.

B&Bs, Inns & Guesthouses

Key West's Conch-style mansions and captains' and cigar-workers' homes date from the 1800s, and many have been marvelously restored to accommodate a thriving tourist industry. Close to 100 intimate hideaways are tucked along the streets, avenues, and lanes of Key West's Old Town, and these charming, romantic inns, bed-and-breakfasts, and guesthouses provide a sense of history, tranquility, and intimacy within the active city.

You'll find few waterfront or water-view guesthouse accommodations. Rather, rooms enjoy tranquil garden views or views of the ever-changing, active streetfront. French doors tend to lead to private verandas with picket fences overlooking lush courtyards where deluxe continental breakfasts, full breakfasts, and afternoon cocktails frequently are served beside peaceful swimming pools, goldfish ponds, or hot tubs. Some guesthouses provide passes that allow use of beach, spa, and fitness facilities at some of the island's full-service resorts.

Key West welcomes diversity, and some guesthouses cater primarily or exclusively to gay travelers. Others are considered all-welcome or gay-friendly. In a separate section at the end of this chapter, we highlight primarily and exclusively gay retreats, many of which maintain clothing-optional policies.

In fact, a few seemingly conservative guest-houses and inns on the island have begun to incorporate a clothing-optional policy; therefore, it is always a good idea to call ahead and check with the property before finalizing your reservation. Rooms do have a maximum capacity. Inquire about this and all other details when you call to make reservations.

Pets tend to be more welcome in Key West guesthouses than in hotels or other accommodations throughout the Florida Keys, but be sure to ask when making your reservation. We will note where pets are permitted. A flat fee or refundable deposit may be required.

As a general rule, guesthouses are for adults only. If a particular property welcomes children, we'll tell you. Otherwise, you may assume that you should either leave the kids at home or look elsewhere in this chapter for kid-friendly accommodations.

At last count, the Key West phone book had listings for close to 100 guesthouses and inns. We have done our best to provide a representative sampling. For a complete list of accommodations, contact the **Key West Information Center** at (305) 292-5000.

ALMOND TREE INN $$$
512 Truman Ave.
(305) 296-5415 or (800) 311-4292
almondtreeinn.com
The Almond Tree Inn sits at the historic crossroads of Truman Avenue and Duval Street in Old Town Key West. Lush tropical landscaping surrounds the 22 elegant, amenity-filled rooms. A tranquil waterfall is on the property, and sundecks surround the pool. Private, off-street parking assures convenience away from the well-traveled Old Town location. A complimentary continental

breakfast is served daily, and beer and wine are offered in the afternoon underneath the pavilion. Some rooms are deluxe king, some are premium king with a king-size bed and a sleeper sofa, and oversize guest rooms have 2 queen-size beds and a sleeper sofa. Guests must be age 25 or older unless accompanied by an adult.

AMBROSIA HOUSE $$$
622 Fleming St.
(305) 296-9838
ambrosiakeywest.com
This delightful bed-and-breakfast compound is really a combination of 6 carefully restored properties on 2 acres. The buildings are nestled among lush tropical landscaping and clear, cool ponds. Located in the heart of Old Town Key West, just 1.5 blocks off Duval, Ambrosia is convenient to shopping, restaurants, and nightlife. The accommodations include suites, town houses, and a stand-alone cottage. All rooms and suites feature individual entrances with French doors opening onto private verandas, patios, or gardens. The walls are adorned with the original works of Key West artists; the beds are dressed in designer linens. Large sunning areas, a lap pool, and a hot tub are also available. Children are welcome, as are pets.

ANDREWS INN & GARDEN COTTAGES $$$
Zero Whalton Lane
(305) 294-7730 or (888) 263-7393
andrewsinn.com
This tiny inn offers a welcome little slice of tranquility and is practically in Hemingway's backyard. You'll find it tucked behind his former house—the only thing that separates the two is a brick wall—on a shaded narrow lane. Guest rooms here are named for

settings in Hemingway's books, such as Paris and Pamplona. Just outside your door, you'll find a lush tropical garden and comfortable lounge chairs situated around a cool, refreshing pool. Andrews Inn offers complimentary mimosas and continental breakfast each morning and cocktails by the pool every afternoon. We should warn you about the neighbors: A representative from that gang of six-toed cats that reside next door at the Hemingway Home is likely to wander over to say hello.

THE ARTIST HOUSE $$$
534 Eaton St.
(305) 296-3977 or (800) 582-7882
artisthousekeywest.com

With the addition of guest suites a block away from the original property, the Artist House now offers accommodations at two levels—in a charming Victorian mansion and in modern villas. The one you choose is a matter of personal taste. What the Artist House Guest Villas might lack in old-world charm, they more than make up for by being exceptionally bright and roomy. Each of the 6 suites has been recently renovated and includes a fully equipped kitchen. The 3 rooms in the house have been renovated as well. Private sundecks and a heated swimming pool round out the amenities. Children age 5 and older are permitted.

AUTHORS OF KEY WEST
GUESTHOUSE $$
725 White St.
(305) 294-7381 or (800) 898-6909
authorskeywest.com

Writers visiting Key West often select this private 3-building compound as their outpost, as each room is named for one of Key West's

legendary authors, like Ernest Hemingway or Tennessee Williams. The main 2-story, 8-room house is lined with lush tropical foliage and offers a 2-sided sundeck. Two poolside Conch houses, built around the turn of the 20th century, are also available for rent; both have small private porches. Rooms within the main house are equally diverse, offering views of the street, the sundeck, or the gardens. Continental breakfast is served daily in the lounge or by the swimming pool. The inn provides off-street parking, and bicycles are available for rent. Pets are not permitted. Note that the entrance to Authors is on Petronia Street.

AZUL KEY WEST $$$$
907 Truman Ave.
(305) 296-5152
azulkeywest.com

Here is the other bookend of Azul properties mentioned early in this chapter (see the Azul del Mar listing). This graceful Queen Anne mansion, built for wealthy cigar baron Walter James Lightbourn, was completed in 1903. In 1992 it was transformed into a hotel, and in 2007 the home was beautifully restored to its current charming splendor. Listed on the National Register of Historic Places, Azul Key West offers guests stylized bedrooms with flat-screen TVs, Wi-Fi, and a shimmering pool. Breakfast fare is a "Tropical Continental" featuring fruit, yogurt, and cereal. Book the room that takes you up two flights of stairs to the treetops. Spending the night among the stars and clouds is as close to heaven as this "paradise" can get you.

THE BANYAN RESORT $$$$
323 Whitehead St.
(305) 296-7786 or (866) 371-9222
banyanresort.com

The Banyan Resort is a collection of 8 beautifully preserved and refurbished Conch-style homes, 5 of which are listed on the National Register of Historic Places. One of these buildings formerly served as a cigar factory. The homes boast 38 contemporary studios, suites, and duplexes, with full kitchens. Some units have been sold as condominiums; others are available as time-shares and guest accommodations. All accommodations have French doors leading to private patios and verandas that overlook gardens filled with jasmine, frangipani, rare orchids, and two magnificent 200-year-old banyan trees. The Tiki Bar serves drinks and light bites throughout the day. Bicycle rentals are available on the premises. Children, with restrictions, are permitted. Limited off-street parking is available at an additional charge.

BLUE PARROT INN $$
916 Elizabeth St.
(305) 296-0033 or (800) 231-2473
blueparrotinn.com

Built in 1884 with wood pegs that are more hurricane-friendly than nails, the Blue Parrot Inn offers 9 guest units. Rooms vary in size, number of beds, and decor. The only blue parrot in residence here is a stuffed one; however, the cats you'll see wandering the grounds are very much alive. A heated swimming pool surrounded by extensive decking sets the scene for a leisurely continental breakfast consisting of fresh fruit, bagels, English muffins, and home-baked quiche or fruit breads served every morning. The atmosphere at the Blue Parrot is friendly and intimate. Guests must be at least 16 years of age, and no pets are allowed. Curbside parking is free; off-street parking is available for an extra charge.

CASA 325 $$–$$$
325 Duval St.
(305) 292-0011 or (866) 227-2325
casa325.com

Casa 325 offers spacious suites, lofts, and studios in a vintage Victorian building that has been recently restored and decorated in a tropical island theme. Located right on Duval Street, but still managing to feel secluded, the suites feature queen-size beds, kitchenettes with refrigerators, microwaves, wet bars, and ceiling fans. A center courtyard showcases gardens and a swimming pool on this quaint property. The location is on the lower end of Duval Street, near the historic Red Barn Theatre and right in the middle of numerous bars, restaurants, and attractions.

CENTER COURT HISTORIC INN &
**   COTTAGES** $$$
916 Center St.
(305) 296-9292 or (800) 797-8787
centercourtkw.com

Center Court is a fine example of the historic preservation for which Key West is so justly famous. Constructed in 1874, the main guesthouse is surrounded by a collection of former cigar-makers' cottages. Each cottage has its own bright and cheerful personality, as well as a fully stocked kitchen, barbecue grill, and private hot tub. The main building houses a spacious, airy breakfast room; dining takes place out on the back porch overlooking a swimming pool, spa, and exercise pavilion. A spiral staircase alongside one of these cottages leads to a clothing-optional sundeck. Breakfast is complimentary for guests in rooms; cottage guests have the facilities to fix their own. Children are allowed in the cottages and suites. Pets are permitted for an additional fee per night.

CHELSEA HOUSE $$$

709 Truman Ave.
(305) 296-2211 or (800) 845-8859
historickeywestinns.com

Built in 1870 for a British ship captain who hauled tobacco from Havana and later became the first general manager of Duval Street's La Concha Hotel, Chelsea House was later converted to a guesthouse by the captain's grieving widow to provide lodging to Key West's military visitors. The Conch-style mansion serves as the main guesthouse. A full acre of property, shared with the neighboring Red Rooster, is likely the largest of all of Key West's guesthouse properties. Here, a private garden with massive palms and flowering plants forms an L-shaped alcove visible from the windows, French doors, and balconies of some of the rooms in the main house.

THE CONCH HOUSE HERITAGE INN $$$

625 Truman Ave.
(305) 293-0020 or (800) 207-5806
conchhouse.com

Since the 1800s this historic 2-story estate has been passed down from generation to generation. The current owners are Sam Holland Jr. and his mother, Francine Delaney Holland. She is the great-granddaughter of Cuban émigré Carlos Recio, a close friend of Cuban revolutionary Jose Martí. The inn is listed on the National Register of Historic Places and combines old-world decor with modern amenities. The 10 bedrooms in the main house feature high ceilings, wood shutters, wraparound porches, and picket fences. A poolside cottage offers 3 guest rooms decorated with Caribbean prints and wicker. Guests may have their continental breakfast in the dining room or on the veranda. Children older than age 12 are permitted at the inn.

CUBAN CLUB SUITES $$$$
LA CASA DE LUCES $-$$$
DOUGLAS HOUSE GUEST ROOMS $$-$$$$

419 and 422 Amelia St.
(305) 294-5269 or (800) 833-0372
casadeluces.com or douglashouse.com

Cuban Club Suites, La Casa de Luces, and Douglas House Guest Rooms share guest check-in and lobby facilities on Amelia Street, but Cuban Club Suites is actually in a separate building at 1102 Duval St. Cuban Club's 2-story luxury suites are condominiums occupying second and third floors above boutiques that are open to the public. La Casa de Luces offers 8 units ranging from 2 small rooms sharing a bath to large garden suites. Complimentary continental breakfast is delivered to guest rooms each morning; there is no swimming pool, but guests are provided passes to a nearby resort. Off-street parking is available. Families are welcome, and dogs are permitted if management is notified at the time the reservation is made.

Douglas House is a collection of 6 Victorian homes, 4 of which are more than 100 years old. Each house contains 2 to 5 spacious units for a combined total of 15. All units have private baths and outdoor entrances, and each unit is furnished differently. Within the Douglas House compound are 2 swimming pools and a hot tub surrounded by gardens. Continental breakfast is served poolside each morning, and coffee perks throughout the day. Pets are permitted for an extra fee. Children younger than age 16 are not allowed during the high season.

CURRY MANSION INN $$$$

511 Caroline St.
(305) 294-5349 or (800) 253-3466
currymansion.com

Curry Mansion Inn is located on the grounds of the estate that once belonged to the Currys, Florida's first homegrown millionaire family. The 22-room mansion is today a museum, housing a selection of turn-of-the-20th-century furnishings and memorabilia. It is also the centerpiece for a guesthouse that is consistently rated among the best in Key West. Guests at the Curry Mansion Inn do not actually stay in the mansion; they do, however, have full access to it. Guest accommodations consist instead of 28 rooms adjacent to the mansion, most of which open onto a pool. A complimentary breakfast buffet is offered poolside each morning; complimentary cocktails are served each evening from 5 to 7 p.m. Ask about beach privileges at nearby oceanfront resorts; Curry Mansion Inn has agreements with several.

CYPRESS HOUSE $$$$
601 Caroline St.

CYPRESS HOUSE GUEST STUDIOS $$$
613 Caroline St.
(305) 294-6969 or (800) 525-2488
cypresshousekw.com

The 40-foot heated lap pool surrounded by lush tropical gardens on the grounds of this 100-year-old mansion is among the largest at any of Key West's inns. The New England–style, 3-story home, constructed of cypress, is listed on the National Register of Historic Places. Six of 16 rooms have private baths. Porches on the first and second floor are accessible to guests. A breakfast buffet is served poolside, as is a nightly complimentary cocktail hour with beer, wine, and snacks. Pets are not permitted. Four luxury suites and 2 guest rooms distinguish Cypress House Guest Studios (formerly William Anthony House), located 3 doors up the street at 613 Caroline St.

DUVAL HOUSE $$$$
815 Duval St.
(305) 294-1666 or (305) 294-1667
duvalhousekeywest.com

This 2-story inn may be set on busy Duval Street, but its pigeon plums, banyans, and hibiscus successfully guard it from intrusion. Lounge poolside amid traveler's palms and light jazz music, linger on a shady hammock, or chat with others in the gazebo. The inn's breakfast room maintains a library of books, board games, magazines and newspapers, and a weather chart listing temperatures throughout the world. In the 1880s Duval House was inhabited by cigar workers. Today the 28 standard and deluxe rooms and apartments are furnished with English antiques, white wicker, and French doors. All are air-conditioned and all except the 2 apartments and 2 front rooms look out onto the gardens.

EDEN HOUSE $$$$
1015 Fleming St.
(305) 296-6868 or (800) 533-5397
edenhouse.com

For years Eden House was known as a hangout for writers, intellectuals, and Europeans. Over the past few years, owner Mike Eden has added several enhancements. Constructed of wood and concrete, the facility categorizes units by luxury rooms and efficiencies; private rooms and efficiencies with bath or shower; semiprivate rooms with shared baths; and European rooms with double or twin-size beds, a sink, and a bath and shower in the hall. Many units have French doors leading to porches and decks near the center of the facility, where gardens surround a swimming pool, hot tub, and gazebo. Children are permitted, but pets are not. Bicycle rentals are available, and guests are treated to a cold drink at check-in. Be sure to check out the elevated sundeck and hammock area.

THE FRANCES STREET BOTTLE INN $$
535 Frances St.
(305) 294-8530 or (800) 294-8530
bottleinn.com

Tucked away in a quiet residential neighborhood on the edge of Old Town, this charming inn takes its name from the owner's collection of antique bottles and cobalt-blue glassware displayed in every window and along several interior shelves. The atmosphere here is quiet and intimate. The Bottle Inn has just 8 guest rooms, each with a private bath and air-conditioning. White wicker chairs line a gracious porch across the front of the house, and in the lush tropical gardens, a complimentary continental breakfast is served each morning under the poinciana trees. Concierge service is available. Although the grounds are too small to allow for a pool, there is a hot tub. This is a pet-friendly inn.

*THE GARDENS HOTEL $$$$
526 Angela St.
(305) 294-2661 or (800) 526-2664
gardenshotel.com

In 1930 the late Key West resident Peggy Mills began collecting various species of orchids from Japan, Bali, and other exotic parts of the world. As neighboring homes were placed on the market, Mills would purchase and level them, adding to her garden until it encompassed a full city block. Before Mills passed away, her gardens gained the attention of botanists worldwide, and they have been restored to much of their original splendor at the Gardens Hotel. A complex of 5 guesthouses and a carriage house,

the hotel offers 17 units set around a tiki bar, swimming pool, hot tub, fountain, and a winding path of bougainvillea, orange, jasmine, palm, mango, breadfruit trees, and more.

*HERON HOUSE $$$
512 Simonton St.
(305) 294-9227 or (888) 861-9066
heronhouse.com

HERON HOUSE COURT $$$
412 Frances St.
(305) 296-4719 or (800) 932-9119
heronhousecourt.com

Centered on a 35-foot swimming pool decorated with a mosaic of a heron, and a Chicago brick patio and sundeck, every one of the 23 rooms at the Heron House features unique woodwork and stained glass created by local artists. Platform-style oak beds are handcrafted, and all accommodations have French doors leading to private porches or balconies overlooking the English-style country gardens. Coffee is served in the breezeway. A private sundeck is clothing optional. The Heron House also has a sister property known as Heron House Court, which is similarly styled and resides in a early 20th-century building that is listed on the National Register of Historic Places. There is a heated outdoor pool and hot tub on the property, and guests enjoy complimentary continental breakfast and beer and wine during happy hour on the weekends.

ISLAND CITY HOUSE HOTEL $$$
411 William St.
(305) 294-5702 or (800) 634-8230
islandcityhouse.com

At Island City House, two 1880s homes and a cypress wood house designed to resemble a cigar factory encompass an enclave lined with brick walkways and lush tropical gardens. Wood decking surrounds the hot tub and swimming pool. Central to Island City House is its charming courtyard patio: Antique iron benches and bistro-style tables are set around a fountain and fishpond where a complimentary breakfast is served daily. Island City House itself is a Conch-style mansion with 12 suites. The Arch House maintains 6 studio and two-bedroom suites. At the Cigar House, built on a cistern and the former site of a cigar factory, spacious suites feature French doors leading to private patios and decks. Children are permitted; those younger than age 12 stay free.

THE KEY WEST BED & BREAKFAST— THE POPULAR HOUSE $$$
415 William St.
(305) 296-7274 or (800) 438-6155
keywestbandb.com

When strong winds blow through the city of Key West, you can feel the 3-story Key West Bed & Breakfast move with them, for this 1890 home was built by shipbuilders skilled in crafting structures able to weather any storm. With the exception of one suite, all of the inn's 8 guest rooms feature a mix of bright colors, elegant Victorian furnishings, exposed Dade County pine, and 13-foot ceilings. The suite at the front of the house is noted for its 5-foot arched Palladian window, which provides a view of the sunset above the city's rooftops and trees. Continental breakfast is served outdoors, where tables and chairs line the backyard wood deck. All rooms are air-conditioned, and most have ceiling fans.

☀LA MER HOTEL AND DEWEY HOUSE $$$$
504 and 506 South St.
(305) 296-6577 or (800) 354-4455
southernmostresorts.com

La Mer Hotel and Dewey House are Key West's only oceanfront bed-and-breakfasts. The two properties are connected by tropical green gardens with swaying palm trees, a fountain, a dipping pool, and loads of romantic charm. La Mer is a turn-of-the-20th-century Conch house with 11 rooms. Each room is elegantly decorated with private balconies or patios. The Dewey House was once home to John Dewey, educator and philosopher, and remained a private residence until 1997. While here, you will be treated to deluxe continental breakfast and afternoon tea served with fresh fruit and cheese. Guests must be 18 years of age, and no pets are permitted. Both properties feature privileges to Southernmost Hotel and Southernmost on the Beach.

LIGHTHOUSE COURT $$$
900 Whitehead St.
(305) 294-9588 or (877) 249-9588
historickeywestinns.com

Lighthouse Court is a historic compound of 10 Conch houses dating from 1890 to 1920. Covering half a city block in Old Town, the location is ideal for sightseeing. It's directly next door to the Lighthouse Museum, across the street from the Hemingway Home, and a block away from Duval Street. The half-acre grounds offer charming brick paths dotted with tree swings and hammocks. Chaise lounges and a sundeck beckon you out of the heat of the tropical sun. If you really want to embody the aura of old Key West, reserve the Hemingway Suite: The 1,000-square-foot penthouse overlooks his Key West home and has views of the lighthouse from the living room, sundeck, and bedroom.

*THE MARQUESA HOTEL $$$$
600 Fleming St.
(305) 292-1919 or (800) 869-4631
marquesa.com

Conde Nast Traveler has named the Marquesa to their "Gold List of the World's Best Places to Stay." This cluster of homes dates from the 1880s. Each standard room, deluxe room, junior suite, standard suite, and terrace suite is furnished with an eclectic collection of antique English and West Indian reproductions that evoke the ambience of an exquisite English plantation. Accommodations are spacious, with oversize marble baths. Many rooms feature French doors and private porches overlooking 2 pools and the garden. At the east end of the garden, brick steps accented by a fountain lead to a newer building of complementary architecture. Breakfast (available for a nominal fee) includes a feast of baked goods fresh from the oven of the highly praised Cafe Marquesa (see the Restaurants chapter).

THE MERMAID AND
THE ALLIGATOR $$$
729 Truman Ave.
(305) 294-1894 or (800) 773-1894
kwmermaid.com

In the enclave known as the heart of Key West's historic district, this charming and inviting 1904 Victorian home awaits its guests. Full breakfast is served, and in the evening guests can enjoy a complimentary glass of wine poolside. Located an easy 3-block walk to Duval Street, you are close enough to all attractions but far enough away to enjoy a relaxing atmosphere. Among the bonuses of staying at the Mermaid and

the Alligator are the resident pooches Caya and Havana. These lovely, friendly, adorable, jet-black flat-coated retrievers will welcome you and put a smile on your face.

OLD TOWN MANOR $$$$
511 Eaton St.
(305) 292-2170
oldtownmanor.com

Listed on the National Register of Historic Homes and written about in *Key West Gardens and Their Stories* by Janis Frawley-Hold, Old Town Manor still remains a peaceful bed-and-breakfast with grandeur. Built in 1886 in Greek Revival style, there are 2 significant buildings on the property: a 3-story home and a carriage house that at one time served as a dry goods store. This property was one of Key West's first ornamental gardens, and today the century-old palms still stand. Steps off Duval Street, in the hub of Old Town, the last century has caught up to this one. The place is delightfully furnished, using the practice of feng shui with touches in keeping with the history of the past. Continental breakfast is included with your room.

THE PALMS HOTEL $$
820 White St.
(305) 294-3146 or (800) 558-9374
palmshotelkeywest.com

The main Conch-style house with its wrap-around porches was built in 1889. It features Caribbean influences and is listed on the National Register of Historic Places. All 20 rooms are painted in pastels and furnished with wicker and Caribbean-style decor; rooms in the main house have separate access to the porch. Private entrances, private baths, and ceiling fans are standard. A deluxe continental breakfast is served each morning at the full-service poolside tiki bar, and the large heated swimming pool is open around the clock. The Palms has a small parking lot on the street directly behind the hotel; on-street parking is also available. Children are permitted; pets are allowed with advance approval.

THE PARADISE INN $$$$
819 Simonton St.
(305) 293-8007 or (800) 888-9648
theparadiseinn.com

Bahamian-style houses and cigar-makers cottages are home to the 15 suites and 3 cottages of the Paradise Inn. Painted white with Caribbean-blue Bahamian shutters, all units have high ceilings, large marble baths, natural oak flooring, and unique window dressings that combine stagecoach and handkerchief valances with wood mini-blinds. French doors lead to outdoor porches in all but one cottage, and the interior decor features distressed pine, botanical prints, and pale shades of tan. The inn's diverse garden features Barbados cherry and avocado trees and bromeliads. Even the pool and hot tub, separated by a lily pond, evoke luxury. A complimentary breakfast is served in the lobby.

PILOT HOUSE GUESTHOUSE $$$
414 Simonton St.
(305) 293-6600 or (800) 648-3780
pilothousekeywest.com

This 100-plus-year-old Conch-style home provides rooms and suites that mix antique furnishings with functional pieces. Frangipani and royal poinciana trees thrive in the yard, and a gumbo-limbo grows through the roof of what is known as this facility's spa building. Set along the brick-patio backyard is a Spanish-style stucco cabana building that offers 6 suites. Passageways rather than doors create privacy for each area of these

suites, and all entrances face the swimming pool. The backyard swimming pool, at 15 by 30 feet, is larger than most in Key West, and an in-ground spa for 12 is sheltered from the sun by a tin roof with lattice. Both are clothing optional. No off-street parking is provided.

ROSE LANE VILLAS $$$
522-524 Rose Lane
(305) 292-2170 or (800) 294-2170
roselanevillas.com

The Rose Lane Villas are actually in a treasure of a home built in 1886 for Dr. William Warren. This charming oasis greets you when you step onto the front porch, and the cheery wicker furniture beckons you to stay and rest a spell. Steps from Duval Street, you'll feel a million miles away from it all in the seclusion of Rose Lane Villas. All one-, two-, and three-bedroom villas have kitchens complete with full refrigerators and all essentials. Rooms have a welcome basket from the owners filled with coffee, tea, bottled water, and snacks. If you just want to read a book or nap, outside by the in-ground pool is the perfect spot to capture a few rays.

✳SANTA MARIA SUITES RESORT $$$$
1401 Simonton St.
(305) 600-5165 or (866) 726-8259
santamariasuites.com

An island unto itself, steps away from vivacious Duval Street and the Atlantic Ocean, you'll discover Santa Maria Suites Resort. Voted as one of the "12 Sexiest Hotels" by *Forbes Traveler*, this "uptown" resort is definitely a dream come true! The 35 luxurious two-bedroom, two-bath suites with glass-front balconies overlook a sensual pool surrounded by exotic tropical greenery. All suites have state-of-the-art kitchens with wine chillers, flat-screen TVs, Wi-Fi, washer and dryer, housekeeping, and private parking. Put on those Jimmy Choos and pop that bottle of Cristal—the modern and chic Santa Maria Suites Resort is one to savor. The resort also houses the chic sushi restaurant Ambrosia (see the Restaurants chapter).

SIMONTON COURT HISTORIC INN AND COTTAGES $$$
320 Simonton St.
(800) 944-2687
simontoncourt.com
Situated on 2 acres of property that once boasted a cigar factory, Simonton Court offers 10 varied structures among a number of buildings. The original building is a Victorian-esque mansion with maritime influences and houses the most luxurious rooms and suites on the property. Within the Inn are 9 rustic old Key West–style rooms featuring high ceilings and heavily shuttered windows. On the "rustic" side are Simonton Court's 2-story cottages. The Manor House suite offers a spacious two-bedroom complex with a full kitchen and private outdoor pool. Simonton Court's 2-story Townhouse Suites are extremely plush, decorated in Grand Floribbean–style antiques and white linens. Simonton Court's tropically landscaped gardens, antique brick pathways, swimming pools, and hot tub all come aglow at night, with lighting emphasizing all the right places.

SOUTHERNMOST POINT GUEST HOUSE $$$
1327 Duval St.
(305) 294-0715
southernmostpoint.com
Throughout Key West you will discover all kinds of things dubbed "the southernmost"—a southernmost hockey rink and Southernmost Motel, for instance. The Southernmost Point Guest House, across from the Southernmost House, is a showy, 3-story, Conch-style mansion built in 1885 for E. H. Gato Jr., son of Key West's first cigar manufacturer. The home is notable for its wraparound porches and private balconies, some of which afford partial ocean or garden views. Rooms come in varying sizes, but all have private entrances, private baths, and ceiling fans. All guests are given a key to the hot tub (large enough for 12 people). Lounge chairs are provided amid the guesthouse's tropical gardens of banana, coconut palm, breadfruit, and mango trees.

SPEAKEASY INN $$$
1117 Duval St.
(305) 296-2680
speakeasyinn.com
The Speakeasy, a turn-of-the-20th-century inn, offers spacious rooms in its main Duval Street house plus 3 spacious suites in a back-alley building along Amelia Street. The original building was the home of Raul Vasquez, a cigar selector at the Gato cigar factory whose true passion was rum-running between Key West and Cuba. The newer building, built as a residence for the owner's stepdaughter, offers what is referred to as the Gallery Suite, considered to be the best offering in the house. This and other rooms at the Speakeasy also offer private tiled baths, refrigerators, wet bars, and ceiling fans.

TRAVELERS PALM INN AND GUESTHOUSES $$$
815 Catherine St.
(305) 304-1751
travelerspalm.com

The recently renovated Travelers Palm consists of 3 new cottages that are completely eco-friendly. Owners Roxanne Fleszar and Michel Appellis met on the property in 1996 and eventually purchased it in 2000. The extensive renovations garnered them a Certificate of Excellence from the Historic Florida Keys Foundation. Captain's Quarters is the largest and most modern of the cottages and can accommodate up to 4 people. This two-bedroom, two-bath cottage also features a full kitchen, living room, and dining room with a front porch and side decks that contain a gas grill. All the cottages have access to the on-site solar-heated pool replete with a stone waterfall.

WEATHERSTATION INN $$$$
57 Front St.
(305) 294-7277 or (800) 815-2707
weatherstationinn.com
The Weatherstation Inn could easily be considered one of this town's best-kept secrets in luxury guesthouse accommodations. Guests here are just 2 blocks off bustling Duval Street, but they'd never know it. Rarely does any sound intrude. This 2-story, 8-room guesthouse sits on the grounds of the Old Navy Yard inside the gated Truman Annex compound, just down the street from Harry Truman's Little White House. The beach at Fort Zachary Taylor is a short walk away (see the Attractions chapter). With its glistening hardwood floors and elegant island furnishings, the inn calls to mind the plantation homes of days gone by in the British and Dutch West Indies. The balconies and decks overlook lush tropical landscaping, and amenities include a heated pool, concierge service, and complimentary continental breakfast.

WESTWINDS INN $$
914 Eaton St.
(305) 296-4440 or (800) 788-4150
westwindskeywest.com
This complex encompasses a 2-story New England–style home, 2-story Conch houses, and poolside cottages. The majority of guests are couples. Room decor is wicker throughout, with queen-size beds in suites, private entrances to the cottages and Conch houses, and some furnished private and shared porches. Some rooms in the main house share a bath. Suites include one-bedroom cottage and Conch units with kitchenettes and kitchenless accommodations that sleep several guests. In back of the compound, brick walkways wind through gardens of hibiscus, bromeliads, and other flowers and shrubs, and the kidney-shaped swimming pool with waterfall is sizable. Continental breakfast is served poolside.

Gay Guesthouses
ALEXANDER'S GUESTHOUSE $$$
1118 Fleming St.
(305) 294-9919 or (800) 654-9919
alexghouse.com
The main 3-story building of Alexander's, a Conch-style design, was built around the turn of the past century and has since been renovated. Two additional 2-story Conch houses combine for a total of 17 guest rooms. This guesthouse, which attracts both gay men and women, is gay owned and operated. The rooms at Alexander's are relatively basic, equipped with queen-size beds. All rooms have private baths, and two share shower facilities. Throughout the inn, eclectic local art mixes with poster prints. A highlight is the cobalt-blue tiled swimming pool surrounded by lush tropical flora. Second- and third-level tanning decks are clothing

optional. An expanded continental breakfast is served by the pool each morning; wine and cheese are offered every evening.

BIG RUBY'S GUESTHOUSE $$$
409 Appelrouth Lane
(305) 296-2323 or (800) 477-7829
bigrubys.com

Formerly the home of a sea captain, the main guesthouse at Big Ruby's, like its 5 additional on-site structures, is New England–style clapboard architecture on the outside with contemporary styling on the inside. All 3 buildings of this exclusively gay male and female property share a clothing-optional sunning yard and swimming pool. An outdoor rain-forest shower amid the vines allows for rinsing before and after swimming. Continental and full cooked-to-order breakfasts are served poolside, as are wine and juice in the early evening. Big Ruby's is set back about 20 feet from the narrow, one-way lane through which it is accessed, and all of the buildings are surrounded by orchids and bougainvillea. Limited off-street parking is provided on a first-come, first-served basis.

EQUATOR RESORT $$$
818 Fleming St.
(305) 294-7775 or (800) 278-4552
equatorresort.com

The building that houses this state-of-the-art, all-male resort looks as though it might have been around for a while, but it is new. It was simply designed to blend with the surrounding structures in this Old Town neighborhood. When it came to the guest rooms, the architects opted for upscale with no attempts at conserving space. All 18 rooms are bright and spacious, and each features Mediterranean tile floors, incredibly comfortable beds, in-room refrigerators, genuinely

ample closets, and plenty of walking-around space. Common areas are equally well designed, with a clothing-optional pool, 8-man outdoor whirlpool, lush tropical gardens, a sundeck, and covered patio. A complimentary full breakfast is served daily; complimentary cocktails and snacks are offered every evening except Sunday.

Pet-Friendly Accommodations

Household pets are members of the family, but traveling with them can create a dilemma. Here in the Florida Keys, which is one of the pet-loving capitals of the world, you will find properties that welcome one and all. In the Upper and Middle Keys, try Marina Del Mar, Casa Morada, Blackfin Resort, and White Gate Court. In Key West, consider the Westin Key West, Francis Street Bottle Inn, Chelsea House, Old Town Manor, and Rose Lane Villas. Visit aaa .com or floridakeys.com for more listings.

OASIS GUESTHOUSE AND
CORAL TREE INN $$$
822 and 823 Fleming St.
(305) 296-2131 or (800) 362-7477
keywest-allmale.com

With its Main, Lopez, and Margaret Houses, the Oasis offers 20 guest rooms on 3 fronts that share a yard. Guests at the facility, which caters to gay men, check in at Main on Fleming. The pool and the sundeck surrounding it are clothing-optional. Also owned by Oasis proprietors is the Coral Tree Inn across the street. This handsome 11-room facility is designed to reflect an upscale European retreat and also caters to gay men. The clothing-optional Coral Tree has a 24-man hot tub and sunning area, and guests here and at the Oasis share facilities. Both establishments are known for their hospitality. Continental breakfast is served each morning, tropical cocktails are offered by the pool every afternoon, and wine and hot hors d'oeuvres are served in the evening.

PEARL'S KEY WEST $$$
525 United St.
(305) 292-1450 or (800) 749-6696
pearlsrainbow.com
Lesbian-owned and -operated, Pearl's Key West is an adult-only gay-friendly resort. Pearl's includes 2 clothing-optional swimming pools, 2 hot tubs, and 38 guest rooms. All standard guest rooms at the Rainbow House feature queen-size beds, private baths, TV, air-conditioning, and ceiling fans. The priciest accommodation is a deluxe poolside suite consisting of a king bedroom, private bath, and separate living room with big-screen TV. Pearl's Rainbow is located half a block off Duval on the ocean side of the island. Shops, bars, and restaurants are within a reasonable walking distance.

RESTAURANTS

Take in the glorious sights in the Florida Keys, then treat your taste buds to a culinary holiday they will never forget. We are an island of restaurants offering stone crabs, yellowtail snapper, cracked conch, *ropa vieja,* and key lime pie.

Surrounded by water, the Florida Keys yields a bounty that easily could qualify as the eighth wonder of the world. We confidently can boast that nowhere else in the continental US—oh, why not say it, the universe even—will you find fresher, more innovatively prepared fish and seafood than in our restaurants. Be sure to sample our special natural resources, served any way you like. We import a few raw materials in the feather and flesh categories as well, so your palate will be truly well rounded. (For preparing your own fare, see the Specialty Foods, Cafes & Markets chapter.)

Enjoy the relaxed atmosphere of our restaurants, where even the most upscale dining carries a laid-back apparel code. Be it a roadside cafe or a resort dining room, you need dress no more formally than "Keys casual," typically an ensemble of shirt and shorts, shoes or sandals. Men may leave their sport jackets at home, and don't even think about bringing a suit to the Keys unless it is the swimming variety. The same code applies to women; we don't discriminate here. The occasional restaurant, such as Cheeca Lodge, Pierre's, or Little Palm Island, affords you the chance to dress up a bit more if you like—but the choice is yours.

The decor of a restaurant doesn't hold to the strict expectations of other parts of the country, either. You'll find that the most unassuming hole-in-the-wall cafe, diner, or bistro may serve the best food in town. Don't drive by. Some of our culinary treasures are hidden away off the beaten track. We'll help you find them.

OVERVIEW

We have organized the restaurants of the Keys by cuisine type, and then location.

Free on-site parking is available at virtually all of our recommended establishments in the Upper, Middle, and Lower Keys. However, most restaurants in Key West do not have on-site parking. Most restaurants suggest that you make reservations, especially during the high season. Those that do not take reservations will be noted.

Many restaurants serve limited alcoholic beverages. You may infer that unless we specify that an establishment offers a full-service bar (usually the larger restaurants or resort facilities), only beer and wine will be served.

Accessibility varies greatly in restaurants throughout the Keys. While many of our establishments are at ground level, and some second-story locations within large resorts may have elevators, steps sometimes must be negotiated and some bathrooms may be too tiny to accommodate a wheelchair. If this is of particular concern to you, be sure to call the restaurant to see exactly what arrangements might be made to fit your needs.

Unless otherwise specified, you may assume that our recommended restaurants are air-conditioned. Those that provide outdoor seating or accessibility by sea will be highlighted. Children are generally welcome in Florida Keys restaurants. The odd exceptions or age restrictions will be stated.

The dollar sign price code indicated in each restaurant listing will help you gauge the cost of your dining experience (see key below). Some of our restaurants include soup or a house salad with an entree; at others, entrees are strictly a la carte. Most of our restaurants accept major credit cards but rarely a personal check. If plastic is not acknowledged, we alert you in advance so that you won't be caught short of cash.

Price Code

Our price-code rating reflects the cost of dinner entrees for two, without cocktails, appetizers, wine, dessert, tax, or tip.

$. . . . . **Less than $25**
$$ . . . . **$25 to $40**
$$$ . . . . **$40 to $60**
$$$$ . . . . **More than $60**

Boondocks Grille & Draft House, Ramrod Key, Classic American & Southern, $$, 89

Braza Leña Brazilian Steakhouse, Islamorada & Key West, Brazilian, $$$, 84

Burdines Waterfront and Chiki Tiki Bar & Grille, Marathon, Classic American & Southern, $, 87

Butterfly Cafe, Marathon, Seafood, $$$, 111

The Buzzards Roost, Key Largo, Seafood, $$, 109

Cabana Breezes, Key Colony Beach, Contemporary American, $, 94

The Cafe, Key West, Contemporary American, $$, 97

Cafe Largo, Key Largo, Italian & Pizza, $$, 103

Cafe Marquesa, Key West, Contemporary American, $$$$, 97

Camille's Restaurant, Key West, Classic American & Southern, $$, 90

Chico's Cantina, Key West, Mexican, $$, 108

China Garden West, Key West, Chinese, $, 84

Coconuts Restaurant & Night Club, Key Largo, Classic American & Southern, $$, 85

The Commodore Waterfront Restaurant, Key West, Seafood, $$$, 113

Conch Republic Seafood Company, Key West, Seafood, $$, 114

Craig's Restaurant, Tavernier, Classic American & Southern, $$, 85

DJ's Diner and Coffee Shop, Key Largo, Classic American & Southern, $, 86

Dion's Quick Mart, Key West, Classic American & Southern $, 90

El Meson de Pepe, Key West, Cuban, $$, 100

El Siboney, Key West, Cuban, $$, 101

Finnegan's Wake Irish Pub & Eatery, Key West, Irish, $, 102

The Fish House Encore Restaurant, Sushi Bar & Lounge, Key Largo, Japanese & Seafood, $$$, 105

Frank's Grill, Marathon, Italian & Pizza, $$, 104

Gilbert's Resort, Key Largo, German, $, 102

The Grand Cafe, Key West, French, $$$, 101

Green Turtle Inn, Islamorada, Seafood, $$, 109

Gus' Grille, Key Largo, Seafood, $$, 109

Half Shell Raw Bar, Key West, Seafood, $–$$, 114

HarbourView Cafe, Key West, Contemporary American, $$$, 97

Harpoon Harry's, Key West, Classic American & Southern, $, 90

Harriette's, Key Largo, Classic American & Southern, $, 86

Herbie's, Marathon, Classic American & Southern, $$, 87

Hideaway Cafe, Grassy Key, Contemporary American, $$$, 94

Hobo's Cafe, Key Largo, Classic American & Southern, $, 86

Hog's Breath Saloon, Key West, Classic American & Southern, $, 91

Hogfish Bar and Grill, Key West, Seafood, $$, 114

Hot Tin Roof, Key West, Contemporary American, $$$, 97

Hurricane Hole Waterfront Bar and Seafood Grill, Key West, Classic American & Southern, $, 91

Islamorada Fish Company and Market, Islamorada, Seafood, $$, 110

The Island Fish Company Tiki Bar & Restaurant, Marathon, Seafood, $$, 112

Island Grill, Islamorada, Seafood, $$$, 110

Jimmy Buffett's Margaritaville Cafe, Key West, Classic American & Southern, $$, 133

Kaiyo Grill & Sushi, Islamorada, Japanese, $$$, 106

Kelly's Caribbean Bar, Grill & Brewery, Key West, Classic American & Southern, $$, 91

Key Colony Inn, Key Colony Beach, Italian & Pizza, $$, 104

Keys Fisheries Market & Marina, Marathon, Seafood, $$, 112

La Trattoria, Key West, Italian & Pizza, $$$, 105

Latitudes Beach Cafe, Key West, Contemporary American, $$$$, 98

Lazy Days Restaurant, Islamorada, Seafood, $$, 110

Leigh Ann's Coffee House, Marathon, Classic American & Southern, $, 88

Little Palm Island Resort & Spa, Little Torch Key, Contemporary American, $$$$, 95

Lobo's Grill, Key West, Contemporary American, $, 98

Lorelei Restaurant & Cabana Bar, Islamorada, Seafood, $–$$$, 111

Louie's Backyard, Key West, Contemporary American, $$$$, 98

Mangia Mangia, Key West, Italian & Pizza, $$, 105

Mangrove Mama's Restaurant, Sugarloaf Key, Seafood, $$, 112

Marker 88, Islamorada, Seafood, $$$, 111

Martin's, Key West, German, $$, 133

Michael's, Key West, Contemporary American, $$$$, 98

Morada Bay Beach Cafe, Islamorada, Contemporary American, $$$, 93

Mrs. Mac's Kitchen, Key Largo, Classic American & Southern, $, 86

nine one five, Key West, Contemporary American, $$$$, 99

No Name Pub, Big Pine Key, Classic American & Southern, $, 129

Num Thai Restaurant & Sushi Bar, Key Largo, Thai, $$, 116

Old Tavernier Restaurant, Tavernier, Mediterranean, $$, 107

Old Town Mexican Cafe, Key West, Mexican, $$, 108

Origami Japanese Restaurant, Key West, Japanese, $$, 106

Panda House, Marathon, Chinese, $, 84

Parrotdise Waterfront Bar & Grille, Little Torch Key, Contemporary American, $$, 95

Pepe's Cafe, Key West, Classic American & Southern, $$, 92

Pierre's Restaurant, Islamorada, Contemporary American, $$$$, 93

Pisces, Key West, Seafood, $$$$, 114

Porky's Bayside, Marathon, Classic American & Southern, $, 88

Prime Steakhouse, Key West, Steak Houses, $$$, 116

Roof Top Cafe, Key West, Contemporary American, $$$, 99

Rusty Anchor Restaurant, Key West, Seafood, $$, 115

Salsa Loca, Key West, Mexican, $, 108

Salute! On the Beach, Key West, Contemporary American, $$, 99

Santiago's Bodega, Key West, Contemporary American, $$$, 99

Sarabeth's, Key West, Contemporary American, $$$$, 100

Señor Frijoles, Key Largo, Mexican, $$, 107

Seven Fish, Key West, Seafood, $–$$, 115

SHOR American Seafood Grill, Key West, Seafood, $$$, 115

Smugglers Cove Resort and Marina, Islamorada, Classic American & Southern, $$, 86

Snapper's Waterfront Restaurant, Key Largo, Contemporary American, $$, 93

The Square Grouper Bar and Grill, Cudjoe Key, Contemporary American, $$, 95

Square One, Key West, Contemporary American, $$$, 100

Strip House, Key West, Steak Houses, $$$$, 116

The Stuffed Pig, Marathon, Classic American & Southern, $, 88

Sundowners on the Bay, Key Largo, Classic American & Southern, $$, 87

Thai Cuisine, Key West, Thai, $, 116

Thai Island, Key West, Thai, $, 117

Tower of Pizza, Key Largo, Italian & Pizza, $, 103

Turtle Kraals Restaurant and Bar, Key West, Classic American & Southern, $$, 92

2¢, Key West, Gastropub, $$$, 102

Uncle's Restaurant, Islamorada, Classic American & Southern, $$, 87

Upper Crust Pizza, Key Largo, Italian & Pizza, $$, 103

Ziggie and Mad Dog's, Islamorada, Contemporary American, $$, 93

BRAZILIAN

Middle Keys & Key West

BRAZA LEÑA BRAZILIAN STEAKHOUSE $$$
MM 83.4 Bayside, Islamorada
(305) 664-4940
421 Caroline St., Key West
(305) 432-9440
brazalena.com

This upscale *churrascaria* (Brazilian steak house) has gauchos dashing to your table with swords of beef, lamb, pork, and poultry. The all-you-can-eatery has more meat than you see at some food stores! Along with this showy presentation is a really delicious salad bar brimming with almost 50 different items from vegetables to seafood. Braza Leña is a fun place to go with great atmosphere. The Islamorada location is open Tues through Sun for dinner, and the Key West location is open daily for dinner.

CHINESE

Middle Keys

PANDA HOUSE $
MM 50 Bayside, Marathon
(305) 743-3417
pandahousechinese.com

One cannot live by Florida Keys seafood alone! This Marathon Chinese restaurant opened its doors in 1997, and the locals pack this place. Their enormous all-you-can-eat lunch buffet is not to be believed. The menu boasts Szechuan, Hunan, and Cantonese cuisines. The friendly staff gets right to the business of making sure your plate is full and you do not leave hungry. It's an ideal spot for families and if you have a crowd to feed. Panda House is open daily and offers free delivery in Marathon.

Key West

CHINA GARDEN WEST $
531 Fleming St.
(305) 296-6177

China Garden West is great for lunch, with chef's specials of pressed duck, subgum wonton, or sea-grass salad. They also have dynamite combo platters offering Asian delights. The China Garden West in Searstown (3300 N. Roosevelt Blvd.; 305-296-5618) has the same menu. The China Garden on Big Pine (MM 30 Bayside; 305-872-8861) is located in the Winn-Dixie Shopping Center. Here you get the same excellent Chinese cuisine that they are known for in Key West. Local delivery is available depending on location in the Big Pine area. All 3 locations are open 7 days a week; takeout is offered, and free delivery is available in Key West with a minimum order of $10.

CLASSIC AMERICAN & SOUTHERN

Upper Keys

✳ALABAMA JACK'S $
58000 Card Sound Rd. (Oceanside),
Key Largo
(305) 248-8741

There are a couple of reasons why one drives the back door into the Florida Keys. Card Sound Road, north of Key Largo, offers incentives to take this scenic excursion. The traffic is not as heavy, the wildlife is more prolific, and you can eat at Alabama Jack's. No trip to the Florida Keys is complete without stopping at this Caribbean honky-tonk. Don't be turned off by the outside of the place; it's what's inside that makes this a true Keys treasure. Alabama Jack's is rated as having the best conch fritters and key lime pie by everyone who manages to find the place. It sits on the water, where you can feed the fish, check out the mangroves, and enjoy the friendly Keys attitude of the staff.

COCONUTS RESTAURANT & NIGHT
  CLUB $$
Marina Del Mar Resort and Marina
MM 100 Oceanside, 528 Caribbean Dr.,
Key Largo
(305) 453-9794
coconutsrestaurant.com

This vibrant outdoor restaurant, cornered between Key Largo Harbor and the swimming pool of Marina Del Mar Resort and Marina, offers lively after-hours entertainment and a variety of culinary specialties, among them tuna tacos, crispy coconut shrimp, crunchy grouper, and several delicious salads. After dinner, head for Coconuts' indoor nightclub and dance the night away or sit back and enjoy the live entertainment (see the Nightlife chapter). Coconuts has a full bar, is open for lunch and dinner, and is accessible by boat. Reservations are recommended. To reach Coconuts, head toward the ocean on Laguna at MM 100; the restaurant is about a quarter mile in on the left.

CRAIG'S RESTAURANT $$
MM 90.5 Bayside, Tavernier
(305) 852-9424
craigsrestaurant.com

Chef-owner Craig Belcher opened his namesake establishment in 1981 with his signature sandwich, which he bills as the "World Famous Fish Sandwich." A diner-style restaurant with an all-day menu, Craig's tries to please every palate, be it down-home or gourmet. The Jon Chicken Sandwich, a grilled chicken breast with Dijon mustard, Cajun seasoning, melted cheese, grilled onions and mushrooms, and bacon, puts a little pep in the ubiquitous *poulet*. Open daily for breakfast, lunch, and dinner, Craig's does not accept reservations.

DJ'S DINER AND COFFEE SHOP $
MM 99.4 Oceanside, Key Largo
(305) 451-2999
djsdiner.com
Established in 1958, DJ's regulars claim "they serve the best breakfast in town," so you'd best be hustling on over to get a table. DJ's serves daily lunch specials, too, like the highly praised blackened tuna Caesar wrap, but no dinners. So, get up early, have a *big* appetite, and enjoy this bright spot in the Upper Keys.

HARRIETTE'S $
MM 95.7 Bayside, Key Largo
(305) 852-8689
This popular roadside diner–style restaurant offers reasonably priced home-style meals in a simple setting. Tables and chairs surround counter dining; local arts and crafts on consignment provide the decor. Harriette's specialty? Ensuring that no guest leaves the restaurant hungry. Open for breakfast and lunch, Harriette's serves filling omelets, oversize homemade biscuits with sausage gravy, burgers, and hot and cold sandwiches. The restaurant caters primarily to a repeat local crowd, so lunch specials change daily. Look for comfort food at Harriette's: meat loaf, pork chops, stuffed peppers, roast pork, and chicken and dumplings. Open daily from 6 a.m. to 4 p.m. on weekdays and to 3 p.m. on the weekends. Reservations are not accepted.

HOBO'S CAFE $
MM 101.7 Oceanside, Key Largo
(305) 451-5888
hoboscafe.net
This place used to look like a hobo on the outside, but now there's nothing but a "homey" feeling about its digs. Keys casual is the norm, with shirts and shoes the required dress, but if you have socks on, you are overdressed. They want you relaxed so that you can wolf down their home-cooked burgers, sweet potato fries, garlic wings, fish sandwiches, and salads and finish things off with a slice of their mouth-pleasing key lime pie. An Insiders' secret is out about one of the best locals' places in the Upper Keys.

MRS. MAC'S KITCHEN $
MM 99.4 Oceanside, Key Largo
(305) 451-3722
mrsmacskitchen.com
You don't show up here for the looks of the place. If good home-cooking is what you want and you're craving plenty of carbs, this is the place to satisfy all of the above. The house is old, bedecked with antiquated license plates that only add to the well-seasoned charm of this Key Largo legend. The menu is long, the sandwiches are hearty, the conch chowder is authentic, and the nightly specials will bring you back—to Mrs. Mac's! Open for breakfast, lunch, and dinner. Closed Sun.

SMUGGLERS COVE RESORT AND MARINA $$
MM 85.5 Bayside, Islamorada
(305) 664-5564
smugscove.com
If you want to find a good place to eat, ask a local. Smugglers Cove, a locals' favorite in Islamorada, puts on no pretensions. What they do put on, however, is a great fish sandwich, among other entrees, that draws raves. Options include peel-and-eat shrimp, oysters on the half shell, chicken wings, and even a kids' menu. What Smugglers lacks in decor and ambience, they make up for in

taste. Smugglers Cove is open 7 days a week for lunch and dinner and is boat accessible.

SUNDOWNERS ON THE BAY $$
MM 104 Bayside, Key Largo
(305) 451-4502
sundownerskeylargo.com
One of Key Largo's most popular places to enjoy the sunset, this open and airy—yet cozy and intimate—establishment overlooks the azure expanse of Blackwater Sound. On the light side, Sundowners' Key Largo fish sandwich wins raves—fresh fish grilled and topped with sautéed onions and American cheese on a kaiser roll. If you prefer a more elaborate meal, try the locals' favorite, Mahi Mahi Meuniere—crispy fish topped with white wine and key lime butter. A large bar, adjoining the indoor dining area, is available for dinner service as well, and busy evenings tend to run on the loud side. The patio and deck afford more privacy. Sundowners offers a full bar and is open for lunch and dinner. Reservations are recommended. The restaurant is accessible by boat.

UNCLE'S RESTAURANT $$
MM 81 Oceanside, Islamorada
(305) 664-4402
unclesrestaurant.com
Mexican tiles, ceiling fans, stained glass, candlelit tables, soft music, and original paintings of Keys flora and fauna set the stage for fine dining at Uncle's. And if you'd prefer to sit under the stars, Uncle's will accommodate you, for it also serves dinner at tables sprinkled on an outdoor deck. The cuisine sparkles with a decidedly Mediterranean flair. Seafood selections are many, including fish du jour prepared five different ways, and there are chicken, veal, beef, pasta, and "Heart Smart" selections as well. Uncle's

offers an extensive wine list and full bar, and is open daily, except Mon, for dinner only. They will happily cook your catch for a fraction of the normal dinner price.

Middle Keys

BURDINES WATERFRONT AND CHIKI TIKI BAR & GRILLE $
MM 47.5 Oceanside, Marathon
(305) 743-5317
burdineswaterfront.com
Take a break and go to this fun-to-be-in-the-Keys eatery. Burdines sits on a channel into Boot Key Harbor, and the view is as good as the food. The Chiki Tiki Bar & Grille sits on the second floor, where you enjoy ocean breezes with a true Keys decor. The service is friendly and you are made to feel welcome and appreciated. The menu holds a bountiful selection, from fresh fish sandwiches to green chile cheeseburgers. If you order nothing else, be sure to get the skinny french fries. They are hand-cut and served with their famous "fry dust." This will put a smile on your tan face. The Chiki Tiki Bar & Grille is open for lunch and dinner daily and is accessible by boat.

HERBIE'S $$
MM 50.5 Bayside, Marathon
(305) 743-6373
Ask anyone: Herbie's is classic Keys. This roadhouse-style watering hole—two simple rooms and a porch with a large bar area and picnic tables—attracts a loyal contingent of locals and snowbirds alike. The conch chowder here is outstanding, packed with conch and chunks of potato. You can order fried shrimp, clam, oyster, or fish baskets or platters, or opt for burgers, dogs, and conch or fish sandwiches. Dinner specials are surprisingly sophisticated, and portions are

generous. They will also cook your catch if you've had a lucky day on the water. Herbie's is open for lunch and dinner Tues through Sat. The restaurant is now air-conditioned, but does not accept reservations or credit cards.

LEIGH ANN'S COFFEE HOUSE $
MM 51.5 Oceanside, Marathon
(305) 743-2001 or (305) 743-6676
leighannscoffeehouse.com
This popular coffeehouse is quaintly closeted in a pale-peach and white Key West–style building on the Overseas Highway. With French doors flung open wide, tile floors, tropical plants, and an eclectic array of rustic furniture and Keys art, this is coffeehouse a la Keys. Chic, clean, and packed with personality, Leigh Ann's food is pretty good, too. Homemade soups rival sandwiches on bagels, croissants, and sub rolls. Specials are made in small batches to ensure freshness. And don't forget the coffee: Choose among cappuccino, mocha coolers, muddy mocha, or macchiato. Leigh Ann's serves beer and wine as well. This is a happening place! Open for breakfast, lunch, and dinner Mon through Sat and until mid-afternoon on Sun.

PORKY'S BAYSIDE $
MM 47.5 Bayside, Marathon
(305) 289-2065
porkysbaysidebbq.com
Looks aren't everything! This tiny, open-air restaurant sits on the water with a picturesque setting among the lobster traps on the commercial fishing docks. Porky's is known for humdinger barbecue and their all-you-can-eat ribs specials every Tues and Wed night. Touted as "swinin' and dinin'," Porky's serves lunch and dinner every day and has live music every night from 6:30 to

9 p.m. Reservations for large parties only are accepted. No credit cards.

THE STUFFED PIG $
MM 49 Bayside, Marathon
(305) 743-4059
thestuffedpig.com
During high-season mornings you'll see a line of hungry diners outdoors reading newspapers and patiently awaiting admittance to the inner sanctum of the Stuffed Pig. This popular cafe packs 'em in for hearty country breakfasts. Try the Pig's Breakfast: two eggs, two pancakes, two sausages, two slices of bacon, potatoes, and toast. Or a Pig's Omelet, a four-egg wonder with the works. If you adhere to less porcine standards, the veggie and egg-substitute omelet will hold the cholesterol. They also serve lunch. The Stuffed Pig is open 7 days a week at the crack of dawn (5 a.m.; an hour later on Sun). They close at 2 p.m. Mon through Thurs and at 3 p.m. Fri through Sun. No reservations or credit cards are accepted.

Lower Keys

BIG PINE RESTAURANT & COFFEE SHOP $
MM 29.5 Bayside, Big Pine Key
(305) 872-2790
The Big Pine Restaurant, sitting next to Big Pine Key's post office, has served this community since the 1950s. The menu highlights traditional American fare: breakfasts of eggs, pancakes, or cereal; lunches of sandwiches or swell burgers; and classic dinners featuring steak, chicken, or fish. Locals head to Big Pine Restaurant for their amazing ribs. Stop in and sit awhile, visit with the Big Pine Key regulars—and enjoy the food! Open Tues through Sat for breakfast, lunch, and dinner and Sun for breakfast and lunch. Closed Mon.

*BOBALU'S SOUTHERN CAFE $$
MM 10 Bayside, Big Coppitt Key
(305) 296-1664

If inexpensive, stick-to-your-ribs food is what you're looking for, then look no more—you have come home. The cuisine at Bobalu's is home-style, hearty, and Southern. The menu includes such entrees as pork chops and authentic fried chicken. The local favorite is the New Haven–style pizza, a Neapolitan-style pie with a crispier crust. Key West's favorite native son, Jimmy Buffett, has been known to dine at the Big Coppitt location on occasion, and he even mentioned this place in his book *Where Is Joe Merchant?* Bobalu's is open in Big Coppitt Tues through Sat for lunch and dinner.

BOONDOCKS GRILLE & DRAFT HOUSE $$
MM 27.5 Bayside, Ramrod Key
(305) 872-4094
boondocks.us.com

Housing the largest miniature golf course in all of the Florida Keys, Boondocks is also home to a grill and draft house with an extensive menu. In addition to the daily happy hour special of 50 percent off all appetizers, like the crispy coconut shrimp and creamy smoked fish dip, Boondocks offers drink and other food specials every weekday. No matter when you go, you will find a celebratory atmosphere under the giant tiki hut that houses the restaurant and bar. They even have a Patio Pet Menu to ensure that Fido is as well fed as you are. Boondocks is open for lunch and dinner daily and has live entertainment on most nights of the week.

*NO NAME PUB $
MM 31 Bayside, N. Watson Boulevard,
Big Pine Key
(305) 872-9115
nonamepub.com

This funky establishment bills itself as "a nice place . . . if you can find it." And you might not find it without a little Insider knowledge. The No Name Pub is topped with a small sign declaring its beginnings in 1936. And N. Watson Boulevard is off the beaten track. Turn west at the traffic light at MM 31 in Big Pine onto Key Deer Boulevard. Proceed to Watson Boulevard and take another right. At the fork in the road, bear right, heading toward No Name Key. Go across a bridge and past a residential subdivision. Just before the No Name Bridge across Bogie Channel, the pub will be on your left, all but hidden under a canopy of large trees. The famous pizza at No Name is deep dish and arrives at your picnic table steaming hot. No Name Pub is open daily for lunch and dinner from 11 a.m. until 11 p.m.

Key West

BLUE HEAVEN $$$
729 Thomas St.
(305) 296-8666
blueheavenkw.com

Blue Heaven—at various times a bordello, a pool hall, a railroad water tower, a cock-fighting arena, a boxing ring (frequented by Papa Hemingway himself), and an ice-cream parlor—is a popular restaurant in historic Bahama Village. Blue Heaven's ambience is as legendary as its Caribbean and vegetarian cuisine. Roosters, hens, and chicks strut all around the picnic tables that fill the restaurant's backyard; so do the resident kitties. Jimmy Buffett's 1995 song "Blue Heaven

Rendezvous" was inspired by this diamond in the rough, and Kenny Chesney confessed to Oprah that it is his favorite restaurant. Blue Heaven has a full bar and serves breakfast with roosters, lunch under the shade, and dinner under the stars daily. Reservations are accepted for parties of 10 or more.

CAMILLE'S RESTAURANT $$
1202 Simonton St.
(305) 296-4811
camilleskeywest.com

The reasonably priced menu at this eclectic local favorite features a wide array of gourmet breakfast, lunch, and dinner specials; it changes daily and nightly. A real crowd pleaser is Paradise Pasta—Key West pink shrimp, lobster, asparagus, and red and yellow peppers in a garlic Alfredo sauce. Weekend breakfast at Camille's is a particular treat, offering pecan waffles, an orgy of eggs Benedict, and eggs galore or eggs whatever—even egg white omelets if you are so inclined. And for lunch, the hand-pulled chicken salad sandwich is always a delicious choice. Liquor and wine are offered. Expect a wait—especially for breakfast. Camille's is open daily for breakfast, lunch, dinner, and happy hour.

✴DION'S QUICK MART $
1127 Truman Ave.
(305) 294-7572
dionsbest.com

Locals turn to Dion's Quick Mart for everything from gas for their car to bread, milk, magazines, and the best fried chicken you have ever tasted. You can smell the aroma of the fryers when you get near the place. Dion's also offers other eats like fried okra and corn dogs on a stick, but chicken is the code of the road here. Call ahead for large

orders. Two additional locations in Key West are at 3228 Flagler Ave. (305-294-4574) and 5350 US 1 on Stock Island (305-296-9901). The location on Truman Avenue is open 24 hours, the shop on Flagler Avenue is open 6 a.m. to 11 p.m., and the Stock Island mart is open 6 a.m. to midnight.

✴HARPOON HARRY'S $
832 Caroline St.
(305) 294-8744
harpoonharrysrestaurant.com

Harpooned and hanging from the ceilings of this hometown-style diner is everything—including the kitchen sink. Across from Key West Historic Seaport, Harpoon Harry's combines Tiffany light fixtures with sleds, carousel horses, and antique toy cars. The restaurant's movie-star wall boasts Elvis, Sophia, and Lucy and Desi. The luncheon menu at Harpoon Harry's is much less eccentric than the decor: Daily blue plate specials consist of baked meat loaf or chicken potpie made from scratch. Breakfast is highlighted by Harry's Special: two extra large eggs, two pieces of sausage and bacon, ham, toast, and jelly served with home fries or grits. Two counters, booths, and tables are available daily for breakfast, lunch, and dinner. Reservations are not accepted.

> **i** If you like to choose a restaurant by its bill of fare, grab a copy of *The Menu*. This quarterly restaurant guide, published by the *Key West Citizen*, features menus from more than 45 Key West eateries. You'll find free copies at hotels, attractions, grocery stores, and newsstands all around Key West. You can also visit their website: keywestmenu.com.

HOG'S BREATH SALOON $
400 Front St.
(305) 296-4222
hogsbreath.com/key-west
Here, nautical charts of Caribbean waters are lacquered onto wood tables, and patrons dine indoors or outside on a brick patio from which large trees sprout. In addition to the favorite fish sandwich served blackened or grilled with lemon, Hog's Breath's smoked-fish dolphin dip and stone crabs (in season) are extremely popular. The restaurant's full-service bar features the medium-bodied Hog's Breath beer, brewed in the Midwest. In case you were wondering, the name of the joint comes from an old saying of the owner's grandmother, that "hog's breath is better than no breath at all." The restaurant is open for lunch and dinner, and live bands play folk rock, rock, blues, and jazz throughout the day and evening. Reservations are not accepted.

*HURRICANE HOLE WATERFRONT BAR AND SEAFOOD GRILL $
MM 4.5 Oceanside, Stock Island
(305) 294-0200
hurricaneholekeywest.com
Situated upon pilings overlooking Cowkey Channel, the location may look informal because it is inside the Hurricane Hole Marina compound, but what awaits the diner is one great meal. The atmosphere and dress code are Keys comfortable. The ample tables and room size of Hurricane Hole give it an airy feel even when the place is packed with folks. The menu is varied enough that it will please everyone's palate. The appetizers range from peel-and-eat shrimp to chicken tenders to bruschetta. The "Fresh Off the Hook" fish of the day is served five different ways, but the most popular entrees include the fish-and-chips. Hurricane Hole is open for lunch and dinner daily, with happy hour specials.

JIMMY BUFFETT'S MARGARITAVILLE CAFE $$
500 Duval St.
(305) 292-1435
margaritavillekeywest.com
Lunch really could last forever at Jimmy Buffett's Margaritaville Cafe, and patrons who steer here quite often remain throughout much of the day. Margaritas are de rigueur and made fresh per order with Margaritaville tequila. "Parrothead" and other island music plays in the background, and decorations include oversize props from stage settings of Buffett tours. The fixin's—lettuce and tomato, Heinz 57, and french-fried potatoes—are not forgotten. Margaritaville is open for lunch and dinner daily, and Buffett himself has been known to stop by, cook a burger, and give an impromptu concert. Live music is offered nightly, beginning at 10:30 p.m. Reservations are not accepted, but those on the waiting list may shop for souvenirs in Buffett's adjacent store.

KELLY'S CARIBBEAN BAR, GRILL & BREWERY $$
301 Whitehead St.
(305) 293-8484
kellyskeywest.com
Named after actress Kelly McGillis, this Caribbean restaurant is on the site of the original Pan American World Airways offices. Outdoor dining is available on a stone patio with gardens. On the second floor Kelly's Clipper Club Lounge invites patrons to relax in an open-air gazebo-style setting. Among the house specialties here are Kelly's Crab Cakes, served with mango salsa and a spicy papaya

remoulade, and the lobster ravioli—lobster-stuffed ravioli with sun-dried tomatoes in an orange-tarragon beurre blanc sauce. Kelly's Caribbean also is home to the Southernmost Brewery, which whips up an all-natural selection including Key West Golden Ale, Havana Red Ale, and Southern Clipper Wheat Beer. The restaurant is open daily for lunch and dinner 7 days a week.

PEPE'S CAFE $$
806 Caroline St.
(305) 294-7192
pepescafe.net

Billed as the "Eldest Eating House in the Florida Keys, established 1909," Pepe's is beloved by locals. Options include oysters served raw or baked, New York strip steaks, filet mignon, pork chops, even barbecue. And Pepe's burgers sound as intriguing as they taste: White Collar Burger, Blue Collar Burger, Slit Ray Burger, and Patty Melt. Be sure to try a margarita here (the lime juice is squeezed fresh) and, for dessert, the brownie pie, served warm with ice cream—ask for Cuban coffee flavor instead of vanilla. The restaurant is open every day for breakfast, lunch, and dinner. Reservations are not accepted and Pepe's is always packed, just like your plate!

TURTLE KRAALS RESTAURANT
AND BAR $$
231 Margaret St.
(305) 294-2640
turtlekraals.com

Turtle Kraals occupies the site of a former turtle cannery, hence the name—which essentially means "turtle pen." Make sure to try the Bucket of Bones, spareribs that have been slowly cooked for up to 14 hours, or the mesquite-grilled oysters on the half shell. Then move on to seafood specialties

like the Best of the Bay, which includes half a Florida lobster tail, Key West pink shrimp, and oysters, all grilled on the open wood-fire grill. You can enjoy all these tasty treats inside in the dockside air-conditioned restaurant or upstairs at the Tower Bar while watching the sun as it sets over the Key West Seaport. Turtle Kraals has a full bar and is open daily for breakfast, lunch, and dinner.

CONTEMPORARY AMERICAN

Upper Keys

ATLANTIC'S EDGE	$$$
NIKAI SUSHI	$$$
LIMONCELLO	$$$

Cheeca Lodge & Spa
MM 82 Oceanside, Islamorada
(305) 664-4651
cheeca.com

The fine-dining room at Atlantic's Edge restaurant located in the Cheeca Lodge & Spa has panoramic vistas of the Atlantic Ocean, with seating indoors and out. A favorite item on the gourmet menu is the apricot-glazed mahi with Yukon puree, broccolini, and Zellwood Farms corn served in a coconut curry sauce. Atlantic's Edge is open for breakfast, lunch, and dinner nightly, offering libations from a full bar. The Nikai Sushi restaurant features an abundance of fresh sushi options, from five different types of tartars to maki and vegetable rolls to specialty rolls like the Keysy Japanesy—a coconut shrimp and avocado roll topped with escolar tartar tempura crunchies and a key lime glaze. Nikai is open for lunch and dinner, with a selection of more than 35 Japanese sakis and wine. Limoncello is a family-friendly Italian restaurant with fresh pasta, hand-rolled pizzas, and entrees like chicken Parmesan served with fresh mozzarella, rapini, and Yukon mash.

MORADA BAY BEACH CAFE $$$
MM 81.6 Bayside, Islamorada
(305) 664-0604
moradabay-restaurant.com

Morada Bay Beach Cafe in Islamorada delivers a tapas-style selection of appetizers and eclectic entrees. Pastel beach tables and low Adirondack-style chairs pepper a wide expanse of sandy beach that fronts the gentle waters of Florida Bay. Curving palms and tiki torches complete the outdoor illusion, and the food is as imaginatively designed as the decor. Any of Morada Bay's fresh fish selections—all imaginatively prepared—will more than satisfy your taste for the sea. This is the perfect place to watch the sun set, as the restaurant perches at the edge of Florida Bay and musicians often stop by for a lively impromptu set. Morada Bay Beach Cafe is open for lunch and dinner daily and serves breakfast Fri through Sun.

PIERRE'S RESTAURANT $$$$
MM 81.6 Bayside, Islamorada
(305) 664-3225
pierres-restaurant.com

Pierre's is the place to go for a romantic dining experience. Flickering candlelight and comfy leather sofas greet you in the downstairs lounge area for predinner libations, and a covered porch welcomes you to sit on cushioned wicker chairs and watch the famed Keys sunset. Walk up the sweeping curved staircase, however, and your dining adventure begins. The decor, tropically British colonial, is elegant yet casual. Dine indoors or out on the covered porch. The culinary stars shine with such signature dishes as herb-grilled mahi mahi, pan-seared scallops, and a constantly changing rotation of the chef's creative offerings. Check your almanac and join in the monthly full-moon

beach party replete with torches, live music, and special tropical drinks. Pierre's is open every evening for dinner only.

SNAPPER'S WATERFRONT RESTAURANT $$
MM 94.5 Oceanside, 139 Seaside Ave., Key Largo
(305) 852-5956
snapperskeylargo.com

The best part of Snapper's is sitting out on the deck near the water overlooking Snapper's Marina—next to the food, that is. Sample some Applewood Smoked Bacon Wrapped Scallops or the local favorite: Matt's Shrimp Fritters with ponzu dipping sauce. Snapper's offers an extensive raw bar as well as sandwiches, burgers, and many selections for landlubbers. There's a lot of action and a frenzied atmosphere, but it's worth the visit. Weekends feature live entertainment nightly in season. The restaurant serves lunch and dinner 7 days a week and brunch on Sun, and is accessible by boat. Reservations are accepted.

✳ZIGGIE AND MAD DOG'S $$
MM 83 Bayside, Islamorada
(305) 664-3391
ziggieandmaddogs.com

Steaks, chops, and seafood are on the menu at this newly renovated Keys landmark. Partners Randy Kassewitz and Miami Dolphins football player Jim "Mad Dog" Mandich turned this historic property (originally built in the 1930s) into a fine-dining establishment offering "something for every palate." Menu items include grilled duck breast served with warm lingonberry sauce, delicious baked jumbo shrimp with mango and crab stuffing, and grilled double-bone pork chop glazed with plum and port wine.

The wine list is extensive. And while the decor may have changed, not to worry—the fish stories still abound in the chic bar area. (Be sure to ask the bartender about Al Capone playing cards in the back room.) Open daily for lunch and dinner; reservations recommended.

Middle Keys

✳ALMA/TOM'S HARBOR HOUSE RESTAURANT $$$$
Hawk's Cay Resort
MM 61 Oceanside, Duck Key
(305) 743-7000
hawkscay.com

Alma is a world-class Latino-themed restaurant with an intimate decor. Adjoining the restaurant is the Bar at Alma, which features a white marble bar at which you can savor drinks and try their outstanding tequila and rum collection. Mojitos anyone? If you plan on coming by boat, call the marina in advance to secure a slip. Alma is open daily for dinner only. Tom's Harbor House Restaurant offers casual seaside dining on a spacious waterfront deck—but don't let the casual atmosphere fool you, the cuisine is just as divine as other fine-dining establishments. Tom's Harbor House is open daily for dinner and offers live entertainment on the weekends.

✳BARRACUDA GRILL $$
MM 49.5 Bayside, Marathon
(305) 743-3314
barracudagrillmarathon.com

Imaginative preparation and presentation showcase the entrees at the Barracuda Grill, a small, lively bistro in the heart of Marathon. Tantalizing stars of the menu are often the char-grilled veal chop, a 22-ounce rib-eye steak, roasted rack of lamb with black raspberry sauce or a sauté of portobello

mushrooms, and mangrove snapper with mango salsa. A daily changing menu of the chefs' creative interpretations rivals the old favorites. Not your typical family restaurant, at Barracuda Mom and Dad can dine sumptuously and keep their kids happy, too. Barracuda Grill opens for dinner Wed through Sat at 5:55 p.m. Reservations are not taken. This popular spot fills up quickly, especially in high season, so come early if you don't want to wait for a table.

CABANA BREEZES $
425 E. Ocean Drive, Key Colony Beach
(305) 743-4849
cabanabreezes.com

Famous bandleader Guy Lombardo once owned this popular landmark back in the 1950s. Different names (the Colony House and the Shamrock) may have come and gone, but the outstanding food and service remain the same. The oceanfront tiki bar with entertainment brings in the crowds, but it is the masterful selections in the cabana that keep this eatery at the top of the locals' hit parade. Menu toppers range from beer-battered fish-and-chips to the new heart-healthy grouper or mahi sandwich—either one is blackened to perfection on a kaiser roll—to bacon-wrapped pan-seared filet mignon. A daily happy hour and live entertainment Thurs through Sun nights ensure that Cabana Breezes remains as popular and lively as ever.

HIDEAWAY CAFE $$$
Rainbow Bend Resort
MM 58 Oceanside, Grassy Key
(305) 289-1554
hideawaycafe.com

The only thing rivaling the direct ocean vistas at Hideaway Cafe is the cuisine. Sure to please the foodie in you, the Hideaway also will intrigue the diner who likes to pig out: The Hideaway Rib Steak is large enough to serve a family of four, and the seafood Wellington is a dream! Other favorites include seafood crepes (a seafood combo rolled in a homemade crepe) topped with flamingo sauce, and seafood puttanesca (shrimp, scallops, and shellfish in a spicy red sauce). Top off your dinner with Bananas a la Hideaway—sautéed bananas in brown sugar and banana liquor. What a gourmet surprise! Hideaway Cafe is open daily for lunch and dinner. The service is "relaxed," so plan to drink in the view along with your libations. Reservations are recommended.

Lower Keys

✳LITTLE PALM ISLAND RESORT & SPA $$$$
MM 28.5 Oceanside, Little Torch Key
(305) 872-2551 or (800) 343-8567
littlepalmisland.com
Dining at Little Palm Island is pure romance. You step into a fairy tale the moment you check in at the mainland substation on Little Torch Key to await your luxurious launch, the *Woodson,* that will spirit you to the island. As you arrive at the island's dock, you'll spot the Great House amid towering coconut palms. Classic European preparations fused with Floridian, Caribbean, and Pan-Asian flavors are the tantalizing offerings from the chef. Insiders know this translates into the meal of a lifetime. Little Palm offers libations from a full-service bar and maintains an extensive wine list. A limited number of reservations are accepted from the general public for lunch and dinner daily. Children must be age 16 or older to dine at Little Palm Island.

PARROTDISE WATERFRONT BAR & GRILLE $$
MM 28.5 Bayside, 183 Barry Ave., Little Torch Key
(305) 872-9989
parrotdisewaterfront.com
Situated high above Big Pine Channel on the gulf, the pavilion-like interior is true Keys atmosphere for a casual feast with a diverse menu. A local favorite is the mahi mahi fingers, lightly broiled and served with fruit chutney. The seared tuna with sesame seeds served with ginger, wasabi, and soy is a real crowd pleaser. The Parrotdise offers a full-service bar. The bar and grill is open daily for lunch and dinner.

✳THE SQUARE GROUPER BAR AND GRILL $$
MM 22.6 Oceanside, Cudjoe Key
(305) 745-8880
squaregrouperbarandgrill.com
Located midway between Key West and Big Pine, this establishment sets out to satisfy your hankering for memorable Keys cuisine. Conch and lobster fritters with Asian dipping sauce are a crowd pleaser, and be sure to try the seared tuna with spicy pineapple sauce. The catch of the day is prepared in a different manner nightly. A children's menu is available, and a dessert certain to bring out the fun for everyone is chocolate fondue with fresh fruit, marshmallows, and pound cake. Open wide and say *a-a-a-h!* The Square Grouper is open for lunch and dinner Tues through Sat, but make sure to call in advance, as they have been known to close for a month or so during the slow summer season.

Key West

✻BAD BOY BURRITO $
1220½ Simonton St.
(305) 292-2697
badboyburrito.com

Hands down, this is the locals' favorite lunch in Key West, be it by delivery or sitting on a bar stool in the tiny establishment. Bad Boy's starts with organic flour tortillas, adds basmati rice and rattlesnake beans, and the rest is up to you. Try the veggie approach and add sautéed mushrooms, tomatilla sauce, shaved cabbage, shredded cheese, grilled green onions, and avocado. Carnivore options include pork carnitas, duck, chicken, and seasoned ground Kobe beef. Bad Boy's also has items on the menu that don't require you to create, like the Cayo Hueso Fish Tacos and Disco Duck Quesadilla. Bad Boy is open and delivers Mon through Sat from 10 a.m. to 6 p.m. No credit cards.

BAGATELLE $$$
115 Duval St.
(305) 296-6609
bagatellekeywest.com

Incongruous among the tourist trappings of lower Duval, Bagatelle sits reservedly amid the fray. Situated on two floors of a gracious old Key West home, Bagatelle serves fresh local ingredients with island inventiveness. Try the tempura lobster tail or the mojo-marinated free-range chicken breast for something different. Wraparound balconies on both levels afford outdoor dining, or you may choose to dine indoors, where the decor favors that of a first-rate art gallery. Bagatelle is a premier spot from which to view the Fantasy Fest Parade (see the Annual Events chapter). Reservations for the evening of Fantasy Fest should be made well in advance of the event, even up to a year. Bagatelle serves breakfast, lunch, and dinner daily. Reservations are suggested.

BISTRO 245 $$$
The Westin Key West Resort and Marina
245 Front St.
(305) 294-4000
westinkeywestresort.com

Imagine, a Sunday brunch buffet table that is 70 feet long—so long you can barely see the other end! Dine indoors or out with a panoramic view of the Gulf of Mexico, all the while indulging in great Florida Keys cuisine. Favorite menu items include the Grouper Antillia, served with chipotle-mango barbecue-grilled shrimp, gingered sweet potato and corn hash, baby arugula, and crispy onions. Regular menu offerings for breakfast, lunch, and dinner Mon through Sat, and the enormous food fest is Sun only.

BLACKFIN BISTRO $$
918 Duval St.
(305) 509-7408
blackfinbistro.com

Stop into this classic bistro-style restaurant for a chance to relax and unwind after the sensory overload of Duval Street. You won't find loud, tropical artwork stuffed into every corner here. Instead, rest your eyes on the soothing island photography, wine options written on a chalkboard, and fresh and clean lines of the cool bistro tables. And the food is just as lovely as the decor. From the yellowfin tuna burger to the grilled ahi tuna, one bite is all it will take to figure out why the locals keep coming back to Blackfin Bistro. Open for lunch and dinner daily.

*THE CAFE $$

509 Southard St.
(305) 296-5515

The Cafe serves mostly vegetarian and vegan food that is full of flavor. Large portions and the fun staff cap off the experience. Simply stated and simply a good place to eat. For lunch, try the falafel, served with bean salad or sweet potato fries for an extra fee. At dinnertime, start with cold peanut noodles to share—soba noodles with edamame, red peppers, peanuts, and black sesame seeds—and follow with the delicious seared yellowfin tuna served with honey-wasabi sauce, organic brown rice, sautéed spinach, and pickled ginger.

CAFE MARQUESA $$$$

The Marquesa Hotel
600 Fleming St.
(305) 292-1244
cafemarquesa.com

Golden walls covered with paintings, pastel tile floors, large mirrors, and a panoramic country-kitchen mural set the scene for one of the finest dining encounters in Key West. Cafe Marquesa, situated in the historic Marquesa Hotel, remains a consistent winner in the restaurant wars. Gracing the white linen tablecloths is an eclectic assortment of innovative dishes. The menu changes regularly, but specialties of the house have included conch and blue crab cake with creole tartar sauce and jicama slaw, peppercorn-dusted seared yellowfin tuna, feta-and-pine-nut-encrusted rack of lamb, and grilled marinated Key West shrimp. Reservations are highly recommended in all seasons. Cafe Marquesa serves dinner nightly

HARBOURVIEW CAFE $$$

Pier House Resort
1 Duval St.
(305) 296-4600
pierhouse.com

This rendering of a classic setting is well worth the price of a dinner tab. Located in the Pier House Resort (see the Accommodations chapter), the menu is full-blown "Floribbean" with all the trimmings. The restaurant lives up to its name with the stunning views of Key West Harbor. Dine inside or out on the harbor and get your taste buds in gear with the white conch chowder—it will make you melt right into your entree of yellowtail, lobster, scallops, or seafood paella. The HarbourView serves breakfast, lunch, and dinner daily.

HOT TIN ROOF $$$

Ocean Key Resort
Zero Duval St.
(305) 296-7701 or (800) 328-9815
oceankey.com

The Hot Tin Roof name comes from Tennessee Williams's (a past resident of Key West) most famous play, *Cat on a Hot Tin Roof*. The dining room and outdoor deck enjoy panoramic views of Key West Harbor and its famed sunset. The chef has combined elements of South American, Asian, and French cuisine in an interpretation of flavors and attitudes of Key West he calls "Conch-fusion." Prime examples include the scallop piccata with pappardelle pasta and tomatoes or the caramelized mahi served with coconut, corn, poblano, and carrots. Hot Tin Roof is open for breakfast and dinner daily.

*LATITUDES BEACH CAFE $$$$
Sunset Key
(305) 294-4000
sunsetkeyisland.com

When you think of dining seaside somewhere on a secluded island, this is the kind of place that comes to mind. Just 5 minutes across the water from the hustle and bustle of Mallory Square, Latitudes might just as well be half a world away. It is that peaceful, that serene. Launches for Sunset Key leave regularly throughout the day from the pier at the Westin Key West Resort and Marina at 245 Front Street. If you are not living or staying on the island, you must make a reservation for your meal at Latitudes with the Westin concierge to secure a boarding pass. Latitudes is open daily for breakfast, lunch, and dinner.

*LOBO'S GRILL $
5 Key Lime Square
(305) 296-5303
loboskw.com

Lobo's is where locals love to lunch. The menu includes burgers, nachos, quesadillas, and salads. But the real standouts are the roll-up sandwiches—a mix of meats, cheeses, fresh veggies, and spreads tucked tightly, then rolled, in a giant flour tortilla. Choose from such selections as the Delhi Chicken (curried chicken salad, Swiss cheese, sprouts, mango chutney, avocado, lettuce, and pineapple) or Porky's Nightmare (honey-baked ham, roast pork, bacon, cheddar, Swiss, lettuce, tomato, onions, and honey mustard). You can eat in or take out; call ahead for quick pickup or free delivery in Old Town.

*LOUIE'S BACKYARD $$$$
700 Waddell Ave.
(305) 294-1061
louiesbackyard.com

Louie's Backyard combines island manor-house ambience with cutting-edge cuisine. A sweeping veranda for outdoor dining overlooks Louie's "backyard," which is actually a prime piece of Atlantic oceanfront property. In the 1970s this spot was a favorite with next-door-neighbor Jimmy Buffett, who often played for his supper. For lunch, try the Not Just Any Fish Sandwich served with potato chips they make every morning. A dinner favorite is the sautéed Key West shrimp with bacon, mushrooms, and stone-ground grits. Louie's Backyard serves lunch and dinner daily. Reservations are recommended. The Afterdeck outdoor oceanside bar is the locals' favorite place for a sundowner and is open all day and into the wee hours (see our Nightlife chapter).

i Hunter S. Thompson, an American journalist and author famous for his flamboyant writing style known as "gonzo journalism," lived in the Keys for part of his life. One of his favorite haunts was Louie's Backyard restaurant.

MICHAEL'S $$$$
532 Margaret St.
(305) 295-1300
michaelskeywest.com

Tucked away in a quiet Old Town neighborhood several blocks off Duval is this casual yet elegant little gem of a restaurant. Since January 1997 owners Melanie and Michael Wilson have been serving up some of the best food on the island. Michael, the former corporate chef for the Chicago-based

Morton's Steakhouses, knows how to cook a piece of beef. His prime beef, rubbed with roasted garlic and Roquefort, has garnered rave reviews and numerous awards. The menu also includes seafood and pasta specialties, and a good selection of fondues is available in the Garden Bar. There is a full bar with a martini menu. Michael's is open nightly from 5:30 p.m. Reservations are recommended for both indoor and outdoor seating.

NINE ONE FIVE $$$$
915 Duval St.
(305) 296-0669
915duval.com
Housed in a stately Victorian home, this James Beard award–winning restaurant is the talk of the town. While you're waiting for your meal, try an appetizer like the tuna dome made with Dungeness crab with a lemon miso dressing, wrapped with sushi-grade ahi tuna. Don't miss the Devils on Horseback—bacon-wrapped dates stuffed with sweet garlic and served with a ginger soy dipping sauce. And for dessert, how about an artisan cheese plate replete with fresh Florida honeycomb? Post-dinner, head upstairs to Point 5 (see our Nightlife chapter) and relax in the hip atmosphere of a wine bar with a cool DJ. Open nightly for dinner. Reservations suggested.

ROOF TOP CAFE $$$
308 Front St.
(305) 294-2042
rooftopcafekeywest.com
High amid the treetops, the Roof Top Cafe looks down on the tourist mecca along Front Street near Mallory Square. And although the restaurant bustles with dining activity, the atmosphere remains unhurried and

removed from the fray. Diners may sit on a second-floor balcony, which extends on two sides of the building, under the canopy of ancient leafy trees. Inside, ceiling fans mounted on the white vaulted ceiling gently move the air about the open-air, pavilion-style dining room. Dinner creations have included mahi mahi with plantain and shrimp stuffing and mango coriander butter, chipotle-glazed roast pork tenderloin, and creamy wild mushroom risotto. Rooftop Cafe is open daily for breakfast, lunch, and dinner. Reservations are recommended.

SALUTE! ON THE BEACH $$
1000 Atlantic Blvd.
(305) 292-1117
saluteonthebeach.com
To "see" Salute is to "see" the "sea"! Right smack dab on Higgs Beach with the Atlantic Ocean as your front yard, Salute has its squatters' rights and rightfully so. Open for lunch and dinner, this locals' hangout is a pet of a restaurant for all of us in the know. Salute serves yummy seafood and great Italian choices, with the antipasto winning hands down. The linguini with mussels, white wine, and butter is also a favorite menu item, as is the Tuscan white bean soup. And don't miss the homemade ice-cream cookie sandwich! But perhaps the best part of this place is the free show that goes on at the beach in front of you.

SANTIAGO'S BODEGA $$$
207 Petronia St.
(305) 296-7691
santiagosbodega.com
Tucked away on a small street with a neighborhood setting, you discover Santiago's Bodega. Wood floors, warm colors, and wide, open windows pouring out onto a porch

for dining under gossamer lanterns capture the setting for this unique tapas experience. The food is fresh and simple with more than 30 selections on the menu, including soups and salads. Smoked salmon carpaccio, fresh yellowfin ceviche, and the local-favorite beef tenderloin topped with blue cheese are on the offering. There are also loads of vegetarian dishes. Wine, beer, lovely sherry, and ports are also served. Service is charming and friendly. Open for lunch and dinner, but be mindful to make a reservation—everyone wants a table!

SARABETH'S $$$$
530 Simonton St.
(305) 293-8181
sarabethskeywest.com

There is a real Sarabeth, and she is an award-winning jam maker, pastry chef, and restaurateur. Not only does her "empire" include four locations in New York City and Key West, but her legendary spreadable fruits and pastries can be purchased on her website as well as in her establishments. The menus include from-scratch pancakes, salads, sandwiches, meat loaf, grilled meats, and fish. The coffee is served in cups so large, they are called bowls. Seating, indoors or out, in this historic 19th-century clapboard building is a wonderful way to make a Keys memory. Sarabeth's is open for breakfast and lunch Wed through Fri, brunch Sat and Sun, and dinner Wed through Sun. Reservations are suggested for parties of four or more.

SQUARE ONE $$$
1075 Duval St.
(305) 296-4300
squareonerestaurant.com

Enjoy a touch of class and a bit of craziness, Manhattan style, at Square One, a casually sophisticated uptown bistro in Duval Square. Dinner options include a whole Florida yellow snapper and grass-fed black Angus tenderloin of beef with sauce options ranging from the classic béarnaise sauce to mint-parsley pesto. Side offerings like the Yukon Gold potato gratin and roasted baby mushrooms with rosemary and lavender round out the custom dishes. Don't worry—a waiter is at the ready to guide you in the right direction should you need help. Outdoor dining is available in the tree-lined courtyard, and there is ample free parking. Square One serves breakfast, brunch, lunch, and dinner. Reservations are recommended.

CUBAN

Key West

EL MESON DE PEPE $$
410 Wall St.
(305) 295-2620
elmesondepepe.com

Situated just off Mallory Square, El Meson de Pepe draws a large post-sunset crowd. A salsa band plays nightly as the sun sinks into the Gulf of Mexico, which adds to the festive and welcoming atmosphere. Look for Cuban-Conch classics on the menu: Mollete a la Pancho; Cuban bread stuffed with picadillo, a spicy combination of ground beef, capers, raisins, olives, and seasonings; and *ropa vieja* (shredded beef). Quench your thirst with Pepe's Lemonade, a refreshing cocktail made with Bacardi Limon, cranberry, and orange juice. El Meson de Pepe is open for breakfast, lunch, and dinner daily. Large groups are welcome, and reservations are appreciated but rarely necessary.

EL SIBONEY $$
900 Catherine St.
(305) 296-4184 or (305) 743-9090
elsiboneyrestaurant.com

A cascade of bilingual chatter washes over the enthusiastic diners at El Siboney, an informal restaurant specializing in Cuban cuisine. Portions are enormous here; the same menu is offered at lunch or dinner. You'll find myriad Cuban twists with beef, including the popular *ropa vieja* and *boliche* (Cuban pot roast). Crab, shrimp, and chicken all get the wonderful Cuban garlic treatment, and you can order paella for two. You can also choose from an array of sandwiches or sides of tamales, yucca, black beans, platanos, and tostones. For a cocktail-with-a-kick, try the homemade sangria, and for dessert (if you have room), try the rice pudding, flan, or natilla. El Siboney is closed Sun. No credit cards.

DESSERTS

Key West

BETTER THAN SEX DESSERT RESTAURANT $
926 Simonton St.
(305) 296-8102
betterthansexkw.com

This romantic place will put you in the mood . . . for dessert. Vintage in music ('30s and '40s), flirtatious in atmosphere (flickering candlelight), and *wowee wowee* in the dessert department, this restaurant serves *only* desserts along with wines and coffees. One such presentation is a Chocolate Cab, a wine goblet coated with lush chocolate then filled with wine. You will be smitten—after all, this is Key West!

FRENCH

Key West

BANANA CAFE $$$
1215 Duval St.
(305) 294-7227
bananacafekw.com

Settle into this quiet open-air bistro and choose from more than 40 breakfast and lunch crepes. The thin, pancake-like crepes are stuffed with veggies, fish, and meat, and they are designated either sweet or savory. The most desirable crepe among patrons is the ratatouille, overflowing with sautéed eggplant, zucchini, peppers, and garlic and topped with a fried egg sunny-side up. Dinner options include such offerings as the local snapper served with Parisian gnocchi in lemon-caper brown butter. Banana Cafe is open for breakfast and lunch daily and dinner Tues through Sat. Reservations are recommended, particularly on weekends.

THE GRAND CAFE $$$
314 Duval St.
(305) 292-4740
grandcafekeywest.com

Southern French cuisine of Provence in a tropical setting is the ambience of the Grand Cafe. Sit on the patio overlooking Duval Street or inside in the air-conditioning among vibrant artwork by local artists. Start with the carpaccio of beef tenderloin, served with shaved Parmesan cheese, red onions, capers, arugula, and white truffle oil, or the bruschetta, crostini piled high with chopped Roma tomatoes and basil pesto. The lunch menu offers crunchy paninis, hot pressed sandwiches served with a small salad of mixed greens with the amazing house vinaigrette dressing. The Grand Cafe prides itself on excellent wine selections and simply grand martinis and is open for lunch and dinner daily. Reservations are recommended.

GASTROPUB

Key West

✳2¢   **$$$**
416 Appelrouth Lane
(305) 414-8626
twocentskw.com
Newly opened at the end of December 2011, 2¢ partners James Beard–honored chef Chris Otten (who also created the local favorite Bad Boy Burrito) with the master-mind behind the local bar hangout the Porch, Chris Shultz. Together, the two Chrises have created Key West's first gastropub and beer garden, and it is a major hit with the locals. The lights are usually low, emanating from metallic chandeliers that are more sculptural than traditional, and the place is typically humming with locals and travelers alike. Grab a table indoors or out in the garden area and order the Thai wings or Gruyère cheese puffs along with a Bell's Two Hearted IPA or other craft beer or glass of wine. Whatever your choice at 2¢, you won't be disappointed.

GERMAN

Upper Keys

GILBERT'S RESORT TIKI BAR AND RESTAURANT   **$**
MM 107.9 Bayside, Key Largo
(305) 451-1133
gilbertsresort.com
Gilbert's Waterfront Tiki Bar and Restaurant is not to be missed. The owners pride themselves on their old-world menu and old Keys charm. Starting at lunchtime, the restaurant

offers daily specials: authentic German schnitzel dinners on Mon, all-you-can-eat shrimp on Wed, and a German buffet tempts you with all the sauerbraten, goulash soup, and Bitburger beer you can hold on Thurs. Of course, Gilbert's also has Keys seafood and steak, but if you are missing hearty ethnic classics, look no further.

Key West

MARTIN'S   **$$**
917 Duval St.
(305) 296-0111
martinskeywest.com
Martin's has taken its expansive German menu with its island flair and shines bright on upper Duval Street. Begin with Pilze a la Martin, toasted bread rounds topped with sautéed mushrooms and herb garlic butter. You'll find classic German dishes such as sauerbraten with spaetzle and red cabbage, and Wiener schnitzel, but Martin's also prepares island seafood creations *à la deutsch*. Yellowtail snapper is encrusted with almonds, flambéed with cognac, and served with a medley of vegetables and wild rice. Choose from a large selection of fine German wines and beers or one of the signature cocktails, like the espresso martini. Martin's serves dinner nightly, and offers Sunday brunch with dining indoors or out in their tropical garden. Reservations are suggested.

IRISH

Key West

✳FINNEGAN'S WAKE IRISH PUB & EATERY   **$**
320 Grinnell St.
(305) 293-0222
keywestirish.com

Try authentic Irish fare at Finnegan's: shepherd's pie, corned beef and cabbage, potato pancakes, or the Dublin chicken potpie. The lovely Irish potato-leek soup, a house specialty, is thick and chunky and served with grated cheddar, chopped scallions, and bacon. And be sure to try a black and tan—half Guinness, half lager—or a pint of bottled cider. They also offer 26 draft beers. Finnegan's Wake is open from lunchtime until 4 a.m. (serving dinner until 10:30 p.m., bar menu until 3 a.m.). You'll find two happy hours here: from 4 to 7 p.m. and from midnight to 2 a.m. Patio dining is available. Reservations will be honored but usually are not necessary. Weekends feature live music.

ITALIAN & PIZZA

Upper Keys

BOARDWALK PIZZA $
MM 88.8 Bayside, Islamorada
(305) 853-3800
boardwalkpizzainthekeys.com
Easy living and easy eating are what make life in the Keys so popular. Boardwalk Pizza creates handmade pizza and bakes the pies in a stone-lined pizza oven. This is a small eatery that is big on taste. Locals rave about the crust, characterized as neither thick nor thin, but light, fluffy, and tender. You'll also find cheesesteaks, subs, calzones, and pasta here. This pizzeria is open daily for lunch and dinner.

CAFE LARGO $$
MM 99.5 Bayside, Key Largo
(305) 451-4885
keylargo-cafelargo.com
This vibrant, third-generation-owned restaurant has been serving up home-style Italian specialties in the Upper Keys for more

than 20 years. The DiGiorgio family offers everything Italian, from pasta to pizza, along with some local delicacies thrown in for good measure. The expansive and diverse menu includes the popular Parmigian Fried Portabella Stix appetizer, tender osso bucco with mushroom risotto, and Florida lobster stuffed with crabmeat and baked with sweet butter and white wine. Specialty drinks include the Key Lime Pie Martini and freshly made sangria by the glass. Cafe Largo has a full bar and extensive wine list, and is open daily at 4:30 p.m.

TOWER OF PIZZA $
MM 100.6 Bayside, Key Largo
(305) 451-1461
Antipasto, Greek salad, minestrone, and a potpourri of great pasta dishes vie with fantastic pizza at Tower of Pizza establishments. Sauces and dough here are homemade, and cheeses are fresh. Locals particularly like the Sicilian-style pie, but you can build your own from a long list of tantalizing ingredients. Delivery is free with a minimum order. The second location is at MM 81.5 Bayside in Islamorada (305-664-8216). Both Towers are open every day for lunch and dinner.

UPPER CRUST PIZZA $$
MM 101.6 Oceanside, Key Largo
(305) 451-4188
Long a favorite pizza restaurant in Marathon, Upper Crust moved up the Keys several years ago and is now winning raves in Key Largo. You can build your own thick-crust pizza with an array of ingredients, but the House Deluxe is a combination you won't want to miss—pepperoni, sausage, mushrooms, green peppers, onions, black olives, extra sauce, and extra cheese. Upper Crust also serves a large variety of pasta dishes and

subs and offers daily specials that are difficult to pass up. Open daily for lunch and dinner.

Middle Keys

FRANK'S GRILL $$
MM 52 Bayside, Marathon
(305) 289-7772
franksgrillmarathon.com
Finding the place makes you work up an appetite, but it's worth looking. Turn at 113th Street and look for the sign. Frank is proud of his restaurant, and he proves it with signature dishes of Italian-American selections. There are more than a dozen pasta dishes on offer. Fish is grilled or blackened, and the catch of the day served Française style is a standout, as is the shrimp scampi. Friendly prices and nice owners make this a winner. Be sure to make a reservation, as Frank's Grill fills up fast! Frank's is open for lunch and dinner Mon through Fri and dinner on Sat.

KEY COLONY INN $$
MM 54 Oceanside, 700 W. Ocean Dr., Key Colony Beach
(305) 743-0100
kcinn.com
The Key Colony Inn is a favorite dining haunt of residents and visitors alike. Besides the varied menu selections—75 entrees—of Italian-style pasta, veal, and chicken dishes, Key Colony offers innovative presentations of Florida Keys seafood, steaks, and interesting daily specials. If dinner conversation is important, request a corner table, which may be a bit quieter, because ceiling acoustics in the restaurant do not filter the noise of a room full of chattering diners. Or if the weather is fine, and it usually is, sit outside on the covered veranda. The Key Colony Inn features a full-service bar and is open for lunch and dinner daily and brunch on Sun

from 11 a.m. to 2 p.m. This place is always packed, and reservations are recommended.

Key West

ABBONDANZA $$
1208 Simonton St.
(305) 292-1199
The specialty at this casual Italian eatery is pasta, of course, in a variety of shapes and with sauces that range from Alfredo to pomodoro. You'll also find such main dishes as chicken marsala and veal parmigiana, plus daily specials. The food is quite tasty, the atmosphere is comfortable, and you're sure to discover that the portions at this restaurant live up to its name, which is Italian for "plenty." Abbondanza is a choice place to have dinner for two or a crowd. There is a full bar, and the menu selections are more reasonably priced than some other Italian restaurants in town. Abbondanza is open daily for dinner and offers free parking. No reservations are accepted.

ANTONIA'S RESTAURANT $$
615 Duval St.
(305) 294-6565
antoniaskeywest.com
Stroll by this Northern Italian restaurant on any afternoon, and you can watch pasta in the making along the marble window-front table. Stringy mozzarella also is made fresh on the premises. The menu changes every evening. Past offerings have included Linguini Al Gamberi, homemade linguini tossed with Key West pink shrimp, fresh tomato, olive oil, crushed red pepper, garlic, and Italian parsley. Even with all the spectacular entrees, patrons simply cannot pass up the homemade desserts. Panna cotta features Italian vanilla ice cream with fresh berries and strawberry sauce. Chocolate fondant is

served warm with two sauces—raspberry and mango. Antonia's maintains an extensive Northern Italian and American wine list. The restaurant is open daily for lunch and dinner.

BIG JOHN'S PIZZA $
1103 Key Plaza
(305) 293-9576
bigjohnspizzakw.com
If you don't feel like going out to a full-fledged restaurant, Big John's Pizza is an eatery located in a New Town shopping center where all the locals go to partake of the best pizza this side of Rome. Sure, there are the usual pizza-chain operations here, but this place is "where the locals know it's good." The couple who owns Big John's takes great pride not only in their food but also in their friendly and cheerful help. The menu offers homemade garlic knots, buffalo chicken salad, 20-inch pizzas, calzones, strombolis, and more. Big John's is open daily for lunch and dinner and offers free delivery anywhere in the city limits of Key West. A minimum order amount is needed for delivery beyond mile marker 2.

LA TRATTORIA $$$
524 Duval St.
(305) 296-1075
latrattoria.us
This upscale SoHo-style New York bistro rates as a Key West treasure. A romantic taste of old Italy favored by locals, visitors, and Keys residents from as far away as Key Largo, La Trattoria redefines the traditional pasta, veal, chicken, lamb, and seafood dishes of the mother country. Try Agnello alla Griglia (lamb with fresh rosemary) or Cheese Tortellina alla Romana, with smoked ham and peas in a parmigiana cream sauce. Penne

Arrabbiata, quill-shaped pasta, delivers a bit of a bite, and the traditional Linguine e Vongole does not disappoint. La Trattoria serves dinner nightly, and reservations are suggested. After dinner, retire to Virgilio's, the charming little cocktail lounge with live music just around the corner (see the Nightlife chapter).

MANGIA MANGIA $$
900 Southard St.
(305) 294-2469
mangia-mangia.com
Meaning "eat, eat" in Italian, Mangia Mangia bestows a passel of homemade fresh pasta (made daily on the premises with semolina and fresh eggs) and finely seasoned sauces. You can always order the basic sauces—marinara, Alfredo, pesto, meat, and red or white seafood—but for something out of the ordinary, try Bollito Misto di Mare: pappardelle with fresh scallops, shrimp, conch, salmon, mussels, and mahi mahi in a garlic white wine clam sauce. Outdoor seating is delightful where the patio area is enclosed with palm trees and flowers. Mangia Mangia serves dinner daily and offers beer and wine. The restaurant does not take reservations; plan to arrive before 6 p.m. to avoid a wait.

JAPANESE

Upper Keys

THE FISH HOUSE ENCORE RESTAURANT, SUSHI BAR & LOUNGE $$$
MM 102.4 Oceanside, Key Largo
(305) 451-0650
fishhouse.com
The owners of the perennially popular Fish House have opened Encore, an upscale

fine-dining restaurant that serves various selections of sushi, sashimi, and other fresh seafood items. From the baby grand piano to the long mahogany bar, the decor is elegant, but you do not need to be similarly attired to dine here. An outdoor patio invites dining amid lush tropical vegetation in all seasons. You'll find plenty of fish on the menu, such as the wildly popular Fish Matecumbe from sibling restaurant the Fish House alongside 10 other fresh fish dishes. After dinner, stop at the piano bar, where you can enjoy tunes from Frank Sinatra to Billy Joel. And, on some lucky evenings, you might even catch a local or two playing along on their own instruments. Encore is open daily for dinner only, and reservations are recommended.

KAIYO GRILL & SUSHI $$$
MM 81.7 Oceanside, Islamorada
(305) 664-5556
kaiyokeys.com
Kaiyo's delightful blend of "Florida Asian" results in an exciting presentation of sushi and Keys-inspired dishes. Ones to try are the crispy ginger pork dumplings with sesame dipping sauce and the whole tempura-fried yellowtail served with rice, bok choy, and three different sauces. Kaiyo's also has 12 types of saki, Kirin beer, and special teas. And where did the restaurant's unusual name come from? In Japanese *kai* means "small body of water" and *yo* means "large body of water." In its cuisine and its ambience, Kaiyo, situated in Islamorada between the Atlantic Ocean and the Gulf of Mexico, successfully marries the mystique of Asia with the mystery of the sea. Kaiyo is open for lunch and dinner daily. The restaurant does not accept reservations or large groups.

Key West

✳AMBROSIA JAPANESE
RESTAURANT $$$
1401 Simonton St.
(305) 293-0304
keywestambrosia.com
Sake it to me! The sun rises brightly on this wildly popular Japanese restaurant. With a plethora of sushi and sakes, as well as great service, you will understand why it is a locals' top pick. Diverse flavors and textures combined with outstanding sauces will beckon you for a return engagement. Don't forget to explore the drink menu, as Ambrosia offers a full bar. They will be happy to see you for lunch and dinner.

BENIHANA $$$–$$$$
3591 S. Roosevelt Blvd.
(305) 294-6400
benihana.com
This famous restaurant chain is a contact sport when it comes to the ancient Japanese art of teppanyaki (literally translated, *teppan* is iron and *yaki* is grilled). I don't know the word for "performance" in Japanese, but as a patron of this restaurant, you get your money's worth. The menu is vast and appealing while your tableside chef performs his magic. A full bar is available, and a private Kimono Room can be reserved for those special occasions with 20 or more people. The view from the front of the building is the Atlantic Ocean, while inside you are serenaded by the knife blades chopping on the sizzling grill. Benihana is open for dinner nightly.

ORIGAMI JAPANESE RESTAURANT $$
1075 Duval St.
(305) 294-0092
The stark white decor of Origami provides a backdrop for the brightly colored tropical

fish adorning the walls. And like the Japanese art of folding paper into decorative or representational forms—origami—the restaurant fashions fresh, local seafood into exquisite sushi and sashimi. The dragon roll must not be missed. Origami also offers traditional Japanese cuisine, such as teriyaki, chicken katsu, steak yakiniku, and tempura. Sit at the cafe-style tables or at the sushi bar and watch the masters at work. Beer, wine, and sake are served. Origami is situated in Duval Square. Free parking is available in the adjoining lot off Simonton Street. Origami is open for dinner daily, and reservations are suggested in high season.

MEDITERRANEAN

Upper Keys

OLD TAVERNIER RESTAURANT $$
MM 90.1 Oceanside, Tavernier
(305) 852-6012
oldtavernier.com
One of the Upper Keys' most popular establishments for more than 20 years, the Old Tavernier marries the Mediterranean and the Caribbean with a continental flair to create a singular cuisine. Diners enjoy traditional Italian favorites such as pasta primavera, baked ziti, fettuccine Alfredo, and chicken or veal parmigiana. Opt for a culinary adventure with a Greek-style whole yellowtail pan-seared, baked, and drizzled with olive oil, oregano, and lemon and served with rice and seasonal vegetables. Guests have the option of dining indoors—where white linen tablecloths are aglow with candles and watercolor sailboat scenes dot the walls—or outdoors on a balcony overlooking a narrow canal. Old Tavernier has a full bar and wine list, and is open daily for dinner only. The restaurant is accessible by boat.

Key West

☀AZUR $$$
425 Grinnell St.
(305) 292-2987
azurkeywest.com
·Toss Greek, Italian, and Iberian cuisines in with a tropical setting and you get a Mediterranean mix called Azur. Selections to consider are the Key West pink shrimp over braised Swiss chard or the wild-caught fresh seafood and shellfish with sweet peas and saffron-infused risotto. Desserts vary but one standout is crème brûlée infused with lavender and topped with berries. The wine and beer list is respectable, with a varied range of prices. Azur's best ingredient is the innovative talent of the two owners who create memorable dishes in this truly outstanding restaurant. Azur is open for breakfast, lunch, and dinner Mon through Sat and brunch on Sun.

MEXICAN

Upper Keys

SEÑOR FRIJOLES $$
MM 103.9 Bayside, Key Largo
(305) 451-1592
senorfrijolesrestaurant.com
Don your sombrero for a taste of Mexico by the sea—Keys style. Señor Frijoles sits on Florida Bay next to Sundowners and offers popular Tex-Mex fare, such as burritos, enchiladas, and quesadillas. But you'll also find some jazzed-up Conch Republic versions, such as blackened tuna tacos filled with crispy cabbage, pico de gallo, and chipotle sour cream with black beans and rice on the side. Feeling parched? Señor Frijoles offers 11 different margaritas made with freshly squeezed lime juice as well as many other

tropical libations and Mexican beers with which you can toast the fabulous Keys sunset. Señor Frijoles is accessible by boat and open for lunch and dinner daily.

Key West

CHICO'S CANTINA $$
MM 4.5 Oceanside, Stock Island
(305) 296-4714
chicoscantina.com

Sit among giant cacti, Mexican tapestries, and a selection of south-of-the-border folk art at Chico's Cantina, a perennial favorite for Mexican cuisine. The food at Chico's is not your ordinary Mexican fare. Complimentary salsa is prepared with fresh tomatoes, onions, and peppers and is so popular among locals that the restaurant sells the stuff in bulk. The sizzling fajitas—with a choice of vegetarian, chicken, beef, chicken-and-beef combo, shrimp, or shrimp-and-beef combo—are accompanied by fresh vegetables, cooked just until crispy. And the fish adobado, grilled in corn husks, packs just the right spicy zing. Daily specials usually highlight local seafood such as yellowtail snapper. Chico's is open daily and serves the same menu for both lunch and dinner. Beer and wine are served; takeout is available.

OLD TOWN MEXICAN CAFE $$
609 Duval St.
(305) 296-7500
oldtownmexicancafe.com

Have a seat in the open-air dining room right on Duval Street or inside, tucked back away from the crowds. No matter where you sit, you are in for a fiesta of flavor. It all starts with the salsa. The freshly made salsa is so good here that when heading back to the mainland, locals first stop by Fausto's—the local grocery store that carries Old Town Mexican

Cafe salsa by the pint—for the perfect hostess gift. But the salsa isn't the only reason to stop in. Authentic dishes like the tortilla soup and the enchiladas verdes keep locals coming back, along with the inventive veggie plates. Old Town Mexican Cafe is open for lunch and dinner daily.

✳SALSA LOCA $
618 Duval St.
(305) 292-1865
salsalocakeywest.com

Salsa Loca offers freshly made Mexican food in a fun, party atmosphere. Be sure to stop by during happy hour for the two-for-one drink specials. You won't go away hungry: The portions are huge, the menu extensive, and the food is excellent. There are 7 different kinds of enchiladas alone, and all come with rice, beans, and a small salad. A local favorite is the mushroom quesadilla served with guacamole, sour cream, salad, and chips and salsa—a vegetarian meal where you won't miss the meat. Salsa Local is open for lunch and dinner daily and delivers to the entire island.

SEAFOOD

It should be noted that practically every restaurant in the Florida Keys serves extremely fresh seafood. We have chosen the restaurants for this category because they specialize in seafood. Each restaurant has menu items for the landlubbers as well.

Upper Keys

BAYSIDE GRILLE $$
MM 99.5 Bayside, Key Largo
(305) 451-3380
keylargo-baysidegrill.com

Situated at the end of a winding drive behind Cafe Largo and perched on the very edge of Florida Bay, Bayside Grille commands one of the premier waterfront vistas in the Keys. Small, casual, and bistro-ish, the open-air Bayside Grille's layout of tables fronted by glass pocket doors enables all diners to drink in the shimmering blue sea while partaking of a palate-tingling selection of offerings. Seafood reigns here: Key West garlic shrimp, island seafood curry, and seafood enchiladas are favorites. But landlubbers will also find a good selection of certified Angus burgers, New York strip and flank steaks, flavorful grilled chicken entrees, and pasta dishes. Bayside Grille offers a full bar and serves lunch and dinner daily.

THE BUZZARDS ROOST $$
MM 106.5 Oceanside, Key Largo
(305) 453-3746
buzzardsroostkeylargo.com
"You hook it and we'll cook it," say the owners of this casual waterfront restaurant in Key Largo. You can also come by boat if you really want to have a waterfront experience. If the fishing wasn't that great on your outing, they offer some tasty menu items that will surely fill your tank. One of the best appetizers is the Corny Blue Crabcakes. This is blue crab meat blended with veggies and roasted corn served with remoulade sauce. The catch of the day is prepared grilled, blackened, Jamaican jerked, broiled, fried, or sautéed in lemon butter and wine. Buzzards Roost also serves delicious cracked conch, which is marinated in garlic, dusted in flour, and sautéed.

GREEN TURTLE INN $$
MM 81.2 Oceanside, Islamorada
(305) 664-2006
greenturtlekeys.com
Sid and Roxie's Green Turtle Inn, which is actually a restaurant, availed itself to an

eager public in 1947. The location now showcases three businesses in harmony: the Green Turtle Inn, Sandy Moret's Florida Keys Outfitters (see the Fishing chapter), and the Wyland Art Gallery. At the Turtle, you can expect a "traditional Keys menu with flair." The "traditional" aspect features Keys lobster or the catch of the day. The "flair" guise stars turtle or conch chowder. The 50-seat restaurant with an open kitchen, full bar with tasting stations, catering, gourmet to go, and a Green Turtle Inn product line makes this a hot hangout in the Upper Keys. Breakfast, lunch, and dinner are served Tuesday through Sunday.

GUS' GRILLE $$
Marriott Key Largo Bay Beach Resort
MM 103.8 Bayside, Key Largo
(305) 453-0000
marriottkeylargo.com
This restaurant serves "Floribbean" dinner specialties such as pan-seared, lightly blackened yellowtail snapper with garlic mashed potatoes, white wine caper sauce, and cilantro-tomato salsa. The executive chef creates your meal right before your eyes in an open kitchen, an upmarket grill-style presentation reminiscent of a tony trattoria. Unobstructed views of Florida Bay and the famous Keys sunset are available from virtually every seat in the house. Booths line the window walls of the light and airy dining room; outdoor patio dining is also available. Walk over the suspension bridge from Gus' Grille to Breezers Bar and Grille for great drinks with luscious sunset views. Open daily for breakfast, lunch, and dinner, Gus' has wheelchair-accessible facilities and an elevator.

The Lime of the Keys

Key lime fruit is very small (1 to 2 inches), round, and a greenish-yellow color at maturity. The tart juice extracted from the limes goes on and into almost everything edible, from fish and meats to salads, drinks, and, of course, desserts. Key limes were grown commercially in southern Florida and the Florida Keys until the 1926 hurricane wiped out the citrus crop. The trees were replaced with a Persian lime, and most remaining key lime trees were found in backyards in the Florida Keys. But commercial production of the key lime trees is once again happening on a small scale, and key limes do seem to be making a slight comeback as a Florida crop in recent years. Once you have tasted a true key lime, any other lime will pale in comparison.

ISLAMORADA FISH COMPANY AND MARKET $$
MM 81.5 Bayside, Islamorada
(305) 664-9271
ifcstonecrab.com

Islamorada Fish Company, primarily a seafood market that opens at 9 a.m. (see the Specialty Foods, Cafes & Markets chapter), also serves lunch and dinner daily until 10 p.m. Eat indoors at the Island Conch House Eatery or outside under umbrella tables that perch on a peninsula jutting into Florida Bay. Islamorada Fish Company's restaurant is so popular that it is not unusual to wait an hour or more for a table. But don't worry: The restaurant abuts World Wide Sportsman's

cavernous sports emporium, so you can browse your wait away, look at the sunset, and wait for your name to be called.

ISLAND GRILL $$$
MM 85.5 Oceanside, Islamorada
(305) 664-8400
keysislandgrill.com

Don't pass up the opportunity to stop here if you see the parking area is full. If you are seated inside, ask for a table near the window, which is right along the canal facing Snake Creek. Outdoor tables are the best choice because you are actually on the dock area of the restaurant. The menu is swimming with seafood. Try an appetizer of spicy seared tuna nachos served over fried wontons with a seaweed salad amid ginger and sweet soy dressing. This dish is so mountainous that it could pass for an entree! Entrees include Low Country shrimp and grits, black Angus New York strip steak, and Island Grill seafood pasta. Open daily for breakfast, lunch, and dinner. Early arrival for any meal is suggested due to parking limitations.

LAZY DAYS RESTAURANT $$
MM 79.9 Oceanside, Islamorada
(305) 664-5256
lazydaysrestaurant.com

Lazy Days provides the ideal setting for kicking back, gazing over the sparkling blue Atlantic, and dining on a revolving selection of seafood offerings. The elevated plantation-style building with turquoise roof, French doors, and wraparound balcony is, indeed, designed for lazy days, for it perches directly on the shoreline of the ocean. Because of this setting, Lazy Days has been featured on the Food Network as one of the best scenic spots on the water to dine.

Some of the menu favorites, such as cracked conch served fried or sautéed with key lime or garlic butter, or jumbo stuffed shrimp baked with crabmeat stuffing and topped with béarnaise sauce and key lime butter, are house standouts. Lazy Days serves lunch and dinner daily.

LORELEI RESTAURANT & CABANA BAR $-$$$
MM 82 Bayside, Islamorada
(305) 664-2692
loreleicabanabar.com

The legend of Lorelei maintains that a nymph's sweet, lyrical singing lured sailors to shipwreck on a rock. Today's Lorelei lures you to a primo perch on the very edge of Florida Bay. The Cabana Bar breaks the day starting at 7 a.m., then serves a casual menu from 11 a.m. to 9 p.m., offering live entertainment nightly starting just before sunset. The air-conditioned Lorelei Restaurant's seafood-inspired menu makes a gustatory decision a difficult task. Landlubbers are accommodated with steak, chicken, ribs, and pasta offerings. The Lorelei Restaurant is open daily for dinner. Happy hour specials are offered from 4 to 6 p.m. Lorelei's family menu offers several complete meals for $15.95 or less, a real value.

MARKER 88 $$$
MM 88 Bayside, Islamorada
(305) 852-9315
marker88.info

Combining bayside ambience with innovative preparation of the Keys' freshest bounty, Marker 88 is a culinary landmark. Favorite dishes include sustainable seafood items like the onion-crusted mahi mahi served with toasted onions and a white wine, key lime juice, and butter sauce. The wine list has more than 250 entries, so you are sure to find the right one to complement your meal. Marker 88 is surrounded by heavy tropical vegetation and rambling docks, and a deck laden with wood outdoor tables and chairs provides the perfect setting for a predinner sunset toast or a starlit after-dinner drink. This boat-accessible restaurant maintains a full bar and is open daily for lunch and dinner. Reservations are recommended.

Middle Keys

ANNETTE'S $$$
MM 49 Bayside, Marathon
(305) 743-5516
notyourmamastreats.com/
our-restaurant.html

An extensive menu and hearty portions distinguish this Marathon restaurant. Annette's sports a nautical decor with dark paneling, wood-plank floors, and memorabilia from the sea. You'll enjoy choosing from the vast selection of pastas, steaks, seafood, and, of course, lots of lobster. Signature dishes include hogfish piccata and broiled Florida lobster. They will also cook your catch for you. Annette's places dessert selections on the menu's first page, so you are sure to be tempted and forewarned to save room. Locals know to ask for the peanut butter cream pie. Annette's is open Mon through Fri for lunch and dinner and Sat and Sun for dinner only.

BUTTERFLY CAFE $$$
Tranquility Bay Beachfront Hotel & Resort
MM 48.5 Bayside, Marathon
(305) 289-0888
tranquilitybay.com

Housed in the main building of the lovely Tranquility Bay Beachfront Hotel & Resort (see the Accommodations chapter), this fine restaurant is truly "Keys casual" with a traditional flair. Its chic but casual design and open, airy, high ceilings flowing out onto a large veranda with breathtaking views of gulf sunsets only enhances the fare. Tropical world cuisine blended with exotic spices and fresh local catches is in evidence on the menu, which changes seasonally. The Caribbean jerk chicken and the horseradish-crusted grouper served with leeks and citrus salad are both excellent choices. A fitting finish would be the TDF (to-die-for) sticky toffee pudding. Don't count the calories—this is why you are on vacation! The Butterfly Cafe is open for breakfast, lunch, dinner, and Sunday buffet. A children's menu is available, and reservations are required.

**THE ISLAND FISH COMPANY TIKI
  BAR & RESTAURANT $$**
MM 54 Bayside, Marathon
(305) 743-4191
islandfishco.com
Perched on a narrow spit of land jutting out into the Gulf of Mexico, the Island Fish Company provides one of the most scenic sunset spots in the Middle Keys and some doggone great food to boot. Whether you feel like a margarita and some quesadillas, a grilled grouper sandwich, or a more substantial meal, the Island Fish Company doesn't disappoint. Try the conch ceviche—unforgettable key lime–marinated pieces of tender conch with onions and peppers in a lime vinaigrette served with tortilla chips—or the Buffalo shrimp, flash-fried Key West pink shrimp tossed in hot pepper sauce and served with ranch dressing and a fried jalapeño pepper. The restaurant is open for breakfast, lunch

and dinner daily, and reservations are not accepted.

**KEYS FISHERIES MARKET &
  MARINA $$**
**MM 49 Bayside, at the end of 35th
Street, Marathon**
(305) 743-4353 or (866) 743-4353
keysfisheries.com
For more than 40 years Keys Fisheries Market & Marina has been the Middle Keys' answer to the eat-the-seafood-right-off-the-boat dining experience. Diners order their selections from an outdoor window, then carry trays to picnic tables overlooking a small marina harbor. Though the place is rustic and informal, the fish doesn't get any fresher than this, because Keys Fisheries is just that, a working fishery and fish market (see the Specialty Foods, Cafes & Markets chapter). Your wisest choices here will be local Keys seafood—such as grouper, yellowtail snapper, or mahi mahi—lobster bisque or chowder, Key West shrimp, and in season, the freshest stone crabs in Marathon served hot or cold, cooked right off the boat. Keys Fisheries Market & Marina is open for lunch and dinner daily.

Lower Keys

MANGROVE MAMA'S RESTAURANT $$
MM 20 Bayside, Sugarloaf Key
(305) 745-3030
mangrovemamasrestaurant.com
This brightly hued roadhouse offers a rustic old garden in the back where you can dine amid the banana trees. The old chairs are painted in a barrage of drizzled primary colors; ceramic fish sculptures adorn the walls. Bright tropical tablecloths cover the simple tables, and painted buoys hang from the trees and suspend from the rafters.

You'll find that seafood gets special treatment—steamed, baked, pan-seared, grilled, stuffed with crabmeat, or rolled in coconut and deep-fried. The restaurant serves lunch and dinner daily and brunch on Sun. Indoor dining is air-conditioned. In addition to a full-service bar, Mangrove Mama's has an extensive wine list. Reservations are suggested for dinner.

Key West

A&B LOBSTER HOUSE $$
700 Front St. (upstairs)
(305) 294-5880
aandblobsterhouse.com

A&B Lobster House, named for its original owners, Alonzo and Berlin, is considered a Key West institution among seafood connoisseurs. Situated beside the water at the foot of Front Street, A&B offers terrific views of the yachts moored at the Key West Historic Seaport. The signature dish of sautéed jumbo scallops served with braised shiitake mushrooms, asparagus, and a lemon-garlic butter sauce is not to be missed. Steaks and pasta dishes are also available. Dine inside or outside on the wraparound porch; in either case, reservations are suggested. After dinner, retire to Berlin's Bar to sample the fine selection of cigars and after-dinner drinks. A&B Lobster House is open daily from 6 p.m.; Berlin's Bar opens at 5:30 p.m. for predinner cocktails.

ALONZO'S OYSTER BAR $-$$
700 Front St. (downstairs)
(305) 294-5880
alonzosoysterbar.com

If you like oysters, Alonzo's is the place to go. You can order them up raw, on the half shell, baked, or batter-dipped and fried. Check the chalkboard daily to find out where the oysters are from and what kind are available.

This casual seaside eatery also serves freshly shucked clams, lobster, conch, mussels, and a variety of dishes made with the native shrimp known as Key West pinks. Alonzo's serves lunch and dinner 7 days a week, and during happy hour the entire right-hand side of the menu is half off. There's plenty of indoor and outdoor seating; reservations are not necessary. Free parking is available.

B.O.'S FISH WAGON $$
801 Caroline St.
(305) 294-9272
bosfishwagon.com

Almost any restaurant in Key West can make you a fish sandwich, but no one can make you a fish sandwich like Buddy Owen. Belly up to the counter and place your order for a fish sandwich grilled or fried; add sides like fries or onion rings only if you're really hungry. The portions here are huge. The menu also features fish-and-chips, the ubiquitous conch fritters, burgers, and hot dogs. To quench your thirst, select from bottle or draft beer, wine by the glass (plastic, that is), sodas, or key limeade. The decor here can only be called Key West eclectic—fishing nets, lobster traps, a muffler shop sign, even an old pickup truck. B.O.'s is open for lunch and dinner Mon through Sat.

THE COMMODORE WATERFRONT RESTAURANT $$$
700 Front St.
(305) 294-9191
commodorekeywest.com

Tables covered in white linen are surrounded by mahogany paneling, brick walls, and lush greenery. Ceiling fans gently whirl, and window walls look out onto the charming harbor of Key West Historic Seaport. The Commodore exudes the elegance of a fine ship, and the establishment offers some top-notch meat and seafood to match the refined ambience. Signature dishes abound. The Commodore Seafood Medley is lobster, shrimp, scallops, and mussels served in a light garlic sauce with vegetables, while the New York strip is first seared to seal in the juices, then broiled and served with your choice of béarnaise, Roquefort, or au jus sauce and a baked potato. The Commodore serves dinner nightly, and reservations are recommended. Free parking is available at A&B Marina.

CONCH REPUBLIC SEAFOOD COMPANY $$
631 Greene St.
(305) 294-4403
conchrepublicseafood.com

The menu here is heavy on seafood. Entrees include seared tuna steak, grilled double-bone pork chops, and the local favorite: jumbo shrimp stuffed with lump crabmeat, wrapped with bacon and served with mango salsa, island rice, and greens. The full-service, 80-seat bar boasts one of the best rum selections around—more than 80 varieties—along with 25 kinds of beer. The full menu is available daily from noon until 11 p.m. Live music is offered nightly, and happy hour is from 4 to 7 p.m. daily. Check out the 80-foot aquarium stocked with local seafood that is the centerpiece of the restaurant, and don't miss the 1,200-pound antique still that stands behind the bar in honor of the rum-runners of yesteryear.

HALF SHELL RAW BAR $-$$
231 Margaret St.
(305) 294-7496
halfshellrawbar.com

The Half Shell Raw Bar is inches from the water and beyond casual. Located in Land's

End Village at the Key West Historic Seaport, the restaurant is known for local seafood. The center of the action is Shucker's station, where mountains of oysters, clams, shrimp, and stone crabs are simply prepared, reasonably priced, and served with plastic utensils on paper plates at picnic tables. The full bar offers beer, wine and frozen drinks. Patrons may opt for outdoor dining on the patio. Reservations are accepted for parties of more than six. Half Shell Raw Bar is open daily for lunch and dinner. Off-street parking is abundant.

HOGFISH BAR AND GRILL $$
6810 Front St., Stock Island
(305) 293-4041
hogfishbar.com

One of the last frontiers of true Keys hangouts, Hogfish Bar and Grill is where the locals go and the fishing boat captains congregate—if you can find it. To get there, take US 1 North out of Key West and across the Cow Key Channel Bridge. At the third stoplight, bear to the right and onto MacDonald Avenue. Follow this for approximately 1 mile and make a right on Fourth Avenue. Take your next left on Front Street and drive almost to the end—you'll see the Hogfish Bar and Grill on the right. Once you are there, belly up to a picnic table and order the signature Hogfish "Killer" sandwich, which is a fish sandwich smothered with onions and mushrooms on freshly baked Cuban bread.

PISCES $$$$
1007 Simonton St.
(305) 294-7100
pisceskeywest.com

This enduring tropical French establishment has won awards and accolades from *Gourmet, Bon Appétit,* and *Wine Spectator* magazines, and the recognition is well deserved. At Pisces, creativity culminates in such delicacies as Lobster Tango Mango— lobster flambéed in cognac with shrimp in saffron butter, mango, and basil—and roast half duckling served with raspberry sauce. One of its finest treasures is Yellowtail Snapper Atocha, sautéed in lemon brown butter with shrimp and scallops. Specials are available nightly. The extensive wine list features some of the best of the vineyards of France and California. Pisces is open for dinner only, and reservations are recommended.

RUSTY ANCHOR RESTAURANT   **$$**
MM 5 Oceanside, 5510 Third Ave.,
Stock Island
(305) 294-5369
You won't find fresher seafood anywhere, for in the back of the Rusty Anchor is a commercial seafood market that supplies many of Key West's restaurants. The restaurant holds rope-edged tables, wood buoys, nautical art prints, and photographs of the fishing fleets of old Key West. Pan-fried yellowtail is their specialty, but make sure to try the teriyaki-grilled tuna sandwich on Cuban bread if it is offered as a special. If seafood is not your favorite, Rusty Anchor also serves burgers, steaks, and ribs. Food is presented picnic style on plastic plates, drinks in plastic cups, and beer out of the can. Open Mon through Sat for lunch and dinner, the Rusty Anchor does not require reservations. It's a great place to bring the kids.

✳SEVEN FISH   **$–$$**
632 Olivia St.
(305) 296-2777
7fish.com

Although the seafood here is excellent, this restaurant, located at the corner of Olivia and Elizabeth Streets, has much more to recommend it. In addition to fresh fish, the menu includes grilled chicken, meat loaf with mashed potatoes, and a New York strip steak cooked the way you like it. Salads— Three Cheese Caesar, mixed greens with balsamic vinegar, or roasted red pepper and goat cheese—are available in two sizes. And for an additional charge, you can add grilled chicken or a crab cake to your greens if you like. Seven Fish is small—go early or you may have to wait—and the tables are quite close together. The restaurant is open nightly 6 to 10 p.m. except Tues. Reservations are recommended.

SHOR AMERICAN SEAFOOD GRILL **$$$**
Hyatt Key West Resort and Spa
601 Front St.
(305) 809-4000 or (888) 591-1234
keywest.hyatt.com
New contemporary decor has brought this popular hotel restaurant back into the spotlight for visitors as well as local diners. While sipping cocktails, enjoy a wall of windows that showcase the beautiful view of the Gulf of Mexico. Offering breakfast, lunch, and dinner, the chefs pride themselves on serving local fresh seafood such as seared sea scallops, shrimp cocktail, and roasted lobster. They also serve beef, pork, and chicken selections. Lighter fare of soups, sandwiches, and salads is equally appealing. Cap the meal with a slice of gluten-free white chocolate mango cheesecake or warm chocolate lava cake.

STEAK HOUSES

Key West

PRIME STEAKHOUSE $$$
951 Caroline St.
(305) 296-4000
primekeywest.com

What a delightful surprise to enter the "Keys swank" atmosphere of Prime Steakhouse. The tables are covered with crisp white linen cloths and tall drinking vessels. The staff is dressed all in black, and the hushed atmosphere takes everyone down about two notches. Even though Prime has a limited menu, each and every selection is superb. They offer a local seafood special prepared Keys style, and their steak selections are outstanding. One of the house specialties is home-fried potatoes that are mashed and then fried. A feast in itself! Desserts are homemade key lime pie with a graham cracker piecrust and a to-die-for chocolate cake that is worth the calories. Prime Steakhouse is open daily for dinner, and reservations are recommended.

✳STRIP HOUSE $$$$
1435 Simonton St.
(305) 295-9669
striphousekeywest.com

Dine outdoors or inside with an ocean view, surrounded by luscious red decor and a collection of vintage Studio Manasse photographs from the 1900s with low lighting, and you have a tropical Strip House atmosphere that has all the fixings for a sensuous dinner. Choose from the main dining room, bar, lounge, or two private dining areas for your evening's pleasure. The trend-setting steak house features prime meats, goose fat potatoes, and truffle creamed spinach. Be sure to ask for their signature 24-layer

chocolate cake—highly recommended! If that is too-o-o much, go for the Australian Homemade Ice Cream offering. The Strip House also services in-room menu items for the Reach Resort (see the Accommodations chapter).

THAI

Upper Keys

NUM THAI RESTAURANT & SUSHI BAR $$
MM 103.2 Bayside, Key Largo
(305) 451-5955

If your taste for Asian food hovers around Thailand or Japan, Num Thai can offer you the best of both worlds: spicy Thai curries and noodle dishes or sushi, sashimi, and traditional Japanese dishes. Japanese offerings include *temaki*, cone-shaped hand rolls; *hosomaki*, medium rolls cut into bite-size pieces; a wide assortment of sushi, by the piece or in dinner combos; and tempura. Or enjoy Thai satays; spicy beef salad; seafood, chicken, or beef curries; or volcano jumbo shrimp, grilled and fired with chili sauce. Pad thai proves to be a hefty portion. Open for lunch Mon through Fri and dinner every day, Num Thai accepts reservations for parties of more than five. American and Asian beers, wine, plum wine, and sake all are offered.

Key West

THAI CUISINE $
513 Greene St.
(305) 294-9424
keywestthaicuisine.com

The salubrious cuisine of Thailand tingles your palate with the afterglow of Thai curry. Thai curry is actually a cooking method, not an ingredient. Together with spices, herbs, and aromatic vegetables, hot chile peppers are ground into a dry paste. At the same time, coconut milk, fish sauce, sugar, and kaffir lime leaves—ubiquitous to every variation of Thai red and green curry—confuse the palate with a riot of sweet-and-sour sensory stimuli. For a traditional delight, try the pad thai, spicy rice noodles sautéed with shrimp, chicken, and egg. Enjoy a selection of Thai and Japanese beers, house wines, plum wine, and sake. Thai Cuisine serves lunch Mon through Fri, is open for dinner nightly, and offers free delivery in Key West.

✳THAI ISLAND $
711 Palm Ave., Garrison Bight Marina
(305) 296-9198
thaiislandrestaurant.com
Located at the foot of the bridge in the historic Garrison Bight, Thai Island has become a favorite of locals looking for amazing Thai cooking without the crowds. Dine on their rooftop patio overlooking the bight as the boats come in with their catches of the day. Start with the tasty Tom Kha Gai or Tom Kha Tofu soup, sour coconut milk blended with chicken or tofu, mushrooms, lemongrass, scallions, and galanga root. Then opt for one of four different kinds of curry with your choice of seafood, beef, chicken, pork, or tofu that promises to be as spicy as you dare. Thai Island is open daily for lunch and dinner, with free parking at Garrison Bight Marina.

SPECIALTY FOODS, CAFES & MARKETS

Here in the Florida Keys, we think our fish is pretty special. It's certainly the freshest—sometimes only minutes from line to linen. Its pedigree is elite; most species are not marketed outside South Florida. And the abounding variety of innovative culinary presentations is astounding. Visitors to the Florida Keys, accustomed to choosing among cod, halibut, haddock, swordfish, and tuna back home, are often overwhelmed when confronted with the bountiful selections from our underwater treasure trove.

When you stop at one of our many seafood markets, you will undoubtedly meet the three royal families of our tropical waters: snapper, hogfish, and dolphin, also known as mahi mahi. The famed yellowtail or the equally desirous mangrove or mutton snapper most often represents the moist, sweet snapper dynasty. The firm, mild-flavored hogfish clan competes in popularity with the large-flaked and sweetly moist dolphin fish (not to be confused with the porpoise dolphin, which is a mammal).

You won't want to miss our Florida lobster, a delicacy any way you look at it (see the "Diving for Lobster" Close-up in the Diving & Snorkeling chapter). And if you have never tasted a stone crab claw, you are in for a treat (see the Close-up in this chapter). To round out your palate, we have provided you with a rundown of delicatessens and shops selling specialty foods.

OVERVIEW

We have listed our recommended seafood markets and specialty food shops alphabetically from the top of the Keys in Key Largo through Key West.

Most places remain open until at least 5 p.m., with the exception of bakeries, which usually open early and often close in the early afternoon. During high season, December through April, many of these markets and stores extend their hours. The off-season often brings abbreviated hours, so you may want to call before you shop.

UPPER KEYS

BOB'S BUNZ RESTAURANT AND BAKERY
MM 81.6 Bayside, Islamorada
(305) 664-8363
bobsbunz.com
The banner out front proclaims BEST BUNS IN TOWN, and these oversize cinnamon rolls live up to the hype. Topped with cream-cheese icing, the buns are undoubtedly one of the local favorites. Also available are "gooey" or sticky buns, bagels, muffins, scones, croissants, key lime pie, cakes, and cookies, which can be ordered online as well. As you might

imagine, this restaurant and bakery is a wildly popular Islamorada breakfast and lunch spot.

CHAD'S DELI AND BAKERY
MM 92.3 Bayside, Tavernier
(305) 853-5566
chadsdeli.com

Lots of good food at reasonable prices and quick service! That is not only a winning combo (just like some of their menu items), it is also what makes Chad's Deli and Bakery a success in the Upper Keys. The waitstaff is very friendly and knows all the regulars by name, which goes a long way in a small place like Tavernier and the Keys. Their specialties are four-way sandwiches, specialty pizzas (try the bacon cheeseburger pizza), calzones, pasta, and salads. They also serve beer and wine to round out your meal.

THE FISH HOUSE SEAFOOD MARKET
MM 102.4 Oceanside, Key Largo
(305) 451-4665
fishhouse.com

Primarily a seafood restaurant (see the Restaurants chapter), the Fish House also offers fresh catch of the day from their small seafood market so that you can be the chef of the day if you like. You'll find just-off-the-boat local favorites such as yellowtail snapper, mahi mahi, grouper, Florida lobster, and stone crab as well as other seasonally caught species.

ISLAMORADA FISH COMPANY AND MARKET
MM 81.5 Bayside, Islamorada
(800) 258-2559
ifcstonecrab.com

Islamorada Fish Company and Market operates out of a 5,000-square-foot facility in the former Green Turtle Cannery building. Thousands of pounds of fresh fish and seafood find their way through the cutting rooms here, much of it displayed in a showy 31-foot display case. Everything is temperature controlled at Islamorada Fish Company, so the dolphin, Florida lobster, snapper, swordfish, stone crab claws, blue crab, Key West pink shrimp, and tuna all stays extra fresh. You can watch the cutters in action from outside the glassed-in cutting room. If you prefer to dine in this charming seafood market ambience, the store has a full-service restaurant (see the Restaurants chapter).

KEY LARGO CONCH HOUSE
MM 100.2 Oceanside, Key Largo
(305) 453-4844
keylargocoffeehouse.com

If you're a coffee connoisseur in Key Largo, you'll want to find your way to the Key Largo Conch House, which is located in a Conch-style house that sits on a lush wooded lot. Choose from among house-blend coffee, gourmet flavors of the day, and espresso drinks. If you prefer a cool drink, how about an iced coffee or a fruit smoothie made with a green-tea base? After making your choice, pick a seat on the wide porch and enjoy the free Wi-Fi in the fresh air. If you're hungry, the Conch House serves freshly baked pastries as well as breakfast, lunch, and dinner.

KEY LARGO FISHERIES
MM 99.5 Oceanside, 1313 Ocean Bay Dr., Key Largo
(305) 451-3782 or (800) 432-4358
keylargofisheries.com

The family-run Key Largo Fisheries ships wholesale to hundreds of clients throughout the country and also offers retail sales at their Key Largo store and via overnight delivery. At Key Largo Fisheries, customers

Close-up

Florida Stone Crab Claws

Now, you Yankees can brag about your blue crabs, and you West Coasters may boast of Dungeness. But here in the Florida Keys we crow about crab claws like none other—those of the Florida stone crabs.

The stone crabs, large nonswimming crabs found in deep holes and under rocks in the waters surrounding the Keys, have the unusual ability to release their legs or pincers if caught or when experiencing extreme changes in temperature. The separation always occurs at one of the joints to protect the crab from further injury. What is unique about this situation is that the stone crab regenerates the severed appendage, a feat it can accomplish three or four times during its lifetime. This makes it a renewable resource.

The stone crab's two claws serve distinct purposes: The larger claw, or crusher, is used to hold food and fight predators. The smaller claw, known as the ripper, acts as scissors for cutting food.

The crabs are harvested commercially in the Florida Keys with baited traps. One or both of the crab's claws are removed (it greatly improves the crab's chances of survival if only one claw is taken). The forearm must measure at least 2¾ inches from the tip of the claw to the joint to harvest it legally. The live stone crabs must then be returned to the water, where in 18 months a new claw will have grown to legal size. It is illegal in the state of Florida to harvest whole stone crabs. They are one of our precious resources.

A stone crab claw has a hard, heavy, porcelainlike shell with a black-tipped pincer. Seafood markets sell stone-crab claws fully cooked. When cooked, the meat inside the shell is sweet and firm-textured. A mild, sweet odor indicates freshness.

The shells must be cracked before serving. If you plan to eat your stone crab claws within an hour of purchase, have the seafood market crack them for you. It is not recommended that you crack the claws until you are ready to eat them.

If you crack the claws yourself, lightly tap the shells with a hammer, a small wooden mallet (available at seafood markets), or the back of a tablespoon. The shells also will crack like a fine china teacup if you hit one claw against the other. Pick the meat from the shell using a small cocktail fork and serve with mustard sauce (cold claws) or clarified butter (resteamed claws).

Stone crab claws are in season from October 15 to May 15. They do not freeze particularly well, but most seafood markets listed in this chapter will ship iced, fresh stone crab claws anywhere in the US.

will find choice seafood, including snapper, mahi mahi, shrimp, and, in season, Florida lobster and stone crab claws. The conch here is imported from the Bahamas and the West Indies, and the scallops are from Boston.

SUNSHINE SUPERMARKET
MM 91.8 Oceanside, Tavernier
(305) 852-7216

There isn't a Tavernier resident who doesn't know about the rotisserie chicken and Cuban bread here. Family owned and operated, Sunshine Supermarket offers some tasty Cuban specialties as well: roast pork, ribs, yellow rice, and black beans and rice, all at reasonable prices and huge portions. The pork is marinated in mojo sauce—a Cuban concoction of oil, vinegar, garlic, and other spices. It is available for chicken as well, upon request, and you can also buy it by the bottle.

THE TRADING POST
MM 81.8 Bayside, Islamorada
(305) 664-2571

This is definitely Islamorada's "super" market. Here you'll discover super grocery selections, supergood deli items, a super meat market with a butcher on hand to help you, super wine offerings, and super hours. The Trading Post is open 24 hours a day, 7 days a week! The store also offers customized catering.

MIDDLE KEYS

FISH TALES MARKET & EATERY
MM 53 Oceanside, Marathon
(305) 743-9196
floridalobster.com

This tiny eatery offers fish and seafood baskets and sandwiches, along with a few heartier specials daily. Fish Tales will cook, smoke, or ship your catch if you've had a productive day on the water. The well-stocked seafood market offers Key West shrimp, stone crabs, tuna, swordfish, the Keys trio (snapper, grouper, and dolphin), and more. Fish Tales Market will ship seafood anywhere in the US. A choice-grade meat counter offers aged steaks, pork tenderloin, and rack of lamb as well.

THE ISLAND FISH COMPANY
MM 54.5 Bayside, Marathon
(305) 743-4561
islandfishco.com

Set your course to this location if you adore oysters! They serve gulf oysters raw, freshly shucked, baked to order with key lime garlic butter, barbecued, Rockefeller, or Moscow style with sour cream horseradish sauce and caviar. How about a seafood tower that is loaded with oysters, clams, shrimp, and a pound of stone crab claws? Moving into other seafood arenas, Island Fish Company comes to the table with conch fritters, calamari, mango crab cakes, spinach crab dip, lobster egg rolls, and smoked fish dip. After just looking at this menu, is there any seafood remaining in the ocean?

✳KEYS FISHERIES MARKET & MARINA
MM 49 Bayside, at the end of 35th St., Marathon
(305) 743-4353 or (866) 743-4353
keysfisheries.com

The fish here is fresh, fresh, fresh, because Keys Fisheries' fishing fleet works out of the marina. You'll find Key West pinks (shrimp), Florida lobster, stone crabs, and all varieties of local fish here, as well as clams, oysters, scallops, squid, conch, and more. Take home homemade soups and seafood salads or spreads if you like. You can also order from the menu of the adjoining eatery (see the Restaurants chapter). They also will fillet, pack, and ship their fish so that you can take your Keys bounty home with you.

LOWER KEYS

✳BABY'S COFFEE
MM 15 Oceanside, Saddlebunch Key
(800) 744-9866
babyscoffee.com

Late last century (ca. 1991), Gary and O. T. left New York City looking for a home for their new coffee-roasting company. They set up shop in a small building on Key West's famed Duval Street named "Baby's Place," formerly "Baby" Rodriguez's cantina where, legend has it, Ernest Hemingway occasionally indulged in shooting craps with the locals. Baby's Coffee grew so large that they had to relocate up the Keys at mile marker 15, and locals still bike up for some fresh brew. They ship their coffee fresh within 48 hours; it is not vacuum-packed or freeze-dried. You'll find all their Key West roasts, Hawaiian roasts, specialty roasts, flavored coffees, and decaf roasts on their website and can buy it by the pound at Fausto's in Key West.

FANCI SEAFOOD
MM 22.5 Oceanside, Cudjoe Key
(305) 745-3887
fanciseafood.com
Shelves and shelves of marinades and seafood sauces will inspire you to try your culinary skills in a new creation when you stop in at Fanci Seafood. The very complete fish and seafood selection lets you choose among the usual Keys finfish (grouper, snapper, and dolphin) and golden crab, stone crab claws, lobster, blue crabs, oysters, and mussels.

GOOD FOOD CONSPIRACY
MM 30.2 Oceanside, Big Pine Key
(305) 872-3945
goodfoodconspiracy.com
A full assortment of health foods, homeopathic remedies, vitamins, organic poultry, and organically grown produce is offered at the Good Food Conspiracy. If you browse the shelves, you'll find interesting specialty foods as well. Part of the Conspiracy is a juice and sandwich bar, which features an "outgoing menu" of healthful selections. In addition to the products and produce, Good Food Conspiracy also houses a holistic health center and even a reverend that performs commitment ceremonies and weddings. Talk about one-stop shopping!

KEY WEST KEY LIME PIE COMPANY
MM 30 Bayside, Big Pine Key
(305) 872-7400 or (877) 882-7437
keywestkeylimepieco.com
Key lime pie, a Florida Keys tradition, is what Key West Key Lime Pie Company is deliciously all about. Lots of people claim to have "award-winning" pie, but the Key Lime Pie Company beat out over 500 competitors to win best pie for their Key Lime Pie Bar at the American Pie Council Championships in 2009. Each handmade, 9-inch pie (also sold by the slice) is frozen, literally melting in your mouth, bite by bite. The company, which has been featured on the Food Network, will ship the pies anywhere in the continental US overnight or provide you with a frozen travel pack so you can take a pie on the road with you or back home by airplane. A second delicious location is at 511 Greene St. in Key West (305-517-6720).

KICKIN' BACK FOOD MART
MM 21.4 Oceanside, Cudjoe Key
(305) 745-2528
Life here in the Keys is really laid back, so why not our grocery stores? This local oasis is easy on and off US 1, offering beer, wine, lottery tickets, an ATM machine, and limited groceries. You won't have to worry about finding a parking spot at Kickin'—it's a gravel parking pad. Pretty simple. That's the way folks here like it!

*MURRAY'S FOOD MARKET
MM 24.5 Oceanside, Summerland Key
(305) 745-3534

This familiar landmark is Summerland Key's lifeline for provisions. Murray's sells most all your food and household needs. Make sure to say hello to Marletti, Tracy, or Sally, who have been managing the market for more than 35 years. Murray's—with its wonderful fresh deli selection, meat counter, daily baked breads, and beer and wine—saves all the locals in the area from driving south into Key West or north to Big Pine just for a gallon of milk.

SUGARLOAF FOOD COMPANY
MM 24 Bayside, Summerland Key
(305) 744-0631
sugarloaffood.com

This tiny treasure encased in a sunny yellow building is bright and upbeat with goodness galore. Homemade tortellini salad to accompany sandwiches stuffed with homemade meat loaf and red onion mayo is a popular choice. Grab a roast beef and Swiss with horseradish aioli on a baguette, a curry pistachio chicken salad, or classic Cobb for a change. Utterly dreamy homemade cookies will have you whistling a happy tune!

KEY WEST

COFFEE PLANTATION
713 Caroline St.
(305) 295-9808
coffeeplantationkeywest.com

While away on vacation, you might just have to check your e-mail. Here at the Coffee Plantation, thanks to the Wi-Fi, you can do just that while enjoying delicious coffee, smoothies, or frappes with light bites like bagels and pastries. They also offer computers with Internet access. Rates and services are reasonable, and the staff is most helpful. The cozy ambience makes this an inviting stop.

✳COLE'S PEACE ARTISAN BAKERY
1111 Eaton St.
(305) 292-0703
colespeace.com

Long a favorite with locals, Cole's Peace Artisan Bakery will become your favorite too. Everything here is authentic, from their famous Cuban bread and mango-cranberry bread pudding to Mexican chocolate cake and their original Ciabatta-Lotta sandwich. Load up on the addictive café con leche to wash down the assorted scones, muffins, and cheese croissants. The wonderful owners will cater your party or event with 48 hours' notice.

CORK & STOGIE
1218 Duval St.
(305) 517-6419
corkandstogie.com

Just as the name implies, head here to the "closest cigar shop to Cuba," which sells original Key West Cigar Factory cigars and bottles of fine wine. Throughout the year Cork & Stogie hosts wine tastings, book signings, and live music Fri and Sat nights. Sit inside or outside on the porch and enjoy your purchases. Hemingway would approve.

CROISSANTS DE FRANCE
816 Duval St.
(305) 294-2624
croissantsdefrance.com

Viva la croissants—and your waistline! Seduction in broad daylight is what awaits you with their pastry selections, which are lovingly created by classically trained pastry chefs. This beloved tiny treasure also dishes up galettes (large, thin buckwheat flour pancakes serves with savory or sweet fillings), quiches, croissants, and brioche sandwiches.

FAUSTO'S FOOD PALACE
522 Fleming St.
(305) 296-5663
faustos.com

This gourmet food emporium has been serving Key West since 1926. The Fleming Street site is its largest and oldest. Here, in addition to the usual bread, milk, produce, canned goods, and kitchen staples, you will find fresh local seafood, premium meats and poultry, and numerous varieties of wine, as well as Beluga caviar, pâtés, rare cheeses, and desserts. The deli counter is especially busy at noontime, when the folks who work downtown line up for hot soup and fresh-made sandwiches. The White Street location (1105 White St.; 305-294-5221) is more like a neighborhood grocery, with a smaller deli counter and a limited selection of produce, bread, frozen foods, and canned goods.

*5 BROTHERS
930 Southard St.
(305) 296-5205
5brothersgrocery.tripod.com

If you're headed downtown along Southard Street any weekday morning between 7:30 and 8 a.m., expect to encounter a traffic jam at the corner of Grinnell Street. It's just the locals pulling over to pick up their "fix" at 5 Brothers, which has been serving this island for more than 30 years. This is where Key West goes for buche, that tiny cup of industrial-strength Cuban coffee that satisfies your caffeine habit with a single swig. This little corner grocery also makes a mean Cuban mix—a combination ham, pork, salami, Swiss, lettuce, and pickle sandwich served on Cuban bread—and great conch chowder (Fri only). For you early birds, 5 Brothers opens at 6 a.m. (closed Sun). The shop is cash only.

FLAMINGO CROSSING
1105 Duval St.
(305) 296-6124

Since 1987 this has been a favorite with locals and visitors alike. Flamingo Crossing is the place to pause for refreshment as you make your way up and down Duval Street. Homemade ice cream is the business here, and it's the closest thing to Italian gelato this side of the Mediterranean. You can choose from such flavors as Cuban coffee, raspberry cappuccino, coconut piña colada, key lime, passion fruit, and green tea, among others. Flamingo Crossing also makes its own sorbet and yogurt.

i Harvesting conch (pronounced *konk*) in Florida waters is illegal. Therefore, most seafood markets import conch from the Turks and Caicos Islands. Firmer in texture than that from most other waters, conch from Turks and Caicos waters is some of the best in the world.

GOLDMAN'S BAGEL, SALAD AND SANDWICH DELI
2796 N. Roosevelt Blvd., Overseas Market
(305) 294-3354
goldmansdeli.com

At this full-service restaurant-deli in the Overseas Market, the hot corned beef and pastrami sandwiches are sliced thin and piled high in traditional deli style, the bagels are baked fresh daily, and the potato salad is tops. You can carry out such delicacies as chopped liver, potato knishes, smoked whitefish, and kosher franks, along with the bagels and an array of flavored cream cheeses sold by the pound. Breakfast and lunch are served at tables along one side and at the counter. Deli platters and catering are also available.

*GRAND VIN
1107 Duval St.
(305) 296-1020

This is *the* place where locals gather to sample fine wines and catch up on the island gossip. Buy a bottle to take back to your hotel room or enjoy a glass (or four) on the porch as you watch the crowds navigate Duval Street. People-watching is a favorite pastime here in Key West, and the porch at Grand Vin offers the best views. Friendly, knowledgeable bartenders and wines of every grape variety imaginable make Grand Vin truly toast-worthy.

*HELP YOURSELF
829 Fleming St.
(305) 296-7766
helpyourselffoods.com

Eating healthy is the way to go, and folks come here for the best in natural and organic eats. No dairy, refined sugars, or bad fats allowed, and the line outside the door proves one thing: People are helping themselves. Choose your greens (mixed, romaine, spinach), your wrap (sprouted grain, gluten-free, whole wheat), and your sauce (coconut lime curry, lemon tahini, basil pesto, miso broth); start piling on the proteins (salmon, shrimp, chicken); enjoy a side (sesame noodles, hummus, bean salad, quinoa tabouli); and top it off with a homemade Ginger Aide or organic smoothie. You feel healthy just reading the menu! As an added bonus, on Mon from 11 a.m. to 4 p.m., they have an open-air, organic-only farmers' market.

KERMIT'S KEY WEST KEY LIME SHOPPE
200 Elizabeth St.
(305) 296-0806 or (800) 376-0806
keylimeshop.com

You can't miss this place because Kermit, the key lime chef (as seen on the Food Network and *The Today Show*), is usually outside waving you into this key lime heaven. Everything inside is made with key lime juice, including oils, cookies, candy kisses, salad dressings, juice concentrate, pie filling, and sweets of all sorts. You'll also find key lime soaps and lotions here. And be sure to look outside for the authentic key lime tree—the source of all this pleasure and a rarity these days in the Florida Keys.

LEMON POINT DELI
825 Duval St.
(305) 453-6155

The Mediterranean comes to Key West in the form of this delightful deli. Start your day with one of their flaky croissants served plain or with Italian ham and cheese. For lunch, the Aegean Sun Salad is a favorite, served with black-eyed peas, orzo, feta, tomato, cucumber, Kalamata olives, red onion, and romaine. Lemon Point also has a vast imported cheese selection that is sold by the pound, as well as deli specialties like Chianti salami, grilled artichokes in oil, and a Greek olive mix that are also sold by the pound. Beer, wine, and other grocery items are also available. Lemon Point offers free delivery in Key West.

MATTHEESSEN'S
419 Duval St.
(305) 296-8014
mattheessens.com

No tourist destination is complete without at least one ice-cream shop, and Mattheessen's proved to be so popular that now there are four. In Key West you'll find more than your fill of this melt-in-your-mouth confection at one of the two Duval Street locations (the second is at 106 Duval St.; 305-296-1616), the White Street shop (1110 White St.; 305-294-8089), or the Front Street shop (300 Front St.; 305-396-7453). All ice creams are made fresh for each location. Traditional chocolate and vanilla are always favorites, of course, but the dulce de leche and Cuban coffee varieties are equally tasty and sinful.

MR. Z'S
501 Southard St.
(305) 296-4445
mrzskeywest.com
Philly-style Italian-American fast food, 24/7! This is Mr. Z's claim to fame in Key West. If you have an urge for a cheesesteak at 3 a.m. or pizza at midnight, one call will curb your craving. Locals don't consider an order complete if it doesn't contain cheese fries. Dieters beware! Eat in the small restaurant on one of the few bar stools or take it to go. There is also free delivery in Old Town. Cash only.

PEPPERS OF KEY WEST
602 Greene St.
(305) 295-9333 or (800) 597-2823
peppersofkeywest.com
Peppers, where chile peppers are the name of the game, bills itself as "the hottest spot on the island." More than 300 varieties of hot sauces already grace the shelves, and more arrive from all over every day. Peppers always has a basket of chips and a few open bottles at the front counter so you can have a taste. Al Roker and Matt Lauer of *The Today Show* barely survived their pepper encounter, so sample if you dare. Peppers bottles its own brands of "hot"— #1, #2, and Goin' Bananas.

RUSTY ANCHOR FISHERIES
5510 Third Ave., Stock Island
(305) 294-5369
Where's the fish? A little Insider help is needed to negotiate for fish at this place, known to locals as having the freshest at the best prices. The fish market is directly behind Rusty Anchor Restaurant, which is on Third Avenue (see our Restaurants chapter), although no sign on Third Avenue indicates the fishmonger's presence. Simply park at the restaurant and they will show you the way to the fishery. Find out about the catch of the day. Rusty Anchor is known for some of the best prices on jumbo stone crab claws and colossal shrimp ("under 15s").

SANDY'S CAFE
1026 White St.
(305) 295-0159
Lodged in the same building as the popular M & M Laundry, this hole-in-the-wall Cuban walk-up joint is one of the best places in the Keys for authentic Cuban "fast food." The lines outside the order windows (with a few bar stools available for seating) indicate how loyal Sandy's customers are. The café con leche, cheese tostada, and Cuban mix sandwiches will have you clamoring for more. Delivery is available in Old Town. No credit cards . . . this is cash and carry only. *Bueno! Bueno!*

✳SUGAR APPLE NATURAL FOODS
917 Simonton St.
(305) 292-0043
sugarapplekeywest.com
A longtime favorite of health-conscious Key Westers, Sugar Apple stocks organic and hard-to-find groceries, vitamins, beauty aids, homeopathic remedies, books, and herbs. A juice bar and deli serve up sandwiches, smoothies, specials, and teas.

NIGHTLIFE

From cool martini bars to quirky dive bars, the Florida Keys has your nightlife needs covered. As a general rule, bars are open later the farther down in the Keys you go, with many establishments in Key West open until 4 a.m. Taverns and pubs in the Upper and Middle Keys are more likely to close between midnight and 2 a.m. Also, a lot of restaurants have separate bar areas in which you can dine as well or continue the party post-dinner. Those typically close around 11 p.m. or sometimes "when the last customer leaves." Hours and entertainment may vary depending on the season or whim of the owners, so it is always best to call ahead.

We encourage you to have fun and enjoy our casual Keys pubs and restaurants, but keep in mind that the DUI limit here is 0.08 percent, less than some other states. Remember, too, that driving-under-the-influence laws apply to all vehicles—scooters, boats, and bikes included. So if you drink, don't drive. Or pedal. Take a cab or take along a designated driver. In Key West, you can request a cab with a bike rack at no extra charge. If you are on foot, pedicabs are a good alternative to transporting yourself, and you can usually flag one down in Key West without any hassle.

UPPER KEYS

BREEZER'S BAR AND GRILLE
Marriott Key Largo Bay Beach Resort
MM 103.8 Bayside, Key Largo
(305) 453-0000
marriottkeylargo.com
Breezer's is an elevated gazebo-sheltered bar overlooking the showy property and wondrous waters of the Marriott Key Largo Bay Beach Resort. This fantasy island setting provides the perfect backdrop for fabulous frozen drinks accompanied by live island-style music on Fri and Sat.

CARIBBEAN CLUB
MM 104.5 Bayside, Key Largo
(305) 451-9970
caribbeanclubkl.com

Bogey and Bacall are alive and well in this famous Key Largo bar and restaurant. The walls are filled with memorabilia from the 1948 classic movie *Key Largo,* even though most of the movie was filmed on Hollywood soundstages and back lots. Great sunset views and live music Thurs through Sun nights draw late-night crowds, making this a popular locals' hangout.

COCONUTS RESTAURANT & NIGHT CLUB
Marina Del Mar Resort and Marina
MM 100 Oceanside, 528 Caribbean Dr.,
Key Largo
(305) 453-9794
coconutsrestaurant.com

A perennial nightclub favorite with a perco-lating dance floor, full bar, and live entertain-ment on Thurs, Fri, and Sat, Coconuts is a weekend favorite where the hardworking locals come to cut loose, catch up, and listen to live music. See our Restaurants chapter for dining options here.

HOG HEAVEN SPORTS BAR
MM 85.3 Oceanside, Islamorada
(305) 664-9669
hogheavensportsbar.com
The congenial outdoor saloon of Hog Heaven Sports Bar sits unassumingly on the waterfront. You can amuse yourself with televised sports, talk with the locals, or head to the point, where a chickee yields seclu-sion that may foster romance. As you might expect, the pork here is heavenly.

*LORELEI CABANA BAR
MM 82 Bayside, Islamorada
(305) 664-4656
loreleicabanabar.com
This bar not only serves great drinks, but the Lorelei also offers one of the best views of stunning sunsets in the Florida Keys, which is celebrated here every night. The bar is a laid-back waterside watering hole and lunch spot all day long, and the views of Florida Bay cannot be beat. See our Restaurants chapter for dining options here.

*SNAPPER'S WATERFRONT RESTAURANT
MM 94.5 Oceanside, Key Largo
(305) 852-5956
snapperskeylargo.com
Snapper's oozes Keys atmosphere, espe-cially the cypress-and-palm-frond chick-ees on the outdoor waterside deck. Menu items are innovative (see the Restaurants

chapter), and patrons enjoy live entertain-ment nightly.

i Planning a fun night out in the Upper or Middle Keys? Keyhopper Transportation has you covered with their "Barhopper" services from Mara-thon to Key Largo. They also do one-day Key West trips and airport runs, but you must plan ahead and book in advance for all their services. Call (305) 587-4400 to book in Key Largo/Islamorada and (305) 393-0146 for more informa-tion in Marathon.

TIKI BAR AT THE HOLIDAY INN KEY LARGO RESORT AND MARINA
MM 99.7 Oceanside, Key Largo
(305) 451-2121
holidayinnkeylargo.com
The outdoor Tiki Bar at the Holiday Inn Key Largo offers fun tropical drinks and cold beers, as well as an extensive lunch menu, perfect for those hot Keys-y afternoons. The Tiki Bar picks up the pace a bit with live music Thurs through Sat; a mix of reggae, rock, and pop attracts an equal mingling of locals and tourists.

MIDDLE KEYS

BRASS MONKEY
MM 50 Oceanside, Kmart Plaza, Marathon
(305) 743-4028
This long-established bar and liquor store is a regulars' hangout in Marathon. The Brass Monkey serves up not only lunch and din-ner but also live music 6 nights a week. The lounge opens early and closes in the wee hours. "That Funky Monkey" is still going strong after more than 30 years!

THE HURRICANE
MM 49.5 Bayside, Marathon
(305) 743-2220
hurricaneblues.com

The Hurricane has been Marathon's favorite place to party for more than 50 years. Open-mike nights are held every Wed, and live bands play most Thurs, Fri, and Sat nights. Open every day of the week, the Hurricane also serves food and is famous for their $5 lunches and late-night pizza. Their prices simply can't be beat in the Florida Keys!

ROCCO'S DOCKSIDE BAR & GRILL
MM 53 Oceanside, 35 Sombrero Rd.,
Sombrero Marina, Marathon
(305) 743-0000
keysy.com/dockside

There are cold drinks and also good eats available here, and as the menu states, "If there is something you don't see on the menu that you may want, just ask!" New owners have breathed new life into this favorite local hangout and still manage to set Rocco's apart from the others for fun in the sun!

SEVEN MILE GRILL
MM 46 Oceanside, Marathon
(305) 743-4481
keysdining.com/7milegrill

You can't miss this watering hole, as it sits off US 1 at the beginning of the Seven Mile Bridge heading south to Key West. When it opens in the morning, you see the many folks lining the bar to sip their favorite beverage and toast the local color that is the Florida Keys. Light fare is on the menu, as are the many drinks of choice.

SUNSET GRILLE & RAW BAR
MM 47 Oceanside, Marathon
(305) 289-3588
sunsetgrille7milebridge.com

Located at the foot of the Seven Mile Bridge, the Sunset Grille & Raw Bar is a great place to grab a drink poolside or under the shade of their massive tiki hut. The sunset is what this grill and raw bar was named for, and the expansive views of the famous bridge certainly make for one gorgeous sunset. There are also daily happy hour specials and live entertainment 7 nights a week as well as pool parties every Sun.

LOWER KEYS

LOOE KEY TIKI BAR
MM 27.5 Oceanside, Ramrod Key
(305) 872-2215
looekeytikibar.com

This open-air tiki bar is where you will find many locals and ardent dive tourists alive and kicking in the Keys. Sandwiches and basket dinners accompany a fine sampling of good conversation from the patrons who frequent this no-pretense bar. Taco and open-mike nights are hosted every Tues by Looe Key's Coral Rick Band, and there is live music nightly.

*NO NAME PUB
MM 31 Bayside, N. Watson Boulevard,
Big Pine Key
(305) 872-9115

Wallpapered with dollar bills and full of good cheer and local color, No Name Pub is a must-do, night or day (see the Restaurants chapter for menu offerings and directions). Off the beaten path about as far as you can go in Big Pine, this small saloon sports a funky bar and a pool table.

PARROTDISE WATERFRONT BAR & GRILLE
MM 28.5 Bayside, 183 Barry Ave., Little Torch Key
(305) 872-9989
parrotdisewaterfront.com

Offering daily happy hour specials on food and drinks, the Parrotdise is a fun, casual meeting hangout perched above the Big Pine Channel. Easily accessible by car or boat, this bar and grill offers wine and beer along with fabulous water views. This is the place locals come to relax, where the live daily entertainment is "just the sounds of quiet on the bay."

KEY WEST

*THE AFTERDECK BAR AT LOUIE'S BACKYARD
700 Waddell Ave.
(305) 294-1061
louiesbackyard.com

The setting at the Afterdeck is exactly what you imagined when you first thought of coming to the Florida Keys—right on the water with beautiful views of the ocean. No trip to the Afterdeck is complete without an Island Cosmo: house-made pineapple-infused vodka and fresh-squeezed lime with a splash of cranberry juice served straight up in a chilled glass. The adjoining restaurant is one of Key West's finest (see Louie's Backyard in the Restaurants chapter).

AQUA NIGHTCLUB
711 Duval St.
(305) 294-0555
aquakeywest.com

Live entertainment at the predominantly gay Aqua Nightclub includes nightly drag shows, karaoke, a weekly "Aqua Idol" competition on Tues night, poker games Sat and Sun, and a dance club complete with DJs every weekend. No matter what time you stop in at Aqua, there will be something fabulous going on.

BLUE MOJITO POOL BAR & GRILL
Hyatt Key West Resort and Spa
601 Front St.
(305) 809-4043
keywest.hyatt.com

Newly revived interior but with the same fabulous view of the Gulf of Mexico and sunset. This pool bar adds all the ingredients, mixed with a tropical punch, for a romantic setting serving appetizers, salads, and sandwiches for light bites. Clink!

BOTTLECAP LOUNGE AND LIQUOR
1128 Simonton St.
(305) 296-2807
bottlecapkeywest.com

Every Fri during happy hour at the Bottlecap, all the tips go to a Key West nonprofit and locals turn up in droves to support their favorite charities. The Bottlecap is home to two rooms, a patio bar, a pool table, and even a Wii and other games, as well as DJs and sometimes live entertainment to keep you occupied all night long.

BULL & WHISTLE
224 Duval St.
(305) 296-4545
bullkeywest.com

This local favorite is actually three bars in one. The Bull is downstairs and features live music in an open-air setting. The Whistle is upstairs and offers pool and video games, along with a great view of Duval Street from the balcony. The Garden of Eden, on the very top, has a great view of Key West . . .

and more. It's the only clothing-optional roof garden in town.

CAPTAIN TONY'S SALOON
428 Greene St.
(305) 294-1838
capttonyssaloon.com

Just half a block off Duval, this watering hole is the site of Hemingway's original bar stool and Key West's first hanging tree, which grows through the roof of the bar. Captain Tony's is part of Key West's history, as it is the original location of Sloppy Joe's. Once owned by Capt. Tony Tarracino, a friend of Jimmy Buffett's and a former Key West mayor, the saloon features walls covered with bras and business cards. Live entertainment is offered nightly.

✳CHART ROOM BAR
Pier House Resort
1 Duval St.
(305) 296-4600 or (800) 327-8340
pierhouse.com

You want to experience a slice of Key West history? Step into this tiny bar located in the Pier House Resort and you will be stepping back in time. Tom Corcoran, author of the popular Alex Rutledge Key West mystery series, used to tend bar here while Jimmy Buffett played for tips. The bar has changed little since then, and the bartender can regale you with many a story about the duo.

✳COWBOY BILL'S HONKY TONK SALOON
618 Duval St.
(305) 295-8219
cowboybillskw.com

The original owner of Cowboy Bill's was a real-life cowboy on the rodeo circuit until

he came to Key West. Mechanical bull and all, this urban cowboy turned tropical, and patrons are in for one wild ride! Open 7 days a week with happy hour daily, Cowboy Bill's has a full menu for eats; a game room with pool, darts, and video games; and 24 TVs a-blaring. Boot scoot across the dance floor to live music, not to mention riding the mechanical bull. Hold on to those cowboy hats—this is not for amateurs!

801 BOURBON BAR AND CABARET
801 Duval St.
(305) 294-9354
801bourbon.com

With a clientele consisting of primarily gay patrons and tourists, 801 offers a first-floor bar with billiards. A second floor features live entertainment with Drag Queen Bingo at 5 p.m. every Sun and drag shows nightly, starring the world-famous Sushi. You might have seen her on CNN New Year's Eve counting down the seconds to the new year while being lowered in a giant red high heel. She even managed to make Anderson Cooper blush.

FAT TUESDAY
305 Duval St.
(305) 296-9373
fattuesdaykeywest.com

Stop in at Fat Tuesday and choose from one of 26 flavors of frozen drinks, including margaritas, piña coladas, and 190-octane rum runners. Our favorite is the Pain in the Ass, a combination piña colada and rum runner. The motto here is "One daiquiri, two daiquiri, three daiquiri, floor," and you can even buy a T-shirt that says just that.

Key West's Burlesque History and Future

Notorious burlesque dancer and actress **Sally Rand** was featured at the 1933 Chicago World's Fair and in the 1934 film *Bolero*. Sally's claims to fame were her trademark fan dance and bubble dance. Ms. Rand was a Key West winter resident for many years, often visiting the troops at the local Navy Hospital. Her historic gingerbread home on Eisenhower Drive is a far cry from its flamboyant mistress. Also, the world's most famous pin-up model of the 1940s, **Bettie Page,** met and married a young man in Key West prior to her retirement and leaving the area. Her spirit lives on with **Marky Pierson's Wonderdog Productions.** Pierson produces variety show and burlesque performances by local favorites like Cheeky Derriere, Dark N' Stormy, Hunny Bunz, and more at various theaters, bars, and restaurants around the island. Visit markypierson.com for more information.

FINNEGAN'S WAKE IRISH PUB & EATERY
320 Grinnell St.
(305) 293-0222
keywestirish.com

Exactly like a good Irish public house ought to be, Finnegan's keeps the merriment going until nearly dawn (4 a.m.) and is among a mere handful of Key West establishments serving food into the wee hours (see the Restaurants chapter). You're sure to find your Guinness here, and you can even down a black and tan. Order one and the barkeep will think you just returned from the Emerald Isle. Enjoy live Irish music on weekends and heed their motto: "Come for the food. Stay for the beer. Leave with the staff."

✳GRAND VIN
1107 Duval St.
(305) 296-1020

Grand Vin is a locals' top pick for its bar and wine shop. Not sure which wine suits you best? Sit at the bar and try a tasting flight of wine, three glasses of different varietals that will have your taste buds singing. Newly expanded seating on the porch and lower patio is great for people-watching through all hours of the day or night.

✳THE GREEN PARROT BAR
601 Whitehead St.
(305) 294-6133
greenparrot.com

Frequented primarily by locals, and known simply as "The Parrot," this eclectic bar is housed in an 1890s-era building half a block off Duval, down Southard Street. Walls are adorned with unusual oversize portraits and a mural of the Garden of Eden. Weekends feature local and national bands playing everything from ukuleles in harmony to blues and zydeco, and the large dance floor is usually crowded.

HARD ROCK CAFE
313 Duval St.
(305) 293-0230
hardrock.com

The Hard Rock Cafe joined the Conch Republic in the summer of 1996. Situated in a renovated, 3-story, Conch-style house on Duval Street, Hard Rock Cafe Key West celebrates historic Key West, the preservation of the Florida Keys' fragile environment, and, of course, rock 'n' roll. This 235-seat Hard Rock is open daily and serves up all-American fare.

HOG'S BREATH SALOON
400 Front St.
(305) 296-4222
hogsbreath.com/key-west
The Hog's Breath features an open-air mahogany bar surrounded by water-sports-related memorabilia, including mounted fish and surfboards. You can try the medium-bodied Hog's Breath beer and sample one of the saloon's famed fish sandwiches. The restaurant (see the Restaurants chapter) is open for lunch and dinner. Live bands play rock, folk rock, blues, and jazz throughout the day and well into the evening. You can purchase T-shirts, hats, and sundry other items emblazoned with the saloon's slogan: "Hog's Breath is better than no breath at all."

JIMMY BUFFETT'S MARGARITAVILLE CAFE
500 Duval St.
(305) 292-1435
margaritavillekeywest.com
Yes, the big man himself does play here once in a while, as do some of the Coral Reefers and bands that have opened for Jimmy on tour. Props from past concerts decorate the walls, ceiling, and even tables. Margaritas are just one of the many frozen drinks offered at the air-conditioned yet open-air bar. You can get a Cheeseburger in Paradise with all the fixin's or pick up some Buffett clothing, recordings, books, and memorabilia at the shop next door (see the Restaurants and Shopping chapters). There is live music nightly, and keep your eyes open: Country

singer-songwriter Kenny Chesney once performed here.

JOE'S TAP ROOM
Behind Sloppy Joe's, Duval and Greene Streets
(305) 294-5717
sloppyjoes.com
Located upstairs behind the world-famous Sloppy Joe's Bar (see listing in this chapter) on Duval Street, Joe's Tap Room is another venue in this popular hangout. Large-screen TV and porch seating are available here. Doors blow open at noon, and they have NFL and college football on HDTV. Gives you a little "home away from home" feeling!

LA-TE-DA
1125 Duval St.
(305) 296-6706
lateda.com
La-Te-Da is a combination hotel, cabaret, restaurant, and bar that has been an icon of the Key West party scene since 1978. They not only offer a bar that faces lively Duval Street, but also live entertainment in their Cabaret Lounge. There is also a Terrace Bar overlooking the beautiful tropical pool. With the great island drinks and delicious food being served here, you may find it difficult to leave.

*MARTIN'S
917 Duval St.
(305) 295-0111
martinskeywest.com
Hands down, Martin's serves the best espresso martini in all of Key West. A favorite with the locals when they are looking to "play through" from happy hour into the wee hours, the espresso martini is tops at Martin's, which makes it with different coffee liquors and no cream. Martin's also offers a good

Key West Bar Card

Looking for a deal on cocktails in Key West? Most establishments have daily happy hour drink specials between 4 and 6 p.m., but you might have to ask for them, as they aren't always advertised. For a drink special any time of day or night at numerous locations throughout Key West, check out the Key West Bar Card. After purchasing the card, you'll get one 2-for-1 drink in any participating bar per day. You can visit as many bars on the card in one day as you like, but you can only use the card once per bar. The card costs $20 to purchase and is good for one calendar year. Key West Bar Cards are sold at various locations around town like the Bottlecap and the Restaurant Store and can also be purchased online before you travel. Visit keywestbarcard.com for more information.

selection of wines, beers, and other martinis to enjoy in their sleek open-air lounge.

✳POINT 5
915 Duval St.
(305) 296-0669
915duval.com
In its lofty aerie above the chic nine one five restaurant, the decor at Point 5 only enhances the drinks. The walls, ceilings, and floors are covered in fabulous Dade County pine, and the second-floor porch beckons you with its cool breezes: Submit to a cheese plate from the bar menu while relaxing at your table on the open-air porch overlooking Duval Street.

✳THE PORCH
429 Caroline St.
(305) 517-6358
Locals head to the Porch, located behind door number 2 in the beautiful Porter Mansion on Caroline and Duval, for craft beers on tap and wine by the glass or bottle. Seasonal selections and popular events like regular wine tastings, 1920s costume parties, and DJ nights are also part of the fun. Beers on tap

include Chimay Blonde Trappist Ale, Magic Hat #9, and Shipyard Export Ale, among others.

RICK'S KEY WEST
202-208 Duval St.
(305) 296-5513
ricksanddurtyharrys.com
Rick's Key West offers eight nightspots in one complex, including a wine and martini bar, a dance club, a VIP bar, and a daiquiri bar. In addition, Rick's Downstairs Bar offers live entertainment from 4 p.m. until midnight. The Tree Bar allows you to sit and sip a spell, all the while watching the sights of Duval Street pass by. The band at Durty Harry's starts at 8 p.m. and plays live rock 'n' roll until 4 a.m. This bar also has a television wall, which shows all major sporting events. And for a little more risqué entertainment, the Red Garter Saloon is a mirror-and-brass adult club. Pick your pleasure.

SCHOONER WHARF BAR
202 William St.
(305) 292-3302
schoonerwharf.com

Close-up

The "Fab Four" in the "Fab" Florida Keys

Most folks plan their trip to the Florida Keys months in advance. "Do You Want to Know a Secret"? On September 11, 1964, a group of four young men made an unexpected stop in "Paradise." That evening, the world-famous **Beatles** were holed up in the old Key Wester Motel on S. Roosevelt Boulevard in Key West. Their landmark concert tour, "Beatles in America," was canceled at the Gator Bowl in Jacksonville, Florida, because Hurricane Dora was pounding the east coast of the state. Their private airplane was diverted to Key West International Airport that evening, where they proceeded to hold an impromptu jam session in the motel bar.

Local musician Coffee Butler just finished his evening gig playing piano at a nearby locals hangout when he got word the "Fab Four" were entertaining the pleasantly surprised guests at the motel. Butler rushed over to the Key Wester and asked if he could make it a five-some, playing until the wee hours of the morning until the bartender and the police informed them Florida law stated no music after 4 a.m.

"Good Day Sunshine" allowed the group to depart that morning and continue on their tour. The Key Wester Motel was demolished in 1999 and replaced with a Hyatt time-share complex. The owners salvaged one piece of musical history by restoring the bungalow in which the Beatles had resided and built the Abbey Road snack bar that sits by the swimming pool.

Dockside at the Key West Historic Seaport is the open-air, thatched-palm Schooner Wharf, which bills itself as "a last little piece of old Key West." The place offers outdoor thatched-umbrella tables, a covered bar, grill, and indoor games, including billiards and darts. Live jazz, rhythm and blues, and island music are featured nightly.

SLOPPY JOE'S BAR
201 Duval St.
(305) 294-5717
sloppyjoes.com

It's no wonder this was Hemingway's favorite watering hole. The upbeat atmosphere of Sloppy Joe's is contagious. The bar opened in 1933 on the site of what is now Captain Tony's Saloon. In 1937 it moved to its current location. Some say that Hemingway did some writing in the back rooms of the bar and kept a few of his manuscripts locked up here. Photos of the author line the walls. Live entertainment is offered from noon to 2 a.m. daily. A gift shop sells T-shirts, hats, and other Sloppy Joe's souvenirs.

SPORTS PAGE BAR AND GRILLE
610 Greene St.
(305) 296-3230

Watch the game of your choice on one of the eight TVs, two of which are projection, or shoot a game of pool while enjoying some jalapeño poppers, cheese fries, or potato skins. If the big game is on, the Sports Page is the place to be.

THE TOP
Crowne Plaza Key West La Concha
430 Duval St.
(305) 296-2991
laconchakeywest.com

High above the city of Key West, with views of Key West Harbor as well as up and down Duval Street, this eagle's-eye perch is one of the most famous bars in all the Keys. The Crowne Plaza Key West La Concha (see Accommodations chapter) was the first upscale lodging facility in the area, and to accommodate its infamous and famous clientele, this bar was developed. Rumor has it Hemingway romanced Ava Gardner and Marlene Dietrich at La Concha and spent many nights high in the sky here at this bar.

TURTLE KRAALS RESTAURANT AND BAR
231 Margaret St.
(305) 294-2640
turtlekraals.com

The lounge portion of this turtle-cannery-turned-restaurant rocks throughout the evening, offering live entertainment (in season) and billiard tables in an open-air, waterfront setting (see the Restaurants chapter). Turtle Kraals's full bar is known for its frozen margaritas, microbrewed beers, and imported beers on tap.

i If you can't wait until "it's five o'clock somewhere" for alcohol, in Key West there are two bars that open with the sunrise. Schooner Wharf Bar (see listing in this chapter) has a "Breakfast Club" where regulars show up at 8 a.m. for a beer buzz rather than coffee. Over at Dons' Place, 1000 Truman Ave., at 7 a.m. you can have an espresso martini made with vodka, Kahlua, Tia Maria, and, oh, I almost forgot, coffee.

VIRGILIO'S
524 Duval St.
(305) 296-8118
virgilioskeywest.com

This fun little New York–style bar is not really on Duval; it's actually situated on Appelrouth Lane, just around the corner from La Trattoria, one of Key West's best Italian eateries (see the Restaurants chapter). Martinis and their cousins—Gibsons, Manhattans, and cosmopolitans—are the specialty here, and on "Martini Mondays" you can pay only $5 for one. Grab a seat at the bar or in one of the overstuffed easy chairs while you sip your cocktail and listen to live music from some of Key West's finest musical talent.

CAMPGROUNDS

J ust as the whooping crane, the Florida panther, and the green sea turtle are on the endangered species list . . . so are campgrounds in the Florida Keys. The locations of most mobile-home parks are on prime real estate. A vast majority of these parks are situated on waterfront/view parcels and are being gobbled up by developers building condos, hotels, or private condotels (condotels are condos privately owned then placed in a pool of properties to be rented by a management company). Whether you enjoy pitching a tent or traveling with a self-contained motor home, the campgrounds of the Keys offer a reasonably priced alternative to motels and resort accommodations. However, you will find that camping rates in the Florida Keys are generally much higher than in other areas of the US. But all our recommended campgrounds have water access, and many are perched at the edge of the Atlantic or the Gulf of Mexico.

A wide range of amenities distinguishes each campground, but one thing is certain: If you wish to camp in the Keys during January, February, or March—those winter months when the folks up north are dusting off their snow boots—you must reserve your site a year in advance. The Keys have a second high season in the summer months, when Floridians locked into triple-digit temperatures head south to our cooling trade winds and warm, placid waters. During sport lobster season, the last consecutive Wednesday and Thursday of July, it is standing room only in the Keys.

OVERVIEW

We have listed our recommended Keys campgrounds and RV parks by alphabetical order beginning in Key Largo and ending at Stock Island. Key West devotes its land use to megahotels and quaint guesthouses, presenting a dearth of recommendable campgrounds.

If you think you might fancy a really unusual camping experience, be sure to see the Camping in the Beyond section in this chapter for information on camping in Dry Tortugas National Park or Everglades National Park.

You may assume that all our inclusions maintain good paved interior roads, clean restrooms and showers, laundry facilities, and 20- and 30-amp electrical service. Most campgrounds accept pets if they are kept on a leash at all times and walked only in designated areas and never on the beach. Exceptions will be noted.

Rates vary by the type of site you secure. Most campgrounds offer a range of options: tent sites, with or without electricity; RV sites with electricity and water; and sites with electricity, water, and sewer. Waterfront sites or sites with boat dockage will be more costly. Extra people or vehicles at a site will incur additional per-diem charges. All water is municipal, piped down to the Keys from Miami. Cable television and telephone hookups are noted when applicable. Back-in and pull-through dimensions vary; call the campground if this is critical for your rig. Toll-free telephone numbers, when stated, are for reservation purposes only. Major credit cards are accepted unless noted to the contrary.

Price Code

Rate ranges are based on a per-diem stay during high season without the 12.5 percent state tax. High season is considered December 15 through May. Some campgrounds also consider the summer months as high season. Weekly and monthly rates are usually available at a reduced cost; be sure to inquire when you make your reservation.

$ . . . . $20 to $40
$$ . . . . $40 to $60
$$$ . . . . $60 to $80
$$$$ . . . . More than $80

THE FLORIDA KEYS

Upper Keys

BLUE FIN ROCK HARBOR MARINA
AND RV RESORT   **$$**
MM 97 Oceanside, Key Largo
(305) 852-2025 or (800) 350-6572
catamaranboatyard.com
Relax and retreat, as the Atlantic Ocean is steps away at this well-established marina and RV resort. On the property you will find fishing, shuffleboard, a swimming pool, a boat ramp with rental boats, and the Mandalay Restaurant and Tiki Bar. A Laundromat is open around the clock. There is 30- and 50-amp service and cable TV; showers and phone connections are for long-term visitors. The park has 24-hour security and can accommodate fifth wheels up to 40 feet.

CALUSA CAMPGROUND RESORT
AND MARINA   **$$**
MM 101.5 Bayside, Key Largo
(305) 451-0232
calusacampground.com
Escape to this family-friendly camp resort on the Gulf of Mexico with all the relaxation you can handle. Paved interior roads lead to gravel pads with full hookups and pull-through sites. Tent sites are also available. Laundry facilities, a clubhouse, LP gas, a swimming pool, playground, boat ramp, and dockage are featured. There is access to the bay and the ocean via Marvin Adams Cut or Tavernier Creek. Pets are welcome for a $5 fee as long as they are on a leash.

⁕JOHN PENNEKAMP CORAL REEF
STATE PARK   **$**
MM 102.5 Oceanside, Key Largo
(305) 451-6300 or (850) 245-2157
floridastateparks.org/pennekamp
Aesthetically, the gravel sites at John Pennekamp Coral Reef State Park don't begin to compare to their waterfront siblings at the Keys' other two state parks, Bahia Honda and Long Key, but a canopy of mature buttonwoods shades most of the sites. The wide range of fabulous recreational opportunities within Pennekamp and its proximity to the nightlife in Key Largo more than make up for any lack of romantic oceanfront ambience (see Beaches & Public Parks in the Recreation chapter).

Florida Keys Wildfire Safety

The dry season in South Florida is November through April. Florida is one of the top 10 states for the number of fires and acres burned, according to the Institute for Business and Home Safety, a Tampa, Florida, nonprofit group. Parts of Florida are facing their driest times in nearly 80 years, so be careful when using fire for anything, including campfires and barbecues. Make sure someone is keeping an eye on the flames at all times. If you park your car on high grass, heat from your vehicle can ignite a blaze, especially if papers and debris are around. Be sure to pick up your trash and dispose of it in metal containers to avoid this potential hazard. Watch for sparks that may fly from grinding equipment, torches, and even lawn mowers. For more helpful tips, visit the Florida Division of Forestry website at floridaforestservice.com.

KEY LARGO KAMPGROUND AND MARINA $–$$
MM 101.5 Oceanside, Key Largo
(305) 451-1431 or (800) 526-7688
keylargokampground.com

Croton and bougainvillea hedges separate the sites in this village-like campground laden with palm trees. About one-third of the condo campsites, with full hookups and free cable television, are available for overnighters. Some sites front the canal and have boat slips. Two beaches look out on Newport Bay, and a heated swimming pool and kiddie pool, shuffleboard, horseshoe pits, and volleyball add to the fun. John Pennekamp Coral Reef State Park is only a mile north of the 40-acre campground. Rates are based on 4 people (2 adults and 2 children younger than age 6) and 1 camping unit per site. A maximum of 6 people are allowed per rental unit at any time.

Middle Keys

LONG KEY STATE PARK $
MM 67.5 Oceanside, Long Key
(305) 664-4815
floridastateparks.org/longkey

Every site is oceanfront when you camp at Long Key State Park. You can't get closer to the ocean than this campground in the Florida Keys. Half of the 60 sites offer water and electric, and all have picnic tables fronting the shallow saltwater flats. The paved road into the campground parallels the Overseas Highway on one side and the ocean on the other. Each deep site runs from the park road to the ocean. Like John Pennekamp Coral Reef State Park and Bahia Honda State Park, Long Key State Park follows a strictly regimented reservation policy. Rates are based on 4 people, 1 vehicle per site, and include all taxes. Only 1 camper and 1 small tent or 2 small tents are allowed per campsite. The park opens at 8 a.m. and closes at sunset. "Well-behaved" pets are welcome in the campground.

Lower Keys

*BAHIA HONDA STATE PARK $
MM 37 Oceanside, Bahia Honda Key
(305) 872-2353 or (850) 245-2157
floridastateparks.org/bahiahonda

Claiming the Florida Keys' best natural beach (2.5 miles long), the 524-acre Bahia Honda

State Park offers campers 3 kinds of sites but no pull-throughs. The roomy sites at Buttonwood can accommodate large motor homes; Sandspur is limited to tents, vans, and pop-ups. Because these sites sit deep in a tropical hardwood hammock, the park is very selective as to which rigs are allowed to camp here. Only 1 car and 1 tent per site are permitted. All these sites have water, and more than half offer electricity. Bayside campsites, accessed by a road passing under the Bahia Honda Bridge, are restricted to tents or small pop-ups. The bridge provides only a 6-foot, 8-inch clearance. These campsites provide water but no electricity.

Three large cabins—each a heated and air-conditioned, two-bedroom duplex with a fully equipped kitchen, full bathroom, and all linens—literally perch on the water near the bayside campsites. You can throw a baited hook from your front porch, rock a little in the old rocker gracing the deck, and catch your dinner without missing the sunset. Each cabin will sleep 6, but you'll have to rough it without television. The cabins can be reserved in person, by telephone, or online up to 11 months in advance. A 2-day deposit by credit card, check, or cash will secure the cabin reservation if it's received within 10 days of your making the reservation.

All campsites at Bahia Honda State Park provide a grill and picnic table. The park has a boat ramp, so you may bring your own craft and try your luck at catching a tarpon under the Bahia Honda Bridge, noted as one of the best tarpon-fishing areas in the state (see the Fishing chapter). "You really don't even have to know what you are doing," counsels the assistant park manager. "Put a live mullet on the end of a line and the tarpon will bite."

BIG PINE KEY FISHING LODGE $
MM 33 Oceanside, Big Pine Key
(305) 872-2351
The Big Pine Key Fishing Lodge abuts a natural oceanside inlet that was a by-product of the dredging of Spanish Harbor Channel for Flagler's railroad. The sites range from rustic grass or dirt tent sites without water or electricity to dockside sites with full hookups. The boat basin, a part of the Big Pine Fishing Lodge since the late 1950s, accommodates small fishing boats up to 25 feet long for a per-foot daily charge. Ample fish-cleaning stations are provided, so you can ready the spoils of the day for the frying pan. The lodge has an oval swimming pool sunken in a raised deck overlooking a peppering of statuesque coconut palms, all grown from seed. Rates are based on 1 or 2 occupants, with 1 vehicle and 1 camping unit. Children younger than age 6 stay free. Air-conditioning, phone outlets, and cable hookups are included in the camping fee.

BLUEWATER KEY RV RESORT $$$
MM 14.5 Oceanside, Saddlebunch Key
(305) 745-2494 or (800) 237-2266
bluewaterkey.com
Bluewater Key RV Resort's 80 spacious gravel sites feature metered utility hookups, including telephone and cable television. Uniquely angled toward the water and buffered with palms and shrubbery, each privately owned site has a stone patio with benches and a round cement table. No tents, pop-ups, or vans are allowed at Bluewater Key; all units must be self-contained RVs. A clubhouse hosts table tennis or informal card games, and the swimming pool attracts sun worshipers from up north. Oceanside flats and deepwater canals surround the property, affording primo fishing for anglers. And if you

want a little action at the end of your day of quiet solitude, you are but 14.5 miles from the center of Key West. Need we say more?

Those reserving waterfront or canal sites may secure their small boats to the floating docks or bulkhead. The high season at Bluewater Key RV Resort is considered Dec 15 to Apr 15. Although the resort accepts reservations for 1 day or 1 week to a month or more depending upon availability, we suggest you book at least a year in advance if you'd like a waterfront spot. Bluewater Key has an onsite manager and is protected from intrusion by a 24-hour, phone-operated security gate.

BOYD'S KEY WEST CAMPGROUND $$$
MM 5 Oceanside, 6401 Maloney Ave., Stock Island
(305) 294-1465
boydscampground.com

Although its brochures state a Key West address, Boyd's is actually on Stock Island, just outside the Key West city limits. Most of the level, shaded sites have cement patios. Bordering the ocean, Boyd's offers a boat ramp, a small marina, extensive dock space, a heated swimming pool, and 4 bathhouses. You can catch the city bus into Key West for unlimited diversions, hang out at Boyd's game room, or watch the large-screen television, which is tucked in a tiki hut near the pool. Rates are based on 2 occupants and 1 camping unit per site. Small dogs are permitted in hard-shell campers only. Fifty-amp service and modem hookup are available.

✳GEIGER KEY MARINA AND CAMPGROUND $$$
MM 10.5 Oceanside, Geiger Key
(305) 296-3553
geigerkeymarina.com

Located in the mangroves "on the backside of Paradise," you'll discover Geiger Key Marina and Campground. The setting on the Atlantic Ocean is what makes this quiet location a hidden gem. Great white herons patrol the grounds in search of pilchards and pinfish. Pelicans look like ornaments in the mangrove branches as they keep a sharp lookout for snapper, grouper, and parrot fish. Geiger Key Marina and Campground is only 10 miles from Key West, yet it seems a million miles away with its laid-back 1950s aura. The property has all the updates, however, with RV hookups, laundry facilities, oceanview private tent sites, transient boat slips, kayak rentals, and fishing charter boats. Their popular restaurant and tiki bar cooks up pig roasts on Sat night; on Sun they whip up a chicken and ribs barbecue. Live music is part of the bar's attraction on Fri, Sat, and Sun night. You can get to this jewel by RV or boat. The marina monitors VHF channel 79 for water-mode arrivals.

LAZY LAKES CAMPGROUND AND RV RESORT $$$
MM 19.5 Oceanside, 311 Johnson Rd., Sugarloaf Key
(305) 745-1079 or (866) 965-2537
lazylakesrvresort.com

Off the beaten path, this 28-acre property with a 7-acre saltwater lake is a real Insiders destination for your full-size RV (99 spots available), Big Rigs, tent sites, or to rent a mobile home. Hike the paths leading around the lake or jump into one of the free kayaks and paddle around for a water view. Lazy Lakes offers 30–50 amp service, laundry facilities, restrooms, a heated pool, general store, and umbrella tables with lounge chairs. During the year they have activities for their guests that include bingo, horseshoes, darts, potluck dinners, and even holiday celebrations. You may never want to leave!

LEO'S CAMPGROUND AND
RV PARK $$$
**MM 4.5 Oceanside, 5236 Suncrest Rd.,
Stock Island
(305) 296-5260
leoscampground.com**
Minutes from downtown Key West, you can ride a bike or take the bus from this campground park. Leo's is ideal for a relaxing spot while in the Lower Keys. Full RV setup with water, sewer, electric (some up to 50 amp), cable TV, barbecues, and picnic tables. On-site also are laundry facilities and a bathhouse. There are tent sites to rent and pets are permitted, but only if traveling in RVs.

SUGARLOAF KEY RESORT KOA
KAMPGROUND $$$
**MM 20 Oceanside, 251 CR 939,
Summerland Key
(305) 745-3549 or (800) 562-7731
koa.com/campgrounds/sugarloaf-key**
Pelicans perched in mangroves near thatched chickees on a palm-speckled beach create an island ambience in this comprehensive KOA on Summerland Key. Nearly 200 gravel, grass, or dirt sites offer a choice of hookups, but no pull-throughs are available. Optional cable hookup is available at an additional charge. The facility offers what you have come to expect from a KOA Kampground—all the necessities plus the amenities of a resort. A full marina covers the gamut of boating and fishing needs. A large heated pool, hot tub, minigolf, horseshoes, and bicycle rentals offer landlubbers relaxing diversions. Volleyball, a game room, and a playground amuse the children. Social activities, crafts, and special events are scheduled

during the winter season. Only 20 miles from Key West and near Looe Key National Marine Sanctuary, Sugarloaf Key KOA Kampground is close to all the action. Rates are based on 2 occupants; children younger than 6 stay free. Some RV trailers are available for rent; call to inquire about amenities and pricing.

SUNSHINE KEY RV RESORT AND
MARINA $-$$$
**MM 39 Bayside, Ohio Key
(305) 872-2217 or (877) 362-6736
rvonthego.com**
Sunshine Key RV Resort and Marina occupies an entire key, officially named Ohio Key. This bustling place, with nearly 400 sites, is more like a small Midwestern town than a camping resort in the Keys. The 75-acre Sunshine Key, with its winding signposted streets and myriad amenities, is friendly and family-oriented. The oceanside portion of Sunshine Key remains a tangle of mangroves, buttonwoods, and palm trees that shield a feathered montage of wildlife popular with bird-watchers. The large marina, which even has a fishing pier, will shelter your boat, and the experts at the bait and tackle shop will put you on the fish. Tennis courts, a heated swimming pool, volleyball, horseshoes, and a full schedule of adult activities in the clubhouse keep things hopping. A game room, basketball courts, a playground, and water sports occupy the children. Rates are based on 2 adults and their accompanying children younger than 12.

CAMPING IN THE BEYOND

If there is a little part of you that longs to forge through uncharted territory and live off the land (or the sea), you can fulfill your fantasies here. Everglades National Park and Dry Tortugas National Park, both day-trip excursions from the Florida Keys, offer unique camping experiences for the adventuresome spirits among you.

i Camping and campfires are not permitted in national wildlife refuges.

Everglades National Park

Canoe or commandeer a small motor craft into the backcountry wilderness of **Everglades National Park.** This 99-mile route, which is recommended for experienced canoeists only, connects **Flamingo** and **Everglades City.** (Allow at least 9 days to complete the trip.) The charted routing through such colorfully named spots as **Darwin's Place, Camp Lonesome, Lostman's Five,** and **Graveyard Creek** encompasses 47 primitive campsites of 3 basic types.

You will need a permit (small fee in season) to camp in one of the backcountry sites. Apply in person at the Gulf Coast or Flamingo Visitor Center up to 24 hours before your trip begins. Everglades National Park also offers camping in 2 in-park campgrounds. Seasonal reservations (Nov through Apr) can be made for these campsites by calling (800) 365-2267 or at the online reservations center, accessed by link from the park's website at nps.gov/ever. Reservations in the winter season are limited to 14 days at one visit, 30 days total per year. Guided tours are offered through North American Canoe Tour. Visit evergladesadventures.com for more information.

- **Chickees:** These elevated, 10-by-12-foot wood platforms with roofs are placed along interior rivers and bays where no dry land exists. A design originally used by the Miccosukee Indians, these open-air structures allow the wind to blow through, keeping the insects away. A narrow walkway leads to a self-contained toilet. You will need to have a freestanding tent, because stakes and nails are not allowed.

- **Beach Sites:** These are set on coastal beaches that have been built up through time from a conglomeration of fragmented shells. Campers are warned that gulf waters can become extremely rough. Loggerhead sea turtles nest on Highland Beach and Cape Sable in the spring and summer. If you see evidence of their nesting, refrain from lighting a campfire nearby. (Campfires are allowed at beach sites only.)

- **Primitive Ground Sites:** These consist of mounds of earth just a few feet higher than the surrounding mangroves. Willy Willy, Camp Lonesome, and Canepatch are old Indian mound sites. Coastal aborigines, who lived here before the Seminole Indians, constructed mounds of shells or soil as dry dwelling sites amid the mangroves. The ground sites, along interior bays and rivers, have a heavier preponderance of insects than either the beach sites or the chickees. Always be prepared for mosquitoes and tiny biting flies called no-see-ums, especially at sunrise and sunset. Mosquito season corresponds with the rainy season, Apr through Oct. We do not recommend you try to camp in the Everglades during these months.

For more information on park or backcountry camping, visit the aforementioned Everglades National Park website, or contact the main park number at (305) 242-7700.

What's Old Is New Again

Everglades National Park is nearly 80 years old and the largest subtropical wilderness in the US. Within this famed park is the historical waterfront village, **Flamingo.** This camping mecca borders Florida Bay to the south that feeds into a sea of sawgrass and pine wilderness. Three plans are now being considered by the state of Florida to rebuild this hurricane-ravaged mecca. On the property is a vintage lodge with cottages and marina. Bringing this famed area back to life will take millions of dollars and time, and the new redevelopment options will be released by the National Park Service to the public in 2013. For more information, visit parkplanning.nps.gov.

Dry Tortugas National Park

Roughing it takes on gargantuan proportions when you consider camping at **Dry Tortugas National Park,** but it's worth the effort, because this remote bit of Paradise has been preserved in a virginal state. You'll find the 11 palm-shaded tent sites—available on a first-come, first-served basis—in a sandy area on **Garden Key** in front of Fort Jefferson. You must pack in all your supplies, including freshwater; only saltwater toilets, grills, and picnic tables are provided. There is no food, freshwater, electricity, or medical assistance of any kind on the island.

You must take your chances on securing a campsite, because reservations are not taken for the individual sites. A small fee per person, per night must be paid upon arrival at Fort Jefferson. (The park service says securing a site usually is not a problem.) Campsites accommodate up to 8 people. You can reserve a group site for as many as 15 people, however, by contacting the park service, (305) 242-7700. If the group site is available when you submit your completed application, a permit reserving the site will be issued. You may stay up to 14 days at either individual or group sites, but keep in mind you must bring complete provisioning

for the duration of your stay and pack out your trash.

You may have left the civilized world behind you in Key West, but the arena of natural splendor surrounding you in the Dry Tortugas is endless. Tour **Fort Jefferson** (self-guided), America's largest 19th-century coastal fort. The walls of the fort are 50 feet high and 8 feet thick.

A white coral beach, nature-made not man-made, provides a tropical backdrop for doing nothing at all. But you can **snorkel** just 60 yards off the beach or dive the seemingly bottomless blue waters, which, preserved as a sanctuary, are filled with fearless battalions of finfish and squadrons of crawfish that are oblivious to your presence.

Bird-watching is superb. Sooty and noddy terns by the thousands gather in the Dry Tortugas from the Caribbean, nesting on nearby Bush Key. Single eggs are laid in depressions in the sand, and parent birds take turns shading them from the hot sun. The entire colony leaves when the babies are strong enough.

Getting to the Dry Tortugas presents a bit of a challenge—and expense. Seaplane is the fastest means of transportation to the Dry Tortugas, but it's also the most expensive. You can also reach the Dry Tortugas by sea. (See the Recreation chapter for information on the *Yankee Freedom II* ferry service to Fort Jefferson.) The National Park Service provides a list of sanctioned transportation services to the Dry Tortugas, which means they are insured and bonded and they maintain good safety records. The park service advises that the criteria are stringent and the list is constantly monitored. Contact the park service, (305) 242-7700, to get the current recommendations. The Dry Tortugas National Park website is nps.gov/drto.

BOATING

The voice of the sea speaks to the soul, no more so than in the Florida Keys. Surrounded by the shimmering aquatic prisms of the Gulf of Mexico and the Atlantic Ocean, the Keys volunteer unlimited vistas for watery exploration. Our depths secret famed fishing grounds (see the Fishing chapter) and unparalleled dive sites (see the Diving & Snorkeling chapter). Cruisers from around the world seek out our remote, pristine anchoring-out spots as well as our resort marinas (see the Cruising chapter). And peppering the Keys, from Key Largo to Key West, a proliferation of water-sports facilities afford anyone visiting our shores the opportunity to get out on the water via canoe, sea kayak, water skis, personal watercraft, sailboard, even paddleboard and paddleboat (see the Recreation chapter). The waters surrounding the Florida Keys are protected as part of a marine sanctuary, so regulations concerning the use of personal watercraft are more stringent here than in other parts of Florida. For more information, contact the sanctuary office at (305) 743-2437 or log on to floridakeys.noaa.gov.

The most popular means of wandering our aqueous acres is undoubtedly by boat. The waters encompassing the Florida Keys have been designated a national marine sanctuary since 1990, and the marine zoning plan imposes certain restrictions and responsibilities on all mariners so that our resources may be preserved for all time. (See the Florida Keys National Marine Sanctuary Regulations section of this chapter.) In this chapter we will introduce you to our waters, alert you to the rules of our hydrous highways and byways, and share some safety and navigational tips. We'll provide you with a primer of available public boat ramps, marine supply stores, and boat sales and service businesses, as well as motor and sailboat rentals, boat charters, and other sources to enhance your time on the water.

BODIES OF WATER

The waters of the Florida Keys conceal multiple habitats that sustain an impressive array of sea life not encountered anywhere else in the US. Depths range from scant inches (which often disappear altogether at low tide) in the nearshore waters, the flats, and the backcountry of Florida Bay to the fathoms of the offshore waters of the deep blue Atlantic. And buried at sea 4 to 5 miles from our shores runs the most extensive living coral reef track in North America. (See the Area Overview, Fishing, Diving & Snorkeling, and Cruising chapters for more information on these waters and the creatures dwelling within.)

Flats, Backcountry & Shallow Nearshore Waters

Perhaps the most complex of our waters are the shallows of the nearshore waters, those directly off both our coasts, which vary from a few inches to several feet in depth and sometimes stretch for a mile or more from shore. These "flats" of the Atlantic and back-country waters of the Gulf of Mexico and Florida Bay (that portion of the gulf bordered by the Upper Keys and Everglades National Park) prove a challenge to navigate. Popular with anglers searching for bonefish, permit, tarpon, redfish, snook, and sea trout and inhabited by an array of barracuda, sharks, and lobsters, the shallow waters cover meadows of sea grass punctuated with patches of sand, which also function as the nursery waters for many offshore species.

As a boater in the Florida Keys, you should familiarize yourself with the necessary nautical charts before venturing off the dock. Learn to "read" the water (see the Aids to Navigation section in this chapter) because waters are littered with unmarked shoals. Nearshore waters are best traversed in a shallow-draft flats boat or skiff, or by dinghy, canoe, or sea kayak. Operators of personal watercraft should steer clear of the flats to avoid disturbing the aquatic life dwelling below.

If you do happen to run aground here, turn off your motor immediately; the rotating propeller will kill the sea grass. Usually all you need to do is get out of the boat to lighten the load and push the craft to deeper water. Then trim up your motor and proceed. If this doesn't work, wait until the tide rises a bit and try to push off the flat again.

Intracoastal Waterway

The primary navigable waterway in Florida Bay and the Gulf of Mexico is the Intracoastal Waterway. In the Keys it leads from Biscayne Bay at the mainland, under Jewfish Creek, and then parallels the Keys, accommodating boats with drafts of up to 4 to 6 feet. The Intracoastal runs about 2 to 3 miles off the gulf side of our islands, between shallow nearshore waters and the scattered mangrove islands that lie varying distances from the coast.

The Intracoastal is well marked to about Big Pine Key, where it meets the Big Spanish Channel and heads north into the Gulf of Mexico. (Red day markers should be kept to the starboard, or right, side of the vessel when traveling down the Keys in the Intracoastal Waterway.) From the Spanish Channel to Key West, boaters must pay close attention to nautical charts to navigate safe passage. Boaters will enter Key West through the well-marked Northwest Channel.

Patch Reefs, Hawk Channel & the Barrier Reef

Between the nearshore waters of the Atlantic and the barrier reef some 4 to 5 miles offshore lies a smattering of patch reefs submerged at depths as shallow as 3 feet, with some even exposed at low tide. Surrounding waters vary in depth, but generally are much deeper than the flats and nearshore waters.

Hawk Channel—a safely navigable superhighway frequented by recreational boaters and cruisers—runs the length of the Florida Keys, bordering the reef at depths between 11 and 16 feet. Square red and triangular green day markers guide boaters through these waters; red markers should be kept to the starboard, or right, side of the vessel when traveling down the Keys in Hawk Channel.

Outside this marked area, the waters are scattered with dive sites designated with anchor buoys and red-and-white flags, as well as marked and unmarked rocks and shoals. If red-and-white diver-down flags are displayed, boaters should steer clear. These flags indicate that a diver is beneath the water.

Lighthouses now mark shallow reef areas, which, at one time, claimed ships that encountered bad weather or navigated carelessly close to the coral mountains. Waters covering the coral reef can run as deep as 20 to 40 feet, but as history attests, depths can vary considerably. Always consult your nautical chart and "read" the water.

The Florida Straits

Outside the reef in the Florida Straits, the water depth of the Atlantic increases dramatically to as much as 80 feet, deepening farther with distance from shore. Although on some days these waters are relatively calm, all offshore boaters should check wind and weather advisories before venturing out.

Creeks & Channels

The channels, or "cuts," between our islands often have extremely strong currents that make traveling between bridge pilings a bit dicey. Current continuously flows from the Gulf of Mexico into the Atlantic because sea level in the gulf is slightly higher than that of the ocean. Exercise caution when boating in these waters.

Key West Harbor

The southernmost city's ports have traditionally been gracious, welcoming tall ships, steamships, ferries, barges, powerboats, and seaplanes. Pirates, wreckers, spongers, shippers, naval officers, and Cuban émigrés all have found shelter here in the midst of their work, play, and quest for worldly wealth and freedom.

Key West's port, the deepest in all the Florida Keys, has a main channel depth of anywhere from 13 to 34 feet; it is even deeper on the Atlantic side. Passenger cruise ships now include this island among their ports of call. Key West is ranked among the top busiest cruise-ship ports of call in the world. Also in that ranking are the Virgin Islands, Puerto Rico, and the Caymans. Recreational cruisers often head for Key West's bustling harbor to prepare themselves and their boats for a Caribbean journey.

Like the rest of the Florida Keys, Key West is protective of its coral reefs and sea-grass beds, and despite the fact that harbors run deep, waters in the backcountry are shallow everywhere. First-time and novice boaters often run aground here and by Fleming Key and Sand Key west of the harbor.

AIDS TO NAVIGATION

Nautical Charts

Always use nautical charts and a magnetic compass for navigation when boating in the waters of the Florida Keys. Use electronic means of navigation (GPS) only for confirmation of position. Be sure your vessel is equipped with a VHF marine radio.

The US Coast Guard recommends you follow charts issued by the National Oceanic and Atmospheric Administration (NOAA). To secure nautical charts for the entire Florida Keys, you'll need to purchase a chart kit that includes charts for each section. You can also purchase NOAA charts individually. For instance, to navigate the waters surrounding Key West, the US Coast Guard recommends you use navigational chart No. 11441 for the approaches to Key West Harbor and chart No. 11447 for the harbor itself.

Readily available in many marine supply stores throughout the Florida Keys and Key West (see store listings in this chapter), these charts are accurate based on the date marked on them. Store personnel will be able to help you secure the proper up-to-date chart for the area you will be exploring. Be sure you know how to read the nautical charts before you set off. To view them online before your trip, visit nauticalcharts .noaa.gov.

Channel Markers

In most waters, boaters follow the adage "red, right, return," meaning that the triangular red channel markers should be kept to the right, or starboard, side of the vessel when heading toward the port of origin. This jingle is confusing at best, for in the Florida Keys it does not appear to apply. Red markers should be kept to the starboard side of the vessel when heading down the Keys, from Key Largo to Key West, through Hawk Channel on the oceanside or the Intracoastal Waterway in the gulf. Conversely, when traveling up the Keys, in either Hawk Channel or the Intracoastal Waterway, square green markers should be kept to your starboard side; keep red markers on your vessel's port, or left, side.

When traversing creeks and cuts from oceanside to the gulf, red markers should be kept on your starboard side, and when coming from the gulf, the opposite holds true. In any event, always consult your nautical chart to determine the channel of safe passage

and the corresponding positioning of the navigational markers.

Tide Charts

It's important to determine mean low tides within the waters you plan to travel so that you do not run aground. In the Florida Keys tides typically rise and fall about 1 to 2 feet. During spring, autumn, and a full moon, tides tend to rise to the higher and lower ends of this scale. Boaters should, therefore, rely on a tide conversion chart. Most marinas, bait and tackle shops, and other businesses that cater to boaters can provide tide information for specific areas in conjunction with a current tide chart available from the US Coast Guard.

"Reading" the Water

In the Florida Keys visual navigation often means "reading" the water—that is, recognizing its potential depth by knowing which colors indicate safe passage and which connote danger. As water depth decreases, its underlying sea bottom is indicated by distinctive coloration. Be aware that readings may be difficult in narrow channels and in strong currents where the waters often are murky and restrict visibility. Wear polarized sunglasses to better distinguish one color from another.

The easiest way to remember what each water color signifies is to follow some poetic, but fundamental, guidance:

- **Brown, brown run aground.** Reef formations and shallow sea-grass beds close to the surface cause this color.
- **White, white you might.** Sandbars and rubble bottoms may be in waters much shallower than you think.

- **Green, green nice and clean.** The water is generally safely above reefs or sea-grass beds, but larger boats with deeper drafts may hit bottom. If you are renting a boat, find out what the draft is.
- **Blue, blue cruise on through.** Water is deepest, but changing tides may cause coral reefs to surface. Allow time to steer around them.

WHEN YOU NEED HELP

Although the US Coast Guard and the Florida Marine Patrol work closely together and will make sure you contact the proper party in any event, they do handle different aspects of our waters in the Florida Keys.

Florida Marine Patrol

The Florida Fish and Wildlife Conservation Commission's law enforcement arm is the Florida Marine Patrol. They deal with violations such as environmental crime, fish and crawfish bag limits, and illegal dumping. They also enforce boating safety laws, responding to reports of unsafe boating and wake violations as well as any perceived illegal activity on the water. You can reach the Florida Marine Patrol on a cell phone by dialing *FMP (*367) or on a regular telephone line at (800) DIAL-FMP (342-5367). The Marine Patrol vessels also monitor VHF channel 16.

i *FMP is a free phone call when you are on your vessel and in need of the Florida Marine Patrol.

US Coast Guard

The US Coast Guard maintains three bases in the Florida Keys and Key West. Their mission

is to ensure maritime safety and handle life-threatening emergencies at sea, such as vessel collisions, drownings, onboard fires, or other accidents at sea. The Coast Guard monitors VHF channel 16 at all times. In an emergency call (305) 743-6388. By cell phone, call *CG (*24). If for some reason you do not have a radio or cell phone on board, flag a passing boat and ask someone on it to radio for assistance.

Sea Tow

Run aground? Out of fuel? Motor problems? Instead of calling the Coast Guard, call Sea Tow, a nationally recognized boater assistance service that maintains facilities the length of the Keys. Convey the details of your problem and what you think you need. Don't just ask for a tow if you have run out of gas or need only a minor repair. Describe your problem; the difference in cost between having gas delivered to your stranded boat and a multihour tow back to land could be a lot of money. Sea Tow also will provide free advice, such as projected weather changes or directions in unfamiliar territory.

Call the Sea Tow offices at (800) 473-2869 or visit seatow.com for more information.

VESSEL REGULATIONS & EQUIPMENT

Vessels must be equipped with Coast Guard–approved equipment, which varies according to the boat's size, location, and use. All vessels must either be documented or registered, and the appropriate paperwork must be carried onboard.

Federal, state, and local law enforcement officials may hail your boat so that they can come aboard and inspect it. Among their reasons for imposing civil penalties: improper use of a marine radio and misuse of calling the distress channel VHF channel 16; boating under the influence (a blood alcohol level of 0.08 percent or higher); and negligence. Negligence includes boating in a swimming area, speeding in the vicinity of other boats or in dangerous waters, bow riding, and gunwaling. Boaters without the required Coast Guard–approved equipment on board or with problematic boats that are considered hazardous may be directed back to port.

Vessel Registration

Whether or not you are a resident of the Florida Keys, your vessel must be registered in the state of Florida within 30 days of your arrival if one of our islands is its primary location. Registration renewals require your old registration form and a valid Florida driver's license, if you have one; for registering new boats, bring your manufacturer's statement of origin, dealer's sales tax statement, and bill of sale. If you are registering a used boat you have just purchased, you will need a title signed over to you and a bill of sale, one of which must be notarized, and the previous owner's registration if available.

Boats must be registered annually; only cash is accepted as payment. Excluded from registration requirements are rowboats and dinghies with less than 10-hp motors that are used exclusively as dinghies. All other boats may be registered any weekday between 8 a.m. and 4:45 p.m. at one of the Monroe County Tax Collector's Offices. For a list of locations, call (305) 295-5010 or visit flhsmv.gov/offices/monroe.html.

Required Equipment

The US Coast Guard requires that vessels using gasoline for any reason be equipped with a ventilation system in proper working condition. With the exception of outboard motors, gasoline engines must also be equipped with a means of backfire flame control. In addition, Coast Guard–approved fire extinguishers are required for boats with inboard engines, closed or under-seat compartments with portable fuel tanks, and other characteristics. There are additional requirements for vessels of more than 39 feet and boats used for races, parades, and other specific purposes.

Personal flotation devices, night distress signals, and navigation lights are other required equipment. Visit uscgboating.org or contact the US Coast Guard at (305) 743-6778 or (305) 664-8078 for specific requirements for your size and style of boat.

Recommended Equipment

Regardless of your boat's size, location, and use, the US Coast Guard recommends that you have the following equipment on board: VHF radio, visual distress signals, anchor and spare anchor, heaving line, fenders, first-aid kit, flashlight, mirror, searchlight, sunscreen and sunburn lotions, tool kit, ring buoy, whistle or horn, fuel tanks and spare fuel, chart and compass, boat hook, spare propeller, mooring line, food and water, binoculars, spare batteries, sunglasses (polarized to see water-color variations better), marine hardware, extra clothing, spare parts, paddles, and a pump or bailer.

FLORIDA KEYS NATIONAL MARINE SANCTUARY REGULATIONS

The Florida Keys fall within the boundaries of the Florida Keys National Marine Sanctuary, created by the federal government in 1990 to protect the resources of our marine ecosystem. And while, for the most part, visitors can freely swim, dive, snorkel, boat, fish, or recreate on our waters, there are some regulations to guide these activities. For a complete copy of the regulations and marine coordinates of the areas, contact the sanctuary office at (305) 809-4700 or visit floridakeys.noaa.gov.

ℹ️ Both boat safety and personal watercraft (PWC) safety courses are offered online by the Florida Fish and Wildlife Commission. The courses teach boat safety and Florida boating laws. Upon successfully completing a course, you will receive a Florida Boating Safety Education ID card, which will make you eligible for a discount on boat or PWC insurance. For more information go to boat-ed.com/florida.

Sanctuary-wide Regulations

These mandates focus on habitat protection, striving to reduce threats to water quality and minimize human impact of delicate resources. The following are prohibited in our waters:

- Moving, removing, taking, injuring, touching, breaking, cutting, or possessing coral or live rock
- Removing, injuring, or possessing coral or live rock
- Discharging or depositing treated or untreated sewage from marine sanitation devices, trash, and other materials
- Dredging, drilling, prop dredging, or otherwise altering the seabed, or placing or abandoning any structure on the seabed
- Operating a vessel in such a manner as to strike or otherwise injure coral, sea grass, or other immobile organisms attached to the seabed, or cause prop scarring
- Having a vessel anchored on living coral in water less than 40 feet deep when the bottom can be seen. Anchoring on hardbottom is allowed.
- Except in officially marked channels, operating a vessel at more than 4 knots/no wake within 100 yards of residential shorelines, stationary vessels, or navigational aids marking reefs
- Operating a vessel at more than 4 knots/no wake within 100 yards of a "diver down" flag
- Diving or snorkeling without a dive flag
- Operating a vessel in such a manner that endangers life, limb, marine resources, or property
- Releasing exotic species
- Damaging or removing markers, mooring buoys, scientific equipment, boundary buoys, and trap buoys
- Moving, removing, injuring, or possessing historical resources
- Taking or possessing protected wildlife
- Using or possessing explosives or electrical charges
- Harvesting, possessing, or landing any marine life species except as allowed by the Florida Fish and Wildlife Conservation Commission Rule (68B-42 F.A.C.)

Marine Zoning Restrictions

The sanctuary's marine zoning regulations focus protection on portions of sensitive habitats, while allowing public access in others. Only about 2 percent of the sanctuary's waters fall into the five zoning categories. All sanctuary-wide regulations apply in the special zones as well as a number of additional rules and restrictions.

With certain exceptions, the following activities are prohibited in the Ecological Reserves (ERs), Sanctuary Preservation Areas (SPAs), and Special-Use Research Only Areas:

- Discharging any matter except cooling water or engine exhaust
- Fishing by any means
- Removing, harvesting, or possessing any marine life
- Touching or standing on living or dead coral
- Anchoring on living or dead coral, or any attached organism
- Anchoring when a mooring buoy is available
- Catch-and-release fishing by trolling is allowed in Conch Reef, Alligator Reef, Sombrero Reef, and Sand Key SPAs only.
- Bait fishing is allowed in SPAs by Florida Keys National Marine Sanctuary permit.

Additional Regulations for Tortugas South ER

- Vessels may only enter if they remain in continuous transit with fishing gear stowed.
- Diving and snorkeling are prohibited.

Additional Regulations for Tortugas North ER

- An access permit is required to stop or use a mooring buoy.

- Anchoring is prohibited.
- Mooring vessels more than 100 feet in total or combined length overall is prohibited.
- No access permit is necessary if vessel remains in continuous transit with fishing gear stowed.

Activities Prohibited in Special-Use Research Only Areas

The sanctuary's four Special-Use Research Only Areas are located at Conch Reef, Tennessee Reef, Looe Key (patch reef), and Eastern Sambo. Sanctuary Preservation Areas, Special-Use Areas, and the Western Sambo Ecological Reserve are marked by 30-inch round yellow buoys. Tortugas Ecological Reserve is not marked.

The following activities are prohibited:

- Entry or activity without a Florida Keys National Marine Sanctuary permit
- Discharging any matter except cooling water or engine exhaust
- Fishing by any means; removing, harvesting, or possessing any marine life
- Touching or standing on living or dead coral
- Anchoring on living or dead coral, or any attached organism

Wildlife Management Area Restrictions

Wildlife Management Areas (WMAs) are marked by white-and-orange information/regulatory cylindrical spar buoys and signs. Public access restrictions in these areas include idle speed only/no wake, no access buffer, no motor, and limited closures, and are marked as such.

BOATING

Activities Prohibited in the Key Largo and Looe Key Existing Management Areas

Removing, taking, spearing, or otherwise damaging any coral, marine invertebrate, plant, soil, rock, or other material is prohibited. However, commercial taking of spiny lobster and stone crab by trap and recreational taking of spiny lobster by hand or hand gear consistent with applicable state and federal fishery regulations are allowed.

Spearfishing and possession of spearfishing equipment is prohibited, except while passing through without interruption.

PUBLIC BOAT RAMPS

If you trailer your boat to the Florida Keys, you can launch it at any number of public ramps. Here is a list of boat-launching sites maintained year-round for your use. Parking is limited except at park sites. Please note that for those listings noted with a $, you must pay a launch fee.

Upper Keys

MM 110 Bayside, Key Largo

MM 102 Oceanside, John Pennekamp Coral Reef State Park, Key Largo, $

MM 92.5 Oceanside, Harry Harris County Park, Key Largo, $ (weekends and holidays)

MM 86 Bayside, Founder's Park, Islamorada, $ (except for locals)

MM 79 Bayside, Islamorada, Indian Key Fill

MM 71 Bayside, Islamorada

Middle Keys

MM 54 Bayside, Marathon

MM 49 Bayside, Marathon Yacht Club, 33rd Street, Marathon

Lower Keys

West of Seven Mile Bridge Bayside, Little Duck Key

MM 37 Oceanside, Bahia Honda State Recreation Area, $

MM 33 Bayside, Spanish Harbor Key

MM 27.5 Bayside, SR 4A, Little Torch Key

MM 22 Oceanside, Cudjoe Key

MM 11 Bayside, Big Coppitt Key

MM 10 Oceanside, Shark Key Fill

Key West

BOAT US TOWING SERVICES
MM 5 Oceanside, Stock Island
End of Route A1A, Smathers Beach
(800) 888-4869
Being stranded in a vessel on the water is not fun! Never pay a towing charge again when you join this marine towing and salvage service with 24-hour assistance. Call their 800 number for membership and protect yourself with marine assistance.

MARINE SUPPLY STORES

Marine supplies and NOAA charts recommended by the US Coast Guard may be purchased at the following facilities.

Upper Keys

WEST MARINE
MM 103.4 Bayside, Key Largo
(305) 453-9050 or (800) 685-4838
westmarine.com
West Marine is an expansive store that carries a variety of supplies for sailboats and powerboats. Hardware and electric, safety, plumbing, and maintenance needs can be met at West Marine. There are 3 additional locations at MM 48.5 Oceanside in Marathon (305-289-1009 or 800-685-4838); 5790 Second St. on Stock Island (305-294-2025 or 800-685-4838); and 725 Caroline St. in Key West (305-295-0999 or 800-685-4838).

Middle Keys

See the West Marine listing in the Upper Keys section for their Marathon location.

Lower Keys

SEA CENTER
MM 29.5 Oceanside, Big Pine Key
(305) 872-2243
sea-center.com
Sea Center offers boat sales, services, and supplies, including hardware, electric, and maintenance needs.

Key West

See West Marine in the Upper Keys section for their Stock Island and Key West locations.

KEY WEST MARINE HARDWARE INC.
818 Caroline St.
(305) 294-3519
This is the place to go for every cleat, bolt, snap, or thingamajig your powerboat or sailboat requires, because Key West Marine Hardware has it all. You'll find the complete set of official NOAA nautical charts to the Keys and Caribbean waters along with cruising, fishing, and sailing publications of every description. The stock of fishing tackle is limited, but you can really dress your boat in style with all the add-on amenities offered here. You can also dress yourself: Key West Marine carries a large selection of stylish boating togs.

BOAT SALES, REPAIRS, FUEL & STORAGE

Facilities throughout the Florida Keys carry a wide variety of new and used boats. For boat owners, most of these sales centers provide all the necessary services, including local hauling, repairs, bottom painting, and fuel.

Upper Keys

CARIBEE BOAT SALES
MM 81.5 Bayside, Islamorada
(305) 664-3431
caribeeboats.com
Offshore anglers shop at Caribee for Grady Whites, Pursuits, and Contenders 20 to 36 feet in length. For fishing the backcountry, the facility carries 16- to 21-foot Hewes, Pathfinder, and Maverick boats as well as Boston Whalers. Yamaha and Mercury engines are sold here. Indoor and outdoor storage is available, and certified mechanics are on duty 7 days a week. Bottom painting and boat hauling are provided; Caribee carries 89-octane fuel and sells live bait, frozen bait, and ice. Mobile service is available.

PLANTATION BOAT MART & MARINA, INC.
MM 90 Bayside, Tavernier
(800) 539-2628
plantationboat.com

Plantation Boat Mart sells Glacier Bay, Palmetto Custom, Jupiter, Sea Pro, and Hydrasport brand boats and is a Hurricane dealer. You may also buy Yamaha, Johnson, and Evinrude engines here. Plantation Boat Mart maintains a full-service repair department.

SMUGGLERS COVE RESORT AND MARINA
MM 85.5 Bayside, Islamorada
(305) 664-5564
smugscove.com

Nice package the folks at Smugglers Cove Resort and Marina have developed in the Upper Keys. Their building at the marina has stationary docks that berth up to 70-foot boats in the slips and is located in a lovely nautical setting. Fuel docks are available along with a great ship's store that carries live bait and tackle. You can rent boats here or hang out with one of the captains and go on a charter for backcountry or offshore fishing.

UNIQUE MARINE
MM 93 Bayside, Tavernier
(305) 853-5370
uniquemarine.com

For more than 10 years, Unique Marine has been the established dealer for EdgeWater, ProKat, ShreaWater, SeaQuest, Venture, and Yamaha. This dealership takes pride in educating the public about Catamaran fishing boats. They are there for you long after the sale, as they value long-term relationships with their loyal customers. Stop in and see why Unique Marine continuously receives prestigious customer-service awards from various boat manufacturers year after year.

Middle Keys

THE BOAT HOUSE MARINA
MM 53.5 Oceanside, Marathon
(866) 904-1234
theboathousemarina.com

State-of-the-art dockage exists in Marathon. Owned by the Singh Company (see the Tranquility Bay Beachfront Hotel & Resort and Parrot Key Resort listings in the Accommodations chapter), this complex is like no other in the Keys. It was constructed to withstand 155-mph winds and has high-tech security, online web cams, and auto fire suppression. They offer 40-foot wet and 36-foot dry storage with full-service boat sales and repairs on-site.

KEYS BOAT WORKS INC.
MM 48.5 Bayside, 700 39th St., Marathon
(305) 743-5583
keysboatworks.com

Keys Boat Works provides a comprehensive range of services for boats up to 67 feet in length and maintains 15-ton and 50-ton travel lifts. This full-service yard offers fiberglass work, carpentry, and Awlgrip topside painting. A variety of on-premises businesses contribute to the one-stop shopping for boat service, including diesel mechanics, an electronics specialist, a yacht refinisher, sign painter, and fiberglasser. Keys Boat Works can store vessels up to 60 feet, either in or out of the water. The facility has a capacity for 180 boats.

i If you see a red-and-white diverdown flag displayed while you are boating, stay at least 100 feet away. Divers or snorkelers are in these waters. Motoring between 100 feet and 300 feet from a diver-down flag must be at idle speed.

MARATHON BOAT YARD
MM 48.5 Oceanside, Marathon
(305) 743-6341 or (888) 726-9004
marathonboatyard.com
Marathon Boat Yard has become the first in the Florida Keys to be designated as a "Clean Boatyard." This ensures that the normally messy job of working on boats doesn't harm the environment. Marathon Boat Yard is a full-service marine yard, and on their 2-acre site they handle new boats, yacht brokerage, sportfishing boats, center consoles, cocktail cruisers, flats boats, and more. To reach them by boat: N24 42.441' / W81 06.268'.

Lower Keys

SEA CENTER
MM 29.5 Oceanside, Big Pine Key
(305) 872-2243
sea-center.com
Sea Center carries new Pro-Lines and Anglers and services Johnson and Evinrude engines. Bottom painting and limited boat hauling are available. The facility carries 93-octane fuel and maintains a complete marine store with parts and accessories.

Key West

FISH AND RACE
5555 College Rd., Sunset Marina, Stock Island
(305) 292-2291
fishandrace.com
Three mechanics with one goal in mind: "When you go out on your boat, we want you to come back." Their expert mechanical skills with decades of combined experience help them keep this motto. An extensive inventory of repair parts and a vast selection of new Mercury and Honda outboard engines offer top-of-the-line tune-ups to powerhead and gear-case rebuilding on engines that range in size from 2 to 300 horsepower.

GARRISON BIGHT MARINA
711 Eisenhower Dr., Key West
(305) 294-3093 or (305) 294-5780
garrisonbightmarina.net
This full-service marina offers both long- and short-term dry or in-water storage. Unleaded fuel may be purchased here, too. The marina also rents powerboats (15 to 22 feet) by the hour, half day, full day, or full week. Garrison Bight Marina is a sales and service dealer for Yamaha, Johnson, Evinrude, and Suzuki engines.

i Tycoon Henry Flagler was not only famous for his overseas railroad from Miami to Key West, but also operated three cargo ships that sailed from Key West to Havana, Cuba. Measuring up to 350 feet in length, each one held a capacity of 30 refrigerated railroad cars on board.

OCEANSIDE MARINA KEY WEST
5950 Peninsula Ave., Stock Island
(305) 294-4676
oceansidekeywest.com
Formerly Kings Point Marina, Key West's largest marina facility has wet slips available up to 80 feet and the T-Head accommodates yachts up to 120 feet. Amenities include a complete tackle shop, a large bathhouse with laundry, a restaurant, fuel, and repair services on-site.

PROP DOCTOR OF KEY WEST
MM 5 Oceanside, Stock Island
(305) 292-0012

The owners go by the creed "Boats need to be on the water, not out of the water." A lot of boat owners know that if you shear a prop or damage it by striking something, you could be landlocked for weeks. Now at Prop Doctor, you can be back on the high seas in a few days. They do all the work themselves on Stock Island and do not send the repairs to the mainland. You can call them and they will send a driver out to the marina to pick up the damaged prop and bring it back to you, sometimes in only a matter of hours. Prop Doctor can also handle shafts, struts, and rudders. They plan on keeping you fishing!

KAYAKING

The first kayaks were created by Arctic Indians, the Inuit. Constructed of wooden frames covered in sealskin, the kayaks varied by design from region to region. Today, kayaks are equally creative and beautiful in design. Using one of these ancient forms of water transportation in the eco-sensitive Florida Keys is a great way to reduce our carbon footprint and further protect this fragile spot on Earth. A wonderful and impressive book on kayaking is *Florida Keys Paddling Atlas*, written by Mary and Bill Burnham and published by this book's publisher, Globe Pequot Press.

Upper Keys

BACKCOUNTRY COWBOY OUTFITTERS
MM 82.2 Bayside, Islamorada
(305) 517-4177
backcountrycowboy.com
Living large in the Florida Keys but not wrestling herds of cattle, Backcountry Cowboy Outfitters kayaks a different range and gathers customers to paddle and explore the beautiful waters here. Noted for their guided kayak tours, camping, and kayak equipment, these folks fill your every request and they are open 7 days a week. Ask about their sunset and sunrise trips as well as their full-moon excursions.

FLORIDA BAY OUTFITTERS
MM 104 Bayside, Key Largo
(305) 451-3018
kayakfloridakeys.com
Florida Bay Outfitters is one of South Florida's largest kayak and canoe dealers, with loads of accessories in stock. This place will have you sport paddling in no time! The knowledgeable and dedicated staff know their business. They offers sales and rentals with full- and half-day water trips for one or more.

THE KAYAK SHACK
MM 77.5 Oceanside, at Robbie's Marina, Islamorada
(305) 664-4878
kayakthefloridakeys.com
Explore the backcountry waters by renting a kayak from the Kayak Shack. You can paddle into the unknown by yourself or take one of several guided tours through mangrove canals, to Lignumvitae or Indian Key (see the Attractions chapter), or across the saltwater flats at sunset.

Middle Keys

MARATHON KAYAK
(305) 395-0355
marathonkayak.com
Well-known for kayaking tours throughout the Keys, Marathon Kayak is a top-notch group to outfit and guide you in your journey. After customers purchase their gear, the demo center lets them get the feel for their equipment and product line to ensure

satisfaction. Marathon Kayak offers multiple locations for outings, including the Seven Mile Bridge and Bahia Honda State Park, along with fishing tours and sunset tours.

Lower Keys

REELAX CHARTERS
MM 17 Oceanside, Sugarloaf Key
(305) 744-0263 or (305) 304-1392
keyskayaking.com
Enjoy backcountry trips on the water in the mangroves and across the untouched sand flats of the tranquil Lower Keys with Captain Andrea. The captain has a boat with a 10-foot beam to accommodate kayaks, a grill, cooler, and beach chairs. It is wheelchair accessible.

REFLECTIONS NATURE TOURS
(305) 872-4668 or (305) 872-7474
floridakeyskayaktours.com
Reflections is a mobile nature tour company that trailers their kayaks to a number of tour locations in the Lower Keys to take advantage of the tides and the prevailing winds. With more than 20 favorite kayaking and paddleboarding spots, Captain Bill Keogh can always find a favorable paddling site in any wind condition. Marine life, birds, plant life, and indigenous Keys animals can be viewed up close and personal.

Key West

BLUE PLANET KAYAK
(305) 294-8087
blue-planet-kayak.com
Join in the fun with Blue Planet Kayak and take one of their informative and lively kayak tours. Offering everything from ecotours to sunset, starlight, birding, and custom tours, these folks know their business. They also

rent kayaks for half- and full-day on-your-own paddling adventures. They will pick you up at your lodging location or meet you in the Publix Shopping Center on N. Roosevelt Boulevard in Key West for your convenience and to help you find their marina on Stock Island.

LAZY DOG KAYAKING
MM 4.2 Bayside, Stock Island
(305) 295-9898
lazydog.com
Stop by the Lazy Dog shack and sign up for a 2- or 4-hour kayak tour around Key West. You can rent a single or double kayak or try your hand (and balance) in a standup paddleboat.

POWERBOAT RENTALS

The following rental facilities offer US Coast Guard–approved, safety-equipped vessels complete with VHF marine radios. Rental boat sizes vary from 15 to 27 feet, in a number of configurations: center consoles, bow-riders, cuddy cabins, and pontoon boats. The boats feature options such as compasses, depth finders, Bimini or T-tops, dry storage, swim ladders, and dive platforms. You can rent a powerboat for either a half day or full day. Call the establishments to inquire about specific boats offered, their features, and prices. (Prices are usually quoted without tax or gasoline.)

Purchase the nautical chart you need (see the Aids to Navigation section in this chapter) and bring it with you to the boat rental facility of your choice. Most facilities will provide you with an operational briefing and a nautical chart review before you set off. Some facilities require that you remain within a specific locale at all times; others base this decision on weather conditions.

Upper Keys

ROBBIE'S BOAT RENTALS & CHARTERS
MM 77.5 Bayside, Islamorada
(877) 664-8498
robbies.com

One of the Florida Keys' more interesting boat rental facilities, Robbie's is behind the Hungry Tarpon Restaurant. Visitors come to Robbie's just to feed the many tarpon that lurk close to shore (see the Kidstuff chapter). Boat rentals, too, are popular, since Robbie's is only half a mile from historic Indian Key (see the Attractions chapter). Robbie's rents boats from 14 to 27 feet in length.

Key West

BOAT RENTALS OF KEY WEST
The Galleon Marina, 617 Front St.
(305) 294-2628
boatrentalsofkeywest.com

You can rent Anglers, Hurricane deck boats, and Wellcrafts of 18 to 21 feet, as well as Jet Boats and Jet Skis. Navigational charts are provided and reviewed, along with an overview of local waters and suggestions (based on weather conditions) of directions to take and places to see. A questionnaire and verbal review ensure that boaters are experienced. Jet Ski tours are also available.

i The 26 segments of the Florida Circumnavigational Saltwater Paddling Trail allow kayakers to explore every Florida coastal habitat type, from barrier island dune systems to salt marsh to mangroves. The trail follows around the state of Florida, and segment 15 encompasses the Florida Keys. For maps of the trail and information on primitive campsites specifically for paddlers, visit dep.state.fl.us/gwt/paddling/saltwater.htm.

GARRISON BIGHT MARINA
711 Eisenhower Dr. (corner of Palm Avenue and Eisenhower Drive)
(305) 294-3093
garrisonbightmarina.net

Open 7 days a week, Garrison Bight Marina offers a modern fleet of boats to rent ranging from 15 to 22 feet. They rent by the hour, half day, or full day; weekly charters with guides are also available. You can rent diving equipment here, too, as well as fish finders and GPS for your boat. Happy boating!

SAILING

With an abundance of protected anchorages, harbors, and marinas and warm tropical waters, the Florida Keys are often described by sailors as the "American Caribbean." Our offshore barrier reef provides protection from swells. Our bayside is so sheltered that many skippers with low-draft boats (typically catamarans or small, monohull sailboats) can trim up their sails and guide their craft through the Intracoastal Waterway. Catamarans and monohulls with drafts of 4 or 5 feet fare best along the sometimes shallow Intracoastal; monohulls with 6-foot drafts have difficulty getting out of bayside marinas. These boats may also run aground here. Most oceanside marinas and harbors typically run deep enough to accommodate virtually any type of sailboat (see the Cruising chapter).

Within the Florida Keys, local sailing clubs organize their own informal races. Sailing in the Florida Keys can include cruising, limited bareboat charters, and a combination of snorkeling, fishing, or diving. Many head out simply to enjoy the sail. In order to sail the diverse waters of the Florida Keys, however, boaters must know a rig from a right-of-way.

Sailing Courses

Several facilities throughout our islands offer sailing courses for beginner through advanced levels, along with bareboat certification and brush-up sessions. Prices vary greatly depending upon the duration and complexity of the courses and the number of people participating. Be sure to ask about all your options when you call to book your instruction.

FLORIDA KEYS SAILING
MM 49 Bayside, Marathon
(305) 731-8105
sailfloridakeys.com

You'll find a wide variety of sailing operations at Florida Keys Sailing, located at Keys Fisheries and Marina. The sailing school offers everything from half-day and full-day day-sailing classes to advanced bareboat sailing courses, and almost everything in between. The basic introductory 3-day, Learn-to-Sail keelboat course is designed to provide the new sailor with a solid foundation. In the basic cruising course, students learn to responsibly skipper and crew an auxiliary-powered cruising sailboat within sight of land in moderate wind and sea conditions. Bareboat cruising is the advanced cruising course. Racing clinics aboard J/24 sloops are offered on short windward–leeward courses. Students learn the techniques of starting, luffing, positioning on the racecourse, covering an opponent to win, and defending position.

✳THE SAILING ACADEMY OF FLORIDA
Islamorada
(305) 240-1429
learntosailfloridakeys.com

Safety here is definitely number one. The Sailing Academy of Florida is the 2011 American Sailing Academy (ASA) School of the Year and has their boat inspected for safety regularly by the US Coast Guard Auxiliary. They offer courses as diverse as your needs: The 1-day Basic Keel Boat course covers nautical terminology, knots, communication, proper ways to assist in docking, crew basics, and more. The Basic Coastal Cruising course can last anywhere from 1 to 5 days in a liveaboard and covers charting, troubleshooting, anchoring, mooring, and more. You can even take the ASA Bareboat Chartering course and learn everything from how to provision for a 3- to 7-day trip to how to handle emergency situations like dragging anchor and crew overboard. If you don't see a class when you want to take it, or need to tailor one to your own needs, call or e-mail Captain Edana directly at captainedana@gmail.com and she'll build one just for you.

Bareboat Charters

If you already know how to sail or you prefer to explore our waters on your own, the Florida Keys also offers captained and bareboat charters for anywhere from 2 hours to several weeks. Prices vary depending upon the size of the vessel and the length of the bareboat excursion.

TREASURE HARBOR MARINE INC.
MM 86.5 Oceanside,
200 Treasure Harbor Dr., Islamorada
(305) 852-2458 or (800) 352-2628
treasureharbor.com

Treasure Harbor maintains a fleet of 12 sloops and ketch rigs ranging in size from 19 to 41 feet by Cape Dory, Watkins, Hunter, and Morgan. Skilled sailors can charter any one of these boats on their own, and written and verbal "exams" will test your sailing experience. Professional captains will provide nautical charts, overviews of Florida Keys waters, and suggestions of places to visit from John Pennekamp and the Everglades to Key West and the Bahamas. Skippers are available. A 2-day minimum is required for all boats greater than 25 feet in length, and a security deposit is required. Power trawler yachts and charters are also available.

Sailing Clubs & Regattas

Avid sailors throughout our islands have formed sailing clubs, which sponsor casual regattas. These are not your upscale yacht clubs, but membership does have its privileges—discounted race entry fees and dinners, and the opportunity to meet individuals who share your interests.

✳THE FLORIDA KEYS DRAGON BOAT CLUB
Locations vary
(305) 304-5100
floridakeysdragonboat.com
In 277 BC some Chinese tried to save a poet from being eaten by fish and dragons by beating the water with their paddles. Here in Key West, this primal teamwork is all fun and games. Twenty-two paddlers are on board, including one helmsman and one rummer, who sets the cadence. The boat design originates from ancient China, with its brightly colored scales, fierce horned head, and a dragon tail. The Loch Ness Monster gone Disneyland? This muscle-aching sport is one vicious workout!

i High-profile fleets, intense competition, and superb sailing conditions draw the boat-racing crowds to Quantum Key West, a major international sailing regatta held annually during the third week of January. Typically more than 150 boats in 13 classes compete in this exciting race.

KEY WEST SAILING CLUB
Sailboat Lane, off Palm Avenue, Garrison Bight Causeway, Key West
(305) 292-5993
keywestsailingclub.org
The Key West Sailing Club is a private organization open to anyone for membership. The club itself is located at the base of the Garrison Bight Bridge. The club has 4 Sunfish boats and a Hobie Cat, as well as 4 Optimists, 2 lasers, a Snipe, an American Day Sailer, and a Cape Dory. In addition, a sizable fleet of privately owned JY15s is available for members to use on race days. The club sponsors monthly offshore races for boats 20 feet and larger; call for more information. Group and private instruction is available for both adults and juniors (younger than age 18). Dates and times of courses change seasonally; call for details. Membership requires a onetime initiation fee and annual dues. The membership year begins in Jan, but dues are prorated so anyone who joins later doesn't pay for a full year. A membership entitles members to use club facilities 7 days a week between 6 a.m. and midnight. Membership also grants possible dockage in a wet or dry slip; rates are based on boat length.

UPPER KEYS SAILING CLUB
MM 100 Bayside, 100 Ocean Bay Dr., Key Largo
(305) 451-9972
upperkeyssailingclub.com
Established in 1973, the Upper Keys Sailing Club is based in a club-owned house on the bay and comprises Upper Keys residents of all ages. Races on Buttonwood Bay are held on a regular basis; spectators watch from clubhouse grounds. Two offshore races take place over a 2-week period. As a community service, members provide free 2-day sailing seminars 4 times a year. Seminars combine 2 hours of classroom instruction with extensive time on the water aboard the club's 19-foot Flying Scot. Boaters with Sunfish and Hobie Cats are welcome. Membership requires a onetime initiation fee and annual dues.

HOUSEBOAT RENTALS

Florida Keys houseboats provide all the comforts of home combined with a camplike experience. Whether you seek a weekend excursion or a gently rocking place to spend your vacation, a houseboat rental may very well float your boat.

HOUSEBOAT VACATIONS OF THE FLORIDA KEYS
MM 85.9 Bayside, Islamorada
(305) 664-4009
floridakeys.com/houseboats
Houseboat Vacations of the Florida Keys offers liveaboard vessels that range from two 42-foot-long catamarans that sleep 6 or 8 adults to a 44-foot-long houseboat that accommodates 8. You must have some boating experience to rent one of these floating homes. Boaters must venture no farther than 8 miles offshore along 25 miles of surrounding coastline in Florida Bay. You may not take the houseboats into the ocean. Each houseboat offers a full galley and air-conditioning and features a gas grill on deck. There is a 3-day minimum; weekly rentals are available. Call for current pricing.

CRUISING

Regarded as America's out-islands by seasoned cruisers of motor and sailing yachts, the Florida Keys can justifiably boast about the sheltered harbors and easily navigated waters enveloping the serpentine stretch. Our waters are well marked; our charts, up to date; and the US Coast Guard keeps channels dredged to the proper depth. The Atlantic's Hawk Channel runs along the ocean side of the Keys, protected by the only coral reef in the continental US. The Intracoastal Waterway—called the Big Ditch in the North's inland waters—cuts through the causeway from the mainland at Jewfish Creek and then parallels the Keys through Florida Bay and the Gulf of Mexico. Keys waters are most accessible to boats with drafts of up to 4½ feet, but you can cruise the Keys with 5½- to 6-foot drafts if you're careful.

If you covet first-class creature comforts, put into one of our comprehensive marinas and enjoy the perks of staying at a luxury resort. Do you relish seclusion? Anchor out on the leeward side of a remote, uninhabited key. Or take the best of both worlds and plan a combination of the two.

To help you plan your Keys cruising adventure, we guide you on a tour of our preeminent marinas and little-known anchoring-out destinations (in descending order from the Upper to Lower Keys). Be sure to read our Key West and Beyond section, where the junket continues.

THE FLORIDA KEYS

Marinas

All marinas listed in this chapter take transient boaters, but we suggest you make reservations at least a month in advance during the popular winter season from Dec through Mar. You may assume unless otherwise stated that all our recommended marinas supply hookups for both 30-amp and 50-amp service as well as freshwater. You'll find that provisioning is easy along the 120-mile stretch of the Florida Keys. Most marinas have ship's stores or are within walking distance of a convenience market. The occasional exception is noted.

The marinas keep an active list of expert marine mechanics who are generally on call to handle any repair needs that might develop during your cruise. We highlight fuel dock facilities and availability of laundry, showers, and restrooms. We also point out restaurants and the hot spots for partying while ashore.

There are no restrictions against bringing children and pets unless specifically noted., Keep your pet on your vessel or on a leash at all times.

Dockmasters monitor VHF channel 16, but they will ask you to switch channels once you've established contact. They will give you detailed directions to the marinas.

ℹ️ **"Wet-foot, dry-foot"** is the name of the 1995 revision of the Cuban Adjustment Act of 1996. The revision designates that any Cuban caught on the waters between two nations ("wet feet") would be sent back to their country. Make it ashore ("dry feet"), one would get a chance to remain in the US.

THE MARINA CLUB AT BACKWATER SOUND
MM 104 Bayside, Key Largo
(305) 453-0081
marinaclubkeylargo.com
The future of boat storage is deeded rackominiums, and the Marina Club at Backwater Sound has these newest entries in waterfront ownership. These dry racks are rented through the marina, and the amenities include showers, a lounge, fuel, boat care, restaurant, Wi-Fi access, concierge, diving, and spa services.

MARINA DEL MAR MARINA
MM 100 Oceanside, 527 Caribbean Dr.,
Key Largo
(305) 451-4107 or (800) 451-3483
marinadelmarkeylargo.com
Plan ahead if you want to stay at one of the 137 slips at the Marina Del Mar Marina, which lies within the underwater boundaries of John Pennekamp Coral Reef State Park and the Key Largo National Marine Sanctuary. All but a select few are usually booked far in advance from Jan through Mar. A short

walk to the Overseas Highway will satisfy provisioning requirements. Laundry, shower, and restroom facilities are provided on the premises. Marina rates do not include water and electricity; a minimum daily charge will be levied. Marina Del Mar Resort (see the Accommodations chapter) has tennis courts, a swimming pool, and a hot tub for your use. And don't miss Coconuts, a popular restaurant and percolating nightspot (see the Restaurants and Nightlife chapters). Marina Del Mar is accessed via Hawk Channel, red marker no. 2.

THE PILOT HOUSE MARINA
MM 100 Oceanside, Key Largo
(305) 451-3142
pilothousemarina.com
Sitting alongside the Pilot House Restaurant (see the Restaurants chapter), this marina offers an array of services to boaters. Deep dockage with slips that can accommodate up to 60-foot-long boats, repairs for your boat, 30- and 50-amp, restrooms, showers, laundry facilities, cable TV, Wi-Fi, bait for fishing, diesel, and gasoline are available. Enjoy the tiki bar at the restaurant next door.

PLANTATION YACHT HARBOR MARINA
MM 87 Bayside, Islamorada
(305) 852-2381
pyh.com
You can grab a slip close to the Keys' fabled backcountry at the bayside Plantation Yacht Harbor, a municipal marina located at Islamorada Founder's Park (see the Recreation chapter). This 88-slip marina can accommodate vessels up to 60 feet in length, drawing 5 feet. Mobile marine mechanics are on call to service needy vessels, and a fuel dock supplies both diesel fuel and gasoline. Plantation Yacht Harbor does not have a ship's

store, but a 1-mile walk up the Overseas Highway will put you at a convenience store. You may use the on-site laundry, showers, and restroom facilities. Tennis courts, a swimming pool, a small beach, skate park, playground, dog park, and sports field await your pleasure. Plantation Yacht Harbor Marina is accessed via the Intracoastal Waterway, between markers no. 78 and no. 78A, or via Snake Creek from the Atlantic.

i Due to the city of Key West's bay-bottom lease, cruise ships may only dock at Mallory Square Pier 12 times a year during sunset. The ships must either moor elsewhere the rest of the year or leave at least one hour before sunset so as not to block the view!

ISLAMORADA MARINA
MM 80.5 Bayside, Islamorada
(305) 664-8884
islamoradamarina.com
Facing Florida Bay, the location of Islamorada Marina provides clear passage into the flats and bay of the Florida Keys, Everglades National Park, and the Atlantic Ocean. If you are water-oriented to fishing, kayaking, or just pure enjoyment, this marina is for you.

✳HAWK'S CAY RESORT AND MARINA
MM 61 Oceanside, Duck Key
(305) 743-7000 or (800) 432-2242
hawkscay.com
Probably the best all-around marina in the Keys, Hawk's Cay offers a totally protected boat basin and all the amenities of its fine resort hotel (see our Accommodations and Restaurants chapters). Dock your boat at one of the 52 full-service marina slips (5-foot draft) with 30- and 50-amp service,

freshwater, cable TV, and phone. If you come in a vessel less than 35 feet, you can dock it at one of 32 small-boat slips and stay at the resort. Hawk's Cay maintains an extensive list of qualified marine mechanics in the area and has divers on call. The full-service ship's store sells everything, including groceries, fine wines, boating hardware, fishing tackle, clothing, and paperback books. It also offers video rentals. A full-service fuel dock pumps regular and premium gasoline and diesel fuel. Showers and restrooms are in the ship's store, and the marina is equipped with a pump-out station at the fuel dock. Hawk's Cay Marina is accessed via Hawk Channel at marker no. 44 when traveling down the Keys or at marker no. 45 when approaching from Key West.

DOLPHIN MARINA
MM 28.5 Oceanside, Little Torch Key
(305) 872-2685
dolphinmarina.net
Quiet Little Torch Key is the safe harbor for this delightful marina. Dolphin Marina offers not only boat rentals and dockage but also quaint lodging. The lodging quarters consist of small cottages overlooking Newfound Harbor and cozy apartments with 1 or 2 bedrooms. Just minutes from luxurious Little Palm Island (see the Accommodations chapter), this down-to-earth marina offers all you need for a day afloat on the open waters of the Atlantic. Dolphin Marina has a fleet of Angler boats that you can rent. Alternatively, you can venture out in your own vessel with an experienced fishing or diving guide. The marina and ship's store can stock you with all the supplies for your outing. Boat launching and trailer storage are available if you tow your own boat. Located at 24.39.95 north latitude and 81.23.28 west longitude.

✳LITTLE PALM ISLAND
MM 28.5 Oceanside, Little Torch Key
(305) 872-2524
littlepalmisland.com

Arriving at Little Palm Island by sea, you will be certain you missed your tack and landed in Fiji, because this exquisite jewel is more reminiscent of the South Seas than South Florida. Little Palm Island, the westernmost of the Newfound Harbor Keys, lies 4 nautical miles due north from Looe Key Light. Staying at this marina is a real deal, even though it is the most expensive marina in the Florida Keys. As marina guests you're invited to use all the recreational facilities: sailboards, day sailers, fishing gear, canoes, snorkeling gear, the beach, swimming pool, and sauna.

Little Palm's marina, though small, maintains slips on Newfound Harbor for boats up to 120 feet in length, with a draft up to 6 feet. Smaller boats can be accommodated at 575 feet of dock space on a protected lagoon. The controlling depth coming into the harbor is 6 feet, but the dockmaster will help you navigate around the tides. The dockmaster monitors VHF channels 9 and 16 at all times. Dockhands are available to assist with lines. Because you're staying on an out-island, offshore from the contiguous Keys and their more plentiful water supply, you will be allowed only 1 gallon of water per foot per day. However, the resort offers you use of guest showers and restrooms in the quarterdeck and a laundry facility during your stay, so this water conservation is not a hardship.

Children younger than age 16 are not permitted at Little Palm Island, nor are villa guests allowed to bring pets. Little Palm does accommodate pets of overnight marina guests, but you must keep them on a leash and walk them only in designated areas. In keeping with the tranquil ambience of the island, motorized personal watercraft also are banned. Little Palm Island is accessed via the Atlantic at the entrance to Newfound Harbor, red marker no. 2.

SUGARLOAF MARINA
MM 17 Bayside, Sugarloaf Key
(305) 745-3135

Housed next to the Sugarloaf Lodge, this marina has ramp access, fuel, beer, soda, bait, tackle, and ice. It may be rugged and rough looking, but locals give it a thumbs up.

Anchoring Out

Barefoot elegance, breathtakingly beautiful, and peaceful all describe anchoring out in the pristine waters lacing the Florida Keys. From the northernmost keys of Biscayne Bay to Loggerhead Key at the end of the line, remote havens remain unspoiled, many reachable only by boat. Ibis, white pelicans, and bald eagles winter among select out-islands, and whole condominiums of cormorants take over the scrub of tiny mangrove islets. Gulf waters simmer with snapper, redfish, lobster, and stone crabs. The Atlantic Ocean sparkles with the glory of the living coral reef beneath. So pack up and push off for an Insiders' bareboat cruise of the Florida Keys, from top to toe.

Elliott Key

On the eastern side of Biscayne Bay, the island of Elliott Key, which has the ranger station for Biscayne National Park, guards a complex ecosystem from the ocean's battering winds. A strong current rushes through the shallow channel between Sands Key and Elliott Key, and small-boat traffic is heavy on weekends. Although the fishing and diving here are first rate, take care. At the southern tip of Elliott Key, Caesar Creek—named for notorious pirate Black Caesar, who dipped in to stay out of sight in the 1600s—offers dicey passage to Hawk Channel for boats carefully clearing a 4-foot draft at high tide. The more forgiving Angelfish Creek, farther south at the north end of Key Largo, is the favored route from Biscayne Bay to the ocean in this wild and deserted area. Angelfish Creek is the Intracoastal Waterway's last outlet to the ocean until after Snake Creek Drawbridge for large boats or those heading for Hawk Channel.

Pumpkin Key

Safe anchorage surrounds Pumpkin Key, making this island an ideal choice for winds coming from any direction. Be sure to test your anchorage, because Pumpkin Key's waters cover a grassy sea bottom. Nearby Angelfish Creek—filled with grouper, snapper, and angelfish—almost guarantees dinner. Scoot out the creek to take advantage of the diving at John Pennekamp Coral Reef State Park. Approachable from Hawk Channel or the Intracoastal, this area remains virginal even though it rests in the shadow of Key Largo.

Blackwater Sound

As you anchor in the placid ebony waters of Blackwater Sound, the twinkling lights of Key Largo remind you that civilization is but a dinghy ride away. Anchor along the southeast shoreline of Blackwater Sound for a protected anchorage in east to southeast winds. The Cross Key Canal, which connects Blackwater Sound to Largo Sound, passes under a fixed bridge at the Overseas Highway in Key Largo. If your boat clears 14 feet safely, traverse the canal to dive or snorkel in John Pennekamp Coral Reef State Park.

Tarpon Basin

Enter Tarpon Basin through Dusenbury Creek or Grouper Creek. Both passages teem with snapper and grouper.

> **i** The Atlantic Intracoastal Waterway begins in Boston, Massachusetts, and ends in Key West, Florida. This 3,000-mile scenic and historic course takes you through man-made canals, bays protected by barrier reefs, natural river channels, and estuaries. It is used extensively by commercial and recreational boaters and "snowbirds" heading south for the winter.

Largo Sound (John Pennekamp Coral Reef State Park)

John Pennekamp Coral Reef State Park and the adjacent Key Largo National Marine Sanctuary encompass the ocean floor under Hawk Channel from Broad Creek to Molasses Reef. Exit the Intracoastal Waterway at Angelfish Creek and enter Hawk Channel to proceed to Largo Sound. Enter Largo Sound through South Sound Creek. Park staff supervise this anchorage, which is completely sheltered in any weather. Call on VHF channel 16 to reserve a mandatory mooring buoy in the southwest portion of the sound; anchoring is prohibited. A nominal fee for the moorings entitles boaters to full use of park facilities and its pump-out station. The reefs of John Pennekamp Coral Reef State Park shine brighter than others in the Keys. More sun filters through the shallow water, causing the coral to flourish. Much of this reef breaks the surface of the water during low tide.

Butternut Key & Bottle Key

Don't worry. Those baby sharks you see in the waters surrounding Butternut Key won't hurt you. The skittish infants leave this nursery area when they reach 2 to 3 feet in length. Prevailing winds will determine anchorage sites near these islands, which offer good holding ground. On the Florida Bay side of Tavernier, Butternut Key and Bottle Key showcase voluminous birdlife. Roseate spoonbills breed on Bottle Key, feeding upon the tiny killifish of the flats. A pond on the island attracts mallard ducks in the winter.

Cotton Key

Approach Cotton Key from the Intracoastal Waterway. This anchorage, protected from north to southeast winds, offers the best nightlife in the Keys north of Key West. Take your dinghy around the entire island of Upper Matecumbe and the community of Islamorada. Catch the action at the Lorelei or Atlantic's Edge at Cheeca Lodge (see the Restaurants chapter). Check out the fishing charters at Bud n' Mary's Marina (see the Fishing chapter). Stop in at the Islamorada Fish Company and take ready-to-eat stone crabs back to your boat for a private sunset celebration (see the Specialty Foods, Cafes & Markets chapter). Dinghy through Whale Harbor Channel to the Islamorada Sand Bar, which at low tide becomes an island beach. And, if you'd just like to commune with nature, the forested northeast section of Upper Matecumbe Key hosts a rookery for good bird-watching. **Note:** There is a no-motor zone on the tidal flat.

Lignumvitae Key

Government-owned Lignumvitae Key stands among the tallest of the Keys, at 17 to 18 feet above sea level. A virgin hammock sprinkled with lignum vitae trees re-creates the feeling of the Keys of yesteryear, before mahogany forests were cut and sold to Bahamian shipbuilders. From 1919 to 1953 the Matheson family, of chemical company notoriety, owned the island, where they built a large home and extensive gardens of rare plantings. Hug the northwest side of the island for good anchorage in east to southeast winds. Dinghy to the Lignumvitae Key dock for guided tours conducted by the state parks service. You can also dinghy through Indian Key Channel to historic Indian Key (see the Attractions chapter). Nearby Shell Key almost disappears at high tide, so exercise caution. Pods of playful dolphins romp in Lignumvitae Basin, and a sighting of lumbering sea turtles is not unusual. But be sure to bait a hook—fishing is prolific.

Matecumbe Bight

If winds are not good for anchoring near Lignumvitae, Matecumbe Bight provides good holding ground, except in a north wind. Two miles south, Channel Five—east of Long Key—offers a good crossover between Florida Bay and Hawk Channel for large sailboats. Strong currents run in the channel beneath the bridge, which is a fixed span with a 65-foot overhead clearance.

Long Key Bight

Anchor in Long Key Bight, which is accessed via Hawk Channel oceanside or through Channel Five from the Intracoastal Waterway. Bordering Long Key State Park—a 300-acre wilderness area with a good campground, tables, and grills—the bight is protected yet open. Legendary author Zane Grey angled at the former Long Key Fishing Club during the days of Flagler's railroad. Beachcomb for washed-up treasure on the southeast shores of Long Key.

Boot Key Harbor

Boot Key Harbor in Marathon serves as a good, safe port in a bad blow, but, crowded with liveaboards, it is a bit like anchoring out in Times Square. Enter this fully protected harbor from Sister's Creek or at the western entrance near the beginning of the Seven Mile Bridge. Moser Channel goes under the hump of the Seven Mile Bridge, creating a 65-foot clearance. The draw-span of the old bridge has been removed, but the rest remains. A portion on the Marathon end now functions as the driveway to Pigeon Key (see the Attractions chapter). A stretch on the Bahia Honda end is maintained for bridge fishing and is referred to locally as the "longest fishing pier in the world." The Moser Channel and the Bahia Honda Channel (with 20-foot clearance) are the last crossover spots in the Keys. You must decide at Marathon if you will travel the Atlantic route or via the gulf to Key West. If you need fuel, note that the marina at Sunshine Key is the last bayside marina until Key West.

Big Spanish Channel Area

Leave all traces of civilization behind and head out the Big Spanish Channel toward the out-islands. Proceed with care, for this remote sprinkling of tiny keys is part of the Great White Heron National Wildlife Refuge. Obey no-entry, no-motor, and idle-speed zones. Get your Florida bird guide out of the cabin and count the species.

Little Spanish Key

The western side of Little Spanish Key provides the best protection from northeast to southeast winds. Explore the surrounding

clear waters by dinghy, where the endangered green turtles, which weigh between 150 and 450 pounds, have been spotted feeding on sea grass. Catch your limit of snapper, and share your bounty with the friendly pelicans.

Newfound Harbor

Newfound Harbor—formed by the Newfound Harbor Keys and the southern extension of Big Pine Key—stars as the premier oceanside harbor between Marathon and Key West. Dinghy to exquisite Little Palm Island, the setting for the film PT-109, the story of John F. Kennedy's Pacific experience during World War II. Newfound Harbor lies within easy reach of Looe Key National Marine Sanctuary, a spur and groove coral reef ecosystem popular with divers and snorkelers.

KEY WEST & BEYOND

Welcome to the ultimate cruising destination: Key West. Full of history and histrionics, this vibrant, intoxicating port pumps the adrenaline, pushes the envelope, and provides a rowdy good time for all. And when you signal a turn back into the slow lane again, dust off your charts and head out to the wild beyond of the Dry Tortugas, the end of the line.

Marinas

All of our suggested marinas take transient boaters, but the multiplicity of celebrated special events in Key West dictates that you prudently reserve a slip as far in advance as possible. You may assume unless otherwise stated that all our recommended marinas supply hookups for both 30-amp and 50-amp service as well as freshwater.

Some marinas impose a minimum charge. Key West offers extensive self-provisioning facilities ranging from supermarkets to gourmet take-out shops (see the Specialty Foods, Cafes & Markets chapter). The city also supports a variety of good marine mechanics, which the marina dockmasters will contact on your behalf should the need arise. Contact the dockmaster on VHF channel 16 for directions and read your charts closely.

A&B MARINA
700 Front St.
(305) 294-2535 or (800) 223-8352
aandbmarina.com

A&B Marina is situated in the heart of Old Town, right in the middle of all the action. Most of its 50 transient slips will accommodate vessels with up to 7-foot drafts. A&B offers dockage for vessels up to 140 feet in length. The marina maintains a diesel fuel dock and has a convenience store, air-conditioned shower facilities, a laundry room, and the Commodore Waterfront Restaurant and Alonzo's Oyster Bar. A&B Lobster House, upstairs, has been feeding hungry cruisers since 1947 and still welcomes one and all. People-watching is great from the dockside bar. A&B Marina is accessed from the Atlantic via the Main Ship Channel (Southeast Channel), at markers nos. 24 and 25. From the gulf take the Northwest Channel to the Main Ship Channel.

THE GALLEON RESORT AND MARINA
619 Front St.
(305) 296-7711 or (800) 544-3030
galleonresort.com

The carbonated excitement of Duval Street pulsates only a few blocks away, but the ambience at the Galleon remains unhurried. The 91 dockage slips will accommodate vessels up to 140 feet and 9-foot drafts. One 50-amp service is included in the daily dockage rate, but you can secure another for an additional fee. Fuel is available in Key West Bight or at Conch Harbor Marina. The Galleon indulges you with all the amenities and then some: shower and restroom facilities, a laundry, pump-out station, deli, swimming pool, tiki bar, private beach, fitness center, sauna, patio, and picnic tables. And if that is not enough, book an afternoon of snorkeling at the on-premises dive shop or plan a fishing expedition with one of the charter boats at the dock. Rent a moped or bicycle and explore Key West, or just kick back and relax on the sundeck. Pets are welcome in the marina but not on the adjoining resort property. The Galleon is accessed via the Main Ship Channel at marker no. 24.

KEY WEST BIGHT MARINA
Key West Historic Seaport,
201 William St.
(305) 809-3983
keywestcity.com

Situated in the heart of the Key West Historic Seaport, Key West Bight Marina has 33 deepwater transient slips that will accommodate vessels up to 140 feet in length with a maximum draft of 12 feet. Dockage includes 30-, 50-, and 100-amp power; water and phone hookups; 24-hour security; a pump-out station; trash removal; ice; and bath, shower, and laundry facilities. Docking rates are the most reasonably priced in Key West. Key West Bight Marina is accessed by entering Key West waters via the Northwest Channel to the Main Ship Channel to red marker no. 4 from the Gulf of Mexico, or from the Atlantic via Hawk Channel to the Main Ship Channel to red marker no. 4.

🔍 Close-up

Lighthouses of the Florida Keys

Nostalgic memories are aroused when you think of lighthouses. Rugged, isolated, beautiful in their strength, and haunting in their history, these beacons of light hold the imagination of anyone interested in sea navigation.

General George Gordon Meade's first career may have been a commander of Union forces, but his interest and real love was in pharology. His genius in marine engineering led him to Delaware Bay and the building of lighthouses along that body of water. Known for his screw-pile design in lighthouses, most of his structures remain standing today. Meade came to the Florida Keys, where he designed and built Carysfort, Sombrero, Rebecca, and Sand Key Lighthouses. To end his dignified career, he went on to design the beautiful Fairmount Park in Philadelphia.

Carysfort Reef Lighthouse: Placed on the National Register of Historic Places in 1984, this red lighthouse was built in 1825 and first lit in 1852. Carysfort is the oldest iron screw-pile lighthouse still functioning in the US and the first of this type in the Florida Keys. Named for the HMS *Carysfort,* which ran into the reef in 1770, and automated in 1960, it stands at 112 feet and is shaped in a skeletal octagonal pyramid.

Alligator Reef Lighthouse: This still-functioning lighthouse was built in 1873 and sits 4 miles east of Indian Key off Islamorada. Automated in 1963, this old beauty is an iron pile with a platform and painted white and black. The height is 136 feet and it is skeletal in its shape.

Sombrero Key Lighthouse: Built in 1858 in the skeletal octagonal pyramidal design, brown in color, and automated in 1960, Sombrero still helps boats navigate the waters off Marathon. Not open to the public, this 160-foot lighthouse is operated by the US Coast Guard.

American Shoal Lighthouse: Built in 1880, this lighthouse sits in the Atlantic off Sugarloaf Key. The brown-and-white sentinel was automated in 1963. It reaches a height of 103 feet and was constructed in the skeletal octagonal pyramidal shape.

THE WESTIN KEY WEST RESORT AND MARINA
245 Front St.
(305) 294-4000 or (866) 837-4250
westinkeywestresort.com
The Westin Key West Resort and Marina offers transients all the perks of its lavish property: pool, hot tub, and weight room as well as Bistro 245 and Latitudes Beach Cafe on Sunset Key. About one-quarter of the marina's dock space is available to transients.

The south basin offers floating slips that accommodate vessels with 30-foot drafts; the north basin's 600 feet of rigid dock space handles craft with 15-foot drafts or less. Make reservations up to 6 months in advance to dock at the Westin Key West Resort and Marina. Only 1 block off famed Duval Street, its location can't be beat and it fills up quickly. In addition to daily transient rates, a power fee is levied. Television hookup is included in the dockage fee, and

Key West Lighthouse: Located at 938 Whitehead St. in historic Old Town, this 86-foot black-and-white structure is a real gem. Built in 1847 for the purpose of helping ships navigate the perilous reefs off the Lower Keys, it was listed on the National Register of Historic Places in 1998. It was automated in 1915, then deactivated in 1969. Built in the West Indian vernacular style, it now is open as a museum and operated by the Monroe County and City of Key West Historical Society.

Loggerhead Key Lighthouse: Used as an active aid for navigating Dry Tortugas National Park off Key West, this black-and-white structure was built in 1858 and was automated in 1988. Standing 157 feet, the lighthouse is operated by the National Park Service and is open to the public.

Tortugas Harbor Lighthouse: In Garden Key, off Key West, proudly stands this hexagonal-shaped black beauty that is operated by the National Park Service and open to the public. Built in 1876, activated in 1912, and deactivated in 1921, the lighthouse sits in Dry Tortugas National Park and is only accessible by boat or seaplane.

Sand Key Lighthouse: Seven miles southwest off Key West, this lighthouse with its red and black colors stands 120 feet out of the water. Built in 1826, automated in 1938, and deactivated from 1989 to 1998, it's not open to the public. Built in the square skeletal with center column design, it is listed on the National Register of Historic Places.

Rebecca Shoal Lighthouse: The original skeletal iron structure was assembled in Key West, disassembled, then erected on-site in 1886. The structure was named after lighthouse keeper Rebecca Flaherty and her five children, who were killed in the 1836 hurricane. Forty-three miles off Key West, where the Gulf of Mexico and the Atlantic meet, this is the most remote of all the lighthouses on our list. Totally destroyed by Hurricane Charley in August 2004, all that remains today is a small beacon with an effective beam range seen 9 miles away. You pass this marker on the way to the Dry Tortugas.

the requisite laundry, shower, and restroom requirements are supplied on the premises. Fuel may be obtained half a mile up the channel at Key West Bight. The Westin Key West Resort and Marina owns the private offshore Sunset Key. Guests of the hotel or marina may take a day trip to the island and enjoy its pristine beach, away from the fray of Key West. The Westin Key West Marina is accessed via the Main Ship Channel at red marker no. 14 if coming from the south, or, from the north, via the Northwest Channel at green marker no. 17.

Anchoring Out

The highway may stop in Key West, but the path to adventure continues into the sunset. The Dry Tortugas, the brightest gems in the necklace, mark the real end of the line in the Florida Keys. Once you leave Key West Harbor, you join the ranks of the swashbucklers who have abandoned the safety of civilization to explore the vast unknown. Be sure you know the range and capabilities of your craft, because only self-sufficient cruising vessels can make the 140-nautical-mile trek to the Dry Tortugas and back. There is no fuel, freshwater, provisioning, or facilities of any kind once you leave Key West. Unpredictable foul weather could keep you trapped at sea for days, so make sure you are fueled for 200 miles, and stock the larder for extenuating circumstances.

Key West

If you want to anchor out in busy Key West Harbor, look for a spot west of Fleming Key in about 10 to 15 feet of water. You'll find less current, good holding ground, and less fishing-vessel traffic than around Wisteria Island. The municipal dinghy dock at the foot of Simonton Street is the only official place to land your dinghy, but you might want to arrange secured short-term dockage for your dinghy from one of the marina dockmasters.

Boca Grande Key

A string of shoals and keys snakes west from Key West, offering unparalleled diving and fishing opportunities. Beyond Man and Woman Keys—popular snorkeling spots—Boca Grande Key offers a good day anchorage on the northwestern side with a beautiful white-sand beach. The current is too swift to anchor overnight, but you can snorkel the small wreck visible just north of the island. Be alert to the constantly shifting shoals around the entrance channel. Note also that this island is a turtle nesting ground—all or parts of it are off-limits during specific times of the year, and fines are possible.

Marquesas Keys

About 24 miles from Key West, a broken collar of low-lying, beach-belted islands forms the Marquesas Keys. If you pass Mooney Harbor Key on your way into the inner sanctum, watch for coral heads about 1,100 yards offshore. Prevailing winds will determine at which side to anchor, but you should be able to achieve a protected anchorage. Many a ship crashed on the coral heads in this area, leaving interesting wrecks, but check with the Coast Guard before you dive, because the US Navy has been known to use the area west of the Marquesas as a bombing and strafing range. Explore the big rookery of frigatebirds or take aim with a little spearfishing. This pit stop on the way to the Dry Tortugas rates as an end point in itself. **Note:** A 300-foot no-motor zone is established around the three smallest islands, a 300-foot no-access buffer zone is established around one mangrove island, and an idle-speed-only/no-wake zone is established in the southwest tidal creek.

Dry Tortugas

Open water stretches like a hallucination from the Marquesas to our southernmost national park, the Dry Tortugas. Ponce de León named these islands the Tortugas—Spanish for "turtles"—in 1513, presumably because the waters teemed with sea turtles, which he consumed as fresh meat. Lack of freshwater rendered the islands dry.

The first sight of the massive brick fortress of Fort Jefferson, the colorful history of which began in 1846, is breathtaking (see the Attractions chapter). Unparalleled diving exists in these unsullied waters. Colors appear more brilliant because the waters are clearer than those bordering the inhabited Keys. The entire area is a no-take zone, so don't be alarmed if you spot a prehistoric-size lobster or jewfish. Be sure to snorkel the underwater nature trail. From your dinghy, watch for the nesting sooty and noddy terns in their Bush Key sanctuary (landing is forbidden).

Fishing and anchoring to anything except mooring buoys are strictly prohibited in the 46-square-mile Research Natural Area (RNA) in Dry Tortugas National Park. Overnight anchoring can only occur on sand bottoms within 1 nautical mile of the Harbor Light at Fort Jefferson. Combined with the Tortugas Ecological Reserve and now the RNA, this is the largest no-take marine reserve in the continental US. The popular fishing area in the Dry Tortugas—the anchorage around Fort Jefferson and Garden Key—remain open for recreational fishing.

Loggerhead Key
Just beyond Garden Key dozes Loggerhead Key, called the prettiest beach in the Keys by those in the know. A good day anchorage with a legion of interesting coral, this is literally the end of the line for the Florida Keys. Nothing but 900 miles of water lies between this point and the Mexican coast. Hope you remembered to fuel up in Key West!

FISHING

Angling in the Florida Keys approaches a religion to many. The very essence of the Keys is embodied in gleaming packages of skin and scales, for a day fishing the cerulean waters that lap our islands creates a sensory memory not quickly forgotten. Long after the last bait is cast, tales of captured prizes or the ones that got away evoke visions of the sun, the sea, and the smell of the salt air.

Anglers fish here with an intensity rarely seen anywhere else in the US . . . the world, even. Eavesdrop on a conversation anywhere in the Keys, and someone will be talking about fishing. As you drive down the Overseas Highway and look out at our acres of shimmering waters, you will feel an overwhelming urge to join in the battle of power and wits—fish against angler—that makes the Keys so special.

The Florida Keys have more than 1,000 species of fish; most are edible, all are interesting. To pursue our bonefish, permit, tarpon, snook, or any other species, you will need a saltwater fishing license (see the Fishing Licenses section in this chapter). You must obey catch and season restrictions and size limits. These regulations change often. Ask for an up-to-date listing when you purchase your fishing license.

The Florida Keys fall within the boundaries of the Florida Keys National Marine Sanctuary, created by the federal government in 1990 to protect the resources of our marine ecosystem. And while, for the most part, visitors freely swim, dive, snorkel, boat, fish, or recreate on our waters, some regulations took effect in July 1997 to guide these activities. Refer to the Boating chapter for information on these regulations before you venture into our waters. For a complete copy of the regulations and marine coordinates of the areas, contact the sanctuary office, (305) 292-0311, or check their website, floridakeys.noaa.gov.

CATCH-AND-RELEASE ETHICS

Preserve our natural resources. "A fish is too valuable to be caught only once," the US Department of Commerce, the National Oceanic and Atmospheric Administration, and the National Marine Fisheries Service maintain. We agree. The spirit behind the catch-and-release policy is to enjoy the hunt and the score, but take a photograph of the fish home with you, not the quarry itself.

Taxidermists do not need the actual fish to prepare a mount for you; they only need the approximate measurements. Take home only those food fish you plan to eat.

To properly release a fish, keep the fish in the water and handle it very little whenever possible. Dislodge the hook quickly with a hook removal tool, backing the hook out the opposite way it went in. If the hook can't

FISHING

be removed quickly, cut the leader close to the mouth. Hold the fish by the bottom jaw or lip—not the gills—with a wet hand or glove so that you don't damage its mucus or scales. Have your photo taken with the fish, then cradle the tired fish, rocking it back and forth in the water until it is able to swim away under its own power. This increases the oxygen flow through its gills, reviving the fish and thereby augmenting its chances for survival against a barracuda or shark.

WHERE TO FISH

To introduce you to our complex watery ecosystem and the species of fish dwelling therein, we have divided fishing destinations into four distinct sections: the flats, the backcountry, the blue water, and the bridges.

The Flats

The continental shelf is nature's gift to the Florida Keys. Stretching from the shoreline like a layer of rippled fudge on a marble slab, it lingers for many shallow miles before plunging to the depths of the blue water. In the Keys we rather reverently call this area the flats. Waters ranging from mere inches to several feet in depth cover most of the flats, but some areas completely surface during low tide, exposing themselves to the air and intense sunlight. Changing winds, tides, temperatures, and barometric pressure ensure that conditions in the flats fluctuate constantly.

An unenlightened observer might think the flats uninteresting, for most of this watery acreage is covered with dense turtle grass, shell-less sand, or muddy muck. But far from being a wasteland, the flats are the feeding grounds and nursery for a city of marine families whose members inspire dramatic

tales of daring and conquest from every person who has ever baited a hook here.

The 4,000 square miles of flats, from Key Biscayne to Key West and beyond, yield a trio of prize game fish—bonefish, permit, and tarpon—which, when caught in one day, we refer to as the Grand Slam. And keeping company in the same habitat are the bonus fish—barracuda and shark—that regularly accommodate anglers with exciting runs and fights. Fishing the flats is really a combination of angling and hunting, for you must first see and stalk the fish before you ever cast the waters. The hunt for bonefish, permit, and tarpon requires patience and unique angling skills, but most essentially, you must be at the right place at the right time.

We cannot even begin to teach you how to fish for these formidable fighters of the flats in this chapter. You should hire a professional guide, for which there is no substitute—at least while you are a novice. Guides know the local waters well and keep detailed records of where to find fish under every condition, saving you precious hours and money in the pursuit of your mission (see the Guides & Charters section of this chapter). But we will introduce you to the exciting species you will encounter on our flats, relate their personalities, tattle about their habits, and point you in the right direction so you can learn all you wish to know and share in the angling experience of a lifetime: fishing the flats in the Florida Keys.

First in the see-stalk-cast sequence so important in fishing the skinny waters of the flats is the visible interpretation of the watery hallucination under the surface. To see the fish of the flats, you must have polarized sunglasses to cut the sun's glare so that you can concentrate on looking through your

177

reflection on the top of the water to the shallow bottom. Under the water, fish often look like bluish shadows, or they may appear as indistinct shadings that simply look different from the waters surrounding them.

Most waters of the flats in the Keys are fished from a shallow-draft skiff, or flats boat, although you can wade out from shore in many areas if you prefer. Never motor onto a flat; the fish can hear the engine noise and spook easily. Use an electric trolling motor or, better yet, pole in, using a push pole. A push pole is a fiberglass or graphite dowel, 16 to 20 feet long, with a V-crotch on one end for traversing the soft bottom of the flats and a straight end on the other for staking out. Using it requires body power and coordination and more than a little practice. A flats boat has a raised poling platform that gives the poler or guide a height advantage to more readily distinguish the fish from its shadowy surroundings, in preparation for an accurate cast.

At the turn of the tide, the fish begin to move into the flats, grazing like sheep in a pasture. Guides know where the fish congregate during an incoming (flood) tide and an outgoing (ebb) tide. While it may prove dangerous for the fish to come up on the flats—they expose themselves to predators—the concentration of food is too enticing for them to resist. The fish prefer feeding during the low, incoming tide; the food is still easy to find, but they won't risk becoming stranded on the flats.

i Former president George H. W. Bush once landed a monster 130-pound tarpon in Lignumvitae Channel off Islamorada. After a 45-minute fight with this trophy catch, he tagged the fish and released it back into the wild.

Bonefish: Phantom of the Flats

A sighting of the glistening forked tail of the Gray Ghost—alias of the famed bonefish (*Albula vulpes*) haunting our flats—has been known to elevate the blood pressure of even the most seasoned Keys angler to celestial heights. This much-respected, skittish silver bullet is considered the worthiest of all opponents, a wily, suspicious street fighter, here one moment, gone the next. The bonefish's superior eyesight, acute hearing, keen sense of smell, and boundless speed routinely befuddle anglers, some of whom dedicate their lives to thwarting the fish's Houdini-like escape attempts.

You can spot a bonefish three ways: tailing, mudding, or cruising. When the slender, silvery bonefish feeds, it looks like a washerwoman leaning over to get her laundry out of the basket—head down, bottom up. The fork of the tail will break the surface of the water—a tailing fish. The bonefish feeds into the current because its food source is delivered in the drift. As the fish puts its mouth down into the sand and silt, rooting around on the bottom of the flats, looking for shrimps, crabs, and other crustaceans, the water clouds up. This is called "making a mud." As the mudding bonefish continues feeding, the current takes the cloudy water away so it can see its prey once again. Bonefish require water temperatures of 70 degrees and higher for feeding on the flats.

Spotting a cruising fish takes some practice. Look for "nervous water." The bonefish pushes a head wake as it swims, which sometimes shows as an inconsistency on the surface of the water. On other occasions, a mere movement by the fish underwater will cause the surface water to appear altered. Most of the time that the bonefish is cruising, however, it is swimming in deeper water; you will have to spot it. The back and sides of the bonefish are so silvery, they act as a mirror. The fish swims right on the bottom of the flats in 8 or more inches of water, and the sun shining through the water causes the bottom to reflect off the sides of the fish. So if you think you have seen a ripple of weeds, the image may actually be a bonefish.

The best bait for bonefishing is live shrimp. A guide with an experienced eye will put you on the fish by calling out directions like the hands of a clock. The bow of the boat will always be 12 o'clock. You will be instructed by the guide to look in a direction—for instance, 2 o'clock—and, at a specified distance, to spot the bonefish in preparation for a cast. The cast is the most crucial part of successfully hooking a bonefish. You should be able to cast 30 feet quickly and accurately. A cast that places the bait too close to the fish will spook it and cause the bonefish to dart away at breakneck speed. If the bait is cast too far away, the fish won't find it at all. The bait should land 2 to 3 feet in front of the fish and be allowed to drift to the ocean floor.

Many times the bonefish will smell the bait prior to seeing it because the fish is downcurrent of the bait and swimming into the current. The bonefish begins to dart back and forth and goes in circles, looking for the scented prey. Once the fish locates the source of the scent, it tends to suck in the bait. You, the angler, must make sure there is no slack in the line and that your rod tip is low to the water. Then firmly but gently lift up to set the hook. Hold on tight and raise your rod straight up in the air, holding your arms as high above your head as possible. Once the fish realizes something is wrong—that it's hooked—it will peel away

in an electrifying run, taking out 100 to 150 yards of line in a heartbeat. This whole process—from sighting to hooking—explodes in adrenaline-pumping nanoseconds. Ten to 30 minutes later, after the bonefish makes several pulse-pounding sprints, you can reel in the tired fish to the side of the skiff, where the guide will photograph both victor and spoils. Then quickly release the bonefish so that it may rest up and thrill another angler on yet another day (see the previous section in this chapter on catch-and-release ethics).

i Please watch for manatees in the waters of the Florida Keys. If you see one of these gentle creatures and it appears to be injured, call (800) DIAL-FMP (342-5367) or *FMP (*367), or use VHF channel 16. Stay in deep water and avoid running your motor over sea-grass beds. Obey speed zone and sanctuary signs. Look, but don't touch; please do not feed or give the manatees water. For more information, visit savethemanatee.org.

Bonefishing is a major playing card of the fishing deck we so lavishly deal here in the Florida Keys. Bonefish usually range in size from 5 to 10 pounds, but the size of this fish belies its strength. A 5-pound bonefish fights like a 20-pound wannabe. The Keys are the only place in the continental US where an angler can fish for bonefish. Locals boast that the Keys have the biggest and best-educated bonefish this side of the Gulf Stream. Expect bonefish to grace our flats during Apr, May, June, Sept, Oct, and occasionally into Nov. Cool weather and cold fronts push them into deeper waters from Dec through Mar. The hot weather of July and Aug drives them to cooler, deeper waters as well, although some will stay all year.

Permit: Ultimate Flats Challenge

Though sharing the same waters as the bonefish and stalked in the same manner, the permit (*Trachinotus falcatus*) proves to be a more elusive catch. Spooky, skittish, and stubborn, this finicky eater, which can take out line like a long-distance runner, is so difficult to catch that most anglers never even see one. Three or four times the size of a bonefish—averaging 20 to 30 pounds—the silvery, platter-shaped permit forages in the safety of slightly deeper waters, not risking exposure of its iridescent blue-green back. Its sickle-shaped, black-tipped tail pokes out of the water as it feeds on bottom-dwelling crabs and shrimps, often tipping off its location. The permit's shell-crushing jaws, rubbery and strong, can exert 3,000 pounds of pressure per square inch, enabling it to masticate small clams and crustaceans and dash many an angler's expectations.

The best days to find permit are those glorious, cloudless sunny smiles from Mother Nature, cooled by a slight ocean breeze. Schools of permit will graze the top of the flats and near rocky shorelines in higher tides and poke around in basins and channels during low tides, searching for a meal of small crabs and crustaceans. They often hover above submerged objects such as lobster pots. If you pass above an area littered with sea urchins, be on the lookout for permit searching for gourmet fixings.

Not easily duped, a tailing permit will make you forget all about a bonefish because, if you manage to hook one, you've got a street brawl on your hands that could last an hour or more. When hooked, the permit instinctively heads for deeper water.

In the transition zone between the flats and the blue water, the permit will try to cut the line by weaving through coral heads, sea fans, and sponges. The fish will pause in its run to bang its head on the bottom or rub its mouth in the sand to try to dislodge the hook. If you manage to follow the permit through this obstacle course, you may actually catch it a quarter mile from where you hooked it.

Tarpon: The Silver King

It is little wonder that the tarpon (*Megalops atlanticus*) is dubbed the "silver king," for it wins 9 out of every 10 encounters with an angler. The tarpon's lunglike gas bladder allows it to take a gulp of atmospheric air from time to time, enabling the fish to thrive in oxygen-depleted water. This magnificent superhero of the sea, ranging in size from 50 to 200 pounds, will break the surface and "roll" with a silvery splash as it steals an oxygen jolt and powers on for an intensified fight. The tarpon frequents the deeper flats of 4 to 8 feet or hangs out in the rapidly moving waters of channels, or under one of the many bridges in the Keys. Live mullet, pinfish, and crabs will entice this hungry but lazy despot, which faces into the current, effortlessly waiting for baitfish to be dragged into its mouth. The tarpon's toothless lower jaw protrudes from its head like an overdeveloped underbite, filled with bony plate that crushes its intended dinner.

The successful angler will use heavy tackle and a needle-sharp hook. Hold the rod with the tip at 12 o'clock and wait. When the fish strikes and eats the bait, let the rod tip drop with the pressure, giving minimal resistance. When the rod is parallel to the water and the line is tight, set the hook through the bony structure with a series of short, very strong jabs. Once hooked, the stunned fish runs and leaps repeatedly, with reckless abandon, entering the water headfirst, tail-first, sideways, belly-flopped, or upside down—an Olympian confounding its rod-clutching judge. It is important to have a quick-release anchor when fishing for tarpon because, once the action starts, you must be on your way, chasing the cavorting fish. Be prepared to duke it out, for it is often a standoff as to who tires first, the angler or the tarpon.

Exciting to catch on light tackle is the schooling baby tarpon, which, at up to 50 pounds, sprints and practices its aerobatics like its older siblings. Look for baby tarpon in channels and in harbors.

Tarpon season generally begins in Apr and continues until mid-July. Because the tarpon is primarily a nocturnal feeder, the best fishing is at daybreak and dusk or during the night. This magnificent creature grows very slowly, not reaching maturity until it is at least 13 years old. Since the tarpon is not an edible fish, some people consider killing it akin to murder. If you want a simulated mount of your catch, estimate the length and girth for the taxidermist. Take a photograph with your prize, and release the fish quickly and carefully.

Barracuda: Tiger of the Flats

Look for the barracuda (*Sphyraena barracuda*), which packs a wallop of a fight, anywhere the water is about 2 feet deep, especially grassy-bottom areas. This toothy, intelligent predator has keen eyesight and moves swiftly. The barracuda's inquisitive nature causes it to make investigative passes by your boat, where it is oft tempted to sample your baited offerings intended for other species. Pilchards make good bait for

catching barracuda. Cut off part of the tail fin of a pilchard before baiting the hook. This injury causes the bait to swim erratically, attracting the insatiable 'cuda. When casting to a barracuda, your bait should land at least 10 feet beyond the fish and be retrieved across its line of sight. A cast that lands the bait too close—5 feet or less—will frighten the 'cuda into deep water. If you are using artificial baits such as a tube lure, be sure to retrieve the bait briskly to pique the barracuda's interest.

Humans eat barracuda in some tropical areas, but not in the Keys. The flesh is sometimes toxic, and it is not worth the risk. You are better off quickly releasing the fish so that it might fight another round.

Sharks

Several shark species (order *Selachii*) roam our flats looking for a free meal. Sand sharks and nurse sharks are relatively docile, but bonnetheads and black-tip sharks readily will take a shrimp or crab intended for a bonefish or permit, putting up a determined fight. If you happen to catch a shark, wear heavy gloves and cut the leader with pliers. The shark will swim away and will be able to work the hook loose from its mouth. Digestive acids and salt water will corrode the hook in mere days, causing the fish no permanent harm.

The Backcountry

When Mother Nature bestowed the prolific oceanside saltwater flats on the Florida Keys, she didn't stop at our rocky isles. As the Gulf of Mexico meets mainland Florida, a lively ecosystem flourishes in a body of water known as Florida Bay. Hundreds of tiny uninhabited keys dot the watery landscape, referred to locally as the backcountry.

Loosely bordered by the Keys—from Key Largo to Long Key—and Everglades National Park, backcountry waters offer a diverse habitat of sea grass or mudflats, mangrove islets, and sandy basins. The southernmost outpost of Everglades National Park is at Flamingo, which maintains a marina, boat rentals, houseboats, and guide services.

You'll usually be able to find snappers, sheepshead, ladyfish, and the occasional shark along the grass-bed shorelines, the open bays, and in the small creeks flowing out of the Everglades. The silver king, the mighty tarpon, frequents backcountry creeks and channels, flats, and basins and is rumored to be particularly partial to the Sandy Key Basin in the summer months. But beckoning anglers to these waters is another sporting trio—redfish, snook, and spotted sea trout—which when caught in one day is boasted far and wide as the Backcountry Grand Slam.

Redfish, aka Red Drum

The coppery redfish, or red drum (*Sciaenops oceallatus*), all but disappeared in the 1980s from overfishing, but conservation measures by the state of Florida and the federal government caused a rebirth. This fast-growing fish migrates offshore to spawn when it reaches about 30 inches (4 years). It is a protected species in federal waters. Regulations open a scant 9-inch window for anglers to keep 1 captured redfish per day, which must measure between 18 and 27 inches. All redfish measuring less than 18 inches or more than 27 inches must be released, always. Because it grows so rapidly, the redfish is exposed to harvest for only one year of its life. It is highly coveted for eating, put on the culinary map by New Orleans's Chef

Prudhomme and his famed Cajun blackening process.

As with fishing for bonefish or permit, you will look for redfish on an incoming tide, when they will be rooting for crabs on the shoals and flats. As the water gets higher, the fish work their way up on the flats. You will want to use a shallow-draft boat with a push pole or electric trolling motor and be prepared with polarized sunglasses for enhanced vision in spotting a tailing fish. You'll hear experienced anglers say, "A tailing red is a feeding red." The reddish, squared-off profile of the redfish's tail can be spotted from several hundred feet. When the fish is really hungry, you may see its entire tail exposed, even the shady eyelike spot at the base. Cruising redfish will push a head wake similar to that of a bonefish.

Although a redfish isn't nearly as easily spooked as a bonefish, you should still stay as far away from the fish as possible while still casting a right-on winner. Live shrimps or crabs will entice the fish, which, with poor eyesight, hits almost any bait coming its way. The hooked redfish often sticks around and puts up a hard fight. Attracted to its discomfort, other redfish swim to the scene of the accident. You can often catch another redfish if you can get another baited hook into the water fast enough.

The backcountry of the Florida Keys is one of the few places in the world where you can fish for redfish year-round, although they prefer cooler waters. It is illegal, however, to buy or sell our native redfish, and they must be kept whole until you reach shore. You are forbidden to gig, spear, or snatch the red drum.

Snook

The second member of the Backcountry Grand Slam, the snook (*Centropomus undecimalis*) likes to tuck against the shady mangrove shorelines to feed on baitfish that congregate in the maze of gnarled roots. A falling tide will force the baitfish out of their rooted cages and into deeper holes, where the snook can get at them. But the baitfish aren't the only ones getting snookered. This cagey, sought-after game fish, once hooked, has buffaloed many an angler, vanishing back into the mangroves and snapping its tenuous connection to the rod-wielder like a brittle string. If you win the battle of the bushes or find the snook pushing water in the open or at the mouth of a creek, you still haven't won the war. Once hooked, the snook thrashes about violently, trying to dislodge the barbed intruder. Its hard, abrasive mouth and knife-sharp gill covers can dispense with your line in a flash.

This silvery, long-bodied fish—thickened around the middle—faces its foes with a depressed snout and a protruding lower jaw. A distinctive lateral, black racing stripe extends the length of its body, all the way to its divided dorsal fin. The snook is unable to tolerate waters colder than 60 degrees. And while some anglers feel snook is the best-tasting fish in the Keys, Florida law mandates that in Monroe County you may not fish for snook from Dec 15 through Jan 31, nor in the months of May, June, July, and Aug. The fish must measure between 26 and 34 inches. The limits is 1 snook per person per day. Snook may not be bought or sold, and you must purchase a $2 snook stamp for your saltwater fishing license in order to fish for them.

Spotted Sea Trout, aka Spotted Weakfish

Even though this backcountry prize is called a weakfish, it can be a challenging catch. The weakfish moniker derives from its clan's easily torn mouth membranes. The spotted sea trout (*Cynoscion nebulosus*)—actually a member of the fine-flavored drum family—nevertheless resembles a trout, with shimmering iridescent tones of silver, green, blue, and bronze.

The sea trout's lower jaw, unlike a true trout's, projects upward, and a pair of good-size canine teeth protrude from the upper jaw. These predatory, opportunistic feeders enjoy a smorgasbord of offerings but are particularly fond of live shrimp. The sea trout makes a distinctive splash and popping sound when it feeds on a drift of shrimp. These weakfish are easily spotted in the shallow backcountry waters, popular with light-tackle enthusiasts who enjoy the stalk-and-cast challenge.

Sea trout prefer temperatures between 60 and 70 degrees. Each must measure at least 12 inches to be fished, and the catch is limited to 4 fish per person per day. They are highly ranked as a table food because they are so delicately flavored, but the flesh spoils rapidly. Ice it quickly, and fillet the fish immediately upon returning to shore.

The Blue Water

The Gulf Stream, or Florida Current, moves through the Florida Straits south of Key West and flows northward, along the entire coast of Florida, at about 4 knots. This tropical river, 25 to 40 miles wide, maintains warm temperatures, hosting a piscatorial bounty from the prolific Caribbean that constantly restocks the waters of the Keys. The blue water encompasses deep water from the reef to the edge of the Gulf Stream and is particularly prolific at the humps, which are underwater hills rising from the seafloor. The Islamorada Hump is 13 miles offshore from Islamorada. The West Hump lies 23 miles off-shore from Marathon and rises from a depth of 1,100 feet to 480 feet below the surface.

Blue-water fishing is synonymous with offshore fishing here in the Keys. To an angler, it means big game: billfish, tuna, dolphin, cobia, wahoo, and kingfish. Also offshore, at the edge of the coral reef and the nearshore patch reefs, you will find a pal-ette of bottom fish, snappers, and groupers coveted more for their table value than their fighting prowess, and a grab bag of bonus fish—some good to eat, all fun to catch.

Until you are experienced in our waters, you will need a guide. To troll for big game fish in the blue water, you should book a private charter, which will put you on the fish and supply everything you need, includ-ing the professional expertise of the captain and mate, who know when to hold 'em . . . and when to fold 'em. These charters usually accommodate 6 anglers and, though pricey, provide the most instruction and individual attention. You can divide the cost with 5 other anglers or join with another party and split the tab (see the Guides & Charters sec-tion of this chapter).

Alternately, sign on to a party boat, or head boat, which usually accommodates 50 or more anglers. These boats usually take anglers to the reef for bottom fishing, where you can drop a line and try your luck for snapper, grouper, and even kingfish and some of their sidekicks. Mates on deck untangle lines, answer questions, and even bait your hook. And although it is a little bit like taking the bus during rush hour instead

of a limousine, at $50 per day—rods, tackle, and bait included—a party boat remains the most economical means of fishing offshore. In Key West, try the *Greyhound,* located at Garrison Bight. Call (305) 296-5139 for more information.

Billfish: Marlin & Sailfish

Before you head out to the blue water to hunt for sailfish and marlin, you might want to have a cardiac workup and check your blood pressure because, if your trolled bait takes a hit, it will prove a battle of endurance.

The cobalt-blue marlin (*Makaira nigri-cans*), largest of the Atlantic marlins, migrates away from the equator in warmer months, enigmatically gracing the Keys waters on its way northward. Females of the species often reach trophy proportions—1,000 pounds or more—but males rarely exceed 300 pounds. Tuna and bonito provide the mainstay of the blue marlin's diet, but some blue marlin have been found with young swordfish in their stomachs. Anglers trolling ballyhoo or mul-let have the chance of latching onto a blue marlin, especially in tuna-infested waters. A fighting blue marlin creates a specter of primitive beauty: A creature the size of a baby elephant plunges to the depths, then soars in gravity-defying splendor, only to hammer the water once again and shoot off in a torpedo-like run.

Less often caught in our waters is the white marlin (*Tetrapturus albidus*), which is much smaller than the blue, averaging 50 to 60 pounds and rarely exceeding 150 pounds. Both marlin use their swordlike bills to stun fast-moving fish, which they then consume. Unlike other members of its family, the white marlin's dorsal and anal fins are rounded, not sharply pointed. The upper portion of its body is a brilliant green-blue, abruptly changing to silvery white on the sides and underslung with a white belly. White marlin will strike trolled live bait, feathers, and lures, hitting hard and running fast with repetitive jumps. The white marlin begins its southward migration as the waters of the North Atlantic cool in the autumn.

A shimmering dorsal fin, fanned much higher than the depth of its streamlined steel-blue body, distinguishes the sailfish (*Istiophorus platyperus*) from its billed brethren. Fronted with a long, slender bill, this graceful creature—averaging 7 feet long and 40 pounds in Florida waters—is meant to be captured and released, but stuffed no more. Probably the most popular mount of all time—the flaunted mark of the been-there, done-that crowd—the sailfish, at least in the Florida Keys, is generally allowed to entertain, take a bow, and go back to the dressing room until the next show. Taxidermists now stock fiberglass blanks, so you need only phone in the prized measurements to receive your representative mount.

The migration of the sailfish coincides with that of the snowbirds, those Northerners who spend the frigid months in the balmy Florida Keys. In late autumn and early winter, the sailfish leave the Caribbean and gulf waters and head up the Gulf Stream to the Keys. A fast-growing fish—4 to 5 feet in a year—it seldom lives more than 5 years. Feeding on the surface or at mid-depths on small fish and squid, the sailfish also is amenable to trolled appetizers of outrigger-mounted live mullet or ballyhoo that will wiggle, dive, and skip behind the boat like rats after the Pied Piper. The sailfish, swimming at up to 50 knots, will give you a run for your money, alternating dramatic runs and explosions from the depths with catapults through the air. It delights novice and expert

alike. The inexperienced angler can glory in the pursuit with heavy tackle, while the seasoned veteran can lighten up, creating a new challenge. Both will savor the conquest.

Florida law allows you to keep 1 billfish per day and mandates size limitations. Sailfish must be at least 63 inches; blue marlin, 99 inches; and white marlin, 66 inches. We recommend, however, that you follow the ethical considerations of catch-and-release, recording your conquest on film instead.

Blackfin Tuna

Highly sought by anglers and blue marlin alike, the blackfin tuna (*Thunnus atlanticus*) is set apart from the other six tunas of North America by its totally black finlets. Rarely exceeding 50 pounds, this member of the mackerel family is not as prized as the giant bluefin of North Atlantic waters, but Keys anglers still relish a substantial battle and the bonus of great eating.

Primarily a surface feeder, the blackfin terrorizes baitfish from below, causing them to streak to the surface and skitter out of the water like skipping stones, a move that attracts seabirds. A sighting of diving gulls will tip off the presence of tuna at the feed bag. Blackfin tuna are partial to a chumming of live pilchards but will also attack feathers and lures trolled at high speeds. Tuna fishing on the humps is usually good in the spring months.

Dolphin: Schoolies, Slammers & Bulls

Anyone who has ever seen a rainbow of schooling dolphin (*Coryphaena hippurus*), aka mahi mahi, knows the fish's identity crisis is unfounded. Nothing about this prismatic fish suggests the mammal sharing its name. The dolphinfish resembles a Technicolor cartoon. Its bright green, blue, and

FISHING

yellow wedgelike body looks like the fish just crashed into a paint cabinet, and its high, blunt, pugnacious forehead and Mohawk-style dorsal fin evoke a rowdy, in-your-face persona not wholly undeserved. Once out of the water, however, the brilliant hues ebb like a fading photograph, tingeing sweet victory with fleeting regret.

Second only to billfish and tuna, dolphin are prized by blue-water anglers. Frantic fights follow lightning strikes, and the dolphin often throws in some aerobatics besides. This unruly fighter rates as a delicacy at the table as well, celebrated as moist white-fleshed dolphin fillets in the Keys and South Florida, but marketed as mahimahi elsewhere. Dolphinfish are surface feeders, attracted to the small fish and other tasty morsels associated with floating debris or patches of drifting sargassum weed. Flying fish, plentiful in the Gulf Stream waters, form a large portion of their preferred diet. A school of dolphin will actually attack a trolled bait of small, whole mullet or ballyhoo, streaking from a distance in a me-first effort like schoolboys to the lunch gong. It is not unusual for 3 or 4 rods to be hit at one time, an all-hands-on-deck effort that approaches a marathon. And as long as you keep one hooked dolphin in the water, alongside the boat, its buddies will hang around and wait their turn for a freshly baited hook.

Dolphins are rapidly growing fish, living up to 5 years. The young are called schoolies, generally in the 5- to 15-pound range. Slammers make an angler salivate, as they each weigh 25 pounds and more, and an attacking school can get your heart pumping. Doing battle with the heavyweight, the bull dolphin, quite often happens by accident while you are trolling for some other species. But the bull can hold his own in any arena.

Dolphin season is generally considered to be from Mar until Aug, but the fish tend to stay around most of the year. Limit is 10 per person per day.

Cobia: The Crab Eater
The cobia (*Rachycentron canadum*), the orphan of the piscatory world, enjoys no close relatives and is in a family by itself. Excellent on the table or on the troll, the adult cobia is a favorite bonus fish, often caught during a day in the blue water looking for sailfish. Particularly partial to crabs, the cobia also feeds on shrimp, squid, and small fish. The young cobia is often found in the flats of nearshore bays and inlets around the mangroves and buoys, pilings, and wrecks.

Wahoo
A fine-eating bonus fish, generally caught by fortunate accident while trolling for sailfish or kingfish, the wahoo (*Acanthocybium solandri*) is far from an also-ran. One of the fastest fish in the ocean, the wahoo is a bona fide member of the mackerel family, similar in many ways to the Spanish mackerel. Its long, beaklike snout and slender silver-and-blue-striped body contribute to its prowess as a speed swimmer, for when hooked, the wahoo runs swiftly, cutting and weaving like a tailback heading for a touchdown. This loner rarely travels in schools. Wahoo season is in May, but the fish are here year-round.

Kingfish, aka King Mackerel
Here in the Florida Keys, we call the king mackerel—which goes by assorted aliases in other parts of the country—the kingfish. At the turn of the 20th century, kingfish was the most popular catch off the Keys. Sailfish, then unrevered, were considered

pests because they crashed the kingfish bait. The streamlined kingfish (*Scomberomorus cavalla*) travels in large schools, migrating up and down the coast in search of warm waters. Kingfish commonly frequent the waters of the Keys during the winter months, heading north in the spring.

Kings can be caught by drift fishing, where anglers cut the boat's engines and drift, fishing over the schools. Alternately, you can troll for kingfish with whole mullet or ballyhoo. Some captains prefer to anchor and chum, lacing the slick from time to time with live pilchards. Any method you use, a wire leader is essential when angling for kingfish because the fish displays razor-sharp teeth that it is not reluctant to use. Kingfish caught in our waters commonly weigh in at about 20 pounds, although the fish have been recorded reaching upward of 40 pounds. The kingfish is a good sport fish and also makes a fine meal. Limit is 2 per person per day.

Amberjack

When all else fails in the blue water, you can always find a deep hole and battle an amberjack (*Seriola dumerili*). This powerful, bottom-plunging fish—nicknamed AJ—guarantees a good brawl. Bringing in an amberjack is like pulling up a Volkswagen Beetle with light tackle. Limit is 1 per person per day.

i Just over 20 miles out, southeast of the Middle Keys, is a favorite fishing spot called Marathon's West Hump. This is an underwater seamount that comes up within 480 feet of the surface and is located in waters twice as deep. The constant easterly flow of the Gulf Stream creates the "hump" that draws baitfish, game fish, and fishing enthusiasts!

The Reef Elite: Snapper & the Mackerels

Inhabiting the edge of the barrier reef that extends the length of the Florida Keys and in the smaller patch reefs closer in to shore, several finned species noteworthy for their food value coexist with the brightly painted tropicals and other coral-dwelling creatures. Like a well-branched family tree, these fish encompass many clans, all entertaining to catch and most delectable to eat. Startled anglers have even brought in permit while fishing the wrecks along the reef line. The brooding presence of the barracuda is always a strong possibility on the reef because the 'cuda is partial to raw snapper "stew" or grouper "tartare" when given the opportunity. It thinks nothing of stealing half the hooked fish in one mighty chomp, leaving the angler nothing but a lifeless head.

You will need a boat at least 20 feet long to head out to the reef, some 4 to 5 miles offshore. But with a compass, your NOAA charts, GPS, tackle, chunked bait, and some information gathered locally at the nearest bait and tackle shop, you should be able to find a hot spot on your own. Then all you need to do is fillet the captives, find a recipe, and fry up the spoils.

The snapper family is a popular bunch in the Florida Keys. The prolific cousins—all pleasurable to eat, delightful to catch, and kaleidoscopic to see—confuse Northerners with their dissimilarity. Snappers travel in schools and like to feed at night. Most common on the Keys table is probably the sweet, delicate yellowtail snapper (*Ocyurus chrysurus*), which usually ranges from 12 to 16 inches in length. Big yellowtails, called flags, approach 5 to 6 pounds and 20 inches in length and are prevalent from late summer through Oct. The yellowtail's back and upper sides shade from olive to bluish with yellow spots. A prominent yellow stripe begins at the yellowtail's mouth and runs midlaterally to its deeply forked tail, which, as you would expect, is a deep, brilliant yellow. The yellowtail is skittish, line-shy, and tends to stay way behind the boat. The fish's small mouth won't accommodate the hooks most commonly used in the pursuit of the other snappers. Successful anglers use light line, no leaders, and small hooks buried in the bait.

The mangrove snapper, or gray snapper (*Lutjanus griseus*), though often haunting the coral reef, also can be found inshore in mangrove habitats. Grayish in color with a red tinge along the sides, the mangrove snapper displays two conspicuous canine teeth at the front of the upper jaw. The mangrove is easier to catch than the yellowtail or the mutton snapper. Live shrimp and cut bait, added to a small hook, will induce these good fighters to strike. Anglers enjoy taking mangrove snappers on light tackle.

The brightly colored mutton snapper (*Lutanus analis*) shades from olive green to red, with a bright blue line extending from under its eye to its tail and a black spot below the dorsal fin marking its side. Mutton snappers are most often caught in blue holes, so called because the water color of these deep coral potholes appears bluer than the surrounding waters. You will also find muttons in channels and creeks and occasionally even on a bonefish flat. The fish range in weight from 5 to 20 pounds. Mutton snappers are rumored to be shy and easily spooked by a bait that is cast too closely, but they love live pilchards. Usually caught in cloudy, churned-up water, the muttons provide a fierce confrontation. The limit for snappers is 10 per person per day.

Ergonomically designed for speed, the torpedo-shaped Spanish mackerel (*Scomberomorus maculatus*) distinguishes itself from the king and the cero with a series of irregular, buttercup-yellow spots on its stripeless sides, which look like the freckles on the Little Rascals. Cherished by light-tackle enthusiasts, the Spanish mackerel averages less than 2 pounds and 20 inches in length. Its razorlike teeth dictate you carefully consider your choice in terminal tackle, for slashing your line rates at the top of the Spanish mackerel's getaway tactics. Spanish mackerel migrate into Florida Bay in Feb. Limit is 15 per person per day.

Larger than its Spanish cousin, the cero mackerel (*Scomberomorous regalis*) displays yellow spots above and below a bronze stripe that runs down its silvery sides, from the pectoral fin to the base of its tail. The cero is the local in our visiting mackerel lineup, not straying far from the waters of South Florida and the Keys, where it feeds on small fish and squid. The cero makes excellent table fare when consumed fresh, but fillets do not freeze well.

You may encounter the tripletail (*Lobotes surinamensis*) if you fish around wrecks, buoys, or sunken debris. Nicknamed the "buoy fish," the tripletail has been known to reach 40 pounds and a length of 3 feet. The fish's dorsal and anal fins are so long that they resemble two more tails, hence the name tripletail. The tripletail is a mottled palette of black, brown, and yellow, looking like an autumn leaf. Young tripletails, which like to stay close to shore in bays and estuaries, often are spotted floating on their sides at the surface, mimicking a leaf on the water. The tripletail will put up a valiant fight, and, though not seen on restaurant menus, it will make a tasty dinner. You must catch tripletail with a hook and line only, no snatch hooks.

The Bridges

The bridges of the Florida Keys attract fighting game fish and flavorful food fish like magnets draw paper clips. The state of Florida replaced many of the original bridges of the Overseas Highway with wider, heavier spans in the late 1970s and 1980s, subsequently fitting many of the old bridges, no longer used for automobile traffic, for use as fishing piers. These bridges are marked with brown-and-white signage depicting a fish, line, and hook. (Many of the old bridge structures have been closed because lack of maintenance has left them unsafe. Be sure to fish only from those bearing the county signage.) The fishing bridges offer the general public free fishing access to many of the same species that frequent more far-flung areas of our waters. Parking is provided at the fishing-pier bridges. The Seven Mile Bridge, the Long Key Bridge, and the Bahia Honda Bridge have been designated historical monuments.

The waters beneath the bridges host a lively population of tarpon, mangrove snappers, snook, baby groupers, and yellowtails (see the Flats, Backcountry, and Blue Water sections of this chapter for information on these fish). Grunts (*Haemulon plumieri*) also are commonly caught at the bridges. Though little respected in other Keys waters, this small, bluish-gray fish is, nevertheless, fun to catch and makes a tasty meal. The grunt's name is derived from the sounds escaping the fish's bright orange mouth when it is captured. This grunting sound is actually the grinding of the pharyngeal teeth, which produces an audible noise amplified by the air bladder.

Night fishing is popular from the bridge piers, too. An outgoing tide with a moderate flow inspires the fish to continue feeding after dark. Baitfish and crustaceans, a temptation too great for many of the finned predators to pass up, are funneled through the pilings and out to sea.

Stop in at one of the local bait and tackle shops to get rigged out for bridge fishing. The local fishing experts working in these shops are encyclopedias of knowledge and will be able to guide you as to times, tides, and tackle. Locals recommend you use stout tackle when fishing from one of our bridges. You not only have to retrieve your catch while battling a heavy current, but you also must lift it a great distance to the top of the bridge.

Live shrimp, cut bait, or live pinfish will attract attention from at least one of the species lurking below. You will need to keep your shrimp alive while fishing from the bridge. Put the shrimp on ice in a 5-gallon bucket with an aerator or in a large Styrofoam cooler with an aerator. You can also lower a chum bag (filled with a block of chum, available at all bait shops) into the water. Tie a couple of dive weights to a long rope, lower the chum bag down the surface of a piling on the downcurrent side of the bridge, and tie it off to the railing. Then fish the slick. The chum will drift with the current, attracting sharks and any finfish in the neighborhood.

You will need sinkers on your line in order for your baited hook to drop to the bottom because a swift current pulses under the bridges. Don't launch your cast away from the bridge. Drop your bait straight down, near a piling or downcurrent, at the shoreside of the bridge. Rubble from past construction sometimes piled here creates a current break, allowing the fish a place to rest, feed, or hide in the swirls or eddies. Don't forget to buy a fishing license.

FISHING LICENSES

Florida law states you must possess a salt-water fishing license if you attempt to take or possess marine fish for noncommercial purposes. This includes finfish and such invertebrate species as snails, whelks, clams, scallops, shrimps, crabs, lobsters, sea stars, sea urchins, and sea cucumbers.

Exempt from this law are individuals younger than age 16 and Florida residents age 65 and older. You are also exempt if you are a Florida resident and a member of the US armed forces not stationed in Florida and home on leave for 30 or fewer days, with valid orders in your possession.

Florida residents who are fishing in salt water or for a saltwater species in freshwater, from land, or from a structure fixed to land need not purchase a license. Land is defined as "the area of ground located within the geographic boundaries of the state of Florida that extends to a water depth of 4 feet." This includes any structure permanently fixed to land such as a pier, bridge, dock or floating dock, or jetty. If you use a vessel to reach ground, however, you must have a license. And if you are wading in more than 4 feet of water or have broken the surface of the water wearing a face mask, you also must have one.

You are not required to have a license when you fish with one of our licensed captains on a charter holding a valid vessel saltwater fishing license or if you are fishing from a pier that has been issued a pier saltwater fishing license. Other, more obscure exemptions also apply. Check floridafisheries .com for more information.

A Florida saltwater fishing license is available from most bait and tackle shops and from any Monroe County tax collector's office. You can also obtain a license by calling (888) 347-4356 or online at www.fl .wildlifelicense.com. Residents and nonresidents pay differing amounts for this license. The state defines a resident as anyone who has lived in Florida continuously for at least 6 months; anyone who has established a domicile in Florida and can provide evidence of such by law; any member of the US armed forces who is stationed in Florida; any student enrolled in a college or university in Florida; or an alien who can prove residency status.

There is a penalty for fishing without the required license or stamps of $50 or more plus the cost of purchasing the proper documentation. A $51.50 tarpon tag is required if you insist upon keeping and therefore killing a tarpon instead of releasing it (see the catch-and-release ethics section in this chapter).

TOURNAMENTS

If you're an angler who would like to compete against your peers instead of just yourself, the Florida Keys offers a plethora of exciting tournaments—more than 50 a year—encompassing most of the finned species enriching our waters. These tournaments, scheduled year-round from Key Largo to Key West, award prizes, cash, or trophies in a variety of categories ranging from heaviest or longest to most caught and released in a specified time period.

Generally, the tournaments fit into one of three categories, although some tournaments have multiple divisions. The **billfish tournaments**—white marlin, blue marlin, and sailfish—are the most prestigious and the most expensive. Billfish tournaments are catch-and-release events. Proof of the catch usually requires a photograph and a sample of the leader, which will be tested for chafing. Scoring follows an intricate point system. A catch of a white marlin, a blue marlin, and a sailfish in one day—not your average day, even in the Keys—constitutes a slam.

Dolphin tournaments are more family-type competitions. Anglers use their own boats without guides, and if the dolphin exceeds prespecified poundage, it may be brought in and weighed. Anglers can keep the fish, which are excellent eating.

Flats tournaments—tarpon, bonefish, and permit—are always catch-and-release, usually scored by a point system. A catch on a fly rod scores more points than one retrieved on light tackle. The fish must be measured, a photo must be taken, and the process must be witnessed. We recommend you book one year in advance for tarpon tournaments.

Some of our tournaments are restricted to a specific category of angler—women only or juniors only, for instance—or to a particular type of tackle, such as light tackle or fly rods. Others award a mixed bag of catches ranging from game fish to groupers to grunts. Many of the tournaments donate at least a portion of their proceeds to a charitable organization.

In the following section we introduce you to a sampling of the most important fishing tournaments held annually in the Keys. For a complete listing, visit fla-keys .com/tdcfishingcalendar.

BAYBONE CELEBRITY TOURNAMENT
Sheraton Beach Resort,
MM 97, Key Largo
(305) 664-2002
redbone.org
Event no. 2 in the Redbone Celebrity Tournament Series, the prestigious catch-and-release Baybone tournament is in late Sept or early Oct. The Celebrity Tournament Series, which includes the Mercury S.L.A.M., donates 100 percent of its proceeds to the Cystic Fibrosis Foundation for research. The stalked catch for the Baybone is bonefish and permit, which are photographed against a measuring device and released. Points are awarded for catches on fly, spin/plug, or general bait; nothing heavier than 12-pound test may be used in all divisions. An intricate point system determines the winners, who receive original paintings and sculptures as prizes. Anglers can fish as a 2-person team, or one angler can be paired with a celebrity.

CHEECA LODGE & SPA PRESIDENTIAL SAILFISH TOURNAMENT
MM 82 Oceanside, Islamorada
(305) 664-4651 or (800) 327-2888
cheeca.com
Perhaps the most prestigious of all tournaments in the Florida Keys is this tournament, held in mid-January. The former president, George H. W. Bush himself, typically competes in this event. Preceded by a kickoff meeting, 2 days of intense fishing are followed by an awards banquet at Cheeca Lodge. Fifty boats participate, 2 anglers per boat. Other than those included in the most-catches category, bonefish must weigh at least 8 pounds to qualify. All must be released. Trophies are awarded to winners, and proceeds benefit a variety of Keys environmental groups.

COCONUTS DOLPHIN TOURNAMENT
Key Largo
(305) 453-9794
coconutsrestaurant.com
The largest dolphin tournament in the Florida Keys, Coconuts Dolphin Tournament at

Marina Del Mar in mid-May regularly hosts more than 700 anglers. This 3-day tournament, which awards prizes, runs from 8 a.m. to 3 p.m. each day. The 2011 prize for a dolphin weighing 52.8 pounds was $10,000. You can book a charter to fish the tournament or use your own boat. The director says there has been no proven advantage to having a charter. Scoring is determined by weight of the fish. Since this is a food-fish tournament, anglers may bring in all dolphin of more than 10 pounds.

i The most famous blue-water angler in Key West's collective consciousness remains Ernest Hemingway, who augmented his famous writing with a passion for fishing these waters. Photographs of Hemingway with his prized monster-size tarpon and sailfish cause many a covetous angler to turn green with envy.

ISLAMORADA SAILFISH TOURNAMENT
Islamorada
(305) 852-2102
islamoradasailfishtournament.com

This annual sailfish tournament takes place in Dec. Scoring is as follows: 100 points for each released sailfish. Completed tagging cards must be submitted to the Committee Boat in order to qualify for the most-tagged trophy. Only 12-pound-test lines or less may be used, and live or dead bait as well as artificials are acceptable.

KEY WEST FISHING TOURNAMENT
Key West
(305) 295-6601
keywestfishingtournament.com

This unusual tournament must have been designed for the angler who just can't

fish enough. It lasts from Mar to Nov and encompasses a potpourri of divisions and species. Both charters and individuals can register for the tournament and also participate in a 2-day kickoff tournament-within-a-tournament, which in itself awards cash prizes. Anglers weigh their food-fish catches or record their releases at participating marinas and are awarded citations for their efforts. At the grand finale of the tournament, the tabulated results are announced and all prizes are presented.

LADIES TARPON TOURNAMENT
Marathon
(305) 289-2248

The waters under the Seven Mile Bridge and the Bahia Honda Bridge are invaded by tarpon-seeking women each year in late Apr or early May in this ladies-only tarpon tournament. The number of tarpon caught and released in the 2-day tournament determines the winners of a cache of rods and reels, trophies, and an assortment of jewelry. Points are awarded for catches on 12-pound test and 30-pound test.

LEON SHELL MEMORIAL SAILFISH TOURNAMENT
Key Colony Beach
(305) 289-1310
leonshelltournament.com

This is 2 days of fishing, with the proceeds benefiting the Keys Hospice and Visiting Nurses Association of the Florida Keys. The tournament is named after Leon Shell, best known as the inventor of the Leon Lure, an artificial lure regarded as one of the top bubble-creating lures ever invented. With more than $150,000 donated since its inception, this tournament draws a huge crowd. In the yearly tourney, cash prizes are awarded and the prize for the boat releasing the most sailfish is given out at an awards dinner. Weight fish divisions are given for dolphin, tuna, wahoo, and kingfish. Also, there is a junior division for youngsters ages 9 to 15½ years old.

S.L.A.M. TOURNAMENT
Key West
(305) 664-2002
redbone.org
First in the Redbone Celebrity Tournament Series each year is the S.L.A.M. (Southernmost Light-tackle Anglers Masters) event in early Sept, for the benefit of cystic fibrosis research (also see the Baybone Celebrity Tournament event). Participants in this 2-day fishing event angle to score a Grand Slam: the catch and release of a bonefish, permit, and tarpon in 2 days. Points are awarded for each release in categories of fly, spin/plug, and general bait. Each release is photographed against a measuring device. Like the other tournaments in this series, the S.L.A.M. awards original artworks to its winners. Anglers can fish as a 2-person team, or one angler can opt to fish with a celebrity.

Never discard your fishing line in the water. It can injure marine life, sea turtles, or seabirds.

GUIDES & CHARTERS

There are many captains and guides in the Florida Keys offering their services on the flats, blue water, or backcountry. Our guides are the most knowledgeable in the world—licensed captains who maintain safe, government-regulated watercraft. Hiring a guide allows the first-time visitor or the novice angler an opportunity to learn how to fish the waters of the Florida Keys and catch its bounty without having to spend too much time learning about the fish's habits. And guides will be your best teachers, for they usually have a lifetime of experience. Once you fish our waters, however, you will be the "hooked" species, for this unforgettable angling experience is addictive.

Book a guide as soon as you know when you are coming to the Keys, because the guides here book up quickly, especially during certain times of the year. If you hope to fish our waters with a guide during tarpon season, especially the months of May and June, plan a year ahead. Holidays such as Christmas and New Year's book up quickly also. Traditionally, the months of Aug through Nov are a bit slower. You may be able to wing it during those months, but we wouldn't advise it. Even if you don't take a charter trip, stop at a fishing marina around 4 p.m. and check out the catch of the day.

Blue-water or offshore fishing charters can accommodate 6 anglers. The captain guides the vessel to his or her favorite hot spots, which are anywhere from 6 to 26 miles offshore and usually closely guarded secrets. Often the captain will stop on his or her blue-water trek so the mate can throw a cast net for live bait. The mate will rig the baits, ready the outriggers, and cast the baited hooks for you. Big game fish are usually stalked by trolling, as are dolphin. You need do nothing but relax, soak in the sea air, and wait for the call, "Fish on!" Then the action is up to you.

Blue-water charter boats range in size from 35 to 50 feet. Each generally has an enclosed cabin and a head (toilet) onboard. Everything you need for a day's fishing is provided except your refreshments, lunch, and any personal items you may need. It is customary to tip the mate 10 to 15 percent in cash if you have had a good day.

Guides for flats fishing or backcountry angling usually take a maximum of 2 anglers per boat. The guide will pole the skiff or flats boat through the skinny water, attentively looking for fish from atop the poling platform. This sight fishing dictates both guide and anglers stand alert, all senses engaged. The angler, whether fly fishing or spin casting, casts to the desired location directed by the guide.

Flats boats measure 16 to 18 feet. They are not outfitted with any shading devices, nor do they have a head. Be aware, you may have to use rather primitive facilities. Many of the guides will dip into shore for a pit stop, but others will not, so inquire before you leave the dock. All fly or spin rods, reels, tackle, and bait are provided. Some guides even tie their own flies, providing special furry or feathery creations proven to entice the fish. It is customary to tip the guide 10 to 15 percent in cash if you were happy with the excursion.

When booking a charter, inquire about penalties for canceling your reservation. No-shows frequently will be charged the full price.

Always bring sunscreen, polarized sunglasses, a cap with a long bill lined with dark fabric to cut the glare, and motion-sickness pills (even if you've never needed them before). Anglers are responsible for providing their own lunches and refreshments. Keys tradition is to bring lunch for the captain and mate on a blue-water charter or for the guide on a flats trip.

Many guides are known only on a word-of-mouth basis, but we have compiled a source list of fishing marinas and outfitters you may call to secure an offshore charter or flats or backcountry guide. The chambers of commerce in Key Largo, Islamorada, Marathon, the Lower Keys, and Key West also act as referral sources (see subsequent listings).

Perhaps even more than the rest of the Keys, you'll need a guide to find the fish in the waters surrounding Key West. A busy harbor for centuries, Key West's marinas and bights are a bustling maze to the uninitiated. Many of the more than 60 charter boats in the Key West fleet dock at the City Marina at Garrison Bight, which is accessed on Palm Avenue, just off N. Roosevelt Boulevard. This marina is locally referred to as Charter Boat Row. From 7 to 7:30 a.m. and 3:30 to 5 p.m., the captains are available at their vessels to take direct bookings. You can meet them and their crews, see the offshore vessels, and save money to boot. Booking a charter directly with the captain instead of a charter agency nets you a sizable discount. Other charter boats dock at Key West Bight, in the Key West Historic Seaport.

Some guides are willing to captain your private vessel at a much-reduced charter rate. If this interests you, inquire when you call one of these booking sources. Often hotels maintain a source list of guides or charter captains they will recommend. Inquire when you reserve your accommodations.

Offshore & Backcountry Guide Booking Sources

Establishments acting as booking services will determine your needs and book your flats/backcountry guide or blue-water/offshore charter directly. Cancellation policies vary and change from year to year, so be sure to inquire about procedures and penalties before you book your charter. The top guides in the Florida Keys book out of the establishments listed below. Be sure to log on to their websites to find out more information on the guides they represent.

Upper Keys

BAY AND REEF COMPANY
MM 80.5 Bayside and 81.7 Oceanside, Islamorada
(305) 393-1779
bayandreef.com

BUD N' MARY'S MARINA
MM 79.8 Oceanside, Islamorada
(305) 664-2461
budnmarys.com

FLORIDA KEYS OUTFITTERS
MM 81.2 Oceanside, Islamorada
(305) 664-5423
floridakeysoutfitters.com

WHALE HARBOR MARINA
MM 81.9 Oceanside, Islamorada
(305) 664-4511
whaleharborcharters.com

WORLD WIDE SPORTSMAN INC.
MM 81.5 Bayside, Islamorada
(305) 517-2269
basspro.com

Middle Keys

CAPTAIN HOOK'S MARINA & DIVE CENTER
MM 53 Oceanside, Marathon
(305) 743-2444 or (800) 278-4665
captainhooks.com

Lower Keys

STRIKE ZONE CHARTERS
MM 29.5 Bayside, Big Pine Key
(305) 872-9863
strikezonecharter.com

Key West

In addition to the limited number of fishing marinas and outfitters booking guides or charters, Key West's fishing excursions are put together by charter agencies operating out of booths peppering Mallory Square, Duval, and other major streets of Key West. You also can book party boats at these booths.

CAPT. TONY MURPHY'S SALTWATER ANGLER
243 Front St., at the Westin Key West Resort and Marina
(305) 296-0700
saltwaterangler.com

Chambers of Commerce

These chamber of commerce offices throughout the Florida Keys will provide you with a list of guides for any style of fishing excursion via their phone numbers or websites.

KEY LARGO CHAMBER OF COMMERCE & FLORIDA KEYS VISITOR CENTER
MM 106 Bayside, Key Largo
(305) 451-4747 or (800) 822-1088
keylargo.org

ISLAMORADA CHAMBER OF COMMERCE
MM 82.5 Bayside, Islamorada
(305) 664-4503 or (800) 322-5397
islamoradachamber.com

GREATER MARATHON CHAMBER OF COMMERCE
MM 53.5 Bayside, Marathon
(305) 743-5417 or (800) 262-7284
floridakeysmarathon.com

FISHING

LOWER KEYS CHAMBER OF COMMERCE

MM 31 Oceanside, Big Pine Key
(305) 872-2411 or (800) 872-3722
lowerkeyschamber.com

KEY WEST CHAMBER OF COMMERCE

510 Greene St., Key West
(305) 294-2587 or (800) 648-6269
keywestchamber.org

i More than 10 percent of the International Game Fish Association (IGFA) saltwater line-class and fly-fishing world records have been set in the Florida Keys.

Party Boats

Party boats, sometimes called "head boats," offer a relatively inexpensive way to fish the waters of the Keys. The party boats, US Coast Guard–inspected and certified vessels, generally hold 50 passengers or more, but most average no more than 25 to 30 anglers. Party boats take anglers out to the reef, where they anchor or drift and bottom fish for more than 40 species of fish. Spring and summer seasons sport a plethora of snappers, dolphinfish, and yellowtails, while kingfish and cobia are more apt to make an appearance in the winter months. Porgies, grunts, and some species of snappers show up all year. Occasionally even a sailfish or a big shark has been caught from a party boat here.

Party boats offer rod and reel rentals at a nominal fee per trip. This includes your terminal tackle—hook, line, and sinker—and all bait. If you bring your own fishing gear, bait is included in the excursion fee. You do not need a fishing license on a party boat. While most party-boat information mentions your license is included in the excursion fee, this

actually is only a temporary license, good for the duration of your fishing trip only. Two or more mates will be working the boat, helping you bait hooks, confiding fishing tips, and untangling the inevitable crossed lines.

Most of the party boats have seats around the periphery of the lower deck and a shaded sundeck up top. You are advised to wear shorts rather than swimsuits and durable sneakers or deck shoes, not flip-flops or sandals. Remember, there will be a lot of anglers and many flying hooks on the boat. Put some sturdy cloth between your skin and that accidental snag. Most captains recommend bringing a lightweight long-sleeved shirt for protection against the sun and a jacket to ward off cool breezes. Bring sunglasses, sunscreen, a hat, and motion-sickness pills (many people who never suffered from seasickness before find drifting in the swells causes them mal de mer). Also bring a fishing rag or towel to wipe your hands with throughout the day.

i Before green turtles were placed on the endangered and protected list and no longer allowed to be caught, they were a source of food throughout Florida's history. The pens that held the turtles were called "kraals."

After you land a fish, a mate will help you take it off the hook and will check the species to make sure it is not one of those protected by law, such as Nassau grouper. The mate then will measure the fish to ensure it meets the required size limit, tag it with your name, and place it on ice. At the end of the fishing trip, you may reclaim your catch. The mate will clean your fish, usually for tips. Party boats with a set cleaning-fee policy will be noted in the descriptions. Mates work for tips aboard party boats, the standard tip being 10 to 15 percent if you had a good day and if the mate was helpful.

The following party boats may be booked for day or evening charters. It is always a good idea to arrive at the docks 30 minutes before departure to stow your gear on the boat and secure a good position on deck. All boats have restrooms on board. Most have an enclosed cabin and offer a limited snack bar, beer, and soda. Exceptions will be noted.

In all cases, you are allowed to bring your own cooler filled with lunch and refreshments. All party boats recommended in this section take credit cards unless otherwise stated. Children's rates for youngsters age 12 and younger are often available.

Upper Keys
CAPTAIN MICHAEL
MM 77.5 Bayside, Islamorada
(305) 664-9814 or (877) 664-8498
robbies.com
Rates for children younger than age 5, who will only be "assisting" Mom and Dad, are reduced. The 65-foot *Captain Michael,* with spacious decks and an air-conditioned cabin, is available for private charters, sunset cruises, and wedding receptions. Both day and night party-boat excursions are available.

MISS ISLAMORADA
Bud N' Mary's Marina
MM 79.8 Oceanside, Islamorada
(305) 664-2461 or (800) 742-7945
budnmarys.com
Miss Islamorada is a 65-foot, air-conditioned party/fishing boat that entertains up to 45 people. All tackle, bait, and licenses are provided along with an experienced crew and

clean restrooms. Onboard catering is available for fishing, sunset cruises, corporate meetings, memorial services, and weddings. There is a deli on-site before you leave, should you need last-minute provisions, as none are available on board without prior arrangement. The daily excursion is from 9:30 a.m. to 4:30 p.m.

SAILOR'S CHOICE
Holiday Inn Marina, MM 100 Oceanside, Key Largo
(305) 451-1802
sailorschoicefishingboat.com
Sailor's Choice, a 65-foot, aluminum, custom-built craft with an air-conditioned lounge, offers plenty of shade and seating for anglers on its daily fishing excursions. Children are welcome on both day and evening trips. During the day they can easily see the big fish in the water and seabirds, porpoises, and sea turtles. The 2 daily excursions are from 9 a.m. to 1 p.m. and 1:30 to 5:30 p.m, while the evening excursion is from 7:30 p.m. to midnight.

Middle Keys
MARATHON LADY
MM 53 Oceanside, Marathon
(305) 743-5580
fishfloridakeys.com/marathonlady
Children fish for significantly reduced rates aboard the 73-foot *Marathon Lady.* Inquire when you make your reservations. If you rent a rod and reel for the 4-hour excursion, your tackle is included, but if you prefer to bring your own gear, terminal tackle is available for a nominal fee. The mates will clean your catch for a small fee.

This Isn't Kansas

The months of June through November make up hurricane season in South Florida. Here in the Florida Keys, summer alerts us to keep a watchful eye peeled on the skies over open water for yet another weather concern: water spouts. Water spouts are tornadoes or vortexes that form over open water, and here in the Keys there are as many as 400 to 500 each year. We hold the title as the most frequent spot on earth for water spouts to form. The reason for this is our islands and shallow water heat the air, then add to the mix our high humidity. With that heat, the air rises and the water in the humidity forms water droplets that make up clouds. As the water vapor condenses, more heat is released, thus causing the air to rise faster. Then throw in the east-to-northeast "trade winds" and boom—the perfect water spout. Ranging in height from 18,000 to 20,000 feet, they are dramatic to witness. Rarely do they come ashore, but nevertheless, they bear keeping a watchful eye on, especially if you are in or on the water.

Lower Keys
SEA BOOTS
MM 24.5 Oceanside, Summerland Key
(305) 745-1530 or (800) 238-1746
seaboots.com
With a Coast Guard Masters License under his belt, Captain Jim Sharp has been on the water most of his life. His vast experience (more than 50 years!) fishing the cool blue waters of the Florida Keys and the Bahamas makes an outing with Jim a thrilling experience. On his 6-passenger boat, *Sea Boots*, you are provided fishing license, tackle, bait, and ice for the trip.

Key West
Key West party boats are docked at Charter Boat Row on Palm Avenue off N. Roosevelt. You can call the numbers listed to make reservations, book a space at one of the booths on Duval Street and in the Mallory Square area, or simply come down to the docks and make arrangements directly with the captain. Vessels usually operate at far less than

maximum capacity during most seasons, so finding a spot should not present a problem.

✳GREYHOUND V
Charter Boat Row, City Marina, Garrison Bight
(305) 296-5139
Daily trips are from 11 a.m. to 4 p.m. On any given trip, you are likely to encounter serious local fishermen and women on this boat. In July and Aug, 2 excursions are offered daily. Mates charge a nominal fee to clean your fish.

GULF STREAM IV
Charter Boat Row, City Marina, Garrison Bight
(305) 296-8494 or (888) 745-3595
gulfstreamkeywest.com
The 58-foot *Gulf Stream IV* provides a full-service lunch counter offering sandwiches, beer, and soda. They have his/hers restrooms on the boat and an inside cabin and an outdoor bench, both with seating. The

mates will clean your catch for a small fee. Sunbathers may come along on these party boats for half price.

OUTFITTERS

Upper Keys

SANDY MORET'S FLORIDA KEYS OUTFITTERS
MM 81.2 Oceanside, Islamorada
(305) 664-5423
floridakeysoutfitters.com

The focus here is on fly fishing, and this outfitter's personnel rank as some of the most experienced in the sport. You'll find such brands as Hardy, Sage, and G. Loomis fly rods and Hardy, Nautilis, and Tibor fly reels, plus a wide selection of flies and fly-tying materials. In addition to Simms, Patagonia, and Columbia clothing, Florida Keys Outfitters sells Simms and Patagonia shoes and booties.

WEST MARINE
MM 103.4 Bayside, Key Largo
(305) 453-9050
westmarine.com

West Marine is your one-stop shop for all of your boating and fishing needs. Great inventory, large selection, and helpful sales folks are available to assist with questions. Check out their website for other locations in the Upper Keys.

WORLD WIDE SPORTSMAN INC.
MM 81.5 Bayside, Islamorada
(305) 664-4615 or (800) 227-7776
basspro.com

This 29,000-square-foot superstore is owned by Bass Pro Shops and is stocked to the rafters with a wide assortment of fishing tackle by manufacturers such as Penn, Sage,

Daiwa, Shimano, Orvis, and more. You'll find fly-tying materials and a huge assortment of flies here. A rod and reel repair center is on the premises. Ex Officio, Woolrich, Bimini Bay, Sportif, Tarponwear, and Columbia fishing clothes for both men and women are just a few of the many brands offered. The facility also features a full-service marina accommodating boats up to 42 feet in length. Many of the area guides launch from these facilities. The marina also offers a fuel dock as well as frozen, live, and fresh bait.

> ## Gentle Giants
>
> Two fishermen anchored in the reef off Marathon recently spotted a 19-foot juvenile whale shark. These are the largest sharks in the ocean, with adults measuring 33 feet long and weighing up to 60 tons. Their identifying marks are spotted backs, and they have broad, flat faces. They scoot along feeding on whatever they can filter through their giant mouths. Whale sharks are gentle, and the only danger is getting slapped with their fins or tail. You just never know what you will see in the sea in the scenic Florida Keys!

Middle Keys

THE TACKLE BOX
MM 48, Marathon
(305) 289-0540
thetacklebox.com

The Tackle Box sells anything and everything you'll need for saltwater fishing, as they stock plenty of brand names of rods, reels, and fishing gear. They offer advice, equipment, bait, tackle, or charters for any type of fishing you wish to do. They even sell bowfishing equipment and can clean, recondition, or repair any Penn, Shimano, Daiwa, or other reels quickly and for a reasonable price with one or more of their 20,000 parts in stock.

Lower Keys

REEF LIGHT TACKLE
MM 29.7 Oceanside, Big Pine Key
(305) 872-7679
reeflighttackle.com

Stop in and swap fish stories about the one that did not get away because you came here for your outfitting! They have it all, including a live-bait room. The crew call their inventory "fish candy." They have special fishing seminars every week in season, as well as inside tips on their website. In-store, they offer Penn rod and reel repair as well as a host of rods, reels, tackle, beer, and even unique pieces for sale by local artists. Also in stock are shirts, hats, and polarized eyewear.

Key West

CAPT. TONY MURPHY'S SALTWATER ANGLER
243 Front St., at the Westin Key West Resort and Marina
(305) 296-0700
saltwaterangler.com

The Saltwater Angler specializes in fly tackle. Look for Sage, G. Loomis, Orvis, Tibor, Abel, and Shimano rods and reels. The store also stocks a full assortment of flies and fly-tying materials. You can also select from a complete line of top-brand fishing apparel by Orvis, Patagonia, and Columbia. Books and artwork with an angling theme round out their offerings.

DIVING & SNORKELING

Ranking as the third largest reef system and one of the most popular dive destinations in the world, the Florida Keys' reef runs 192 miles from Virginia Key in Biscayne Bay all the way to the Dry Tortugas in the Gulf of Mexico. A fragile symbiotic city of sea creatures crowds our reef—fish, sponges, jellyfish, anemones, worms, snails, crabs, lobsters, rays, turtles, and, of course, both soft and stony corals—sometimes mixing it up with sunken bounty of a different kind: shipwrecks of yesteryear. Although our coral reef appears sturdy, this toothsome barrier is actually made up of colonies of tiny living animals. These coral polyps develop so slowly that it can take years for some species to grow just 1 inch. The careless toss of an anchor or slightest touch can destroy decades of coral growth in just seconds. When polyps are damaged or killed, the entire colony becomes exposed to the spread of algae or disease, and the reef is at risk.

To protect and preserve our marine ecosystem, Congress established the Florida Keys National Marine Sanctuary in 1990. Extending on both sides of the Florida Keys, the 2,800-square-nautical-mile sanctuary is the second largest marine sanctuary in the US (see the Area Overview chapter). The sanctuary encompasses two of the very best diving areas in the reef chain of the Keys: the Key Largo National Marine Sanctuary, which in turn envelops John Pennekamp Coral Reef State Park, and the Looe Key National Marine Sanctuary.

The state of Florida adjusted its offshore boundaries from 7 miles to 3 miles. This means many of the underwater dive and snorkel sites that used to be referred to as John Pennekamp Coral Reef State Park are now actually part of the Key Largo National Marine Sanctuary. To clear up the confusion, remember: Key Largo National Marine Sanctuary encompasses the waters of John Pennekamp Coral Reef State Park, but Pennekamp is not synonymous with the sanctuary.

OVERVIEW

In this chapter we provide you with a run-down of great reef and wreck dives and snorkel adventures from Key Largo to the Dry Tortugas. Our reefs are not within swimming distance of the shore, so you will need to make your way by boat. If you plan to venture out on your own craft or in a rental boat, be sure to stop at a dive center or marine supply store and purchase a nautical map that denotes the exact coordinates for dive and snorkel sites (see the listings in this chapter). Motor to the reef only if you know the waters, are an experienced boat handler, and can read the nautical charts well. You are financially liable for damage to the reef, so always anchor only at mooring buoys when provided or on sandy areas of the sea bottom. Florida law dictates you fly the diver-down flag, which is red with a diagonal white stripe, to warn other boaters that divers are underwater within 100 feet of your craft.

Probably the most popular and hassle-free way to dive or snorkel in the Florida Keys is to go out with a dive charter. Most reputable dive centers in the Keys belong to the Keys Association of Dive Operators, which sets standards of safety and professionalism. Crews are trained in CPR, first-aid, and handling dive emergencies. Emergency oxygen supplies are kept on board. The dive captains, who must be licensed by the US Coast Guard, judge weather conditions and water visibility each day and select the best sites suited to your experience level. Often their coveted knowledge of little-visited patch reefs and wrecks affords you an experience you could not duplicate on your own. We offer you a guide to dive centers, noting the comprehensive services ranging from instruction and underwater excursions to equipment rentals and sales.

In the Florida Keys, usually neither the crew nor the dive master accompanies divers in the water. Divers spread out across a shallow reef, two by two, swimming in a buddy system. The dive master stays on board and watches everyone from the boat. You must prove your experience level by showing current dive certification and your dive log before you may go out on a dive charter. If you have not made a comparable dive within the past six months, you should hire an instructor or dive master to accompany you in the water. Be sure you are comfortable with the sea conditions and that they are consistent with your level of expertise.

i Funded by Sanctuary Friends Foundation of the Florida Keys, Ken Nedimeyer and a group of volunteers have successfully propagated and transplanted native staghorn corals in the wild. Some of the corals Ken "baby-sat" for 12 years, and by using polyps that settled on his "livestock," the staghorn thickets have been successfully established. Contact the foundation at (305) 289-2288 or visit sanctuary friends.org for more information.

Whether you dive on your own or go out to the reef with a charter, you should be aware of the strong current of the outgoing tidal flow and in the Gulf Stream. It is easy to overlook the current in the fascination of your dive until, low on both energy and air, you must swim against it to get back to the boat. Begin your dive by swimming into the current. To determine the direction of the current, watch the flow of your bubbles or lie back into a float position and see which way the current carries you.

Be careful around bridges. The tremendous energy of the tides passing through the pilings of our bridges creates coral outcroppings that would not normally be so close to shore. Divers and snorkelers without boat transportation to the patch reefs or the gulf waters like to take advantage of this underwater terrain to look for lobsters. Be forewarned: It is very dangerous to dive or snorkel under and around our bridges. The currents are swift and the tidal pull is strong. Boat traffic is often heavy. If you do decide to dive or snorkel here, be sure to carry a diver-down flag with you on a float, and follow the buddy system. The best and safest time to tackle these turbulent waters is just before slack tide, during slack tide, and immediately following slack tide. The time of this cycle varies with wind, the height of the tide, and the phase of the moon.

Whether you'd like to spend a few hours, days, weeks, or a lifetime exploring our coral reefs and wrecks, you'll find in this chapter all you need to know to "get wet," as divers like to say, in the Florida Keys.

In Emergencies

Before you dive, you should check out the **Divers Alert Network (DAN),** a nonprofit, dive safety organization. DAN's mission is to help divers in need of medical emergency assistance and to promote dive safety through research, education, products, and services.

The DAN Emergency Hotline, (919) 684-9111, is available 24 hours a day, 7 days a week, to assist with medical emergencies and to facilitate medical evacuation services. DAN also provides a Medical Information Line, (919) 684-2948, during normal business hours for nonemergency questions. For more information, visit diversalert network.org.

Divers in the Florida Keys are in good hands in the face of a recompression emergency. The **Florida Keys Hyperbaric Center** (305-853-1603) is located at Mariners Hospital in the Upper Keys. Dive shop personnel, instructors, dive masters, and boat captains have joined with members of the local EMS, US Coast Guard, Marine Patrol, NOAA, Monroe County Sheriff's office, and the Florida State Highway Patrol to develop a coordinated evacuation program to get injured divers off the water and to the hyperbaric chamber quickly. In case of a decompression injury, call 911 and get the victim to the nearest emergency room as rapidly as possible.

Great Annual Fish Count

The Reef Environmental Education Foundation (REEF), headquartered in Key Largo, invites divers to participate in the Great Annual Fish Count. First begun in California's Channel Islands in 1992, it now extends beyond US borders into the Caribbean and Canada. More than 120,000 volunteer surveys have been submitted. The information is then used for fish population studies of marine protected areas and artificial reefs, and to see if a particular species is being overfished. No wildlife is harmed in this effort. Visit fishcount.org or reef.org to learn more.

THE KEYS TO THE REEF

Most diving and snorkeling takes place on the barrier reefs of the Florida Keys. These linear or semicircular reefs, larger than the inner patch reefs, have claimed a graveyard of sailing vessels, many laden with gold and silver and other precious cargo. Salvaged by wreckers for centuries, the remains of these wrecks entice experienced divers, some of whom still hope to discover a treasure trove. Lighthouses were erected on the shallower, more treacherous sections of the barrier reef during the 19th century as an aid to navigation. They now also mark popular dive and snorkel destinations.

The coral reef system of the Florida Keys is distinctively known as a spur-and-groove system. Long ridges of coral, called spurs, are divided by sand channels, or grooves, that merge with the adjoining reef flat, a coral rubble ridge on the inshore edge of the reef. The ridges of elkhorn coral thrive in heavy surf, often growing several inches a year. The spurs extend 100 yards or more, with shallower extremities sometimes awash at low tide while the seaward ends stand submerged in 30 to 40 feet of water. Small caves and tunnels wind through to the interior of the reef, home to myriad species of marine plants and animals. The white grooves separating the spurs are covered with coarse limestone sand, a composite of coral and mollusk shell fragments and plates from green calcareous algae. The wave action passing between the spurs of coral creates furrows in the sand floor of the grooves.

Generally, the shallower the reef, the brighter the colors of the corals, because strong sunlight is a prerequisite for reef growth. Legions of fish sway back and forth, keeping time with the rhythm of the waves. While deep dives yield fascinating discoveries—such as long-lost torpedoed ships—for those with advanced skills, sport divers will not be disappointed with the plethora of sea life within 60 feet of the surface. Night dives reveal the swing shift of the aquatic community. While the parrotfish may find a cave, secrete a mucous balloon around itself, and sleep the night through, sparkling corals blossom once the sun sets, and other species come out of hiding to forage for food.

Supplementing our coral barrier and the broken bodies of reef-wrecked ships, artificial reefs have been sunk to create underwater habitats for sea creatures large and small. The Florida Keys Artificial Reef Association, a nonprofit corporation of Keys residents, banded together in 1980 to capitalize on putting to use the many large pieces of concrete that became available during the removal of some of the old Keys bridges. More than 35,000 tons of rubble were deep-sixed throughout the Keys' waters between 1981 and 1987, creating acres of artificial reefs. In recent years, steel-hull vessels up to 350 feet long have been scuttled in stable sandy-bottom areas, amassing new communities of fish and invertebrates and easing the stress and strain on the coral reef by creating new fishing and diving sites. You'll find a comprehensive list of the artificial reef locations at the Florida Fish and Wildlife Conservation Commission website: myfwc.com.

Always use a mooring buoy if one is available. The large blue-and-white plastic floats are drilled directly into the sea bottom and installed with heavy chains or concrete bases, and are available on a first-come, first-served basis. If you are in a small craft, however, it is courteous to tie off with other similar boats, allowing larger vessels use of the mooring buoys. Approach the buoy from downwind against the current. Secure your boat to the pickup lines using a length of your own rope. Snap shackles provide quick and easy pickup and release. Large boats are advised to give out extra line to ensure a horizontal pull on the buoy. If no mooring buoys have been provided, anchor only in a sandy area downwind of a patch reef so that your boat's anchor and chain do not drag or grate on nearby corals.

DIVE SITES

In the Upper, Middle, and Lower Keys parts of this section, we highlight some of the better-known and most enchanting dive and snorkel sites, listed in descending order from the top of the Keys in the Key Largo National Marine Sanctuary to the Looe Key National Marine Sanctuary in the Lower Keys.

Underwater History

In August 2008 underwater archaeology students from across the country took part in a deep mystery 25 feet below the surface off Key Largo. Their discovery of weathered metal bands of a paddle wheel, parts of a smoke-stack, and boiler plates helped them solve the puzzle of the shipwrecked *Menemon Sanford*. This 237-foot side-paddle steamship sank in 1862 while on a secret Civil War mission. The vessel was built in 1854 and named after Captain Sanford, founder of the Sanford Independent Line that later became Royal Caribbean Cruise Line.

In Key West our coral reef system heads west into the sunset as it swings by Cayo Hueso into the untamed and isolated but charted waters leading to the Marquesas and the Dry Tortugas. (The half-day dive excursions based in Key West do not venture as far as these outer, uninhabited Keys. You will have to charter private overnight dive excursions or travel the distance in your own motor or sailing yacht if you wish to explore these waters; see the Cruising chapter.) In the Key West and the And Beyond parts of this section, we highlight 20 of the most interesting dive and snorkel sites from Key West to the Dry Tortugas National Park.

Upper Keys

Carysfort Reef

Situated at the extreme end of Key Largo National Marine Sanctuary, Carysfort Reef appeals to both novice and intermediate divers. British vessel HMS *Carysfort* ran aground here in 1770. The reef, now marked by the 100-foot steel Carysfort Lighthouse, undulates between 35 and 70 feet. Lush staghorn corals, which look like bumpy deer antlers, and masses of plate coral, which overlap each other like roofing tiles, cascade down the 30-foot drop to the sandy bottom. Schools of algae-grazing blue tang and pin-striped grunts circulate among the coral heads of a secondary reef. The HMS *Winchester*, a British man-of-war built in 1693, hit the reef in 1695 after most of her crew died of the plague while en route from Jamaica to England. The wreck, discovered in 1938, was cleaned out by salvagers in the 1950s. It rests southeast of Carysfort Light in 28 feet of water. Location: North Carysfort: Lat. 25° 13.80, Long. 80° 12.74; South Carysfort: Lat. 25° 13.00, Long. 80° 13.06.

The Elbow

Aptly named, the Elbow looks like a flexed arm as it makes a dogleg turn to the right. Prismatic damselfish and angelfish, so tame they will swim up and look you in the eye, belie this graveyard of sunken cargo ships, the bones of which litter the ocean floor. The 191-foot *Tonawanda*, built in 1863 in Philadelphia, ended its short career as a tug and transport vessel in 1866 when it stranded on the reef. The ca. 1877 passenger/cargo steamer *City of Washington,* cut down and sold as a barge, piled up on the Elbow Reef in 1917 as it was towed by the *Edgar F. Luchenbach*. Dynamited so it would not impede navigation, the barge's scattered remains rest near the *Tonawanda* in about 20 feet of water covered with purple sea fans and mustard-hued fire coral trees. The unidentified Civil War wreck, now nothing more than wooden beams held together by iron pins, sits in 25 feet of water. A search of the area may yield a sighting of an old Spanish cannon, probably thrown overboard to lighten the load when one of the ships ran aground. The Elbow, marked by a 36-foot light tower, provides good diving for the novice. Depths at this spur-and-groove reef range between 12 and 35 feet, and currents vary. Location: Lat. 25° 08.82, Long. 80° 15.19.

Christ of the Deep Statue

Perhaps one of the most famous underwater photographs of all time is of the *Christ of the Deep* statue, which stands silhouetted against the sapphire-blue ocean waters bordering Key Largo Dry Rocks. This 9-foot figure of Christ, arms upraised and looking toward the heavens, was donated to the Underwater Society of America by Egidi Cressi, an Italian industrialist and diving equipment manufacturer. Designed by Italian sculptor Guido Galletti and cast in Italy, the statue is a bronze duplicate of the Christ of the Abysses, which stands underwater off Genoa. Surrounded by a flotilla of nonchalant skates and rays, the statue's left hand appears to be pointing to the massive brain corals peppering the adjoining ocean floor. With depths ranging from shallow to 25 feet, snorkeling is outstanding. Schools of electric-blue neon gobies congregate in cleaning stations, waiting to service other fish that wish to be rid of skin parasites. A slow offer of an outstretched arm may net you a goby-cleaned hand. Location: Lat. 25° 07.45, Long. 80° 17.80.

Grecian Rocks

This crescent-shaped patch reef, which ranges in depth from shallow to 35 feet, ranks as a favorite among snorkelers and novice divers. Colonies of branched elkhorn corals, resembling the racks of bull moose or elk, provide a dramatic backdrop for the curious cruising barracuda, which often unnerve divers by following them about the reef but rarely cause a problem. Colossal star corals dot the area, which is populated by a rainbow palette of Spanish hogfish and a scattering of protected queen conch. An old Spanish cannon reportedly is concealed in one of the more luminous of the star coral, placed there some time ago by rangers of John Pennekamp Coral Reef State Park. Look for a small patch of reef near Grecian Rocks where old cannon and fused cannonballs litter the landscape. At low tide this reef rises out of the water. Location: Lat. 25° 06.70, Long. 80° 18.55.

San Pedro Underwater Archaeological Preserve

This shipwreck park named after the Spanish ship *San Pedro* lies in 18 feet of water approximately 1.25 nautical miles south of Indian Key. The ship went down in 1773, and the remains can be found on the white-sand bottom. The park is located approximately 1.25 nautical miles south from Indian Key at GPS coordinates N24 51.802' / W80 40.795'. To prevent anchor damage, make sure to tie up to mooring buoys located at the site. Visit floridastateparks.org for more information.

USS Spiegel Grove

The USS *Spiegel Grove*, a decommissioned landing ship dock (LSD 32), was scuttled as an artificial reef in May 2002 in the waters off Key Largo. The largest vessel ever sunk as an artificial reef in the US, the *Spiegel Grove* did not go down without a fight, however. The ship unexpectedly began to sink ahead of schedule, turtling and sinking upside down and at an angle that kept it from completely submerging. The ship's bow stuck up out of the water for three weeks before a Resolve Marine Group salvage crew rolled it onto its starboard side, allowing it to sink completely on June 10, 2002. The Spiegel Grove rests at a depth of 130 feet, midway between the *Benwood* wreck and the Elbow reef.

Benwood

The English-built freighter *Benwood,* en route from Tampa to Halifax and Liverpool in 1942 with a cargo of phosphate rock, attempted to elude German U-boats early in World War II by running without lights. Unfortunately, the American freighter *Robert C. Tuttle* also took a darkened route. In their ultimate collision, the American ship ripped the *Benwood*'s starboard side open like a can opener. As it limped along, a fire broke out on deck and attracted a German U-boat, which finished her off with two torpedo hits. A memorable first wreck for novice divers, the bow of the ship remains in about 50 feet of water, while the stern rests in but 25 feet. It lies in line with the offshore reef about 1.5 miles north of French Reef. Location: Lat. 25° 03.16, Long. 80° 20.02.

French Reef

Even novice divers can negotiate the caves at French Reef. Swim through the 3- to 4-foot limestone ledge openings or just peer in for a glance at the vermilion-painted blackbar soldierfish, which often swim upside down, mistakenly orienting themselves to the cave ceilings. Limestone ledges, adorned with tub sponges, extend from the shallows to depths in excess of 35 feet. Follow the mooring buoys for the best route. A mountainous star coral marks Christmas Tree Cave where, if you swim through the two-entrance passage, trapped air bubbles incandescently

flicker in the cave's low light. Hourglass Cave sports a shapely column of limestone that divides the space in half, and White Sand Bottom Cave, a large swim-through cavern, shelters a potpourri of groupers, dog snappers, moray eels, and copper-colored glassy sweepers. Location: Lat. 25° 02.06, Long. 80° 21.00.

White Bank Dry Rocks

A garden of soft corals welcomes snorkelers and novice divers to these patch reef twins. With calm waters and depths ranging from shallow to 25 feet, White Bank Dry Rocks extends north and south along Hawk Channel at the southern end of Key Largo National Marine Sanctuary. You will feel as if you are swimming in a giant aquarium, for the lacy sea fans, feathery sea plumes, and branching sea whips create surreal staging for the fluttering schools of sophisticated black-and-yellow French angelfish. Bring an underwater camera. Location: 1.25 miles inshore of French Reef.

Molasses Reef

Shallow coral ridges of this well-developed spur-and-groove reef radiate from the 45-foot light tower that marks Molasses Reef. Mooring buoys bob in deeper water, about 35 feet. Just off the eastern edge of the tower lies a single windlass, all that remains of the so-called Winch Wreck, or Windlass Wreck. Look for Christmas tree worms among the masses of star coral. The conical whorls, resembling maroon and orange pine trees, are actually worms that reside in living coral. If you slowly move a finger toward these faux flowers, they will sense your presence within half an inch and disappear like Houdini into their coral-encased tube homes. Location: Lat. 25° 01.00, Long. 80° 22.53.

USCG Bibb and USCG Duane

Advanced divers will relish the exploration of the two US Coast Guard cutters sunk as artificial reefs 100 yards apart near Molasses Reef. These vessels, ca. mid-1930s, saw action in World War II and the Vietnam War. Both did search and rescue in their later peacetime years and were decommissioned in 1985. A consortium of dive shops and the Monroe County Tourist Development Council bought the cutters, which were subsequently stripped of armament, hatches, and masts, then cleaned. In 1987 the US Army Corps of Engineers sank the 327-foot vessels on consecutive days. The *Bibb* rests on her side in 130 feet of water, with her upper portions accessible at 90 feet. The upright *Duane* sits in more than 100 feet of water, but you can see the wheelhouse at 80 feet and the crow's nest in 60 feet of water. Location: *Bibb:* Lat. 24° 59.71, Long. 80° 22.77; *Duane:* Lat. 24° 59.38, Long. 80° 22.92.

Pickles Reef

Pickles Reef got its name from the coral-encrusted barrels strewn about the ocean floor near the remnants of a cargo ship, called the Pickles Wreck, that carried them to their demise. The kegs are said to resemble pickle barrels, hence the name of the reef, but more likely were filled with building mortar bound for burgeoning construction in Key West. Look for the distinctively marked flamingo tongue snails, which attach themselves to swaying purple sea fans, grazing for algae. Flamboyantly extended around the outside of the flamingo tongue's glossy cream-colored shell is a bright orange mantle with black-ringed leopard-like spots. Don't be tempted to collect these unusual creatures, for the colorful mantle is withdrawn upon death. With depths between 10

and 25 feet and a moderate current, Pickles Reef is a good dive for novice to intermediate skill levels. Location: Lat. 24° 59.23, Long. 80° 24.88.

Conch Reef

Dive charters usually anchor in about 60 feet of water at Conch Reef, but the area actually offers something for everyone. With depths ranging from shallow to 100 feet and currents varying from moderate to strong, beginners as well as intermediate and advanced divers will be entranced here. The shallow section, festive with swirling schools of small tropicals, extends for a mile along the outer reef line. Conch Wall steeply drops from 60 to 100 feet, where sea rods, whips, fans, and plumes of the gorgonian family's deepwater branch congregate with an agglomeration of vaselike convoluted barrel sponges. The coral of Conch Reef was nearly decimated by heavy harvesting in bygone eras; dead stumps of pillar corals can still be seen. Location: Lat. 24° 57.11, Long. 80° 27.57.

Hens and Chickens

A brood of large star coral heads surrounds a 35-foot US Navy light tower within 7 feet of the water's surface on this inshore patch reef, bringing to mind a mother hen and her chicks. Less than 3 miles from shore, this easily accessed 20-foot-deep reef remains popular with novice divers. Plumes, fans, and candelabra soft corals intermingle with skeletons of the coral graveyard (almost 80 percent of the reef died in 1970 after an unusually cold winter). Jailhouse-striped sheepshead mingle with shy notch-tailed grunts and the more curious stout-bodied groupers, but don't be tempted; spearfishing is not allowed here. Remains of the Brick Barge, a modern casualty, and an old steel barge torpedoed during

World War II lie among the coral heads. Location: Lat. 24° 55.9, Long. 80° 32.90.

The Eagle

In 1985 an electrical fire disabled the 287-foot *Aaron K*, a freighter that carried scrap paper between Miami and South America. Declared a total loss, she was sold to the Monroe County Tourist Council and a group of local dive shops and then scuttled for use as an artificial reef. The vessel was renamed the *Eagle* after the Eagle Tire Company, which provided much of the funding for the project. A must-do for advanced divers, the *Eagle* landed on her starboard side in 120-foot waters, though her upper portions lurk within 65 feet of the surface. Densely packed polarized schools of silversides flow and drift within her interior. The tiny fork-tailed fish will detour around divers swimming through the school. Location: Lat. 24° 52.18, Long. 80° 34.21.

Middle Keys

Alligator Reef

Launched in 1820 in Boston, the USS *Alligator* hunted pirates in Florida as part of the West Indies Squadron. A 136-foot light tower now marks her namesake, Alligator Reef, which claimed the copper-and-bronze-fitted warship in 1825. The navy stripped the ship's valuables and blew her up. The *Alligator* rests offshore from the 8- to 40-foot-deep reef, now a bordello of brilliant tropicals, corals, and shells. Location: Lat. 24° 51.07, Long. 80° 37.21.

American, Maryland & Pelican Shoals

American, Maryland, and Pelican shoals lie just offshore of the Saddlebunch Keys. They are east of Summerland and Cudjoe Keys where dive boats depart. Teeming with fish,

these reefs are less visited than others in the Florida Keys.

Coffins Patch

Gargantuan grooved brain corals join staghorns and toxic fire corals at Coffins Patch, a 1.5-mile reef popular with Middle Keys divers. A drift of yellow-finned French grunts and festive angelfish join an escort of mutton snappers, each distinctively branded with a black spot below the rear dorsal fin, as they guard the remains of the Spanish galleon *Ignacio*, which spewed a cargo of coins across the ocean floor in 1733. Location: Lat. 24° 40.60, Long. 80° 58.50.

The Thunderbolt

In 1986 the artificial reef committee bought the *Thunderbolt*, a 188-foot cable-laying workboat, from a Miami River boatyard. The vessel was cleaned and her hatches removed. She then was towed south of Coffins Patch, where she was sunk as an artificial reef. Sitting majestically upright in 115 feet of water, the *Thunderbolt*'s bronze propellers, cable-laying spool, and wheelhouse are still recognizable. A stainless-steel cable leads from the wreck to a permanent underwater buoy. Current is strong at this wreck. Clip a line to the eye on the buoy and walk down the line. This dive is suitable for those with advanced certification. Location: Lat. 24° 39.48, Long. 80° 57.90.

Delta Shoals

This shallow 10- to 20-foot shoal claimed many an unsuspecting ship through the centuries. Perhaps the most colorful history is that of an old vessel that ran aground in the 1850s. The ship yielded no treasure, but recovery of unique relics and elephant tusks led to the name Ivory Wreck. Among the wreckage were leg irons and brass bowls, leading historians to believe this was a slave ship from Africa. Location: Lat. 24° 37.78, Long. 81° 05.49.

Sombrero Reef

A 142-foot lighthouse tower marks this living marine museum. Coral chasms, ridges, and portals support a proliferation of fuzzy, feathery, or hairy gorgonians as well as a salad bowl of leafy lettuce coral. A battalion of toothy barracuda swims reconnaissance, but don't be alarmed. You are too big to be considered tasty. Location: Lat 24° 37.50, Long. 81° 06.50.

Lower Keys

Looe Key National Marine Sanctuary

In 1744 Captain Ashby Utting ran the 124-foot British frigate HMS *Looe* hard aground on the 5-square-mile Y-shaped reef now bearing her name. Remains of the ship are interred between two fingers of living coral about 200 yards from the marker in 25 feet of water. The ballast and the anchor remain camouflaged with centuries of vigorous coral growth. Preserved as a national marine sanctuary since 1981, the 5- to 35-foot-deep waters surrounding Looe Key protect the diverse marine communities from fishing, lobstering, and artifact collecting, all forbidden.

The sanctuary, like Key Largo National Marine Sanctuary in the Upper Keys, offers interesting dives for novice, intermediate, and advanced divers alike. The spur-and-groove formations of Looe Key National Marine Sanctuary are the best developed in the Keys, and you can observe a complete coral reef ecosystem within the sanctuary's boundaries (see the Area Overview chapter).

Astronauts under the Sea

NASA's National Oceanic and Atmospheric Administration's Aquarius underwater laboratory is the site for "splash down." This is tech talk for astronaut training underwater. The lab at Aquarius is a 45-foot-long complex that rests 62 feet beneath the surface, 3 miles off Key Largo in the Florida Keys National Marine Sanctuary. This setting provides a habitat for astronauts training for possible missions in space. During the NASA Extreme Mission Operations, astronauts imitate moonwalks, testing for mobility using specially designed space suits and weights to simulate lunar gravity. Aquarius is also the world's only undersea science facility.

Take a laminated reef-creature guide sheet (readily available in dive shops) on your dive to identify the senses-boggling array of sea life at Looe Key. Look for some of these interesting species: The yellowhead jawfish excavates a hole in the sand with its mouth and retreats, tail-first, at the first sign of danger. The wary cottonwick sports a bold black stripe from snout to tail. The prehistoric-looking red lizardfish rests camouflaged on rocks and coral. The occasional blue-spotted peacock flounder changes color, chameleon-like, to match its surroundings.

Commercial dive charters provide excursions to Looe Key from Big Pine Key, Little Torch Key, and Ramrod Key. Location: Lat. 24° 32.70, Long. 81° 24.50.

The Adolphus Busch

Scuttled in 1998 between Looe Key and American Shoal, this 210-foot freighter is named for one of the founders of the brewing industry. The *Adolphus Busch* sits upright in 100 feet of water. A tower comes within 40 feet of the surface and can be penetrated. *Adolphus Busch* is rapidly becoming a thriving tenement of fish and marine organisms. Location: Lat. 24° 31.81, Long. 81° 27.64.

Key West

Eastern Sambo

An underwater ridge at 60 feet dropping off sharply to the sand line at 87 feet goes by the name of Eastern Drop-off in this immensely popular reef area southeast of Key West. Reddish-brown honeycomb plate corals encrust the sloping reef face, while boulder corals pepper the base at the outer margin of the reef. The Hook, a long spur-and-groove canyon, extends south from the Eastern Sambo reef marker. Look for cruising tarpon during the summer months. West of Eastern Sambo is a site commonly referred to as No. 28 Marker, where sea turtles and nurse sharks make their rounds of the elkhorn coral. Location: Lat. 24° 29.50, Long. 81° 39.80.

Middle Sambo

Coral heads and soft corals cover the sand beneath the 30- to 40-foot depths of Middle Sambo. You won't be alone as you observe the prolific lobsters haunting this area, especially in the summer months. Look for squadrons of tarpon and snook. Location: Lat. 24° 29.71, Long. 81° 41.79.

Western Sambo

Mooring buoys mark this popular reef area with a variety of dives to 40 feet. Fields of branch coral stretch into the blue infinity, while mountains of sheet, boulder, star, and pillar corals cover the dramatic drop from 28 to 40 feet. Small yellow stingrays, which are actually covered with dark spots and can pale and darken protectively when the environment dictates, lie on the bottom with their stout, venomous tails buried in the sand. In the protected midreef area of the Cut, goggle-eyed blennies mill about with a colony of yellowhead jawfish, retreating tail-first into their sand holes when frightened.

Half a mile south of Western Sambo, the remains of the *Aquanaut*, a 50-foot wooden tugboat owned by Chet Alexander, were scuttled in 75 feet of water as an artificial reef. Scattered about amid drifts of mahogany snappers and nocturnal glasseyes, the wreck is alive with spiderlike yellow arrow crabs. Location: Lat. 24° 29.38, Long. 81° 42.68.

The Cayman Salvager

The 187-foot-long, steel-hulled buoy tender *Cayman Salvager*, built in 1936, originally sank at the Key West docks in the 1970s. Refloated and innards removed, she went back down in 1985 for use as an artificial reef, coming to rest on her side. Hurricane-force waves later righted her, and she now sits in 90 feet of water on a sandy bottom. Look for the fabled 200-pound jewfish and 6-foot moray eel residing in her open hold. Location: 6 miles south of Key West, 1 mile southwest of Nine Foot Stake, which is 1 mile west of No. 1 Marker.

Joe's Tug

Sitting upright in 60 feet of water, *Joe's Tug*, a 75-foot steel-hulled tugboat, was scuttled as an artificial reef in 1989. The boat rests inshore from the *Cayman Salvager* on a bed of coral. This is one of the most popular wreck dives in the Key West circuit. Look for Elvis, the resident jewfish, who hangs out at the tug with yet another large moray eel. Location: 6 miles south of Key West.

Eastern Dry Rocks

Shells, conchs, ballast stones, cannonballs, and rigging of disintegrating wrecks litter the rubble zone, coral fingers, and sand canyons of Eastern Dry Rocks. With depths between 5 and 35 feet and only light current, this dive is suited to novices. Location: Lat. 24° 27.50, Long. 81° 50.44.

Rock Key

Twenty-foot cracks barely as wide as a single diver distinguish Rock Key from nearby cousins at Eastern Dry Rocks. A 19th-century ship carrying building tiles from Barcelona went aground on Rock Key, scattering her bounty about the ocean floor. Tiles carrying the Barcelona imprint are reportedly still occasionally recovered. Location: Lat. 24° 27.21, Long. 81° 51.60.

Stargazer

Billed as the "world's largest underwater sculptured reef," *Stargazer* stands 22 feet below the surface, 5 miles off Key West between Rock Key and Sand Key. The creation of artist Ann Lorraine Labriola, *Stargazer* mimics a primitive navigational instrument, its giant steel sections—ranging between 2,000 and 8,000 pounds—emblazoned with constellation symbols and emblems. A "mystery chart" sends divers on an underwater treasure hunt with a series of puzzles that require a certain amount of celestial knowledge to solve. Location: Lat. 24° 27.49, Long. 81° 52.09.

Sand Key

Originally called Cays Arena by early Spanish settlers, Sand Key, 6 miles south of Key West, is partially awash at low tide. Topped by a distinctive 110-foot red iron lighthouse, Sand Key's shape, composed of shells and ground coral, changes with each hurricane and tropical storm. Sand Key shines as a good all-weather dive and, with depths ranging to 65 feet, appeals to all skill levels. The shallows of the leeward side provide good snorkeling. In spring and summer the Gulf Stream movement over the shallows provides great visibility and vibrant colors. You can easily reach Sand Key on your own in a 17- to 18-foot boat on a calm day. Location: Lat. 24° 27.19, Long. 81° 52.58.

Ten-Fathom Bar

Advanced divers peruse a gallery of deep dives on the western end of the outer reef system, which is nearly 4 miles long. The southern edge, Fennel Ridge, begins at about 60 feet deep, giving the site its name, then plunges to the sand line, undulating between 90 and 120 feet. Encrusted telegraph cables at 45 to 55 feet, apparently snaking a line to Havana, cut across the eastern end of the Ten-Fathom Bar, competing with man-size sponges and dramatic black coral.

Near the cable, Eye of the Needle sports a plateau of coral spurs. Deep, undercut ledges shelter the spotted, white-bellied porcupinefish. Divers can swim under a ledge and up through a broad "eye" to the top of the plateau. Depths max out at 120 feet, but you'll see much more between 40 and 80 feet. Be prepared for a sea squadron of fin-driven tropicals to shadow your every move. Location: 0.5 mile due south of Sand Key.

Toppino's Reef (#1 Marker Reef)

Four and a half miles south of Boca Chica Channel and 5 miles south of Key West is one of the most beautiful shallow dive spots in the Keys. Famous for 8- to 10-foot high coral fingers rising from the bottom, marine life congregate to eat off the hard and soft coral. This is a very popular nighttime dive spot in 25 feet of water. The USS *Vandenberg* was sunk near this spot in 2009 (see below, this section).

Western Dry Rocks

Experts will love the unusual marine life at Western Dry Rocks. Novices and snorkelers will, too, because this site ranges in depth from 5 to 120 feet, averaging 30 feet with lots of light. Coral fingers with defined gullies and coral formations laced with cracks and caves showcase species normally found more in the Bahamas than in the Keys. The deep-dwelling candy basslets hide themselves away at 90 feet, while their more gregarious cousins, the orangeback bass, hang out in the open. The dusky longsnout butterflyfish prefer dark recesses, though they will sometimes curiously peer out to see what's happening. Sharks have been witnessed regularly enough to prompt advice against spearfishing. Location: 3 miles west of Sand Key.

Alexander's Wreck

Commercial salvor Chet Alexander bought a 328-foot destroyer escort from the US Navy at the bargain price of $2,000 and sank her (still sporting her deck guns) in about 40 feet of water west of Cottrell Key as an artificial reef in 1972. Though the current fluctuates from moderate to strong, the relatively shallow depths here allow conscientious novices a chance to swim among

fascinating sea creatures: The bodies of the prison-bar-striped spadefish resemble the spade figures in a deck of playing cards. Zebra-striped sheepshead are so curious that if you remain stationary, they may come over to investigate. The flashy metallic gold-and-silver-striped porkfish is apparently the victim of a cruel creator—two bold, black, diagonal bands slash across its glittery head. Location: Lat. 24° 36.97, Long. 81° 58.91.

Cottrell Key

A snorkeler's paradise at 3 to 15 feet, Cottrell Key, on the gulf side, saves the day for divers when the weather is foul on the Atlantic. The grassy banks of the adjoining lakes protect the reef in east-southeast to southwest winds. Ledges and solution holes run for several miles amid intermittent coral heads and swaying gorgonians. The pits, crevices, and coral caves hold great treasures: encrusting orange sponges, which look like spilled cake batter; lustrously mottled cowries, camouflaged by their extended mantles; Florida horse conchs, which will venture out of their long conical spire if you wait patiently; and spindle-shaped freckled tulip snails. Location: Gulf side, 9 miles out of N.W. Channel.

✳USS Vandenberg

Key West has its newest artificial reef: a 13,000-ton, 520-foot-long, 100-foot-tall decommissioned vessel, the *General Hoyt S. Vandenberg*. Located near marker 32 in 140 feet of water, 6 miles off the coast of Key West in the Florida Keys National Marine Sanctuary, and costing nearly $6 million, the *Vandenberg* is one of the premier dive sites in the world. Experts boast you can dive there for days and not see it all. Suitably trained and equipped deep divers can penetrate the superstructure using the multiple horizontal and vertical swim-through flooding and venting holes that are cut into the ship. The *Vandenberg* is a US Air Force missile-tracking ship that was decommissioned in 1983. The ship also tracked US space missions in the early 1960s. Local videographers from Digital Island Media won an Emmy for their work on filming the sinking of the *Vandenberg*.

i Local honorary Conch and ocean explorer Sylvia Earle convinced Google executives to launch Google Ocean. Using existing maps and databases to reveal parts of the ocean world, Google's downloadable programs allow views under the Florida Keys of marine protected areas, dive sites, and shipwrecks. All this without getting your hair wet! Visit earth.google.com/ocean.

And Beyond

The Shipwrecks of Smith Shoals

Between June and August 1942, four large ships met their demise near Smith Shoals, apparent unwary victims of American military mines. The USS *Sturtevent*, a 314-foot-long four-stack destroyer, was only two hours out of port escorting a convoy when two consecutive explosions ripped her apart. She rests in 65 feet of water. The 3,000-ton American freighter *Edward Luchenbach*, en route from Jamaica to New Orleans with a cargo of tin, zinc, and tungsten, joined the *Sturtevent* after hitting the same minefield. The *Bosiljka* also made a navigational misstep, succumbing to an American mine as she carried her pharmaceutical cargo from New Orleans to Key West. Groupers, jewfish, snappers, and cobia populate the sunken 277-foot Norwegian ship *Gunvor*, taken by a mine on her way to Trinidad from Mobile,

Alabama. The wreckage is scattered in 60 feet of water. Location: Lat. 24° 45.30, Long. 81° 01.18.

Marquesas Keys

This group of 10 mangrove islands surrounded by shallow waters has alternately been called the remains of a prehistoric meteor crater and an atoll. The ring of keys was named for the Marquis de Cadierata, commander of the 1622 Spanish fleet that included the wrecks *Atocha* and *Santa Margarita*. The wrecks were partially salvaged until 1630 by the Spanish, who enticed slave divers to search the remains, promising freedom to the first diver to recover a bar of silver from the site. Mel Fisher rediscovered the ships in 1985. Fisher, the famous 20th-century salvor, found a mother lode of treasure in the holds.

The Marquesas Keys evidence little human influence, for they remain uninhabited. Clusters of coral heads shrouded in groupers and snappers mark the southern edge of the islands. Twenty-five miles from Key West, the Marquesas appeal to divers cruising in their motor yachts or on an overnight charter, and to hale and hearty day-trippers. West of the Marquesas several wrecks dot the suboceanic landscape. Exercise caution before diving, however, because the US Navy has been known to use them as bombing and strafing targets from time to time. Before you strap on your tanks, check your radio for a Coast Guard bulletin regarding this area. Location: 25 miles west of Key West.

The Northwind

The *Northwind*, a large metal tugboat belonging to Mel Fisher's Treasure Salvors Inc., tragically sank in 1975 while working on the *Atocha* project. Said to have a malfunctioning fuel valve and a leaky bulkhead, the *Northwind* capsized while at anchor, taking Fisher's son and daughter-in-law to a watery grave. The vessel lies on her side in 40 feet of water 3.5 miles southwest of the Marquesas.

Cosgrove Shoal

A 50-foot skeletal lighthouse marks the northern edge of the Gulf Stream, 6 miles south of the western Marquesas. This rocky bank runs for miles, a prehistoric dead reef where caves and ledges support gardens and forests and social clubs of marine fin and flora. A contingent of giant barracuda patrols the shallows, and black coral grows up from the depths, which extend beyond recreational diving capacities. Be sure to take the strong outgoing tide into consideration before you dive here. Location: 6 miles south of the western edge of the Marquesas.

Marquesas Rock

Moderate to strong currents and depths to 120 feet dictate that this dive is only suited to advanced skill levels. A can-buoy marks the rocky plateau of Marquesas Rock, the cracks and crevices of which reveal a potpourri of sea life. A school of jacks, apparently attracted by your bubbles, may make a swing past. Saucer-eyed reddish squirrelfish, with elongated rear dorsal fins resembling squirrel tails, mind their own business in the shaded bottom crevices. Occasional sightings of sailfish, sperm whales, and white sharks have been reported. Keep in mind that when diving at Marquesas Rock you are 30 miles from the nearest assistance.

Florida Keys Menace

The lionfish, a small fish with spines that are venomous, is prolific and voracious and has been spotted in Florida Keys waters. The lionfish is native to the Pacific Ocean and has been known to upset local ecosystems off the coast of North Carolina as well as in the Bahamas. REEF and the Florida Keys National Marine Sanctuary sponsor derbies throughout the year with cash prizes to help rid our waters of this invasive species. Since 2010 more than 1,500 lionfish have been removed.

Dry Tortugas National Park

The end of the line in the Florida Keys, the Dry Tortugas lie some 60 miles beyond Key West. Small boats are discouraged from making the trip because strong tidal currents flowing against prevailing winds between Rebecca Shoals and the reef of the Tortugas can be treacherous. There is no fuel, freshwater, or facilities offering provisions, nor will you find any emergency assistance. Nonetheless, if your vessel is self-sufficient, if you are with a charter out of Key West, or you have traveled to the Dry Tortugas by seaplane or ferry to camp on Garden Key (see the Recreation and Campgrounds chapters), you are in for the treat of a lifetime.

The eight-island chain is guarded as our southernmost national park. All living creatures below are protected from collection or capture, so a virtual mega-aquarium exists beneath the sea. The constant Gulf Stream current cleanses the waters, allowing visibility of 80 to 100 feet over the 100-square-mile

⊕ Close-up

Diving for Lobster

Now, you Easterners may conjure up scarlet visions of the mighty Maines, but when we say lobster here in the Florida Keys, a totally different creature comes to mind. Equally delectable and much in demand, the **Florida lobster**, or spiny lobster, is actually a crustacean whose relatives include crabs, shrimp, and crawfish. Unlike its Downeast cousin, the Florida lobster is clawless. Ten spiderlike legs support its spiny head and hard-shell body, and radarlike antennae make up for bugged eyes and weak eyesight. But its best defense, and the one most coveted by hungry humans, remains its powerful tail muscle, which propels the lobster backward at breakneck speed.

Diving for lobster is a popular sport in the waters of the Florida Keys. Like any other hunt, you will need to understand your intended prey, for self-preservation will be their only consideration. Nocturnal feeders, spiny lobsters hide underwater in crevices, between rocks, in caves, under artificial reefs, near dock pilings, or in dead coral outcroppings during the day. They are not easy to spot. They occasionally peek out from their protective holes, but most often only a single antenna will be visible. The good news is that a whole gang may be hiding out together.

So how do you catch these potentially tasty morsels locals call "bugs"? We have found a few basic tools—and tricks—to help swing the scales in your favor:

- You will need a pair of heavy-duty dive gloves, for the two large horns on the lobster's head and the sharp spines of its whipping tail can draw blood.

- To store your captive prizes, get an easy-to-open mesh game bag that has a fastener that you can hook to your weight belt. Be sure this bag does not drag over the reef, which would damage coral and other marine life.

- A probe, or "tickle stick," which is a long metal or fiberglass rod with a short, 90-degree bend on one end, allows you to wisely refrain from poking your arm into a crevice or hole in order to coax out a lobster. That hole could just as easily house a moray eel as a lobster.

- And finally, a lobster net is a must if you hope to capture the tickled lobster.

To harvest lobsters in the Florida Keys recreationally, you must possess a valid Florida saltwater fishing license with a current crawfish stamp (see the Fishing chapter). Florida law mandates lobster hunters carry a device to measure the carapace of each lobster. (The carapace is that portion of the lobster shell beginning between the eyes and extending to the hard end segment just before the tail.) The carapace should measure at least 3 inches; otherwise, the lobster—deemed a "short"—must be returned to the sea. The measuring device is most often made of plastic or metal and can be attached to a string and secured to your game bag. Measure the lobster before you put it in your bag; do not bring it to the boat to be measured.

Look for lobsters in the patch reefs on the ocean side. Patch reefs can usually be found by using the NOAA navigational charts. Look for relatively shallow areas (15 to 20 feet) surrounded by deeper water (25 to 30 feet). If your boat is equipped with a chart recorder, use this device to detect bottom contours and the presence of fish. Look for irregular bottom areas, which will usually mean coral outcroppings and sponges. When you find the suspected patch reefs, check them out with a quick dive to the bottom before anchoring your boat. You will need to scuba dive for lobsters in the patch reefs.

Alternately, look for lobster "holes" in the shallow gulfside waters and, wearing mask, snorkel, and fins, free-dive for the crustaceans—a one-breath challenge for sure. These areas will appear as patches of brightness in the turtle-grass floor as you skim across the water in your skiff. Sandy sea bottom looks bright also, so you must slow to idle speed and look for a hunk of coral. It helps to throw a buoy marker at this spot (connect a dive weight to a Styrofoam buoy with a length of line), because these coral outcroppings are few and far between. Send a dive scout over the side to bird-dog the outcropping for antennae, and with a little luck, the hunt will begin.

These crusty crustaceans are a wily group. When frightened, the lobster will contract its powerful tail and propel itself like a bullet backward to the far recesses of its shelter or deep into the sea grass. Tickle your way to victory. Slowly slide your tickle stick behind the lobster and tap its tail. Bothered from behind, the lobster is persuaded to slowly leave its shelter to investigate. Once the lobster is out of the hole, place the net behind (yes, behind!) the lobster with the rim firmly resting on the sandy bottom if possible. Tap the lobster's head with the tickle stick. This time, irritated, the lobster will propel backward into your net. Quickly slam your net down on the seafloor so the lobster cannot escape. Then secure the net closed with your other hand. The lobster may thrash and become tangled in the net.

Holding the netted lobster firmly with one hand, measure the carapace. Carefully remove the lobster from the net. If the lobster is a short, release it to be captured another day. If it is legal size, place it securely in your game bag, tail-first. One thrust of the vigorous tail could negate all your efforts. Also, be careful not to release any other "bugs" you have already bagged. If you see a dark spot or reddish orange nodules under the tail, this lobster is an egg-bearing female. By Florida law you must release her.

Place your captured lobsters in the saltwater-filled bait well of your boat or store them on ice in a cooler with a lid. Do not wring the tails from the lobsters until you get back to shore. It is against Florida law to separate the tail from the body while on Florida waters. Once on dry land you may pull the tails, which by law must measure more than $5\frac{1}{2}$ inches. There is negligible meat in the body of the Florida spiny lobster, so it may be discarded unless you want to boil it to make lobster stock. After wringing the tail, break an antenna from the severed body of the crawfish. Insert the antenna, larger end first, into the underside base of the tail and then pull it out. The spiny thorns of the antenna will snag the intestinal tract, which will be removed with the antenna. If you wish to freeze the lobster tails, place them in small plastic ziplock bags, fill the bags with freshwater, and place the bags in the freezer for up to six months.

living coral reef. Just off the beach on the west side of Loggerhead Key slumbers a snorkeler's paradise. About a mile offshore lies the remains of a 300-foot, steel-hulled French wreck. Divers report that a monster-size jewfish estimated to be 150 years old resides under the wreck. Other wrecks are littered about the ocean floor, claimed by the reef during centuries past.

DIVE CENTERS

As you drive down the Overseas Highway from Key Largo to Key West, you will notice banner-size, red-and-white diver-down flags heralding one dive shop after another. More than 100 such establishments are listed in the phone book alone. To help you navigate this minefield of choices, we supply you with the best ammunition: information.

Many of the dive operations offer the same basic services and will take you to similar, if not the same, spots. But each also differs in many ways. Snorkelers and divers often are taken to the reef in the same excursion, for the varied depths of our spur-and-groove reefs can be experienced with multiple levels of expertise. Snorkel-only trips also are an option. The size of dive excursions varies greatly, ranging from 20 individuals or more to a small-boat group called a six-pack.

Dive rates are based on a two-tank, two-site daylight dive. If you don't have your own equipment, full-gear packages—generally including two tanks, buoyancy compensator, weight belt, regulator, octopus breathing device, gauges, and occasionally mask, snorkel, and fins—are available. A wet suit is advisable in winter. Always ask exactly what is included if you need a full-gear package. All our recommended dive centers make a

one-tank, night-dive excursion on request unless otherwise specified.

Virtually all of our listed dive centers offer optional dive packages, either for multiple days of diving or for hotel-dive combinations. If you plan to dive on several days of your holiday, you will save money with a package, but you will be limited to diving with one exclusive dive center.

You may assume, unless otherwise noted, all featured dive centers rent full equipment and maintain a retail dive shop where you can purchase equipment, accessories, and underwater camera housings if needed. You may also count on the fact that all recommended dive centers offer a one-day "let's give it a try" resort course. These courses are based on participation of two or more people. Private courses also are available at a considerably higher fee. Many of our recommended dive centers offer a wide selection of Professional Association of Diving Instructors (PADI), National Association of Underwater Instructors (NAUI), and other advanced classes.

You will be required to show your certification card and logbook, and you must wear a buoyancy compensator and a submersible pressure gauge. Snorkels are required equipment for all divers. To dive deeper than 60 feet, considered a deep dive, you must hold advanced certification or a logbook entry showing dives to equivalent depths within the last six months. If you cannot meet these specifications, you will be required to be accompanied by an instructor or guide, which often entails an additional fee. You must wear an octopus (an emergency breathing device to share air with your dive buddy) or carry spare air for a deep dive, and you must be equipped with a depth gauge or a timing device. You do not need advanced certification to participate in a night dive, but you must own or rent a dive light and carry a Cyalume stick as a backup lighting system.

All dive centers request you check in at least 30 minutes prior to the excursion's departure. Allow even more time if you are renting a full-gear package. We list the dive centers in alphabetical order from Key Largo through Key West.

Upper Keys

AMY SLATE'S AMORAY DIVE RESORT
MM 104.2 Bayside, Key Largo
(305) 451-3595 or (800) 426-6729
amoray.com
From this resort, you can hop out ,of bed onto the deck and take off for a scuba excursion. The Amoray Dive Resort's villa lodging options, complete with hot tub and pool, cater to your every diving whim (see the Accommodations chapter). Amoray's catamaran will whisk you to the reefs of the Key Largo National Marine Sanctuary for a two-tank dive. Night dives are available.

CAPTAIN SLATE'S ATLANTIS DIVE CENTER
MM 106.5 Oceanside,
51 Garden Cove Dr., Key Largo
(305) 451-3020 or (800) 331-3483
captainslate.com
Divers of all skill levels enjoy outings with the Atlantis Dive Center. Snorkelers can make a snorkel-only excursion to one destination aboard a glass-bottomed boat, or they can accompany divers to two reef locations. Snorkeling rates here include mask, snorkel, fins, and safety vest. A special feature of Captain Slate's is the custom underwater wedding package. Divers are married in front of the *Christ of the Deep* statue at Key Largo

Dry Rocks. Vows are made via underwater slates as guest-divers watch the ceremony from the ocean floor and guest-snorkelers view the proceedings from overhead. Guest landlubbers are accommodated in the glass-bottomed boat, where the perspective varies yet again. Videos and still-photography of the blessed event are also available.

CORAL REEF PARK COMPANY
MM 102.5 Oceanside, John Pennekamp Coral Reef State Park, Key Largo
(305) 451-6300 or (800) 326-3521
pennekamppark.com
Snorkel-only excursions in John Pennekamp Coral Reef State Park leave the docks 3 times daily. The shallow-reef sites vary, depending upon where the least current, least wave action, and best visibility conditions exist. The snorkel trip lasts 2.5 hours, with 1.5 hours of actual snorkeling time at Molasses Reef, White Bank Dry Rocks, Grecian Rocks, Key Largo Dry Rocks, or Cannon Patch. Another option is a 4-hour sail and snorkel aboard a 38-foot catamaran. If you want to stay close to shore, you can rent mask, snorkel, and fins and paddle around in the water off Cannon Beach, where, yes, there really are a couple of sunken cannon and ancient anchors.

DIVERS DIRECT
MM 99.6 Oceanside, Key Largo
(305) 451-0118 or (800) 348-3872
diversdirect.com
Divers Direct, a water lover's emporium with 6 locations in the state of Florida (see the website for details), offers one of the largest selections of men's, women's, and children's clothing along with snorkeling and scuba gear, kayaks, surfboards, wakeboards, kids' equipment, videos, books, and a repair service. In business since 1984, the owners are

divers as well. They have trained their staff to be knowledgeable of their products and make sure their customers have the right gear for the right dive.

FLORIDA KEYS DIVE CENTER
MM 90.5 Oceanside, Tavernier
(305) 852-4599 or (800) 433-8946
floridakeysdivectr.com
The Florida Keys Dive Center is one of the few that offer technical diving. This refers to diving beyond the limits that apply to recreational diving. New compressors blend trimex, a gas containing varied blends of helium, nitrogen, and oxygen. Partial pressure blending puts 100 percent oxygen into special scuba tanks in addition to pre-blended enriched. The Florida Keys Dive Center is also one of only two PADI 5-Star Career Development Centers in the Keys.

> **i** The Florida Keys National Marine Sanctuary has devised a Shipwreck Trail that directs you to nine historic shipwreck sites along our coral reef. Underwater site guides for each of the wrecks are available at local dive shops. The guides provide shipwreck and mooring-buoy positions, the history of the wrecked ships, a site map, and information on marine organisms you may encounter.

HORIZON DIVERS
MM 100 Oceanside, Ocean Drive,
Building #1, Key Largo
(305) 453-3535 or (800) 984-3483
horizondivers.com
Horizon Divers offers a full hour of bottom time studying large varieties of fish species found in the waters off Key Largo. Videotape or photograph the sea life in these waters

while polishing your diving skills. Whether you're novice or advanced, Horizon Divers has instructors to help you hone your skills. Advanced divers can dive in the area wrecks and in waters up to depths of 140 feet.

*JOHN PENNEKAMP CORAL REEF STATE PARK BOAT RENTALS & DIVE CENTER
MM 102.5 Oceanside, Key Largo
(305) 451-6300 or (800) 326-3521
floridastateparks.org/pennekamp
The Pennekamp State Park Dive Center prides itself on being the "only authorized dive center" in John Pennekamp Coral Reef State Park, although all the Key Largo dive centers advertise themselves as diving the park. The only dive center actually situated inside Pennekamp's grounds, this company's scuba shuttles regularly visit such novice sport dives as Molasses Reef, French Reef, Christmas Tree Cove, the wreck of the *Benwood,* and the *Christ of the Deep* statue. All dives are less than 60 feet, and certification requirements are stringent. If you have not dived in the past 2 years, you must hire a guide. If you have not dived in 3 years, you will have to take a review course. Pennekamp does not offer night dives.

OCEAN DIVERS
MM 100 Oceanside, 522 Caribbean Dr.,
Key Largo
(305) 451-1113 or (800) 451-1113
oceandiversid.com
Ocean Divers has had over 500,000 divers come through their dive center. Diving with Ocean Divers, which opened in 1977, brings a different adventure, because this company tries to maintain a rotating schedule of set dive sites if conditions allow. Visiting the popular sites within the Key Largo National

Marine Sanctuary, Ocean Divers slips into Eagle Ray Alley and Fire Coral Cave at Molasses Reef, and between the stands of the rare day-feeding pillar coral. Divers who enjoy wreck dives can visit the *Bibb*, the *Duane*, and the *Spiegel Grove*. Night dives are regularly offered and upon request. Ocean Divers is adjacent to Marina Del Mar Resort. It maintains 2 dive shops; the second is located at MM 105.5 Bayside, Key Largo.

RAINBOW REEF
MM 100 Oceanside, Key Largo
MM 83.4 Oceanside, Islamorada
(305) 451-7171 or (800) 457-4354
rainbowreef.us
Rainbow Reef, with 2 locations, offers extensive dives to coral and artificial reefs, ledges, walls, and centuries-old wrecks. Oh, and don't forget the fish! Depths range from 18 to 120 feet, with each dive site offering its own unique qualities. The charters hit all the spectacular spots from Pennekamp State Park down to Alligator Reef. Rainbow Reef has small (12 persons max) boats to help make your dive personal and pleasurable. They are a full-service PADI 5-Star Gold Palm Instructor Center. See you beneath the sea!

SILENT WORLD DIVE CENTER INC.
MM 103.2 Bayside, Key Largo
(305) 451-3252
silentworldkeylargo.com
Silent World regularly visits the Elbow, Key Largo Dry Rocks, the *Benwood*, French Reef, Carysfort Reef, and other popular sites within Key Largo National Marine Sanctuary.

Middle Keys

ABYSS DIVE CENTER
MM 54 Oceanside, at the Holiday Inn Marina, Marathon
(305) 743-2126 or (800) 457-0134
abyssdive.com
The Abyss Dive Center in Marathon subscribes to the less-is-more theory of diving, which guarantees lots of personal attention. The company takes a maximum of 6 divers or snorkelers to 48 sites spread over the reefs at Sombrero Key, Coffins Patch, Yellow Rocks, and Delta Shoals. Abyss will take you to the *Thunderbolt* if your certs are current or your dive experience warrants, or you can hire an instructor and explore the wreck with a guide.

HALL'S DIVING CENTER
MM 48.5 Bayside, Marathon
(305) 743-5929 or (800) 331-4255
hallsdiving.com
If you are an advanced certified diver or have an 80-foot dive under your weight belt, head out to the *Thunderbolt* with Hall's. Divers of other skill levels will enjoy diving the Middle Keys' 25- to 90-foot reef specialties, from Looe Key to Coffins Patch and especially around Sombrero Reef. Snorkelers may accompany divers at shallow reef locations. In addition to standard equipment, a deluxe full-gear package, featuring top-of-the-line Nitrox clean gear, is available. Hall's also rents and provides certification in the use of a rebreather and offers such specialty dives as marine interaction dives and diver propulsion vehicles. Or you can rent mask, snorkel, and fins and explore the shallow gulf waters or the Atlantic Ocean off Sombrero Beach with a buddy.

TILDEN'S SCUBA CENTER
MM 49.5 Bayside, at the Blackfin Resort and Marina, Marathon
(305) 743-7255 or (888) 728-2235
tildensscubacenter.com

Long known as a top-notch dive center in the Florida Keys, Tilden's heads to such reef locations as Coffins Patch, Porkfish Reef, and Shark Harbor and takes advanced divers on guided excursions to the *Thunderbolt* and the *Adelaide Baker* wrecks. Tilden's reports that the Middle Keys reef tracts are very healthy. Tilden Scuba Center operates one of the largest dive vessels in the Middle Keys—it's licensed to carry 40 passengers—but limits its excursions to 24 divers and snorkelers.

Lower Keys

✳LOOE KEY REEF RESORT & DIVE CENTER
MM 27.5 Oceanside, Ramrod Key
(305) 872-2215 or (800) 816-3483
diveflakeys.com

The friendly crew at Looe Key Reef Resort whisks you off to the Looe Key National Marine Sanctuary, where you will visit 3 sites with at least an hour of bottom time at each location. On Wed and Sat divers visit 2 reef sites plus the wreck of the *Adolphus Busch*. The other days divers visit 3 reef sites. Snorkelers may accompany divers. Looe Key Reef Resort & Dive Center offers dive/lodging packages at its adjoining motel. The dive boat leaves from its mooring directly behind the motel, so schlepping your gear is not a burden here.

STRIKE ZONE CHARTERS
MM 29.6 Bayside, Big Pine Key
(305) 872-9863 or (800) 654-9560
strikezonecharter.com

Docked out back, Strike Zone Charters' glass-bottomed catamarans are ready to transport you to the Looe Key National Marine Sanctuary for a spectacular two-tank dive. Strike Zone now also visits one of the Keys' newest artificial reefs, the *Adolphus Busch*.

i Soldiers Undertaking Disabled Scuba (SUDS) is a nonprofit organization designed to help improve the lives of injured soldiers returning from Iraq and Afghanistan. As part of soldiers' physical rehab, SUDS often takes them to Key Largo to finalize their scuba certification. For more information, visit sudsdiving.org.

UNDERSEAS INC.
MM 30.5 Oceanside, Big Pine Key
(305) 872-2700
underseasinc.com

In the Lower Keys when you've said, "Looe Key National Marine Sanctuary," you've said it all. And when you need a dive center, Underseas will take you to depths to satisfy all levels, from snorkelers and novice divers to those with advanced skills. Looe Key is endlessly fascinating. Departures are at 8:30 a.m. and 1:30 p.m.

Key West

✳CAPTAIN'S CORNER DIVE CENTER
125 Anne St.
(305) 296-8865 or (305) 304-0437
captainscorner.com

Captain's Corner Dive Center's scuba and snorkel excursions feature wreck and reef dives, and double wreck dives are available by special arrangement. During daylight saving time months, twilight wreck and reef dives are available on Tues, Thurs, and Sat. First you dive a wreck, then watch the sunset from the deck of the boat. After dark, experience the after-hours sea life during a reef dive. Private trips may be booked to the wreck of the *Nuestra Señora de Atocha*, 30 miles west of Key West. Captain's Corner always has instructors in the water with you, so you can sign on even if you are a novice diver. The boat departs from 631 Greene St., corner of Greene and Elizabeth Streets, at the Conch Republic Seafood Restaurant.

DIVE KEY WEST INC.
3128 N. Roosevelt Blvd.
(305) 296-3823 or (800) 426-0707
divekeywest.com
Dive Key West offers "reef du jour," customizing the schedule based on diver demand and weather conditions. It concentrates on the 30-foot reef lines where the light is better and the colors are more brilliant, allowing you more bottom time. The inner reefs have large stands of coral and a high concentration of tropical fish, while at the outer reefs you will see less coral, more big sea fans and sponges, and larger finfish. For your 2-dive combo you can choose between a wreck and a reef or 2 reefs. Dive Key West visits the wrecks of the *Cayman Salvager, Joe's Tug,* and the *Alexander,* which, at 90 feet, 60 feet, and 30 feet, respectively, offer a skill level for everyone.

LOST REEF ADVENTURES
261 Margaret St., on Key West Bight
(305) 296-9737 or (800) 952-2749
lostreefadventures.com
Lost Reef Adventures customizes its dive trips a day before departure based upon the skill levels and dive-site desires of interested divers. Excursions visit the celebrated *Joe's Tug,* the *Cayman Salvager,* and *Alexander* wreck sites and reefs from the Western Sambos to the Western Dry Rocks. Lost Reef offers night pilgrimages seasonally. First you can pay homage to the sun as it sinks into the water, then you will take the plunge for a one-tank twilight dive.

Pin Wreck

Off Grassy Key, in 14 feet of water, archaeological divers from the Florida State Division of Historical Resources and Florida Keys National Marine Sanctuary discovered a timeworn pile of rubble known as the Pin Wreck, named for the shiny copper alloy and wooden fastening pins found on the ocean floor. The 130-foot wreck is one of a few found in Hawks Channel that flows between Marathon and Grassy Key. Divers also confirmed, from further examining the wreck, that turtles have used the old posts and alloy fasteners to scratch themselves. By doing so, they have kept corrosion off the metal parts.

SEADUCTION
1605 N. Roosevelt Blvd., on Garrison Bight
(305) 296-9914 or (800) 853-3483
seaduction.com/keywest
Mornings find Seaduction's dive boat exploring 2 wrecks or 2 reefs. Wrecks visited include *Joe's Tug,* the *Cayman Salvager,* and the *Alexander,* whose shallower depths invite exploration by those of all experience levels. Seaduction offers trips to a wreck and a reef or 2 reefs in the afternoons. These excursions visit the Sambos, Rock Key, Sand Key, and the Dry Rocks. Snorkelers are welcome on the afternoon excursions, or they may opt for a snorkel-only trip. Night dives are also offered regularly.

RECREATION

I f you want to scuba dive or snorkel, fish, sail, or motor in our abundant waters, see the related chapters in this book. For a plethora of other stimulating diversions, read on. We show you where the action is—from skydiving, parasailing, and water sports to sunset cruises, ecotours, and bicycling. You'll find out about our beaches and public parks in this chapter. And if the weather isn't fine—which is rare—or you would just like to stay indoors, we tell you where to see a first-run movie or even a local play.

OVERVIEW

Expect to pay a fee for your recreational choices. We will indicate which diversions are free. Recreation facilities are organized by category from Key Largo to Key West.

AIR TOURS & SKYDIVING

KEY WEST BIPLANES
Key West International Airport
3469 S. Roosevelt Blvd., Key West
(305) 294-8687
keywestbiplanes.com
For a bird's-eye view of Key West and beyond, take a ride in a vintage open-cockpit biplane. Key West Biplanes' sightseeing plane rides take you over the coral reef to view shipwrecks in Fleming Key Channel, along the south shore of Key West, to Boca Grande Key, across the backcountry waters, and up the Keys as far as Little Palm Island (see the Accommodations chapter). Tours range from 6 minutes to more than an hour. Prices are based on 2 people riding in the front seat. They also offers aerobatic rides.

SKYDIVE KEY WEST
MM 17 Bayside, Lower Sugarloaf Airport, Sugarloaf Key
(305) 745-4386
skydivekeywest.com
Try tandem skydiving from 10,000 feet over the Lower Keys and Key West with Skydive Key West. First-timers are welcome. Allow 1 hour per person for this venture, including training and the jump. Soft landings are provided on Lower Sugarloaf Key. Skydive expeditions aboard a Cessna 182 depart Sugarloaf Airport between 10 a.m. and sunset 7 days a week. Skydivers are advised not to scuba dive for 24 hours before their jump. Videos and photographs are available for purchase as souvenirs. Jumps are by reservation only, and you must be at least 18 years of age to take the plunge.

BEACHES & PUBLIC PARKS

Life's a beach, the T-shirts say, but first-time visitors to the Keys who expect to find soft, white, endless sand along the ocean are bound to be disappointed. The coral reef protects the Keys from the pounding surf that grinds other shorelines into sand, and so most of ours must be carted in by the truckload. Nevertheless, if stretching out in the sand tops your recreational must-do list, humans and nature have teamed up here to bring you a stretch or two. Some of our parks and beaches charge admission fees, and most have specific hours of accessibility.

Keys beaches do not maintain lifeguard stations. Riptides are rare here, but jellyfish are not. Swim at your own risk, and never venture out alone or after dark.

i For your safety, Florida has warning flags posted on our public beaches statewide. Double red lines: no swimming at all. Yellow: medium hazard, moderate surf and/or currents. Green: low hazard, calm conditions but exercise caution. Purple: dangerous marine life.

Upper Keys

ANNE'S BEACH
MM 73.5 Oceanside, Islamorada
At low tide, tiny Anne's Beach holds enough sand to accommodate several blankets, but it attracts sun worshipers by the dozens. Swimming waters are shallow. A wooden boardwalk meanders for about 0.3 mile along the water, through the mangroves, and 5 picnic pavilions jut out from the boardwalk. Parking is limited. To find Anne's Beach, slow down along the Overseas Highway southwest of Caloosa Cove Resort and look toward the ocean for 2 small parking lots. The boardwalk connects the lots. Blink and you'll miss it. There is no charge.

BEACH BEHIND THE LIBRARY
MM 81.5 Bayside, Islamorada
This stretch of beach has no more official name than its general location, but it does offer a playground, restrooms, and showers. There is no admission charge.

DAGNY JOHNSON KEY LARGO HAMMOCK BOTANICAL STATE PARK
MM 106 Oceanside, Key Largo
(305) 451-1202
floridastateparks.org/keylargohammock
Encompassing almost 2,500 acres stretched over nearly 11 miles of north Key Largo, this state park is a jewel. The park is located in a tropical jungle of mangrove swamp, coastal rock barren, and a rockland hammock. Some of the resident species are rare tree snails, the Schaus swallowtail, the silver-banded hairstreak, and mangrove and hammock skippers. There is a guided walk every Thurs and Sun on a beautiful 0.5-mile nature trail. A backcountry permit, obtained at John Pennekamp Coral Reef State Park (see listing in this section), gives you access to an additional 6 miles of tranquil Keys flora and fauna.

FOUNDERS PARK
MM 87 Bayside, Plantation Key
(305) 853-1685
islamorada.fl.us/newsite/founderspark
Islamorada, Village of Islands, is proud of its green spaces. One of its gleaming examples is the 40-acre municipal Founders Park on Plantation Key. This multipurpose park offers fun for the entire family—including the family dog! The park features playgrounds, sandy beaches, a dog park, baseball diamonds, picnic areas, an Olympic-size pool with restrooms, bocce, and tennis courts, a vita course with 18 exercise stations, a

skate park, and unforgettable views of the Gulf of Mexico. Various community events are held here throughout the year, so check local publications. Some fees may apply to some areas.

FRIENDSHIP PARK
MM 101 Oceanside, Key Largo

This park sports a playground, a Little League field, swings, and a basketball court. It's perfect for those lazy afternoons with children in tow, and it's especially inviting for picnics. The park is open from 8 a.m. until dusk or when a Little League game is scheduled. Admission is free.

HARRY HARRIS PARK
MM 92.5 Oceanside, Tavernier
(305) 852-7161

Bring the kids along to Harry Harris, where a small beach fronts a tidal pool protected by a stone jetty. You'll find a playground, ball field, volleyball net, in-line skating park, and picnic grounds. Restrooms are also available. To reach the park, follow signs leading toward the coast along the oceanside by mile marker 92.5 (Burton Drive). Stay on Burton Drive about 2 miles and follow the signs to the left. Admission is free, except on weekends and federal holidays when non-residents (persons residing outside Monroe County) must pay a per-person admission fee as well as a docking fee to use the boat ramp. The park is open from 8 a.m. to sunset.

INDIAN KEY BEACH
MM 78 Oceanside, Islamorada

Although there isn't much of a beach here, a swimming area and boat access are available. Admission is free.

⁕JOHN PENNEKAMP CORAL REEF STATE PARK
MM 102.5 Oceanside, Key Largo
(305) 451-1202
floridastateparks.org/pennekamp

Well known to divers and snorkelers as the first underwater state park in the US, John Pennekamp also serves a wide palette of diversions within its land-based boundaries. You can explore most of the fascinating habitats of the Florida Keys here (see the Area Overview chapter), and enjoy campfire programs, guided walks, and canoe trips. The park offers a nature trail, beaches, picnic areas, campsites (see the Campgrounds chapter), restrooms, showers, and water-sports concessions (see listings in this chapter) where you can rent any equipment you might desire, from scuba gear to sailboats. Expect to pay a nominal admission fee per person and per vehicle. The park is open from 8 a.m. to sunset.

KEY LARGO COMMUNITY PARK
MM 99.6 Oceanside, Key Largo

This huge community park offers playgrounds, ball fields, a skate park, and tennis and volleyball courts. It is co-located with Jacob's Aquatic Center (see listing in the Water Sports section of this chapter).

⁕LIGNUMVITAE KEY BOTANICAL STATE PARK
MM 78.5 Bayside, Islamorada
(305) 664-9814

The only way to get to this park is by boat. The trails here provide real insight to an almost untouched tropical spot. Tours are available by calling the number above.

*LONG KEY STATE PARK
MM 67.5 Oceanside, Long Key
(305) 664-4815
floridastateparks.org/longkey

A long, narrow sand spit makes up the "beach" at this state park, which is fronted by a shallow-water flat. You can rent a canoe and enjoy the calm, easily accessible waters while you bird-watch and fish in ideal conditions. The picnic area is equipped with charcoal grills. Long Key State Park offers superb, newly renovated oceanfront campsites (see the Campgrounds chapter), restrooms, and shower facilities. Expect to pay a nominal admission fee per person and per vehicle. Long Key State Park is open from 8 a.m. to sunset.

SEA OATS BEACH
MM 74 Oceanside, Islamorada

Featured on the front page of *USA Today* after Hurricane Wilma flooded this part of US 1, Sea Oats Beach has now been refurbished to the tune of $5.4 million. This long stretch of beach offers a full mile of open water with grass flats for wade fishing for bonefish and tarpon. It is not unusual for a flats skiff to go poling by or to see folks just hanging out on the beautiful white sand with the sea oats blowing in the Atlantic breeze.

Middle Keys

CURRY HAMMOCK STATE PARK
MM 56.2 Oceanside, Marathon
(850) 245-2157

The newest addition to the state park scene in the Florida Keys is Curry Hammock, at Little Crawl Key just north of Marathon Shores. Exuding an untouched charm all its own, the park offers a mix of tropical hammock, mangrove swamp, and a wide expanse of the coral rock sand that passes for a beach in the Keys. Grills and picnic tables abound, many tucked beneath shady buttonwood trees. The kids will enjoy the swings and slides, and anglers will like the shallow, productive bonefish flat that fronts the shoreline. A cut of deeper water on the north side of the park affords the chance for a "real" swim and maybe some snorkeling as well. Changing rooms and restrooms are fresh, clean, and new. A number of roofed pavilions protect picnic tables and grills from the elements. A nominal fee for entry is charged by honor system. Camping is not allowed here. So far, this little gem remains relatively undiscovered.

MARATHON COMMUNITY PARK
MM 49 Oceanside, Marathon

The city of Marathon can be very proud of their 23-acre public park, which offers 2 softball fields, 4 tennis courts, playgrounds, picnic area, 3 basketball courts that are also used as a roller-hockey rink, a jogging path, pavilion, band shell, and restrooms. The park is free.

SOMBRERO BEACH
MM 50 Oceanside, Sombrero Beach Road, Marathon

This spacious, popular public beach offers a picnic area, playground, restrooms, and sweeping views of the Atlantic. Swimming waters run deep off Sombrero Beach. The Marathon Chamber of Commerce and volunteer organizations work to keep this gem of a beach in pristine condition. There is no admission charge, and parking is plentiful.

Lower Keys

✳BAHIA HONDA STATE PARK
MM 37 Oceanside, Bahia Honda
(305) 872-2353
floridastateparks.org/bahiahonda
Across the Seven Mile Bridge from Marathon, Bahia Honda State Park sparkles like a diamond and boasts the best natural beach in all of the Florida Keys. Narrow roads wind through the mangrove thickets, many of which have been fitted as campsites (see the Campgrounds chapter). Tarpon fishing beneath the Bahia Honda Bridge attracts seasoned anglers and novices alike, and the park has its own marina with boat ramps and overnight dockage. Bahia Honda offers picnic facilities, restrooms, guided nature walks, and charter boat excursions. Expect to pay a nominal admission fee per person and per vehicle. The park is open 8 a.m. to sunset.

BIG PINE KEY PARK
MM 31 Oceanside, end of Sands Road, Big Pine Key
Monroe County spent $5 million on this community park that includes a playground, baseball field, basketball and roller-hockey courts, a skate park, and a central building containing a concession stand. Located on the property is an all-purpose field for other sports programs plus jogging trails circling the park.

LITTLE DUCK KEY BEACH
MM 39 Oceanside, Little Duck Key
With restrooms and picnic shelters, this beach makes for an ideal lunch spot. The small beach provides a swimming area but no lifeguards. Open from 8 a.m. until dusk, the beach is free to the public. And don't be confused by the name. This beach is on Little Duck Key, not Duck Key. You will find it on the left side of the Overseas Highway, just this side of Bahia Honda, as you are traveling south toward Key West.

Key West

BAYVIEW PARK
Truman Avenue and Jose Martí Drive
You will definitely notice Bayview Park if you are driving into Key West on N. Roosevelt Boulevard, which becomes Truman Avenue. On your left as the road narrows and you head into Old Town, Bayview Park is one of the few free green spots still left in Key West. Look for the gazebo. Several picnic tables are strewn throughout the park and come highly recommended for a shady afternoon lunch.

✳FORT ZACHARY TAYLOR HISTORIC STATE PARK
Truman Annex at the end of Southard Street
(305) 292-6713
floridastateparks.org/forttaylor
Look to the left of the brick fort for a pleasant, although rocky, beach with picnic tables and barbecue grills. The locals call this place "Fort Zach"; this is where they come in droves to sunbathe and snorkel. The water is clear and deep, and you're likely to see many colorful fish congregating around the limestone-boulder breakwater islands constructed just offshore. When it gets too hot on the beach, head for the shade—there's plenty of it available under the lofty pine trees in the picnic area. The beach area is open 8 a.m. to sunset. An admission fee to the park is charged.

HIGGS BEACH AND C. B. HARVEY REST BEACH
Atlantic Boulevard

These twin beaches are so close together, they are often mistaken for each other. Higgs Beach offers a playground, picnic tables, and nearby tennis courts. It is between White and Reynolds Streets on Atlantic Boulevard. The beach is open sunrise to 11 p.m. Admission is free.

C. B. Harvey Rest Beach is smaller than Higgs Beach and is dwarfed by the massive White Street Pier. This pier is a favorite with anglers and dog walkers and is sometimes called the "unfinished road to Cuba." Rest Beach has the same hours as Higgs Beach. Right across the street is an extensive playground called Astro City, a favorite with the kids. (See the Kidstuff chapter for more kid-friendly activities.)

SMATHERS BEACH
S. Roosevelt Boulevard

Across from Key West International Airport, Smathers is a long strip of sand that bustles with food vendors, water-sports concessions, and beautiful bods in itsy-bitsy, teeny-weeny suits. Admission here is free, but bring plenty of quarters for the streetside parking meters. If you don't mind carting your beach gear a few extra yards, free parking is available on the far side of S. Roosevelt. The beach is open sunrise to 11 p.m.

BICYCLING

You'll be able to get a "wheel" deal when you rent a bike and cycle the Keys. Rentals are offered by the day, 24 hours, multiple days, week, or month. Most of these establishments sell parts and new bicycles, do repairs, and rent helmets and other gear. Remember, Florida state law requires helmets for cyclists younger than age 16.

Upper Keys

Among the best places to bike the Upper Keys are Harry Harris Park, where bicycle lanes are provided, and on the bicycle paths in the median and along the ocean side of the Overseas Highway in Key Largo. Down the Keys, you may safely cycle through Islamorada's Old Highway, which borders the Overseas Highway on the ocean side. A bike path on the bay side finishes a tour through Upper Matecumbe Key and on through Lower Matecumbe Key, thereby making it possible to safely cycle from about mile marker 90 to approximately mile marker 72.

BILL'S DISCOUNT BIKE SHOP
MM 102 Oceanside, Key Largo
(305) 453-4070

Mostly new, high-end bikes at discount prices for all of your biking needs. Bill's is a nice shop offering service with a smile.

Middle Keys

In Marathon you'll need to cycle on the old Seven Mile Bridge to Pigeon Key (a good 2-mile-plus jaunt), use the Key Colony Beach bicycle lane (turn onto the Key Colony Causeway at mile marker 53.5 to get to Key Colony), or pedal along the relatively traffic-free streets of the Sombrero residential area (turn onto Sombrero Beach Road, mile marker 50, next to Kmart).

OVERSEAS OUTFITTERS
MM 48 Bayside, Marathon
(305) 289-1670
overseasoutfitters.com

Overseas Outfitters is the place to go in the Middle Keys to make that active lifestyle come alive. They carry Oakley and Maui Jim sunglasses and Adidas activewear for women, along with bike sales, service, and rentals. If whizzing down the road on in-line skates is your ticket to ride, they have those here as well.

Lower Keys

The Lower Keys span 30 miles, but toward the end of the Keys, you will have the best luck finding rental bikes on Stock Island and Key West (see section below).

BIG PINE BICYCLE CENTER
MM 31 Bayside, Big Pine Key
(305) 872-0130
This is the best source for bicycle rentals in the upper portion of the Lower Keys.

Key West

A & M RENTALS
523 Truman Ave.
(305) 896-1921
amscooterskeywest.com
A & M Rentals provide their customers with free pickup and drop-off in the city of Key West. Here you can rent bikes by the day or week, scooters by the hour or the week, and electric cars for 2- or 4- hour rides.

✳THE BIKE SHOP
1110 Truman Ave.
(305) 294-1073
thebikeshopkeywest.com
Since 1981 the Bike Shop has offered the best bicycle products and services to locals and travelers alike. They rent one-speed cruisers and carry a full line of components and accessories (piggy bike horn anyone?) along with Trek, Gary Fischer, Giant, and Haro bikes.

EATON BIKES
830 Eaton St.
(305) 295-0057
eatonbikes.com
Ever fall in love with a bicycle? If not, this may be a first! The guys at Eaton Bikes are two hip entrepreneurs who will *ooh* and *aah* you with their artistic, intricate designs on bicycles, choppers, lowriders, and electrical bikes. The Eaton Bike boys will even custom design one to ensure you are a true pedal pusher! Their cycles are as beautiful to look at as they are to ride. Walk in and pedal out—I promise that!

ISLAND BICYCLES
929 Truman Ave.
(305) 292-9707
islandbicycle.com
Island Bicycles offers a full selection of bicycles for sale and rent. Repairs and accessories are also available here.

MOPED HOSPITAL
601 Truman Ave.
(305) 296-3344
mopedhospital.com
Moped Hospital rents single-speed bicycles with coaster brakes, baskets, high-rise handlebars, soft seats, balloon tires, and locks by the hour, day, or week.

RECYCLE BICYCLES
MM 4.5 Oceanside, Stock Island
(305) 294-7433
The screaming green building gets your attention even if you don't need a bike. Inside the folks offer a full-service bicycle shop and free pickup and delivery on bike repairs.

BOAT EXCURSIONS & SUNSET CRUISES

Our crowning glory rests in our encompassing waters. Explore the backcountry and the waters of Everglades National Park on group ecotour expeditions (see the Area Overview chapter) or take a glass-bottomed boat trip to the reef to view the fascinating creatures residing there. Relax aboard a sunset cocktail cruise or fire up for a casino cruise. Expect to pay a fee for all these adventures.

Upper Keys

AFRICAN QUEEN
MM 100 Oceanside, Holiday Inn Docks, Key Largo
(305) 451-2121 or (800) 465-4329
holidayinnkeylargo.com
Board the legendary *African Queen*—featured in the Humphrey Bogart and Katharine Hepburn movie of the same name—in Key Largo for daily 1-hour cruises and sunset or charter excursions during the autumn and winter months.

CAPT. STERLING'S EVERGLADES ECO-TOURS
MM 102 Bayside, Dolphin Cove, Key Largo
(305) 853-5161 or (888) 224-6044
pennekamp.com/sterling
Venture 17 miles into the waters of Everglades National Park, in and around mangrove and bird rookery islands (see the Area Overview chapter) aboard a 23-foot pontoon boat. Tours are limited to 6 passengers and depart twice daily. The Key Largo Flamingo Express charter takes you through Crocodile Dragover, the Dump Keys, and 38 miles to Flamingo in Everglades National Park. And then there's the Crocodile Tour, a

nighttime adventure that takes you in search of the elusive Florida saltwater crocodile.

CARIBBEAN WATERSPORTS ENVIRO TOURS
MM 97 Bayside, at the Key Largo Grande Resort and Beach Club, Key Largo
(305) 852-5553
caribbeanwatersports.com
Glide through the Everglades with Caribbean Watersports' 2-hour guided Hobie Sailing Safari and explore uninhabited mangrove islands all along Florida Bay. Environmental tours (see the Area Overview chapter) provide the same guided ride in a 17-foot rigid inflatable Zodiac that has a fiberglass hull, stabilizing inflatable side pontoons, and a quiet electric trolling motor. Tours are limited to 6 people; you must call ahead to reserve a spot.

JOHN PENNEKAMP CORAL REEF STATE PARK
MM 102.5 Oceanside, Key Largo
(305) 451-1621
floridastateparks.org/pennekamp
Pennekamp State Park's glass-bottomed catamaran, the *Spirit of Pennekamp*, carries as many as 150 people on 2.5-hour tours of the reef. Tours are offered 3 times daily. The 38-foot catamaran *Salsa* departs the park marina twice daily for a sailing/snorkeling adventure.

KEY LARGO PRINCESS GLASS BOTTOM BOAT
MM 100 Oceanside, at the Holiday Inn Docks, Key Largo
(305) 451-2121 or (800) 465-4329
keylargoprincess.com
This princess carries passengers on narrated 2-hour tours that drift above the reef. A full

bar is on board, and guests can buy hot dogs and snacks. *Key Largo Princess* tours are offered 3 times daily. Family rates and private charters are available. The boat is wheelchair accessible.

THE *NAUTILIMO*
MM 82 Bayside, Islamorada
(305) 942-3793
nautilimo.com

To see a 1983 Cadillac stretch limousine on the sea is a trip—literally. Giving the boat its shape is a wood-rib frame mounted on a 23-foot Carolina skiff, powered by a 100-hp engine. After the fiberglass covering was installed, the details brought the boat to life. Salvaged from a discarded Cadillac, the dashboard, mirrors, and grill are authentic. To complete the look, the *NautiLimo* was generously covered in pink paint. A trip out on this one-of-a-kind boat lasts 2 hours and covers 9 miles of beautiful Florida Bay country. All that is missing is Elvis!

QUICKSILVER CATAMARAN
MM 100 Oceanside, at the Holiday Inn Docks, Key Largo
(305) 451-0105
quicksilversnorkel.com

Daily sails through the sanctuary waters of John Pennekamp Coral Reef State Park vary with the season aboard the 50-foot catamaran *Quicksilver*. Discounts and family rates are available on snorkel/sunset sail combinations. Private and group charters also can be arranged. Gear rental is extra.

Middle Keys

HAWK'S CAY RESORT AND MARINA
MM 61 Oceanside, Duck Key
(305) 743-7000 or (888) 313-5749
hawkscay.com

Sail aboard the 40-foot custom sailing catamaran at up to 20 knots or sign on for a more leisurely sunset cruise. Or rent a sea kayak for a self-guided ecotour of the out-islands near Duck Key. All these excursions may be booked at Hawk's Cay. Many other water-related activities are available at Hawk's Cay, including chartered fishing excursions to the backcountry or the reef. For those with other interests, other amusements are available, including personal watercraft and small-boat rentals, water-skiing, pontoon party barge rentals, and parasailing.

KEY LIMEY CHARTERS
MM 61 Oceanside, Duck Key
(305) 293-1814
keylimey.com

This is the only private charter that will whisk you away at 35 knots into the backcountry waters of Florida Bay to the Arsnicker Keys, 7 miles northwest of Lower Matecumbe, to see the fabulous white pelicans. These ultimate snowbirds winter in the Keys from Nov until about the end of Mar. The flock often numbers 500 or more around the tiny islets of the Arsnickers. Captain John Skidmore stealthily poles his flats boat through the shallows so as not to alert the birds to your presence. Bring your camera! Captain Skidmore is also an expert flats fishing guide, specializing in bonefish, permit, tarpon, redfish, snook, and other backcountry species. You can combine the bird-watching excursion with some guided backcountry fishing if you like.

SPIRIT CATAMARAN CHARTERS
MM 47.5 Oceanside, 56223 Ocean Dr., Marathon
(305) 289-0614

A 40-foot catamaran named *Spirit* takes passengers snorkeling to popular Middle

Keys reefs twice a day, makes family charter cruises to Pigeon Key, offers marine biology tours with classrooms of children, and sets off for a daily sunset cruise at the end of the day. Call in advance to make reservations.

TURTLE ISLAND WATERSPORTS
MM 50 Oceanside, Marathon
(305) 289-0888
tranquilitybay.com/adventure/
watersports.htm

Located at Tranquility Bay Beachfront Hotel & Resort (see the Accommodations chapter), Turtle Island Watersports can equip you for fun activities, both above and beneath the water. They offer snorkeling, parasailing, kayaks, boat rentals, fishing charters, Hobie Cats, sunset cruises, WaveRunner rentals, island tours, and scuba diving.

Lower Keys

STRIKE ZONE CHARTERS
MM 29.5 Bayside, Big Pine Key
(305) 872-9863 or (800) 654-9560
strikezonecharter.com

This 5-hour backcountry out-island excursion, which includes a fish cookout on a secluded island, will entice your entire family. See the Kidstuff chapter for more details, and see the Diving & Snorkeling chapter for Strike Zone's underwater offerings.

Key West

✳DANGER CHARTERS
407 Caroline St.
(305) 296-3652
dangercharters.com

Don't let the moniker fool you: *Danger* and *Danger Cay* are the names of the Chesapeake Bay skipjack sailboats, not any situation you will encounter on this adventurous charter. Up to 6 people board the skipjack, and right away the captain assigns one of his new crew as first mate. The fun begins as the new mate learns the intricacies of tending to a sailboat and tacking into the wind. The boat soon travels to the backcountry, where the crew disembarks into 3 double kayaks and journeys through the mangrove islands. Then the sailboat moves to another location, where snorkeling gear is donned. Finally, after much adventure, the boat sails back home. Excursions last about 5 hours. Full-day trips, sunset cruises, and specialized bird-watching trips are also available. Call for details and pricing. Their traditional wooden power yacht, *Roamer*, takes you to a pristine reef, where the staff serves you a picnic lunch. Kayak to an out-island in the backcountry and enjoy your yacht-for-a-day.

DREAM CATCHER CHARTERS
5555 College Rd., Bayside
(305) 304-0497
chartersofkeywest.com

How romantic for a couple or great fun with a group of 6—cruising Key West Harbor in your own personal 29-foot powerboat. Your captain handles all the navigating as you enjoy the company and the lovely view of Key West from the water. The trip is approximately 2 hours. Sodas and water are provided, and the sunset is free!

FURY CATAMARANS
237 Front St.
(305) 294-8899 or (877) 994-8898
furycat.com

Climb aboard one of Fury's 65-foot catamarans for a sail by day or night. Fury offers two 3-hour trips to the reef daily for snorkeling—one in the morning, one in the afternoon—plus a 2-hour champagne sunset sail each evening. You can buy separate tickets for day snorkeling or sunset sailing, or purchase a combination snorkeling/sunset sail ticket. Fury also offers snuba excursions. (Snuba, a cross between scuba diving and snorkeling, involves a cylinder of compressed air attached to a raft and connected to two 20-foot-long regulator hoses that participants use for breathing.) Beer, white wine, sodas, and snorkeling/snuba gear are included in the price of your ticket. In addition, Fury offers parasailing as well as a land-sea excursion package that includes a trip to the reef and a tour of Key West aboard either the Conch Tour Train or Old Town Trolley.

MOSQUITO COAST ISLAND OUTFITTERS
MM 4.2 Oceanside, Stock Island
(305) 295-9898
lazydog.com

The gang at this outfitter offers guided backcountry tours that include a narration of the trees, birds, fish, coral, sponges, sea grass, and sea creatures (see the Area Overview chapter). Single and double kayaks are available; half the trip is devoted to snorkeling. Gear, snacks, and bottled water are included in the fee. They even have a 2-hour paddle tour for you and your dog! Children are welcome but must be at least 9 years old to participate.

RESTLESS NATIVE CHARTERS
201 William St.
(305) 394-0600
restlessnative.com

Sail away for the day on this luxurious 50-foot catamaran yacht while you enjoy a gourmet lunch with wine, beer, or soda. Sailing aboard this beauty, with her 28-foot beam, you can expect a smooth and unforgettable time on the water. Onboard are 2 kayaks for individual pursuits, swinging air chairs, and hammocks, or you can get dragged from the cargo net, snorkel on the reef, or walk the sandbar. The *Restless Native* can only carry 6 passengers, with crew, so this is like having your own private vessel to explore the waters off Key West.

SEBAGO CATAMARANS
201 William St., at the Key West Historic Seaport
(305) 292-4768 or (800) 507-9955
keywestsebago.com

Head out to the reef for a snorkeling/sailing adventure aboard Sebago's 60-foot catamaran or cruise Key West Harbor at sunset. Complimentary drinks are served on both excursions. Sebago also offers parasailing as well as a 6-hour "Island Ting" trip that includes kayaking, snorkeling, and sailing, plus a luncheon buffet. Call for details.

WHITE KNUCKLE THRILL BOAT RIDE
MM 4.5 Oceanside, at the Hurricane Hole Marina, Stock Island
(305) 797-0459
whiteknucklethrillboatride.com

Hold on to your head, keep your arms inside the boat, and your feet on the footboards—you are in for one wild ride! This is not a boat ride for the faint of heart nor your elderly relatives. With a velocity of about 50 mph, this boat is a mix of an Everglades airboat and a Jet Ski with a screaming group of about 12 on board. Twisting, turning, and spraying salt water every which way, you return to the dock exhilarated and soaking wet. A photographer is on hand to capture that look on your face as the "White Knuckle" makes a 360-degree turn—priceless.

i There are six beaches in the Key West area: South Beach, at the end of Duval Street (no facilities); Dog Beach, next to Louie's Backyard restaurant (no facilities); Higgs Beach, at the end of Reynolds Street (facilities); Rest Beach, home to White Street Pier (facilities within walking distance); Smathers Beach, on S. Roosevelt Boulevard (facilities); and Fort Zachary Taylor, entrance through Truman Annex at Southard Street (facilities).

YANKEE FLEET FERRY TO FORT JEFFERSON AND DRY TORTUGAS NATIONAL PARK
Key West Historic Seaport
(305) 294-7009 or (800) 322-0013
yankeefreedom.com

A voyage to Dry Tortugas National Park, 70 miles west of Key West, requires a full day. But if you have the time, be sure to include the adventure in your itinerary. Not only is this a spectacular ride back in history, it's a chance to experience what the Florida Keys are truly all about. Ponce de León named the 7 islands *las Tortugas* (the Turtles) in 1513. The word *Dry* was later incorporated into the name to let seafarers know that there is no freshwater available here.

You'll be able to take a tour of the massive, historical Fort Jefferson on Garden Key and enjoy calm seas, pristine natural sand beaches, and some of the best snorkeling anywhere. The protected waters surrounding the Tortugas sparkle with all the sea creatures of the coral reef, plus a few shipwreck remains. And because this area has been designated a no-take zone, the creatures you see get a chance to grow larger than those you might otherwise encounter. Do remember, however, that

there is no food, freshwater, electricity, public restrooms, or medical assistance at Fort Jefferson.

The *Yankee Freedom II*, a 100-passenger, high-speed catamaran, whisks passengers from Key West to Fort Jefferson in less than 2.5 hours. *Yankee Freedom II* departs promptly at 8 a.m. and returns at 5:30 p.m. daily. Fare includes round-trip transportation; snorkeling gear; en route commentary by a naturalist-historian; a 45-minute guided tour of Fort Jefferson; continental breakfast of bagels, doughnuts, cold cereal, and juice; and lunch consisting of cold salads and a make-your-own sandwich bar. Coffee, iced tea, and water are complimentary; you can buy sodas, beer, wine, and mixed drinks on board. Passengers are not permitted to carry alcohol to the Dry Tortugas.

Only campers staying the night on Garden Key may bring large coolers (see the Campgrounds chapter). Campers pay slightly higher fees for passage aboard *Yankee Freedom II* to accommodate their gear.

GOLF & TENNIS

Putters and players drive the Keys links, and racqueteers of all ages love our courts. Read on and be on the ball. Expect to pay for court time by the hour. Greens fees are reasonable at the public course in Key West, and if you belong to a country club back home, be sure to contact Sombrero Country Club in Marathon, (305) 743-2551, to see about reciprocal privileges.

Upper Keys

ISLAMORADA TENNIS CLUB
MM 76.8 Bayside, Islamorada
(305) 664-5341
islamoradatennisclub.com

This facility maintains 4 clay and 2 hard courts, 5 of which are lit for extended play into the evening hours. Private lessons, clinics, round-robins, and tournaments are offered to the general public, and Islamorada Tennis Club will arrange games at all levels. A pro shop and boutique are on the premises. Same-day racquet stringing is available.

Middle Keys

BOONDOCKS GRILLE & DRAFT HOUSE
MM 27.5 Bayside, Ramrod Key
(305) 872-4094
boondocks.us.com
Boondocks is a family-fun park that allows kids of all ages to enjoy a round of miniature golf. Some of the larger hotels offer minigolf for their clients, but this is the only public minigolf course in the Keys. With its large rock formation shaped like a huge boulder, the state-of-the-art 18-hole course comes complete with waterfalls, tunnels, ponds, tiki hut clubhouse, and towering, giant cavemen. The lush tropical landscaping at this attraction gives it Keys believability. Boondocks is a fun place to hold birthday parties, tournaments, or fund-raisers. This family-friendly destination is a "must do" while here.

Key West

BAYVIEW PARK TENNIS
1310 Truman Ave.
(305) 294-1346
The tennis courts at Bayview Park are open to all on a first-come, first-served basis. Reservations are neither required nor accepted. There are no court fees, and courts are lit until 10 p.m.

ISLAND CITY TENNIS
1310 Truman Ave.
(305) 294-1346
These public tennis courts are owned by the city of Key West and keep the lights on till 9 p.m. Island City Tennis is right on Truman Avenue, which leads to Duval Street. It is first-come, first-served and is very popular with visitors as well as locals. There is a pro shop on the premises operated by a father and son team that are a delight. In fact, the father teaches tennis at Key West High School.

KEY WEST GOLF CLUB
MM 5 Bayside, Stock Island
(305) 294-5232
keywestgolf.com
The only public 18-hole course in the Keys, this par-70 course designed by Rees Jones offers a clubhouse, pro shop, and lessons. Greens fees are hefty in high season but about a third less in the off-season. For late-afternoon golfers, special "twilight" fees are available after 2:30 p.m. Monroe County residents receive discounts, but you must reside here year-round to qualify. Call for details.

KITEBOARDING

Here is a list of shops that provide thrill seekers a source and means for their fix of over-the-edge athletic thrills. Hold your breath—you are now in the deep end so get ripping!

THE KITE HOUSE
Key West
(305) 879-0549
thekitehouse.com
Ten years ago perhaps only 10,000 people were involved with the sport of harnessing

the wind. Today over 500,000 agile folks partake in this exhilarating hobby. Kiteboarding is not for the amateur, so the owner of this business urges everyone to take a few lessons with a PASA (Professional Airsport Association) instructor. After the lessons the instructor gives you practice runs, then you get into your power zone and you're off!

OTHERSIDE BOARDSPORTS
MM 83 Bayside, Islamorada
(305) 853-9728
This shop offers board-sports-minded athletes a chance to skateboard, kiteboard, wakeboard, and wakeskate. With knowledgeable instructors, you will be off and boarding in no time.

SEVEN SPORTS KITEBOARDING
MM 84.7 Bayside, Plaza 88, Islamorada
(305) 853-5483
sevensports.com
Private lessons from PASA-certified instructors for beginners, intermediate, or advanced boarders in the thrilling sport of kiteboarding keeps Seven Sports busy. You can also test your nerve on a SUP board and master the art of paddleboarding. That's standing *up* on a board, in case you didn't know!

WATER SPORTS

Pick your pleasure and make a splash—parasailing, waterskiing, and kayaking. You'll find personal watercraft and paddleboat rentals in this section. For a rundown of scuba diving/snorkeling trips to the reef, see our Diving & Snorkeling chapter. Expect to pay a fee for these watery endeavors.

Upper Keys

CORAL REEF PARK COMPANY
MM 102.5 Oceanside, John Pennekamp Coral Reef State Park, Key Largo
(305) 451-6300 or (800) 326-3521
pennekamppark.com
Coral Reef Park Company rents snorkeling equipment at Pennekamp Park for unguided exploration of the nearshore Pennekamp waters off Cannon Beach, or you can sign on with one of the snorkeling tours to the reef (see the Diving & Snorkeling chapter for details). Rent canoes or kayaks here and paddle the mangrove water trails. Small boats also are available for hire.

H2O SPORTS
MM 84.5 Oceanside, at Pelican Cove, Islamorada
(305) 664-4435 or (800) 445-4690
pcove.com
On the beach at Pelican Cove, hook up with H2O Sports' personal watercraft and 16-foot skiffs for round-trip visits to the Sand Bar (a popular snorkeling and swimming site). A reef boat takes snorkelers on excursions, and 16-mile, guided personal watercraft tours depart before sunset and head through the backcountry.

IT'S A DIVE WATERSPORTS
MM 103.8 Bayside, Marriott Key Largo Bay Beach Resort, Key Largo
(305) 453-0000 or (800) 809-9881
marriottkeylargo.com
It's a Dive offers personal watercraft and kayak rentals. Parasailing, waterskiing, and scuba instruction are available, and snorkeling trips aboard a glass-bottomed boat depart twice daily.

✳JACOB'S AQUATIC CENTER
MM 99.6 Oceanside, Key Largo
(305) 453-7946
jacobsaquaticcenter.org
Jacob's Aquatic Center is a 3-pool complex with a 25-meter, 8-lane competition pool and contiguous diving pool with 1- and 2-meter diving boards. This facility is suitable for scuba and Red Cross certification, synchronized swimming, youth swim teams, masters' swimming, swim lessons, water aerobics/Pilates, gymnastics, and water polo. They also have an interactive pool/water park featuring a pirate ship, "spray" gym, and "beachfront" entry. Co-located with the Key Largo Community Park (see listing in this chapter).

OVER UNDER ADVENTURES
MM 82 Oceanside, Islamorada
(305) 852-8015
overundercharters.com
This company offers on-the-water vacation packages, and they will even pick you up in Miami or Fort Lauderdale and bring you to the Florida Keys. Come join the fun for a full week of fishing, backcountry exploration, or diving. If you drive or fly into the Keys, they have boat locations all the way from Islamorada to Key West for clients.

Middle Keys

HAWK'S CAY RESORT AND MARINA
MM 61 Oceanside, Duck Key
(305) 743-7000 or (888) 313-5749
hawkscay.com
The water-sports facility at Hawk's Cay offers parasailing, pontoon, or center-console boat rentals, personal watercraft and kayak rentals, water-ski and wakeboard rentals, as well as instruction. A scuba center and sailing school are also on the premises.

Key West

✳KEY WEST WATER TOURS
MM 4.5 Oceanside, Stock Island
(305) 294-6790
keywestwatertours.com
Ride a WaveRunner and take in an aerial view of Key West—you can do them both at Key West Water Tours. Take a WaveRunner on a 27-mile guided tour around Key West or ride for an hour in a 4-square-mile play area. Parasail to see dolphins, sharks, stingrays, and other marine life from a lofty perch. Both activities will be a Kodak moment!

THE KEYS TO KEY WEST
5555 College Rd., Bayside
(305) 292-7212 or (888) 362-3474
gotothekeys.com
The folks at the Keys to the Key West claim they throw the largest island party in the Keys. This inclusive package is billed as "do it all in one day," and even their website comes with a warning label: "This trip will wear you out!" The package trip involves WaveRunner riding, Sunfish sailboating, banana boat rides, kayaking, knee boarding, snorkeling, windsurfing, and parasailing. Trips are from 10 a.m. to 4 p.m. with lunch, sodas, and water served. Be sure and eat a hearty breakfast before this outing!

PARAWEST WATERSPORTS INC.
700 Front St., at A&B Lobster House
(305) 292-5199
This parasailing enterprise prides itself on offering excursionists the most free falls and dips in Key West. Regular rides of 8 to 10 minutes include heights of 300 feet with one free fall and one dip; longer, higher rides of 10 to 12 minutes reach 600 feet and include several free falls and dips. Most parasailing is done behind Christmas Tree Island

and Sunset Key. Single and double personal watercraft also are available for rent. Renters must remain within a limited riding area.

SUNSET WATERSPORTS
Smathers Beach
(305) 296-2554
This outfit offers something for everyone. Parasailing, Hobie Cats, kayaks, and sailboards are all provided on Smathers Beach. For an all-inclusive day trip, take the "Do It All." From the Key West Seaport, a 44-foot catamaran takes you out about 3 miles to a shallow wreck. From there, take turns exploring with personal watercraft, waterskiing, and just about anything else they can imagine.

PHYSICAL FITNESS

Upper Keys

FROGGY'S FITNESS
MM 91.8 Bayside, Tavernier
(305) 852-8623
froggysfitness.com
Froggy's Fitness is a 6,500-square-foot fitness center that features free weights, treadmills, Stairmasters, elliptical machines, and more. In addition to customized personal training, Froggy's offers yoga, boot camp, Pilates, aerobics, and kickboxing classes as well as indoor cycling. The center provides individualized diet and nutrition plans and body-fat testing. You can purchase gym wear, aerobics footwear, vitamins, protein supplements, and other health foods here, too.

KEY LARGO YOGA
Key Largo
(305) 879-0377
keylargoyoga.com
Yoga teacher Kathy Shirley will come to your home or hotel, or even meet you at Founders Park for a private, semiprivate, or group yoga session. She has been practicing yoga for more than 10 years and completed the 200-hour training for Vinyasa yoga. If you've never taken yoga but always wanted to try, a private or semiprivate session in the great outdoors will let you experience the beauty in the heart of the Keys while doing some good for your heart as well.

＊PILATES IN PARADISE
MM 98.8 Bayside, Key Largo
(305) 453-0801
pilatesinparadise.net
Owner and instructor Christi Allen is a certified Romana's Pilates instructor with more than 1,500 hours of training in the Pilates method from teachers all over the country. Allen is also a certified nutrition and lifestyle coach and therefore takes a holistic approach to fitness, which is reflected in her classes. Pilates in Paradise offers classes in mat, tower, reformer, and combo, which is a little bit of everything. Private instruction is also available.

Middle Keys

BODIES IN MOTION
MM 50.5 Oceanside, Marathon
(305) 292-2331
bodiesinmotiononline.com
Head to this "little studio with a lot of heart" for yoga, fitness, and flexibility classes. Yoga is taught every Mon, Wed, Fri, and Sat at 9:30 a.m. and Tues at 7 p.m. Private sessions are available, and all levels are welcome. Body work and massage therapy are also offered, as well as Cranial Release Technique, a hands-on process that creates the relaxation of nervous system, fascial, and muscle tissue tension throughout the entire body. Breathe out already!

KEYS FITNESS CENTER
MM 49.5 Oceanside, Marathon
(305) 289-0788
floridakeysfitness.com
Offering fitness equipment by Paramount, Life Fitness, and Nautilus, Keys Fitness Center also sports a separate free-weights room for the serious workout addict. The facilities offer private showers and a relaxing sauna. Personal trainers are bilingual. Keys Fitness Center is open Mon through Fri from 6 a.m. to 9 p.m., Sat from 8 a.m. to 6 p.m., and Sun from 9 a.m. to 4 p.m.

YOGA ON THE SEA
Spirit Snorkeling
MM 47.5 Bayside, Marathon
(305) 289-0614
yogaonthesea.com
How many people can say they've done yoga on the ocean? Calling all yogis! Spirit Snorkeling offers a yoga sunset cruise aboard their 34-foot catamaran taught by an Ananda instructor. No need to worry about the motion of the ocean, as the construction of the watercraft is such that it is almost as wide as it is long, allowing for much more stability than other craft. All levels are welcome. Call for schedules and availability. *Namaste* indeed!

Lower Keys

PIRATE WELLNESS CENTER
MM 21.4 Oceanside, Cudjoe Key
(305) 744-3348
piratewellnesscenter.com
Pirate Wellness Center houses a multiuse studio, treatment rooms, a steam room, and locker rooms in their comfortable 5,000-square-foot building. The studio is the location for classes including step aerobics, yoga, cardio, and strength training. There are also treadmills, recumbent and upright bikes, rowers, free weights, and Smart Strength training machines. Personal training is available as are day, week, and "snowbird" passes.

Key West

BIKRAM YOGA STUDIO OF KEY WEST
927 White St.
(305) 292-1854
bikramyogakeywest.com
This is the real thing and is not for wimps. Classes are 90 minutes long, and you will need to bring or rent a yoga mat for $1 on the premises. At Bikram Yoga the room is kept warm so your muscles will stretch more easily. To that end, it is recommended that ladies wear leotards and men wear bathing suits. Renowned yoga experts often give seminars here and classes are held daily; call for details.

BODY ZONE SOUTH
2740 N. Roosevelt Blvd., Overseas Market
(305) 292-2930
bodyzonefitnessclub.com
A full range of exercise equipment is available here, including Nautilus equipment, treadmills, stationary bikes, stair climbers, and plenty of free weights. Classes include indoor cycling, yoga, and core strength. Personal training and massage are available as well. The juice bar and play care for children are both convenient services. Body Zone South is open daily.

*COFFEE MILL DANCE & YOGA STUDIO
916 Pohalski St.
(305) 296-9982
coffeemilldance.com
The Coffee Mill is the place in Key West to get moving! Instructors include members of the

Key West Contemporary Dance Company, and classes are taught for beginners and advanced dancers (or wannabe dancers) of all ages. Coffee Mill's extensive class list includes yoga, ballet for beginner adults, aerobics, Pilates, Capoeira, Zumba, jazz, and even belly dancing. Classes are held daily, and visitors are welcome.

ISLAND GYM
1119 White St.
(305) 295-8222
keywestislandgym.com
This facility is open 7 days a week for serious athletes. Island Gym hosts a full range of free weights as well as indoor and outdoor workout spaces. Personal training and group fitness sessions are also available, and wireless headsets allow you to watch TV on flat screens while working out on the elliptical or treadmill.

PARADISE HEALTH AND FITNESS
1706 N. Roosevelt Blvd.
(305) 294-4120
paradisehealthandfitness.com
In addition to a full-circuit weight room, Paradise offers a wide range of group classes, including yoga, Pilates, extreme fitness, and lower and upper body challenges for all ages and fitness levels. They also offer ballroom and salsa classes on the weekends for beginners or advanced dancers. Personal trainers

are on staff to assist you and will make home visits if you're so inclined. Short- or long-term memberships as well as daily rates are available.

*STAY FIT STUDIO
804 White St.
(305) 294-0693
stayfitstudiokeywest.com
Start off another perfect day in paradise with an invigorating workout with Stay Fit Studio. They have classes in spinning, Pilates, boot camp, and yoga, among many others. Stay Fit will also come to you. Whatever your fitness level, they will work with you. Their certified personal trainers are experts in their fields and will tailor a workout specifically for your needs. Stay Fit also offers massages and facials so you can truly relax post-workout.

*ULTIMATE ATHLETICS
(305) 394-4065
ultimateathletics.com
Ultimate Athletics will take you on a workout outdoors while you enjoy the beautiful Key West scenery. If you are looking to find the best route to run, do a swim workout in the ocean, do yoga on the beach, or cycle up the Keys, Ultimate Athletics will get you there. Coach Bill Elkins is a certified USA-T trainer and will build a custom plan for you, whether it is for an hour, day, week, or monthlong stay.

ATTRACTIONS

Don't wait for a rainy day (you might not have one) to explore our historical sites, out-islands, museums, nature preserves, and marine research centers. You'll find the majority of our most popular land-based diversions bordering the Overseas Highway, for our string of islands is not very wide. So put on your sandals, grab your hat, and don't forget the sunscreen! You are about to set out on an adventure in the Florida Keys.

Price Code

Codes are based on adult admission.

$	Less than $5
$$	$5 to $10
$$$	$10 to $20
$$$$	More than $20

HISTORIC HOMES & MUSEUMS

Upper Keys

FLORIDA KEYS HISTORY OF DIVING MUSEUM $$$
MM 83 Bayside, Islamorada
(305) 664-9737
divingmuseum.org

The Florida Keys History of Diving Museum displays historic diving equipment and research documents representing more than 3,000 years of underwater exploration from around the world and the Florida Keys. The self-guided tours begin with "Timeline of Diving" (starting with breath-holding diving), an "Art McKee Exhibit" (regarded as the father of recreational diving), "Parade of Nations" (a collection of historic hard-hat dive helmets from around the world), a gallery featuring underwater lighting and communication (which led to today's scuba sport diving),

and the gallery "Into the Abyss" (showcasing diving suits). World-renowned maritime-life artist Guy Harvey, along with David Dunleavy and local schoolchildren, have created a breathtaking sea-life mural to catch your eye on the exterior of the museum.

Middle Keys

MUSEUMS OF CRANE POINT $$$
MM 50.5 Bayside, Marathon
(305) 743-9100
cranepoint.net

The small, interesting Museum of Natural History and the adjoining Florida Keys Children's Museum (see the Kidstuff chapter) sit on the skirt of the Crane Point hammock. The museum houses a potpourri of Keys icons and exhibits. Creatures of the reef have been authentically re-created in tropical splendor and are accompanied by an audio of the sounds of the deep. The museum provides a self-guided tour pamphlet that also lists some of the unusual tropical hardwoods you'll see along the nature trails. Crane Point is open daily. One admission charge allows access to both trails and museums. Children age 4 and younger get in free.

Key West

*AUDUBON HOUSE & TROPICAL GARDENS $$$
205 Whitehead St.
(305) 294-2116 or (877) 294-2470
audubonhouse.com

In 1832 John James Audubon did spend time on the grounds of John Geiger's huge garden. Legend has it that Audubon sketched the white-crowned pigeon and the Geiger tree he found in the garden here. During his stay in the Keys, Audubon produced 18 sketches of native wildlife. Original lithographs of these drawings are on display at the Audubon House. The house and environs, however, are more reminiscent of the family of Captain John Geiger, a wrecker who built the house and lived here with his family. Set your own tour pace with a free pair of headphones and a tape that brings the house alive. Audubon House is open daily.

CURRY MANSION INN $
511 Caroline St.
(305) 294-5349 or (800) 253-3466
currymansion.com

This imposing home evokes images of an opulent old Key West, although the 3-story Conch house now serves as the focal point for a bed-and-breakfast inn and a museum. Built in 1905 by Milton Curry, Florida's first homegrown millionaire, the inn's public rooms display a selection of antiques and memorabilia. Poke around in the attic, and you'll find an 1899 billiard table among the old dresses and luggage. From the attic you can climb the widow's walk for a panoramic view of Key West Harbor. Self-guided tours are available daily between 9 a.m. and 5 p.m. See the Accommodations chapter for information on overnight stays in the adjacent buildings.

EAST MARTELLO MUSEUM $$
3501 S. Roosevelt Blvd.
(305) 296-3913
kwahs.com

This enchanting, artifact-filled former fort will bring you up to speed on Key West history. Built during the Civil War, the brick fortress was never completely finished because the circular Martello design became antiquated before it was ever armed. Operated today as a museum and gallery by the Key West Art and Historical Society, the 8-foot-thick walls support pictures, artifacts, and historical documents. Featured in the small gallery are the charming wood carvings of Key West's Mario Sanchez and funky welded sculptures by the late Stanley Papio of Key Largo, fabricated from bedsprings, toilet fixtures, and other so-called junk. You can climb the citadel to the lookout tower for an unobstructed view of the Atlantic coast. East Martello Museum is open daily.

FLORIDA KEYS HISTORICAL MILITARY MEMORIAL FREE
One Mallory Square

Flush with military history, Key West honors its best with this handsome memorial dedicated to those who have proudly served their country and the military events directly affecting Key West and the Keys. Beginning in 1822, when the US Navy raised the American flag over Key West, through the era of the Spanish-American War, World Wars I and II, Korea, the Cuban missile crisis, Vietnam, Desert Storm, Iraq, and the ongoing war on drugs, this simple, elegant display stands proud as a sentinel reflecting a community paying homage to these historical events and brave souls.

ATTRACTIONS

✳HARRY S. TRUMAN LITTLE WHITE HOUSE $$$
111 Front St.
(305) 294-9111
trumanlittlewhitehouse.com

President Harry S. Truman came to Key West for the first time in 1946 and went on to spend 11 working vacations in the commandant's quarters, dubbed the Little White House. You'll be able to view Truman's Winter White House as it looked when he spent his 175 working vacation days here. The family quarters, poker porch, dining room, and living room are open to the public. President Eisenhower spent two weeks here recuperating from his second heart attack, and Kennedy held a summit meeting here before the Bay of Pigs action. Jimmy Carter visited with his family in 1996 and again in 1997 for New Year's Eve, and Bill and Hillary Clinton spent a weekend here in 2005. Guided tours are conducted daily.

✳HEMINGWAY HOME AND MUSEUM $$$
907 Whitehead St.
(305) 294-1136
hemingwayhome.com

Once the home of Key West's most famous writer, Ernest Hemingway, the Hemingway Home and Museum ranks as Key West's most popular attraction. Built by wrecker Asa Tift in 1851, the home took on historical significance when Ernest and Pauline Hemingway moved in. Pauline spearheaded extensive remodeling, redecorating, and refurnishing and fitted her backyard with the island's first swimming pool. Hemingway wrote several of his most celebrated works, including *For Whom the Bell Tolls*, *Death in the Afternoon*, *The Green Hills of Africa*, and *To Have and Have Not*, from his pool-house office out back. The

Hemingways lived in this Key West home from 1931 to 1939. Be sure to look for the infamous six-toed cats!

i Looking for a quiet, tranquil place to catch your breath? Just a few blocks off the hustle and bustle of Duval Street is the serene Stations of the Cross Gardens on the grounds of historic St. Mary Star of the Sea Catholic Church. This half-acre garden is open to travelers and islanders alike.

KEY WEST LIGHTHOUSE AND KEEPER'S QUARTERS MUSEUM $$
938 Whitehead St.
(305) 294-0012
kwahs.com

This 1847 structure, inland on a Key West street just across from the Hemingway Home, affords visitors a bird's-eye view of Key West from atop its 90-foot light tower (88 steps to the top). Why a lighthouse so far from the water? It was positioned here to avoid the fate of its predecessor on Whitehead Point, which toppled in a hurricane the previous year. The keeper's quarters houses maritime memorabilia and a gift shop. The lighthouse museum is open daily for self-guided tours. Children younger than age 6 are admitted free. Adults may purchase a combination ticket for admission to this museum, the East Martello Museum, and the Key West Museum of Art and History at the Custom House (see descriptions elsewhere in this chapter).

✳THE KEY WEST MUSEUM OF ART AND HISTORY AT THE CUSTOM HOUSE $$
281 Front St.
(305) 295-6616
kwahs.com

The Custom House is on the National Register of Historic Places and remains one of the finest examples of Richardsonian/Romanesque Revival architecture in existence. Inside you will find 7 galleries and a gift shop. Exhibits of artwork and historical artifacts change periodically; however, those on the second floor traditionally focus on the history of Key West. Be sure to continue up the stairs to the third floor. There are no exhibit galleries here, but the works of folk artist Mario Sanchez, which line the walls between the closed office doors, are worth the climb. There's a great view from the arched window overlooking Sunset Key and the harbor here, too. The museum is open daily.

✳ MEL FISHER MARITIME HERITAGE SOCIETY AND MUSEUM $$$
200 Greene St.
(305) 294-2633
melfisher.org

For 16 years "today's the day" was the hope of treasure salvor Mel Fisher, who finally struck pay dirt on July 20, 1985. Finding the *Nuestra Señora de Atocha*, which Fisher estimated to be worth $400 million, ensured his legacy as treasure hunter extraordinaire. Heavy gold chains, jeweled crosses, and bars of silver and gold are among the artifacts on display at the permanent first-floor exhibit. In 2007 Mel Fisher's Treasures subcontracted a company to salvage the shipwreck site of the *Santa Margarita*. Their discovery of this 1622 Spanish galleon yielded a metal box full of pearls, gold artifacts, and chains. The second-floor exhibit changes frequently—call for details. A museum shop offers a variety of pirate and nautical gifts. The museum is open daily.

RIPLEY'S BELIEVE IT OR NOT MUSEUM $$
108 Duval St.
(305) 293-9939
ripleys.com/keywest

Ripley's Believe It or Not is world-famous for strange, fantastic, weird, and just hard-to-believe artifacts. In the Ripley's Key West location, they house a Key West gallery with items from Ernest Hemingway (reading glasses, a typewriter, and a shrunken torso) and Count von Cosel, who stole the body of his beloved and kept her in the fuselage of a plane in his backyard. There is also a Boutique of Weird Clothing displaying a vest made of human hair, a giant pair of shoes, and even a pair of Madonna's underwear. And if all that weren't enough, they also have a portrait of Vincent van Gogh made from butterfly wings. You know you're not in Kansas anymore!

SAN CARLOS INSTITUTE FREE
516 Duval St.
(305) 294-3887
institutosancarlos.org

Founded in 1871 by Cuban exiles, the San Carlos Institute was established to preserve the language and traditions of the Cuban people. Dubbed "La Casa Cuba" by legendary poet and patriot José Martí, the institute helped unite the exiled Cuban community. The current building was completed in 1924 and operated as an integrated school until the mid-1970s. With the perseverance of the Hispanic Affairs Commission, a state agency headed by Rafael Penalver, restoration of the San Carlos was completed and the institute reopened on January 3, 1992, 100 years to the day after José Martí's first visit in the late 19th century. Today the San Carlos Institute is a museum, library, school, art gallery,

The Schooner Western Union Maritime Museum

The Schooner *Western Union* is one of the oldest working wooden schooners in the US. The Schooner Western Union Preservation Society is the not-for-profit corporation founded for the purpose of restoring, maintaining, and operating the historic **Schooner Western Union Maritime Museum** in Key West. In addition to the restoration of the schooner, they operate the boat as a maritime museum with an educational outreach program that includes historical tours, children's activities, and private excursions. This proud 130-foot vessel is built of mahogany timbers and Dade County pine. The beam is 23½ feet, the draft is 8 feet, and the sail area is a whopping 4,800 square feet. Even though the Schooner *Western Union* is a sailing vessel, the ship has two engines to steady it at sea. Book her for a sunset sail. You can also reserve the Schooner *Western Union* for weddings and special events. Located at 202 William St., Key West; call (305) 292-1766 or visit schoonerwestern union.org for more information.

theater, and conference center. The institute is open weekends.

WEST MARTELLO TOWER JOE ALLEN GARDEN CENTER   FREE
Atlantic Boulevard and White Street
(305) 294-3210
keywestgardenclub.com
Built in 1862, the West Martello Tower, like the other forts on the island, was never involved in an actual war. It was, however, used for target practice by the US Navy, which accounts for its somewhat shabby condition. Today the tower is also the Joe Allen Garden Center, and the Key West Garden Club operates here. Use the self-guided tour to spot local flora, including a key lime tree, or just find an inviting spot to relax. West Martello is open Tues through Sat in season. The schedule may vary; call for more information. Admission is free, but note that shirt and shoes are required.

WILDLIFE

Upper Keys

DOLPHIN COVE $$$$
MM 101.9 Bayside, Key Largo
(877) 365-2683
dolphinscove.com
Dolphin Cove, situated on a 5-acre lagoon in Key Largo, offers an in-water encounter with bottlenose dolphins in addition to myriad other water activities. Structured and natural dolphin swim encounters are offered daily. The encounter is preceded by a 30-minute boat ride in the waters of the backcountry, where you will receive an orientation briefing about the dolphins and about the interactions you will experience. Dolphin Cove also offers guided ecological tours of the Everglades National Park backcountry waters and Florida Bay. Other interesting trips into Florida Bay are offered on request, such as guided snorkel trips, kayak tours, sunset cruises, and even a private nighttime

crocodile search in the nearshore waters of the Everglades.

DOLPHINS PLUS $$$$
MM 100 Oceanside, Ocean Bay Drive, Key Largo
(305) 451-1993 or (866) 860-7946
dolphinsplus.com

This marine mammal research and education facility offers you the opportunity to enter the world of the bottlenose dolphin for a compatible swim. The 2.5-hour natural swim, offered twice daily, teaches you all about dolphins, including their social pod structure, communication methods, and anatomy. You'll learn how to conduct yourself in the water for your 30-minute swim with the dolphins. Dolphins Plus also offers a 2-hour, structured interaction program 3 times daily where you can be in the water and involved directly with the dolphins. After an educational briefing, you will experience a structured water session encompassing platform behaviors and in-water behaviors. Participants in all programs must call for reservations. Directions to Dolphins Plus are complicated. Call the center or check the website for detailed instructions.

*FLORIDA KEYS WILD BIRD CENTER   FREE
MM 93.6 Bayside, Tavernier
(305) 852-4486
fkwbc.org

Dedicated to the rescue, rehabilitation, and release of ill, injured, and orphaned wild birds, the Florida Keys Wild Bird Center will fascinate visitors of all ages. Artificial environmental hazards such as entanglement with anglers' lines or fishhooks also can render the birds injured and helpless. This rapid-care aviary treats the wounds, supervises the convalescence, and releases the birds back into the wild. Meanwhile, you may walk along a boardwalk path through the birds' natural habitats, which have been discreetly caged with wire enclosures. Signage and brochures provide environmental education of Keys habitats. The Wild Bird Center is open daily during daylight hours. The center is funded by public donations; there are no admission fees. Look for the Florida Keys Wild Bird Center signs as you drive down the Keys.

THEATER OF THE SEA $$$$
MM 84.7 Oceanside, Islamorada
(305) 664-2431
theaterofthesea.com

With continuous performances offered daily, Theater of the Sea is the Florida Keys' showiest marine entertainment facility. The natural saltwater lagoons, created by excavations for Flagler's railroad, are home to popular marine creatures like dolphins, stingrays, sharks, and sea turtles. Special programs are offered for an additional fee, which includes park and show admission. The Trainer-for-a-Day program allows you to assist the trainers in feeding and caring for the dolphins and sea lions. The Swim with the Stingrays program includes 15 minutes of instruction and 30 minutes in the water snorkeling with the stingrays, sea turtles, and other marine life. Swim with the Dolphins and Swim with the Sea Lions programs are also offered.

Middle Keys

THE DOLPHIN CONNECTION $$$$
MM 61 Oceanside, at Hawk's Cay Resort, Duck Key
(888) 251-3674
dolphinconnection.com

The Dolphin Connection's Dolphin Discovery provides an interactive, 25-minute, in-water encounter with bottlenose dolphins. You will not actually swim with the Connection's dolphins, but you'll get to know them up close and personal. You'll be able to touch, feed, pet, and play with them from the security of a submerged platform (great for nonswimmers or those people with physical limitations). Dockside Dolphins is a 30-minute, behind-the-scenes look at dolphin training sessions. Participants learn how the professionals at Dolphin Connection train the dolphins and then, from the dock, take part in an actual training procedure. You'll be able to feel, feed, and pet the dolphins but not have to get into the water. Advance reservations are required for all programs.

DOLPHIN RESEARCH CENTER   **$$$$**
MM 59 Bayside, Grassy Key
(305) 289-1121 or (305) 289-0002 (for reservations)
dolphins.org

Look for the giant statue of a dolphin and her calf that heralds the Grassy Key home of the Dolphin Research Center, which offers a variety of fascinating dolphin encounters. One-hour, narrated walking tours introduce you to the dolphins in their natural environments, where you'll witness their training sessions. The half-day Dolphin Encounter enables you to learn how people interact with the dolphins. In the DolphinSplash program, meet the dolphins without swimming. In Meet a Dolphin, you can observe a dolphin behavior session and then join the trainer at the dock for a personal introduction to the dolphin. In Paint with a Dolphin, you can help a dolphin paint a T-shirt for you. There are many other programs available, so call for more information.

✳MARATHON WILD BIRD CENTER   **FREE**
MM 50.5 Bayside, Marathon
(305) 743-8382
marathonwildbirdcenter.org

Safely protected in a wooded, 64-acre Crane Point Hammock park, the Marathon Wild Bird Center is a licensed wildlife rehabilitation facility that specializes in migratory birds. Incorporated in 1998, they work with local veterinarians and other caring individuals who are concerned with the rescue, rehabilitation, and return of wild birds back into their natural setting of the Florida Keys. Their website gives step-by-step detailed instructions on the care of orphaned baby birds.

Lower Keys

THE BLUE HOLE   **FREE**
MM 31 Bayside, Key Deer Boulevard, Big Pine Key
(305) 872-2411

You may wonder why all those cars are parked on the side of Key Deer Boulevard, for from the roadside the area looks like an uninhabited stand of slash pines. Park your vehicle and join the crowd. A few steps into the thatch palm understory you'll see a large, water-filled barrow pit, known as the Blue Hole. Inhabiting this incongruous water hole are a couple of resident alligators, the only known gators in the Keys. If you're lucky, you may catch a glimpse of one of these elusive reptiles. Ducks and wading birds stay out of the alligators' path. The Blue Hole is 0.25 mile north of the intersection of Key Deer and Watson Boulevards. There is no charge for visiting the Blue Hole.

✳NATIONAL KEY DEER REFUGE AND WATSON NATURE TRAIL   **FREE**
MM 30.5 Bayside, Key Deer Boulevard, Big Pine Key
(305) 872-2239
fws.gov/nationalkeydeer

The National Key Deer Refuge protects the habitat frequented by the key deer, a small species—most are around 3 feet high—that is found nowhere else in the world (see the Area Overview chapter). Some areas of the refuge, which encompasses a large portion of Big Pine Key, are off-limits to visitors and marked accordingly. National wildlife refuge signs mark the boundaries of the refuge, which is open for daytime public access on designated trails. The key deer are protected by law, and even feeding them is a misdemeanor offense. You can sometimes spot key deer beside US 1, but you are more likely to see them along the back roads and especially on No Name Key, where there are fewer human inhabitants.

Key West

KEY WEST AQUARIUM   **$$$**
1 Whitehead St., at Mallory Square
(800) 544-5927
keywestaquarium.com

Key West's oldest tourist attraction (built in 1934) and still one of the most fascinating our southernmost city has to offer, the Key West Aquarium affords you a diver's-eye view of the marine creatures of our encompassing waters. Stroll at your leisure alongside the backlit tanks re-creating our coral reefs, but don't miss the guided tours offered 4 times daily, when you'll witness the feeding of the various species. You'll marvel at the feeding frenzy of the sharks and sawtooths; the nurse sharks and stingrays flipping and splashing for their rations; and the tarpon, barracuda, game fish, and sea turtles recognizing the hands that feed them in the outdoor Atlantic Shores Exhibit, created to look like a mangrove lagoon. The aquarium is open daily.

THE KEY WEST BUTTERFLY & NATURE CONSERVATORY   **$$$**
1316 Duval St.
(305) 296-2988 or (800) 839-4647
keywestbutterfly.com

The Key West Butterfly & Nature Conservatory celebrates the lives of butterflies around the globe. Visitors first stop at the Learning Center for a brief introductory film on the wonders of the butterflies' world before proceeding to the Miracle of Metamorphosis exhibit. Here you can watch the actual butterfly-hatching process and observe the stages of development from egg to caterpillar to chrysalis. When mature, the butterflies are released into a 5,000-square-foot glass-enclosed greenhouse featuring more than 3,500 tropical trees and plants. The gardens are a horticulturalist's nirvana—lush and tropical vegetation inhabited by 30 to 50 species of exotic butterflies, such as blue morpho and emerald swallowtail, and myriad birds from all over the world.

KEY WEST WILDLIFE CENTER   **FREE**
1801 White Street
(305) 292-1008

This is a branch of the Marathon Wild Bird Center (located at the Museums of Crane Point; see listing in this chapter) treating sick, injured, and orphaned animals with a mission to educate the public about birds and other wildlife in the Keys. This shelter lies on the grounds of the McCoy Indigenous Park, full of rare and native species of flora. At any given time approximately 100 animals, ranging from seabirds to raccoons to chickens, are recovering here; you can see them during visiting hours. Key West Wildlife Center will rescue animals anywhere from the Seven Mile Bridge to the Dry Tortugas. The park is open daily from sunup to sundown. Admission is free, but donations are appreciated, and volunteers are always needed.

OUTDOOR SITES

Upper Keys

GREEN TURTLE HAMMOCK   FREE
MM 81 Bayside, Islamorada
This historic 8-acre property is now a passive park. The area provides a natural outdoor recreation and education setting, including nature trails, a wildlife observation platform, and a launch with dockage for kayaks and canoes to paddle across Florida Bay. A historic cottage doubles as an interpretive center as well as an amenity for the adjacent Florida Keys Overseas Heritage Trail.

HURRICANE MONUMENT   FREE
MM 81.6 Oceanside, Islamorada
Honoring the hundreds of residents and railroad workers in Islamorada who lost their lives in the Labor Day hurricane of 1935, this monument depicts the fury of nature's elements with a bas-relief of high seas and wind-battered palm trees. Carved out of local coral limestone, the Hurricane Monument may be freely viewed just off the Overseas Highway.

INDIAN KEY STATE HISTORICAL SITE   FREE
MM 77.5 Oceanside, Indian Key
(850) 245-2157
floridastateparks.org/indiankey

A colorful history paints Indian Key, a 10-acre oceanside island about 0.75 mile offshore from Lower Matecumbe Key. Now uninhabited, this tiny key has yielded archaeological evidence of prehistoric Native American cultures. Physician Henry Perrine sat out the Second Seminole War here, which proved a misguided decision, for Indians attacked the island in 1840 and he lost his life after all. Fires destroyed all the structures except for the foundations. Indian Key is accessible only by boat. The historical site is open from 8 a.m. to sundown. Ranger-led tours are at 9 a.m. and 1 p.m. Robbie's Marina, MM 77.5 Bayside (305-664-9814; robbies.com), offers the only regularly scheduled tour transportation to the island. Reservations are preferred.

✳LIGNUMVITAE STATE BOTANICAL SITE $
MM 77.5 Bayside, Lignumvitae Key
(850) 245-2157
floridastateparks.org
Named for the lignum vitae tree, Lignumvitae Key—our highest island at 17 feet above sea level—supports one of the best examples of a virgin hardwood hammock in the Florida Keys. Also on the island is the 1919 home of the Matheson family, who owned the island for many decades. One-hour ranger-guided walks at 10 a.m. and 2 p.m. allow visitors to tour the house and the hardwood hammock. You may not enter the hammock unless accompanied by a ranger. Park officials suggest you come equipped with mosquito repellent and sturdy shoes. Like Indian Key, Lignumvitae Key may be accessed only by boat, and limited private dockage for small craft is available (see previous listing for information on Robbie's Marina, which offers transportation to the key).

PIONEER CEMETERY   **FREE**
MM 82 Oceanside, at Cheeca Lodge, Islamorada

Their gravestones defiled in the hurricane of 1935, the founding fathers and mothers of Islamorada—the Parkers, Pinders, and Russells—still rest in the Pioneer Cemetery, now a part of the extensive grounds of Cheeca Lodge. The angel statue marking the grave of Etta Dolores Pinder was found on the highway, miraculously intact except for a broken arm and wing. In 1989 Cheeca Lodge and University of Miami historian Josephine Johnson researched the cemetery, leading to the designation of the Pioneer Cemetery as a historical site by the Historical Association of Southern Florida. You'll find the tiny Pioneer Cemetery surrounded by a white picket fence near the beach on the Cheeca Lodge grounds. The cemetery is open for free viewing by the general public.

WINDLEY KEY FOSSIL REEF STATE GEOLOGIC SITE   **$**
MM 85.5 Bayside, Windley Key
(850) 245-2157
floridastateparks.org/windleykey

Quarried long ago by workers building Flagler's East Coast Railroad Extension, the fossilized coral reef that forms the bedrock of the Keys (see the Area Overview chapter) is exposed here for all to see. Borrow the in-house trail guide, which interprets what you'll discover on Windley Key's 4 trails. The state site is open Thurs through Mon. Guided tours are offered at 8 a.m. and 5 p.m.

Middle Keys

PIGEON KEY NATIONAL HISTORICAL SITE   **$$$**
Old Seven Mile Bridge, at MM 47 Oceanside, Marathon Bayside, Pigeon Key
(305) 289-0025, (305) 743-5999 (gift shop), (305) 743-5999 (ferry)
pigeonkey.net

Though undoubtedly Pigeon Key was known to Native Americans and Bahamian fishermen in the early days of the Keys, it was Henry Flagler's East Coast Railroad Extension that put the tiny 5-acre key on the historical map. And it is the volunteer-staffed Pigeon Key Foundation that keeps it there. The island is connected to the mainland by a bridge that was originally built for the railroad. The hurricane of 1935 flooded Pigeon Key and caused so much damage to the railroad that the company decided not to rebuild (see the History chapter). When the Seven Mile Bridge was built over the railroad spans in the late 1930s, Pigeon Key became headquarters for the Bridge and Toll District.

Key West

AFRICAN CEMETERY AT HIGGS BEACH   **FREE**
Atlantic Boulevard

In 1860 the slave trade brought thousands of young slaves from West Africa to the New World. Hundreds were brought to Key West to be eventually shipped back home to West Africa. Unfortunately, many died in transit, and the bodies were buried in mass graves in the Higgs Beach area. In 1993 these events come to the attention of a local historical researcher, and in 2007 a concrete slab was poured over the grave site and the African

Cemetery at Higgs Beach sign was erected as a first step in creating a lasting memorial.

✳DRY TORTUGAS NATIONAL PARK   **FREE**
(305) 242-7700
nps.gov/drto

Visit Dry Tortugas National Park for a spectacular ride back in history. Accessible only by boat or seaplane, the Dry Tortugas lie almost 70 miles west of Key West. Ponce de León named the seven islands "Las Tortugas" in 1513, presumably for the multitude of sea turtles (*tortugas*). The "Dry" moniker was added later to indicate the islands' lack of freshwater. You'll be able to take a self-guided tour of Fort Jefferson on Garden Key, America's largest 19th-century coastal fort, which operated as a military prison. Fort Jefferson's most famous inmate was Dr. Samuel Mudd, who was convicted of conspiracy after he set the broken leg of President Lincoln's assassin, John Wilkes Booth. The protected waters surrounding the Tortugas sparkle with all the sea creatures of the coral reef as well as a good many shipwreck remains. With natural sand beaches and calm seas, snorkeling and swimming are a must.

✳FLORIDA KEYS ECO-DISCOVERY CENTER   **FREE**
35 E. Quay Rd., Truman Waterfront
(305) 292-0311 or (305) 809-4700
floridakeys.noaa.gov/eco-discovery.html

The 6,400-square-foot Eco-Discovery Center is operated by the National Oceanic and Atmospheric Administration's Florida Keys National Marine Sanctuary, the National Park Service, and the US Fish and Wildlife Service. Located at historic Truman Waterfront, the center's high points are a 22-minute film

by David Talbot, the award-winning director of *Free Willy* fame. Talbot takes you on an exciting trip from land to under the sea. In the Eco-Discovery Center you can utilize touch-screen computers to learn more about the Keys, its habitats and coral reefs, and walk through a version of the Aquarius undersea lab (see sidebar in the Diving & Snorkeling chapter). To add to the marvels of this complex, there is a "green" roof that covers the main structure—talk about being eco-friendly!

✳FORT ZACHARY TAYLOR HISTORIC STATE PARK   **$**
Truman Annex at Southard Street
(305) 292-6713
forttaylor.org

This Key West military bastion served the Union well during the Civil War, when it guarded against Confederate blockade runners. So impressive were its defenses, the fort was never attacked. It saw continuous usage by the military until the federal government deeded the structure to the state of Florida for use as a historic site. The Florida Park Service opened Fort Zachary Taylor to the public in 1985. The surrounding park offers a beach for fishing, swimming, or snorkeling, as well as picnic areas equipped with tables and grills, outside showers, a snack bar, and restroom facilities. It also offers one of the best, unobstructed views of the sunset.

✳KEY WEST AIDS MEMORIAL   **FREE**
Foot of White Street and Atlantic Boulevard
keywestaids.org

The names of many of the victims of the AIDS epidemic are inscribed on this memorial, which consists of flat granite slabs embedded in the walkway approaching White

Street Pier. Built with private funds and dedicated on World AIDS Day, December 1, 1997, the memorial has room for 1,500 names. At the unveiling, it contained 730. New names are engraved annually and dedicated in a ceremony that takes place each December on World AIDS Day. Members of a volunteer group—Friends of the Key West AIDS Memorial—maintain and protect this site.

✳KEY WEST CITY CEMETERY   FREE
Bordered by Angela, Frances, and Olivia Streets and Windsor Lane
(305) 292-8177
keywestcity.com/cemetery

Built in 1847 after the horrific hurricane the year before washed out the sand sanctuary at the island's southernmost point, the Key West City Cemetery lies right in the center of town. Carved with symbols and prosaic sayings, such as I TOLD YOU I WAS SICK and DEVOTED FAN OF JULIO IGLESIAS, the gravestones are a living legacy for those lying beneath. The Historic Florida Keys Foundation's self-guided tour pamphlet lists graves of Key West's most prominent or notorious deceased citizens, with brief profiles and the meaning of the carved symbols on the gravestones. Pick up a free Historic Key West City Cemetery Self-Guided Tour pamphlet at the Monroe County Public Library, 700 Fleming St., or at the Key West Chamber of Commerce at 510 Greene St.

✳KEY WEST HISTORIC SEAPORT
AND HARBORWALK   FREE
201 William St., at the Key West Bight
(305) 294-1100
keywestcity.com

Formerly known as Key West Bight, this once-seedy piece of prime waterfront real estate was where shrimpers, spongers, and turtle traders came to unload their daily catch, tell tall tales of the sea, quaff a few brews, and just generally hang out. With the relocation of the shrimp boats to Stock Island and the demise of sponging and turtle hunting, this area has undergone a complete metamorphosis. Tall ships still tie up here, but so do million-dollar yachts. Shops, restaurants, and raw bars now line the wooden boardwalk that stretches from the foot of Front Street to the foot of Margaret Street. Vessels bound for the Dry Tortugas leave from here, as do many of the snorkel and sunset cruises and fishing charters (see our Recreation chapter for details).

KEY WEST HISTORICAL MEMORIAL
SCULPTURE GARDEN   FREE
Mallory Square
(305) 294-4142

Located on Key West's original shoreline just behind Mallory Square, this tiny fenced-in "garden" pays homage to three dozen men and women whose lives and deeds have had tremendous impact on the southernmost city. Here you will find the stories and likenesses of such former influential citizens as wreckers Asa Tift and Captain John Geiger; writer Ernest Hemingway; president Harry S. Truman; railroad magnate Henry Flagler; Sister Louise Gabriel, whose Grotto to Our Lady of Lourdes is said to have protected Key West from hurricanes for more than 75 years; and land developer Charley Toppino. All of the bronze busts, as well as the imposing wreckers sculpture, are the works of sculptor James Mastin of Coral Gables, Florida.

KEY WEST SHIPWRECK MUSEUM $$$
1 Whitehead St., Mallory Square
(305) 292-8990
keywestshipwreck.com

Relive the days of wreckers, lumpers, and divers at the Key West Shipwreck Museum, where actors, video footage, and interactive presentations re-create vestiges of Key West's once-lucrative wrecking industry. During the 1800s about 100 ships passed by the port of Key West daily, many running aground on the reef. Asa Tift, a 19th-century wrecker and the original owner of what would one day become the Hemingway Home, tells his story of salvaging the goods of the SS *Isaac Allerton,* which was downed by a hurricane in 1856 (see our Kidstuff chapter). Shows run every 30 minutes, daily.

i Get out of the hotel or house, stop the shopping and fishing, and take a nature call at the Key West Tropical Forest & Botanical Garden. There are exciting events going on all the time, including Hot Havana Nights, the annual summer party; Brunch with Mom in the Garden, which blooms in May; and Jewels of the Tropical Forest, which glitters in Febuary. In April, Migration Mania offers kids the thrilling experience of bats, birds, butterflies, and reptiles up close and personal.

KEY WEST TROPICAL FOREST & BOTANICAL GARDEN $
5210 College Rd., Stock Island
(305) 296-1504
keywestbotanicalgarden.org
Maintained by volunteers from the Key West Botanical Garden Society and funded by donations since 1935, this 11-acre garden represents the last undeveloped native hardwood hammock in the environs of Key West. Despite its proximity to US 1 and a busy public golf course, the garden is surprisingly peaceful. It features exotic and native plants that can be viewed from a series of walking trails and is home to numerous birds and butterflies, especially during the spring and fall migration seasons. On any given day, you're apt to see a turtle sunning itself on a log or an egret searching for food in Desbiens Pond. You can also sit in the quiet, restored Toppino Nature Chapel.

MALLORY SQUARE SUNSET CELEBRATION FREE
1 Whitehead St.
(305) 292-7700
sunsetcelebration.org
Key West is famous (or perhaps infamous) for this sunset celebration. Buskers and street players, vaudevillians and carny wannabes strut their stuff every day as the sun sinks into the Gulf of Mexico over Sunset Key off Mallory Square. Beverage and food vendors hawk refreshments while fire-eaters, furniture jugglers, tightrope walkers, and sword swallowers compete for your attention. A footbridge links Mallory Square to the pier at the adjacent Westin Key West Resort and Marina, where the likes of vaudevillian Jeep and his dog Moe and Dominique's high-flying cats delight the crowd. This daily event, a Key West tradition since 1984, is free to all, but pack your pocket with small bills because the performers play for tips. The fun starts approximately an hour before sunset at Mallory.

MILE MARKER 0 FREE
Corner of Whitehead and Fleming Streets
Key West is truly the last resort and here's the proof: The official green-and-white Mile Marker 0 signifying the end of US 1 is posted at this corner. Have someone snap a picture

of you in front of the sign. It will make a wonderful reminder of that very moment you finally arrived at the end of your road . . . that's providing some souvenir hunter hasn't made off with the sign, which happens with great regularity. Tampering with highway signs (including those enticing green mile markers) is against the law, by the way. If you must own one, replicas of Mile Marker 0 are available for purchase in many Key West shops.

NATIONAL WEATHER SERVICE STATION   FREE
1315 White St.
(305) 295-1316
srh.noaa.gov/eyw

Weather observation in Key West dates back at least as far as 1832, when rainfall measurements were taken at the Sand Key Lighthouse. In 1870 the first observation station was opened on Duval Street. The National Weather Service relocated to different spots during the 1900s. In 2006 a new $5.1 million station opened on White Street, bringing the art and technology of weather reporting into the 21st century. Key West sits in a prime location between the Gulf of Mexico and the Atlantic Ocean, making it an important stop along international shipping lanes. Forty percent of the world's shipping relies on the Key West Weather Station for weather data. Tours of this architectural marvel are available Mon through Fri by appointment only.

THE SOUTHERNMOST POINT   FREE
Corner of Whitehead and South Streets

Look for the traffic jam at the Atlantic end of Whitehead Street and you'll see the giant red, white, green, and yellow marker buoy that designates the southernmost point of the continental US. And standing in front

of it, in the street, blocking traffic trying to turn left onto South Street, preens a never-ending stream of Key West visitors, trying to capture the moment they stood closer to Cuba than anyone else in the country. Call it touristy, even tacky, if you like, but the crowds seem to love it.

GUIDED & SELF-GUIDED TOURS

Key West

CITYVIEW TROLLEY $$
330 Elizabeth St.
(305) 294-0644
cityviewtrolleys.com

Experience Key West and learn about its rich history from the comfort of this new hop-on/hop-off open-air trolley service. The seats are comfortably padded, and the conductors will regale you with tales of Key West's past and present as you leisurely cruise around the island aboard the trolley. There are 9 stops on the route, including Mallory Square, La Concha, the White Street Pier, the Southernmost Point, and the Hemingway Home. The first tour begins at 9:30 a.m., with the last reboard at 4:30 p.m., and trolleys run at a 30-minute frequency.

CONCH TOUR TRAIN $$$
303 Front St.
(305) 294-5161 or (800) 213-2474
conchtourtrain.com

The quirky little Conch Tour Train is a great way to garner an overview of Key West in the shaded comfort of a canopied tram. You'll pass by most of the attractions we've written up in this chapter, sometimes twice, because in tiny Key West the train weaves a circuitous route that often changes from one hour to the next depending on road construction and special events that necessitate street closures. Tours start at Mallory Square or Flagler Station on Caroline Street. Children younger than age 4 ride free. The tour lasts 90 minutes, with one 10-minute rest break at the Conch Tour Train ticket station, 501 Front St.

GHOST TOURS OF KEY WEST $
(305) 294-9255
hauntedtours.com

Love a good ghost story? Ghost Tours offers you the chance to get an in-depth introduction to the most famous ghosts of our island. Highlights include a visit to the city's original hanging tree. Tales of Robert, a haunted doll said to have been possessed by an evil spirit, intensify the mystery. Disbelief and awe surround the deeds of the German count who dug up the body of his true love, dressed her in a bridal gown, and serenaded her for seven years. Narrated by a spooky, caped, lantern-bearing guide, this 1-mile tour wends its way through Key West after dark and lasts about 90 minutes. Tours leave nightly from the lobby of the Crowne Plaza La Concha, 430 Duval St. Reservations are recommended.

GHOSTS & LEGENDS OF KEY WEST $$
(305) 294-1713
keywestghosts.com

Each evening at 7 and 9 p.m., Ghosts & Legends of Key West leads visitors to our southernmost city on a shadowy saunter down the narrow lanes of Old Town. The second ghostly attraction in Key West (see Ghost Tours of Key West above), Ghosts & Legends meets at the corner of Duval and Caroline Streets at the Porter Mansion. Guides share dark narratives of haunted mansions, voodoo superstitions, a secret leper colony, and pirate lore, hitting such "low" spots as the

old city morgue and St. Paul's Cemetery. This 90-minute jaunt may put you in touch with Key West's restless spirits. Reservations are required.

LLOYD'S TROPICAL BIKE TOUR $$
(305) 294-1882
lloydstropicalbiketour.com

Lloyd is one of Key West's most colorful characters and will lead you on a leisurely 2-hour bike tour of the island, machete in hand. He is an expert on all things Key West, having lived on the island for more than 40 years. Don't worry—if you haven't been on a bike since before you had your first margarita, you will still be able to enjoy yourself. During the tour in the historic Old Town area, you might stop along the way to hear stories from other locals and sample the local fruits. As Lloyd says, "There is always some kind of fruit in season, perhaps something you've never tried before, like a sapodilla or a Surinam cherry. Just sit back, pedal along effortlessly on our flat island, and relax. It all makes so much sense." And we couldn't agree more.

OLD TOWN TROLLEY TOURS OF
KEY WEST $$$
3840 N. Roosevelt Ave.
(305) 395-4958 or (800) 213-2474
historictours.com/keywest

Join the Old Town Trolley Tour for an informative, convenient entry into Key West. The trolley stops at most major hotels, handy if you're staying in the southernmost city. Day-trippers will appreciate the free parking at the Key West Welcome Center, where you can pick up the tour. The trolleys depart every 30 minutes, and you can get off at any of the 12 stops and reboard the same day. All along the way the tour guide will treat you to a Key West history lesson, full of anecdotes and legends. Old Town Trolley Tours run daily.

PELICAN PATH   **FREE**
Key West Chamber of Commerce, 510 Greene St.
(305) 294-2587
Visitors who like to wander on their own should be sure to first pick up a copy of the Pelican Path brochure at the chamber of commerce on Greene Street. This handy compact walking guide and map offers a short history of Key West as well as a suggested route that will take you past 50 of our most prominent historic structures. Most of the buildings described in this brochure are now private homes and guesthouses. Don't be surprised, however, if you can't spot those yellow-and-blue Pelican signs described in the brochure as path markers; many of them have disappeared over the years. Even so, the Pelican Path remains relatively easy to follow and is a great way to get acquainted with island history.

WILD DOLPHIN ADVENTURES   **$$**
William Street, Old Historic Key West Bight
(305) 304-8000
wilddolphinadventures.com
Relax and get away from the Key West crowds by taking an adventure on the *Coral Reefer* out onto the Gulf of Mexico and interacting with beautiful wild Atlantic bottlenose dolphins. This is an ecology tour that gives you the opportunity to watch a resident pod of dolphins in their natural habitat where they live and play. On your outing you will see local marine life, birds, coral reefs, sponges, rays, and more. Snorkeling is also available on these trips. Seating is limited, and reservations are recommended.

KIDSTUFF

There is so much for the little ones to do in the Keys: observe dolphins in their natural habitat, swim with sea creatures in our tropical waters, learn about the ecosystem of the Florida Keys at our museums and parks, and lots more! In this chapter we list highlights of kid-friendly activities by category in each area of the Keys.

ARTS

Upper Keys

BLUEWATER POTTERS
MM 102.9 Oceanside, Key Largo
(305) 453-1920
bluewaterpotters.com
Watch skilled artisans work the clay by hand to form creative and functional shapes for spoon rests, dinnerware, lamps, and fun decorative pieces.

Key West

MALLORY SQUARE
Waterfront at Front Street
sunsetcelebration.org
The free nightly sunset celebration at Mallory Square draws hundreds of people to experience an island tradition featuring street performers and vendors. Adults and kids gather on the waterfront square to applaud tightrope walkers, jugglers, and animal acts striving to top the fiery sunset over the Gulf of Mexico. Bonus: Your kids might even get drafted to help the performers.

BEACHES, PARKS & PLAYGROUNDS

Upper Keys

ANNE'S BEACH
MM 80 Oceanside, Islamorada
This small beach offers a scenic walkway and great views of the shallows surrounding Islamorada. It has restrooms and picnic tables.

FOUNDERS PARK
MM 87 Bayside, Plantation Key
(305) 853-1685
Islamorada.fl.us
Many activities at this well-maintained waterfront park are free to out-of-town guests who bring their hotel room keys. Founders Park offers an Olympic-size pool with diving area; a shallow-water beach; water-sports rentals; ball fields; a fishing jetty; bocce, tennis, and basketball courts; a vita course with 18 exercise stations; a multipurpose path; a skate park; and a dog park.

FRIENDSHIP PARK
MM 100 Oceanside, Key Largo
This free community park offers a ball field, playground, and tennis courts.

HARRY HARRIS PARK
Turn off US 1 at Burton Drive, MM 92.5
Oceanside, Key Largo
This gorgeous oceanfront park has been updated with a new toddler playground. You can watch your kids from a convenient covered picnic area. Entry to the park is free Mon through Fri. On weekends it's free for kids under 12, with a small charge for others.

✳JOHN PENNEKAMP CORAL REEF
   STATE PARK
MM 102.5 Oceanside, Key Largo
(305) 451-6300
pennekamppark.com
The depths of the sea can be discovered at John Pennekamp Coral Reef State Park, the nation's first underwater preserve. Pennekamp can be explored by glass-bottomed boat or on scuba diving or snorkeling excursions. (See the Diving & Snorkeling chapter for more information.)

KEY LARGO COMMUNITY PARK
MM 99.6 Oceanside, Key Largo
This huge park has it all: playground, ball fields, tennis courts, volleyball court, and more. It is co-located with the Jacob's Aquatic Center pool facility (see the Camps & Outdoor Activities section in this chapter for more information).

OLD SETTLER'S PARK
MM 92 Oceanside, Key Largo
This small community park is free and offers swings and slides for children to play on.

WINDLEY KEY FOSSIL REEF GEOLOGIC
   SITE
MM 85.5 Bayside, Islamorada
(305) 664-2540
floridastateparks.org/windleykey

Examine the fossilized imprints of ancient shells and marine organisms you'll find in the coral quarry walls of the Windley Key Fossil Reef Geologic Site. If you bring paper and crayons, you and the kids can make a crayon rubbing of your favorite fossil.

Middle Keys

COCO PLUM BEACH
Turn off US 1 at Coco Plum Drive, MM 54.5 Oceanside, Marathon
This small, natural beach is an enjoyable stop, but one with few amenities. It is a quiet, dog-friendly beach with clean-up baggies provided.

MARATHON COMMUNITY PARK
MM 49 Oceanside, Marathon
Marathon Community Park features 4 tennis courts, a tennis wall, 3 combination hockey/basketball courts, 2 Little League fields, and 2 soccer fields. There is also an X-treme skating park, 2 shuffleboard courts, 2 bocce courts, a batting cage, concession stand, amphitheater, picnic areas, and restrooms. This facility is wheelchair accessible. The park hours are 7 a.m. to 10 p.m.

ROTARY FIELD OF DREAMS
MM 52 Oceanside, Marathon
Your children will be talking about this large playground long after you leave the Keys. It offers a wooden replica of Thomas the Train, plus plenty of tunnels, swings, and a sandbox with a toothy, make-believe shark. There is plenty for toddlers and older kids as well.

✳SOMBRERO BEACH
MM 50 Oceanside, Marathon
This 12.6-acre beach is one of the most popular stops in Marathon and offers walkways, picnic areas, and a roped-off swimming area.

The kids can play in the sand or look for crabs and crustaceans. There is no admission fee. Turn off US 1 at Sombrero Beach Boulevard and drive to the end to reach the beach.

Lower Keys

BAHIA HONDA STATE PARK
MM 37 Oceanside, Big Pine Key
(305) 872-2353
floridastateparks.org/bahiahonda
This state park has 2 beaches. A small one near the concession stand at the south end of the park is calm, sheltered, and roped off for safety. The other, the Sandspur, is much longer. You can wade in the soft sand through waters that vary from several inches to 3 feet deep looking for sea creatures and washed-up treasure (see the Recreation chapter for more on beach options).

BAY POINT PARK
MM 15 Oceanside, Saddlebunch Key
This community park offers a soccer field, basketball and tennis courts, and a small playground with swings.

BLUE HERON PARK
Lytton's Way, off Key Deer Boulevard, Big Pine Key
This well-equipped community park offers basketball courts, playgrounds, pavilions, and portable toilets.

✳VETERAN'S MEMORIAL PARK AND BEACH
MM 39 Oceanside, west end of Seven Mile Bridge, Little Duck Key
This convenient beach offers beautiful views of the Atlantic Ocean and offers covered picnic tables for those who need shade. It is a nice spot to show children the shallow-water flats habitat of the Keys.

WATSON FIELD AND SOUTH STREET PLAYGROUND
Key Deer Boulevard and South Street, Big Pine Key
You'll find a baseball diamond here and behind that a small playground, a volleyball court, and the Susann Thisler Tennis Courts.

Key West

✳ASTRO CITY
Atlantic Boulevard
This well-equipped playground is conveniently located just across the street from Higgs Beach. It is a popular stop for families on their way to and from the beach, White Street Pier, or Old Town.

BAYVIEW PARK
Truman Avenue and Eisenhower Street
This large park offers plenty of room for a family ball game. You'll also find a fully-equipped playground, basketball court, tennis courts, and restrooms. Los of community events take place here.

✳FORT ZACHARY TAYLOR HISTORIC STATE PARK
Truman Annex at the end of Southard Street
(305) 292-6713
floridastateparks.org/forttaylor
This historic fortress at the southwest end of Key West is a fascinating place to roam. The grounds offer a sandy beach with picnic tables and restrooms. Children will enjoy watching the boats sail by out of Key West Harbor. The fort was named after the 12th president of the US.

KEY WEST MARINE PARK
Atlantic Ocean from White Street to Duval Street

The waters along the southwest end of Key West have been cordoned off with buoys to create safe areas for swimming and snorkeling. You'll view numerous species of coral, tropical fish, and birds at this park set up by the local group Reef Relief.

CAMPS & OUTDOOR ACTIVITIES

Upper Keys

✳JACOB'S AQUATIC CENTER
320 Laguna Ave., Key Largo
(305) 453-7946
jacobsaquaticcenter.org
Your children can splash for hours at the fun water park at Jacob's Aquatic Center. A mock-up of a pirate ship looms in the center of a shallow splash pool that's perfect for toddlers. Older kids will also enjoy swimming in an adjacent pool. Polite and astute lifeguards are on hand, and swim lessons and training are available.

Middle Keys

CAMP ADVENTURE
City of Marathon Parks and Recreation, Marathon
(305) 289-5888
marathonflorida.org
For 7 weeks, from June through mid-July, the weekly camp, with exciting themes that change each week, keeps kids ages 6 to 13 entertained, educated, and active. Parents can register children for single or multiple weeks. Because of the camp's popularity, it is first-come, first-served to sign up.

✳PIGEON KEY MARINE SCIENCE SUMMER CAMP
MM 47 Oceanside, Marathon
(305) 289-0025
pigeonkey.net
This hands-on science expedition into the living history of Pigeon Key and the Florida Keys can be either a day or overnight camp. Students ages 8 to 18 learn about habitats, marine life, and the fragile ecosystem we live in. Classes are usually at the end of June through mid-July.

Lower Keys

BOONDOCKS GRILLE & DRAFT HOUSE
MM 27.5 Bayside, Ramrod Key
(305) 872-4094
boondocksus.com
Featuring the only public miniature golf course in the Florida Keys, Boondocks is a favorite place for families to play a round or four.

✳SEACAMP
MM 29.5 Oceanside, Big Pine Key
(305) 872-2331
seacamp.org
This marine science educational program for teenagers is located at the tip of Big Pine Key. Campers visit coral reefs, sandy and grassy areas, mudflats, and natural tide pools, all of them rich in sea plants and animals basic to the study of marine science. Camp facilities include a dining and recreation hall, science laboratory, deepwater harbor, arts and crafts building, infirmary, sailing shelter, teaching shelter, and commercial kitchen.

⊙ Close-up

Things That Go Bump in Plain Sight . . .
Robert the Doll

This straw-filled toy doll was a gift, given to Key West resident Robert Eugene Otto as a child by his Jamaican nurse in the early 1800s. The nurse, upset for being dismissed by Robert's mother, handmade the stuffed doll in the likeness of young Master Otto, and some say it was voodoo cursed. The doll was even given young Mr. Otto's first name of "Robert." With his unblinking eyes, faded sailor suit, and the mysterious stories surrounding him, Robert has become a legend in his own right. Living in their family home on the corner of Eaton and Simonton Streets (see the Artist House listing in the Accommodations chapter), young Eugene became very attached to Robert and even blamed the doll for mishaps and unusual events, saying "Robert did it!" Eventually, the toy was banished to the attic where, as the story goes, he would taunt schoolchildren from the window so much that the kids would take a different route to school.

When Mr. Otto died in the 1970s, Robert was given a home in a glass case at the **East Martello Museum** (see the Attractions chapter), where he resides today. Despite rumors of ruined photographs and unexplained events at the museum from time to time, Robert is the most popular exhibit. In the summer of 2008, Robert took a road trip, leaving Key West for the first time in more than 100 years. He was featured at the Atlantic Paranormal Society Convention in Clearwater, Florida. Trick or treat, any time of the year . . .

MUSEUMS

Middle Keys

FLORIDA KEYS CHILDREN'S MUSEUM AT THE MUSEUMS OF CRANE POINT
MM 50.5 Bayside, Marathon
(305) 743-9100
cranepoint.net
Your children can learn all about hermit crabs and then dress up in pirate clothes and hop aboard a 17th-century galleon. Afterwards, they can learn about the native Keys inhabitants, the early explorers, the pioneers, and the developers of the "Railroad that Died at Sea."

Key West

KEY WEST SHIPWRECK MUSEUM
1 Whitehead St.
(305) 292-8990
keywestshipwreck.com
History comes to life here with re-creations of the salvage and wrecking era through live actors, film, and artifacts from the wreck of the *Isaac Allerton*, which sank off the Keys in 1856. The business of salvaging goods from ships wrecked on Florida Keys reefs made Key West the richest US city per capita in the mid-1800s. Wrecking master "Asa Tift" guides guests through the museum, explaining the unique industry, and invites them to climb the facility's 65-foot lookout tower.

WILDLIFE

Upper Keys

DOLPHIN COVE
MM 101.9, Bayside, Key Largo
(877) 365-2683
dolphinscove.com

DOLPHINS PLUS
31 Corrine Place, Key Largo
(866) 860-7946
dolphinsplus.com
Both Dolphin Cove and Dolphin Plus offer structured as well as natural dolphin swim and wade programs for children as young as 3 years old.

LAURA QUINN WILD BIRD SANCTUARY
MM 93.6, Bayside, Tavernier
(305) 852-4486
fkwbc.org
This Upper Keys landmark is home to more than 100 ill, injured, or orphaned wild birds, all housed in a natural setting on more than 5 acres. Bird lovers can visit a daily pelican feeding, set for 3:30 p.m., that typically draws hundreds of wild pelicans hungry for fish.

✳ROBBIE'S MARINA
MM 77.5 Bayside, Islamorada
(305) 664-9814 or (877) 664-8498.
robbies.com
Feeding the tarpon at Robbie's Marina is something that is not to be missed. You can purchase a cup of baitfish, the tarpon's favorite snack, at the marina. Visitors pay just $1 for dock access and $3 for a pail of baitfish to hand-feed the giant tarpon, the popular Keys fish that hang around on an almost year-round basis. Robbie's also offers small powerboats and kayaks for rent, and a party fishing boat on which you can go reef fishing off Islamorada.

THEATER OF THE SEA
MM 84.5 Bayside, Islamorada
(305) 664-2431
theaterofthesea.com
Islamorada's lush 17-acre tropical oasis features a variety of fish and marine life, native birds, colorful parrots, sea turtles, crocodiles, and exotic plants. General admission includes live performances by dolphins in the main lagoon (created by excavations for Henry Flagler's railroad; see the History chapter), sea lions, and parrots; a guided tour of marine-life exhibits; petting the sharks in the touch tank and dolphins in another tank; and a glass-bottomed boat tour of the facility's natural saltwater lagoon. Theater of the Sea also hosts swim programs with dolphins, stingrays, and sea lions. (For more on Theater of the Sea, see the Attractions chapter.)

Middle Keys

**CAPTAIN HOOK'S MARINA & DIVE
  CENTER AQUATIC LEARNING CENTER**
MM 53.1 Oceanside, Marathon
(800) 278-4665
Captain Hook's has been around for more than 50 years, so you can bet they know the Florida Keys waters extremely well. A highlight of visiting Captain Hook's is their fishpond and marine life exhibit, including their 48,000-gallon outdoor aquarium. Every day at 4 p.m. you can watch nurse sharks, eels, and other big fish receive their evening meal. It's free fun.

CRANE POINT HAMMOCK
MM 50.5 Oceanside, Marathon
(305) 743-9100
cranepoint.net
This 63-acre environmental and archaeological preserve includes attractions like the Adderley House, built in 1906 by a Bahamian

immigrant; a touch tank that features sea urchins and starfish; a large lagoon with nurse sharks and tropical fish; nature trails full of interesting sinkholes and mangroves; and the Marathon Wild Bird Center for injured and orphaned birds.

DOLPHIN RESEARCH CENTER
MM 59 Bayside, Grassy Key
(305) 289-1121
dolphins.org

The Dolphin Research Center is a teaching and research facility with fun-filled interactive programs, including painting with a dolphin and becoming a trainer for a day. The facility also features a water recreation "sprayground" for families. Visitors can initiate whale, manatee, and dolphin sounds while splashing through sprays of water that shoot out of marine- and island-themed figures such as a supersize dolphin tail.

Lower Keys

THE BLUE HOLE
MM 31 Bayside, Key Deer Boulevard, Big Pine Key
(305) 872-2411

This freshwater sinkhole is home to a couple of curious alligators, and they'll swim almost up to the viewing platform. Keep your puppy on a leash, because its barking will ring the alligators' dinner bell. You'll see turtles in the Blue Hole, and key deer come around at dusk. There is no admission charge.

✳THE HORSESHOE
MM 35 Bayside, just over the Bahia Honda Bridge, Big Pine Key

Stop here as you head down the Keys. In the Horseshoe you'll see a natural aquarium of colorful tropical fish, with no danger from

sharks or barracuda because they can't get in.

✳NATIONAL KEY DEER REFUGE VISITOR CENTER
MM 30.5, Bayside, Key Deer Boulevard, Big Pine Key
(305) 872-2239
fws.gov/nationalkeydeer

Just before sunset, simply drive or ride a bike cautiously to the end of Key Deer Boulevard and you're bound to see key deer strolling out of the woods to feed. The key deer is an endangered species that lives only in the Lower Keys. These shy, appealing creatures are about 3 feet tall and can be found grazing all around Big Pine Key, especially during early morning hours and around dusk. The deer are wild and healthy, so please don't feed or touch them. For more information, stop by the refuge headquarters at the National Key Deer Refuge Visitor Center.

NO NAME KEY BRIDGE
Big Pine Key

This scenic bridge that links No Name Key to Big Pine Key is a popular spot to take kids fishing. The evening sightseeing is also excellent for birds and key deer. We suggest you park your car and walk along the pedestrian walkway.

STRIKE ZONE CHARTERS
MM 29.5 Bayside, Big Pine Key
(305) 872-9863 or (800) 654-9560
strikezonecharter.com

Hop aboard a glass-bottomed boat for a 5-hour ecological tour of the Lower Keys backcountry with Strike Zone Charters. You'll learn the history of the key deer, the tiny out-islands, the hurricanes, the wreckers, and the Indians. You'll see bald eagle nesting sites, great white herons, egrets, and dolphins feeding in the wild. You can snorkel and fish a little, too. And to top it all off, you'll enjoy a fish cookout picnic on a private island.

Key West

✳DOLPHIN WATCH
Key West Harbor
(800) 979-3370
dolphinwatchusa.com
Book a trip with Key West's original dolphin charter, Dolphin Watch, and observe the wild dolphins as they frolic in their natural habitat. The boat is a custom-made 31-foot catamaran and they only book 6 people per trip, so you and your family will have no trouble viewing the magnificent creatures, along with other sea life including turtles, rays, fish, and maybe even a manatee or two.

✳THE FLORIDA KEYS ECO-DISCOVERY CENTER
33 E. Quay Rd., Truman Waterfront
(305) 809-4750
floridakeys.noaa.gov
This 6,400-square-foot facility showcases natural wonders both on land and underwater. Highlights include a walk-through version of the Aquarius, a manned underwater research habitat located off Key Largo, and interactive exhibits that spotlight the Keys' diverse environments. A 2,500-gallon living reef tank with corals and tropical fish completes the experience. With its touch screens, stunning photos, and roomy theater, this educational center has become a hit with families. It's a fun way to learn about reef and mangrove habitats indoors. The center is operated by the Florida Keys National Marine Sanctuary, and admission is free.

KEY WEST AQUARIUM
1 Whitehead St.
(888) 544-5927
keywestaquarium.com
Opened in 1934, the aquarium was one of the first family-friendly attractions in the Keys. Today it's home to groupers, moray eels, barracuda, tropical fish, tarpon, sharks, parrotfish, and more. A touch tank features small sea creatures that children can touch and feed. Guided tours of the aquarium include shark feeding and even an opportunity for guests to "pet" a shark.

THE KEY WEST BUTTERFLY & NATURE CONSERVATORY
1316 Duval St.
(305) 296-2988
keywestbutterfly.com
This is a wonderland housing thousands of tropical plants and hundreds of the delicate creatures known as "flowers of the sky." The solarium and nature exhibit, which is one of only three major butterfly facilities in Florida, features a 5,000-square-foot glass-domed tropical butterfly habitat.

KEY WEST NATURE PRESERVE
Two entrances on Atlantic Boulevard between White and Bertha Streets
The City of Key West acquired this undeveloped oceanfront property and turned it into an accessible natural area. Wooden walkways and trails take visitors through mangrove forests to a quiet strip of beach. Children will enjoy seeing butterflies, lizards, and birds.

ANNUAL EVENTS

No one knows how to throw a party better than residents of the Florida Keys. Come dress with us in period attire as we relive eras of our past. Or join locals and folks from across the world in a challenging road race on a bridge spanning miles of open sea.

We also have boat parades, bikini contests, battle reenactments, and our own unplugged, underwater concert. Or try your angling skills in one of our many fishing tournaments (see the Fishing chapter for an expanded listing). Immerse yourself in Florida Keys arts and culture at our historical observances, music festivals, or arts and crafts fairs.

And my, how we love to eat. From Key Largo to Key West, food festivals abound. These events provide an inexpensive means of sampling incredibly fresh seafood and menu items from leading local restaurants.

OVERVIEW

The following selection of festivals and events is a sampling of what we offer annually in the Florida Keys. Additional events occur sporadically from year to year. Dates and locations often change, and admission prices vary. Call the local chambers of commerce for details: Key Largo, MM 106 Bayside, (305) 451-1414 or (800) 822-1088; Islamorada, MM 82.5 Bayside, (305) 664-4503 or (800) 322-5397; Marathon, MM 53.5 Bayside, (305) 743-5417 or (800) 262-7284; Lower Keys, MM 31 Oceanside, (305) 872-2411 or (800) 872-3722; Key West, 510 Greene St., (305) 294-2587 or (800) 527-8539. You can pick up the annual *Attractions & Events* brochure at any of these chambers. You also will find annual event information on the official website of the Monroe County Tourist Development Council: fla-keys.com.

JANUARY

ART UNDER THE OAKS
MM 89.5 Bayside, Plantation Key, Islamorada
(305) 360-8556
artundertheoaks.com
Begun in 1982, Art under the Oaks, held in the gardens on the grounds of San Pedro Church, is always a tremendous community gathering. This 1-day celebration in mid-Jan is held in a natural setting under a lovely canopy of oak trees. It offers homemade crafts, fine art from local artists, specialty food booths, self-guided nature tours of the gardens, children's arts and crafts, raffle items, and live music. Because of the large turnout, free shuttle bus service runs from the Plantation Key School's parking lot to the event.

CHEECA LODGE & SPA PRESIDENTIAL SAILFISH TOURNAMENT
MM 82 Oceanside, Cheeca Lodge, Islamorada
(305) 664-4651 or (800) 327-2888
cheeca.com

In 1989 when George H. W. Bush was our president, he came to Islamorada on holiday and to fish. This exciting 3-day tourney has been taking place for more than 20 years in mid-Jan and is part of the Florida Keys Gold Cup Sailfish Championship and world Billfish Series. Cash prizes and trophies are awarded in this catch-and-release event.

✳KEY WEST CRAFT SHOW
Whitehead Street, Key West
(305) 294-1241
keywestartcentercom

Key West ends the month of Jan with a weekend-long exhibit of original crafts. Among the one-of-a-kind items offered for sale, you'll find handmade jewelry, leather goods, wood carvings, kitchen accessories, and exquisite hand-thrown pottery from Pottery by Grace, a fifth-generation Conch (potterybygrace.com). Exhibitors come from throughout the Keys and the US. The crafts show takes place in the street—on Whitehead Street between Eaton and Greene. Admission is free.

✳KEY WEST FOOD AND WINE FESTIVAL
Various locations throughout Key West
(800) 474-4319
keywestfoodandwinefestival.com

The Key West Food and Wine Festival is 4 fun-filled days of culinary delights and funky events you would only expect to experience in Key West. The festival's signature events are the Kick Off Your Flip-Flops Barefoot Beach Party; the Grand Tasting, with a refined selection of wines; and Duval Uncorked, which leads guests along Duval Street for a mile-long food and wine tasting extravaganza. There are also neighborhood strolls, one-of-a-kind fund-raisers like coconut bowling, various informative seminars, and an outdoor wine market.

ℹ️ If you are "road tripping" south to the Florida Keys, remember that Florida's Turnpike (built in 1957) is a toll road. If you travel on I-95 or US 1 in Florida, there are no tolls.

✳KEY WEST HISTORIC HOUSE AND GARDEN TOURS
Various locations throughout Key West
(305) 294-9501
oirf.org

Olde Island Restoration, a nonprofit organization that encourages preservation of Key West's many historical structures, sponsors this popular tour—spanning Dec, Jan, Feb, and Mar—to show off some of the city's finest private properties. Typically each event features 5 or 6 privately owned homes. Tours explore shotgun-style cottages, Conch-style mansions, and everything in between. The tours are self-guided, but participants may meet at the Olde Island Restoration offices along Mallory Square and then embark on a Conch Train bound for the tour site. Scheduled dates vary from year to year. There is an admission fee.

✳KEY WEST LITERARY SEMINAR
San Carlos Institute, 516 Duval St., Key West
(888) 293-9291 or (888) 293-9291
kwls.org

Originated in 1983 and dedicated to the celebration of the written word, the Key West Literary Seminar is a very important gathering of notable authors and their admiring public. Key West's San Carlos Institute serves as the home base for these sessions, but events occur at various locations throughout Key West. Writing workshops, tours of legendary local authors' homes, and cocktail parties also are offered to seminar participants. Included in the core seminar price, these parties offer the opportunity to mingle with panel guests. Workshops and tours cost an additional fee. The 4-day event is typically held during the second week of Jan. Call for information on registration and workshop fees, but reserve early. These events are typically sold out up to a year in advance. The 2013 headliners include James Atlas, Rosalind Brackenbury, and Edmund White, among others.

SCULPTURE KEY WEST
Fort Zachary Taylor Park, Key West
(305) 295-3800
sculpturekeywest.com
Sculpture Key West may be viewed by land, seen by boat, or observed by air. Showcased in Jan, this annual event has grown from a handful of Key West locals to a nationally and internationally prominent exhibition showcasing world-renowned contemporary sculptors.

FEBRUARY

CIVIL WAR HERITAGE DAYS
Fort Zachary Taylor, at Truman Annex at Southard Street, Key West
(305) 292-6850
History comes alive at Fort Zachary Taylor (see the Recreation and Attractions chapters)

during the first 2 weeks in Feb, when the fort is the setting for a Civil War battle reenactment. During the event the fort is filled with activity, with many enthusiasts wearing the uniforms of Union and Confederate soldiers. Other participants in period attire portray merchants and citizens. Events include the capture of a blockade runner, with the captain of the vessel standing trial. Key West was the only Southern city that stayed in the Union throughout the Civil War, and the fort was a key point in guarding the shipping lanes to Union ports.

✳GIGANTIC NAUTICAL FLEA MARKET
MM 87 Bayside, Islamorada
(305) 664-4503 or (800) 322-5397
giganticnauticalfleamarket.org
The Upper Keys Rotary Club has been producing this giant flea market for more than 15 years. New and used boats, clothing, marine equipment, electronics, dive gear, antiques, fishing gear, and nautical arts and crafts are just some of the items available. Held at the end of Feb in Founders Park on Plantation Key (see the Recreation chapter), the entrance fee is a suggested donation of $5, which goes to the Rotary scholarship fund. There is a free shuttle from Coral Shores High School at MM 89.9 due to limited parking.

OLD ISLAND DAYS ART FESTIVAL
Whitehead Street, Key West
(305) 294-1241
keywestartcenter.com
If you appreciate art, your heart is bound to beat faster at the sight of several blocks of exhibits by talented local artists. Inspired by this southernmost city, they take this opportunity to showcase their vivid creations. Virtually all artistic media are represented in this

juried weekend-long show, usually held at the end of Feb, including oil, watercolor, and acrylic paintings; graphics; wood, metal, and stone sculptures; glasswork; and photography. Judges provide merit awards within each category. Old Island Days Art Festival exhibits line Whitehead Street from Greene Street to Caroline and into Truman Annex. No charge for browsing.

PIGEON KEY ART FESTIVAL
MM 49 Oceanside, Marathon
(305) 743-5999
pigeonkey.net
Hundreds of artists from throughout the country apply to display their works in this annual early Feb show, but only 70 are selected by the judges to participate. The festival is typically held at the Marathon Community Park. Live entertainment features the music of steel-drum bands, jazz groups, classical ensembles, and country-and-western performers. Local restaurants sell food, and raffle drawings include original artwork donated by each participating artist. All proceeds are donated to the Pigeon Key Foundation for restoration of the island. Artists pay entry fees, and half the show's work has a Florida theme.

MARCH

CONCH SHELL BLOWING CONTEST
Sunset Pier at Ocean Key House, Duval Street, Key West
(305) 294-9501
oirf.org
Come to this fun "Conch Honk." The Conch Shell Blowing Contest offers adults and children the opportunity to sound off. Prizes are awarded to the loudest, the funniest, and the most entertaining conch-shell blowers

in several divisions. This 1-day, springtime event takes place on the waterfront and on various dates each year, but usually in Mar or Apr. Participation is free.

KEY WEST GARDEN CLUB FLOWER SHOW AT WEST MARTELLO TOWER
Atlantic Boulevard and White Street, Key West
(305) 294-3210
keywestgardenclub.com
Established in 1949 by former Key West politician Joe Allen, the Garden Club organizes monthly educational seminars for the public. Plant-swapping sessions also are popular. The group holds a prejuried show every other year. Held at the Joe Allen West Martello Tower, home of the Key West Garden Club, the show features some 800 entries of floral arrangements, potted plants, palms, rare tropical flowers, and hybrids. Judges from garden clubs throughout the state of Florida award ribbons and prizes in several categories. The flower show is typically held during the spring, not necessarily always in Mar. There are admission costs.

APRIL

*CONCH REPUBLIC INDEPENDENCE CELEBRATION
Various locations throughout Key West
(305) 296-0213
conchrepublic.com
This 10-day festival officially commemorates Key West's attempt to secede from the US on April 23, 1982, after the US Border Patrol established roadblocks at the end of the mainland to screen for drugs and illegal aliens. Independent Key Westers rebelled, creating their own flag and attempting to secede. The secession fizzled, of course, but

locals here find the brief attempt at independence a reason to party nevertheless. Around this same time every year, officials of the fictitious Conch Republic—secretary general, prime ministers, navy, air force, and all—host events like picnics, balls, Conch cruiser car shows, the Red Ribbon Bed Race down Duval Street, and what has been dubbed "the world's longest parade."

⚡**SEVEN MILE BRIDGE RUN**
Seven Mile Bridge, Marathon
(305) 395-7040
7mbrun.com

For more than 30 years, men and women from around the world have flocked to this 7-mile roadway, which spans the open water between Marathon and Bahia Honda. In the wee morning hours, these spirited individuals participate in the most scenic competition of its kind: a run across one of the world's longest bridges. Designed to raise money for local schools and youth groups, the run is said to be the only one in the world held completely over and surrounded by water. Prizes are awarded in various categories. Usually the run begins on the Marathon end of the Seven Mile Bridge. Expect to pay an entry fee. Spaces are limited, so if you plan to run, reserve your spot early.

WORLD SAILFISH CHAMPIONSHIP
Key West
(866) 550-5580
worldsailfish.com

Presented in mid-Apr, this 3-day sailfish challenge is one of South Florida's most illustrious tourneys. Winners of previous sailfish tournaments, elite anglers, and celebrity participants are challenged in this event. VIP registration is available for teams wanting to rub elbows with the likes of baseball greats Johnny Bench and Wade Boggs, and sometimes even fish with a celebrity teammate. Cash prize money, reaching six figures, is awarded to the team for the largest confirmed number of sailfish caught and released during this hard-fought championship.

MAY

CINCO DE MAYO CELEBRATION
Schooner Wharf Bar, 202 William St.,
Key West
(305) 292-3302
schoonerwharf.com

In 1994 the first Cinco de Mayo Celebration kicked off with all the sizzle and salsa anyone could handle. Still going strong, this zany festival is usually held the first week of May. In honor of the victory of the Mexican army over the French at the Battle of Pueblo in 1862, current revelers pay homage with everything from a taco-eating contest to taking shots of tequila, eating hot jalapeño peppers, and drinking beer in record time.

HARRY S. TRUMAN LEGACY
SYMPOSIUM
111 Front St., Key West
(305) 294-9911
trumansymposium.com

From 1945 to 1953 president Harry S. Truman spent 11 working vacations on the Key West Navy Base in what was to be known as the Little White House. The annual Truman Legacy Symposium, held in mid-May, offers a reception and lunch with a VIP tour of the house. Guest speakers, like Florida senator Bob Graham, discuss the various roles Truman played in shaping our nation's history. Topics change each year, as do the speakers. Truman's grandson, Clifton Truman Daniel, usually is in attendance and gives one of the keynote addresses.

✳KEY WEST SONGWRITERS FESTIVAL
400 Front St., Key West
(305) 292-2032
kwswf.com

You may not recognize the names of the performers at this annual event in early May, but if you're a country music fan, you'll almost certainly know their songs. For more than 15 years, this festival has been bringing over 100 of the country's foremost performing songwriters to the Key West stage. The Songwriters Festival revolves around 5 days and nights of more than 25 free shows staged at the most popular drinking holes and hot spots throughout Key West.

> **i** Heading into "love bug" territory is not an invite for Valentine's Day. In the months of late May and early June, heading north from the Florida Keys, you run smack dab into these pesky critters—literally—which splat all over windshields, hoods, and grills of cars, not to mention your sunglasses and body parts if you are cycling.

JUNE

THE ORIGINAL FKCC SWIM AROUND KEY WEST
Key West
(305) 809-3562
fkccswimaroundkeywest.com

Sponsored by the Bone Island Swim Club, this is the only sanctioned, insured, and US Coast Guard–permitted race around Key West. The event is a 12.5-mile swim clockwise around the island of Key West.

Age groups 18 through 65 and older can register.

JULY

FOURTH OF JULY FIREWORKS
Bayside, Key Largo
(305) 451-1414 or (800) 822-1088

View this 30-minute fireworks display from land or, if you are a boater, by sea. Funded by local merchants, the show typically begins at 9 p.m. The best coastal viewing spots are the Caribbean Club, Señor Frijoles, Sundowners, and Marriott Key Largo Bay Beach Resort. Some of these facilities host barbecues with live entertainment. Admission is free, but you must be a patron to enjoy the view from a private business. Food and drinks are sold separately.

✳HEMINGWAY DAYS FESTIVAL
Hemingway Home and Museum
907 Whitehead St., Key West
(305) 294-2587
fla-keys.com

Celebrate the legendary author's birthday with residents of the old man's former hometown by the sea. There's a street fair, a short-story competition, and a Hemingway look-alike contest at what was one of his favorite haunts, Sloppy Joe's (see the Nightlife chapter). This weeklong event centers on the author's July 21 birthday. Fees for some events are required.

> **i** The Monroe County Tourist Development Council maintains an online calendar of events. For the latest month-by-month listings of festivals, gallery showings, and theater productions, visit fla-keys.com.

JULY 4TH FIREWORKS
White Street Pier, White Street and Atlantic Boulevard, Key West
(305) 294-2587 or (800) 648-6269

The Key West Rotary Club sponsors this pyrotechnic extravaganza every July 4 beginning at 9 p.m. and lasting approximately 30 minutes. Best viewing spots are Higgs Beach and the Casa Marina. There is no admission charge; the fireworks are funded strictly by donations.

✳STAR SPANGLED EVENT AT SOMBRERO BEACH
MM 50 Oceanside, Marathon
(305) 743-5417 or (800) 262-7284

On July 4 follow a parade to the beach, where fireworks decorate the sky, and enjoy all-American hot dogs, hamburgers, and fish sandwiches. Live entertainment is provided, games are available for the kids, and an afternoon volleyball tournament welcomes last-minute sign-ups. Many people see the fireworks display from the decks of their boats, anchoring offshore for the extravaganza. No admission or entry fee is required. Food and games are priced individually.

✳UNDERWATER MUSIC FESTIVAL
MM 31 Oceanside, Big Pine Key
(305) 872-2411 or (800) 872-3722
lowerkeyschamber.com

Whether you dive, snorkel, or merely swim, you can enjoy 6 hours of prerecorded, commercial-free music—from Beethoven to the Beatles to the humpback whale song—in synchronicity with tropical fish swimming across the reefs of the Looe Key National Marine Sanctuary. Dance the day away underwater, and look out for surprises such as mermaids and the Keys' very own Snorkeling Elvises. On land, you'll find a variety of foods, arts and crafts, and family games at the Lower Keys Chamber of Commerce, MM 31 Oceanside. Admission to both the concert and the food festival, usually held the second Sat in July, is free. See the Diving & Snorkeling chapter for a list of dive and snorkel charters that will take you to the reef.

SEPTEMBER

FLORIDA KEYS BIRDING AND WILDLIFE FESTIVAL
MM 56.2 Bayside, Marathon
(305) 289-2690
keysbirdingfest.org

Held at Curry Hammock State Park in Marathon, this exciting annual event celebrates nature with guided kayaking tours, birding talks, field trips, and astronomy. There are guest speakers throughout the event offering expert presentations on various bird-related topics. The festival is usual held the last weekend of Sept, which coincides with Florida wildlife at the peak of the birding season.

FLORIDA KEYS POKER RUN
Miami through Key West
(305) 393-4827
petersonsharley.com

Revved up in 1972, bikers have traveled our roads into Key West for this highly successful and popular motorcycle run. For this event in early Sept, more than 10,000 motorcyclists ride from Miami to Key West, stopping at various points within our islands to pick up playing cards. At the end of the ride, the player with the best poker hand wins, and all enjoy live bands, field events, and runs-within-a-run on Duval Street. Bikers can also get their machines blessed before returning home. Entry is free; each poker hand costs a nominal fee.

S.L.A.M. CELEBRITY TOURNAMENT
Key West
(305) 664-2002
redbone.org
First of the annual Celebrity Tournament Series is the Southernmost Light-tackle Anglers Masters (S.L.A.M). Anglers try to score a Grand Slam by catching and releasing a bonefish, permit, and tarpon in 2 days. Usually held in early Sept; proceeds benefit the Cystic Fibrosis Foundation. (See the Fishing chapter for additional details.)

WOMENFEST KEY WEST
Various locations throughout Key West
(305) 294-4603 or (800) 535-7797
womenfest.com
Each week after Labor Day, thousands of women from all over the country and the world gather in Key West for a bit of female bonding, and have been doing so for more than 30 years. They include women from diverse races, religions, professions, and sexual orientations. This 7-day celebration is produced by the Key West Business Guild and includes women-only water sports, pool and dance parties, cocktail parties, comedy shows, and concerts. Some guesthouses on the island, like the popular Pearl's (see the Accommodations chapter), will be women-only for that week.

OCTOBER

BAYBONE CELEBRITY TOURNAMENT
Sheraton Beach Resort, MM 97 Bayside,
Key Largo
(305) 664-2002
redbone.org

For more than 20 years, the Baybone Celebrity Tournament has been in the Celebrity Tournament Series as a catch-and-release tourney in pursuit of bonefish and permit. Proceeds benefit the Cystic Fibrosis Foundation. Usually held in early Oct. (See the Fishing chapter for more information.)

FANTASY FEST
Various locations throughout Key West
(305) 296-1817
fantasyfest.com
Usually held in late Oct, this is Key West's biggest party of the year—a citywide celebration similar to Mardi Gras in New Orleans, with different themes that dictate the floats and costumes every year (see the Close-up in this chapter). The theme for 2012 was "A-Conch-Alypse."

GOOMBAY FESTIVAL
Petronia Street, Key West
(305) 294-2587 or (800) 648-6269
Designed to showcase the cultural customs of the city's Bahamian community through food, music, and crafts, this grassroots affair has grown to include African, Filipino, and Latin traditions, too. Try some festival fare and one of the Bahamian-inspired food booths, dance in the streets to the music of African and steel drummers or calypso bands, then stop by the straw market to see straw hats and fruit baskets being woven. The festival stretches from the corner of Petronia at Duval down to Emma Street and encompasses many of the streets that make up a good share of the neighborhood known as Bahama Village. Goombay is held the first weekend of Fantasy Fest (see Close-up).

Close-up

Fantasy Fest

Kookier than Carnival and merrier than Mardi Gras, Fantasy Fest is Key West's own decadent decibel of dreamy delight.

Fantasy Fest was originally conceived as a way to boost tourism in an otherwise soft season. It succeeded—and how! Today, more than two decades after its conception, this event more than doubles the island's population for one week in October, culminating with the arrival of some 70,000 revelers on Duval Street for the Saturday-night parade.

Fantasy Fest is a nine-day adult Halloween celebration that commences on a Friday night with the Royal Coronation Ball, where the King and Queen of Fantasy Fest are crowned. The competition is open to all, and campaigning for the titles begins as early as late August. The winners are the ones who "buy" the most votes (translation: They raise the most money for AIDS Help Inc.). The closer it gets to Fantasy Fest, the fiercer the competition becomes and the more creative the candidates are.

The final tally takes place at the Coronation Ball. The man and woman—or man and man-in-drag—are dubbed "royalty" only after emerging from a field of entrants. The King and Queen receive regal robes, crowns, and scepters and preside over all official Fantasy Fest events. The real winners in all of this, however, are the people served by AIDS Help Inc.

Each year Fantasy Fest features a new theme, which is emblazoned on posters and T-shirts promoting the events—all of which are for sale, of course. During the celebration week you can enjoy a preview of some courageous/outrageous costumes at the Masked Madness and Headdress Ball, and even enter your pet (and yourself) in the Pet Masquerade and Parade. No species is excluded. Visit fantasyfest.com or call (305) 296-1817 for more information.

NOVEMBER

AMERICAN POWERBOAT ASSOCIATION WORLD CHAMPIONSHIP RACE
Waters off Key West
(305) 296-6166
superboat.com

Just as Key West begins to recover from Fantasy Fest, the big boats roar into town to compete in a week's worth of offshore races that culminate in the naming of the world's champ. These are no little, putt-putt motorboats; they are high-performance ocean racers costing more than $1 million each and boasting speeds of 125 to 150 mph. Close to 50,000 fans line the waterfront to view the competition, which generally takes place in the first half of Nov. There's no charge to watch, and the best viewing spots are along Mallory Square and at the harborside hotels—the Pier House, Ocean Key House, Hyatt, and Westin. Even if you're not a particular fan of powerboats, these are something to see.

DECEMBER

BOOT KEY HARBOR CHRISTMAS BOAT PARADE
Marathon
(305) 743-5417 or (800) 262-7284
floridakeysmarathon.com

Sponsored by the Marathon Power Squadron, this parade begins at sundown on the first Sat in Dec. The best public viewing areas include Faro Blanco Marina, Boot Key Harbor Bridge, and the Dockside Lounge on Sombrero Road, where judging ceremonies are held immediately following the parade.

CHRISTMAS AROUND THE WORLD AT MARATHON GARDEN CLUB
MM 50 Bayside, Marathon
(305) 743-4971
marathongardenclub.org
This monthlong, annual display by the Marathon Garden Club features more than a dozen Christmas trees, each decorated in the traditional style of a different country. Expect to pay an admission fee.

CHRISTMAS BOAT PARADE
Bayside, Key Largo
(305) 451-1414 or (800) 822-1088
keylargo.org
Deck the boats with boughs of holly . . . Come watch a festive parade of between 30 and 50 lighted boats glow its way through Blackwater Sound. Prizes are awarded in various categories. At recent events we've spotted Santa Claus catching a sailfish and Frosty the Snowman water-skiing. As with the Fourth of July Fireworks, the best coastal viewing locations are the Caribbean Club, Señor Frijoles, Sundowners, and Marriott Key Largo Bay Beach Resort. Some of these facilities host barbecues with live entertainment. Admission is free, but you must be a patron at any of these facilities to enjoy the view. Usually held in early Dec.

KEY COLONY BEACH BOAT PARADE
MM 53.5 Oceanside, Key Colony Beach
(305) 743-5417 or (800) 262-7284
floridakeysmarathon.com
A more intimate, equally spectacular version of the Key Largo boat parade, this one is held along the landmark canals of Key Colony Beach, usually in early Dec. Admission is free.

✳KEY WEST HOLIDAY PARADE
Begins on Truman Avenue
(305) 294-2587 or (800) 648-6269
keywestcity.com
Fun for kids and grown-ups as well, this street parade has floats from various businesses around the area. Lots of color and music, and some floats even toss candy canes for a sweet taste of holiday spirit. Santa and Mrs. Claus appear at the end of the line so as not to disappoint the sleepyheads in the crowd dreaming of sugar plums. This event is usually held the second weekend in Dec.

KEY WEST LIGHTED BOAT PARADE
Various locations throughout Key West
(305) 294-2587 or (800) 648-6269
keywestcity.com
Lighted boat parades are common throughout our islands, and Key West is no exception. In addition to the magical entourage of skiffs, schooners, and cruisers, viewers may enjoy the pre-parade sunset activities at Mallory Square. The boat parade begins at Schooner Wharf Bar at the foot of William Street, but you can get the best view from Mallory Square and the pier beside the Hilton Resort and Marina. The boat parade is typically held in early Dec. Participation is free, but call Schooner Wharf at (305) 294-2587 to reserve your spot.

KEY WEST TRIKW TRIATHLON
Key West
trikw.com

This annual triathlon consists of a swim in the warm Gulf of Mexico waters on the first leg, biking the Overseas Highway, then running along the Atlantic Ocean to the finish line. There is also an expo with information booths on all things healthy in the Keys. Start training now!

LIGNUMVITAE CHRISTMAS
Islamorada
(305) 664-0655

A historic Keys coral rock home from the 1900s is decorated inside and out with all the floral blossoms in bloom on the island. See angels created out of palm fronds, with grape vines in place of holly. If you are talented, you may spend time creating your own ornaments using such things as grape leaves, sea beans, and shells. Travel by boat and you will be greeted by guides at the dock dressed in period costumes to enhance the magical spell of an era gone by. Robbie's Marina (see the Boating chapter) provides the transportation for this 2-day event.

NEW YEAR'S EVE ON DUVAL STREET
Key West
(305) 294-2587 or (800) 648-6269
keywestcity.com

Times Square has nothing on us when it comes to ringing in a new year. We close off the street and, in typical Key West style, party outdoors till the bars close at 4 a.m. So come New Year's Eve, grab your hat and horn, and head for Duval to watch the conch shell drop from the top of Sloppy Joe's Bar (or the red high heel at Bourbon Street Pub) at the stroke of midnight. Just don't wear your best silks and satins for this celebration, because it will be raining champagne for sure! Round out your New Year's revelry with an "ooh" and an "aah" as you watch the fireworks explode above Key West Harbor. CNN televises this countdown, so be on your best behavior as you smile at the cameras.

✳NUTCRACKER KEY WEST
Tennessee Williams Theatre, 5901 West College Rd., Stock Island
(305) 304-1726
nutcrackerkeywest.com

The children of Key West, under the direction of founder Joyce Stahl, will leave you breathless with their annual artistic production of the *Nutcracker*. This classic ballet is all done with fabulous professionalism, but with a Keys twist. King Neptune, the queen, and her cavaliers perform their magic along with local kids who dance as baby chicks, toy soldiers, angelfish, reef fish, and tiny shrimp. Worthy of a standing ovation every time, performances are scheduled in the first week of Dec.

✳POPS IN THE PARK
Founders Park, MM 87 Bayside, Plantation Key
(305) 853-7294
islamorada.fl.us

Come one and all to the Pops in the Park, held in mid-Dec, and enjoy the free outdoor concert featuring the music of Christmas and Hanukkah. Bring a blanket or lawn chair for this family gathering, and capture the true spirit of the holiday season.

ARTS & CULTURE

Creative juices flow freely in the Florida Keys. Is it the sunshine? Or maybe the profusion of riotous colors everywhere you look? Perhaps our pervasive nothing-is-impossible, sky's-the-limit attitude is a contributing factor. Or maybe it's the fact that when you're in the Keys, you take the time to smell the bougainvillea.

Key West is the cultural center of the Florida Keys. This scintillating port has long attracted free spirits and adventurers—wreckers, sailors, spongers, shrimpers, and pirates—who played an enormous role in Key West's settlement and development. An enigmatic quality inherent in the essence of Key West draws fertile minds and searching souls to its inner sanctum like moths to a flame. From Ernest Hemingway to earnestly trying, Key West has hosted for a time the famous, the infamous, and the obscure.

Join us for an Insiders' look at the arts, from Key Largo to Key West, some traditional, others not so. Enjoy our music, theater, and dance while you are here and tour our myriad galleries. Or, if your timing is right, catch an arts festival, literary seminar, or theater gala for a creative night out. Be sure to check the Annual Events chapter for descriptions of special arts festivals and events.

ARTS ORGANIZATIONS

The Florida Keys Council of the Arts (keysarts.com) is considered the official arts organization of the Florida Keys. They provide services to visual and performing artists in the Keys by offering grants, showcasing art in public places, and sponsoring various festivals and events throughout the year. This and other arts organizations are listed alphabetically.

Upper Keys

ART GUILD OF THE PURPLE ISLES
MM 101.4 Oceanside, Key Largo
(305) 451-2396
purpleislesartguild.com

Established in 1966, this Upper Keys artists society has more than 1,000 visitors viewing its annual event, held in the Key Largo Public Library from mid-Feb through the first part of Mar. You can vote for "Best in Show" in watercolor, oil, acrylic, sculpture, 3-D, photography, digital art, and student art. In addition to the show, the guild meets once a month in the Library Community Room and invites anyone to join them for the camaraderie and to enhance their talents.

ARTS & CULTURE

Lower Keys

LOWER KEYS ARTISTS NETWORK
MM 30.5 Bayside, 221 Key Deer Blvd., Big Pine Key
(305) 872–1828
artistsinparadise.com
Formed in 1994, the Lower Keys Artists Network has about 50 members, and anyone in the Lower Keys interested in art is welcome to join. Meetings are held in season at Artists in Paradise, a co-op gallery in Big Pine. Members assist in judging student art competitions and work with the public library to provide arts and crafts programs for children. The group raises funds for art scholarships through corporate sponsorships. Lower Keys Artists Network also provides demonstrations and seminars on all forms of art, including watercolor, wood sculpture, food sculpture, stained glass, and etching.

Key West

FLORIDA KEYS COUNCIL OF THE ARTS
1100 Simonton St.
(305) 295-4369
keysarts.com
The Florida Keys Council of the Arts acts as the "chamber of commerce" of arts throughout the Keys. The council's stated mission is "to connect artists and arts organizations with each other, with local audiences, and with the important tourism economy." They maintain an artist registry and website, where you'll find complete, year-round listings of the arts and entertainment events in the Keys. In addition, they get the cultural word out to the public via a weekly calendar in five local newspapers and a quarterly brochure of events. The arts council both writes and provides grants that benefit individual artists, arts organizations, schools, and libraries. It is supported by Monroe County and private donations and has several hundred members throughout the Florida Keys.

THE STUDIOS OF KEY WEST
600 White St.
(305) 296-0458
tskw.org
The Studios of Key West (TSKW) is a nonprofit cultural organization located in the historic Armory building in Key West. Founded in 2006, TSKW is Key West's only multidisciplinary arts center. They host artists-in-residence in their studio spaces and hold lectures, concerts, performances, and workshops. TSKW's mission is "to build audiences and support the advancement of established and emerging creative people in the Florida Keys." Check their online catalog regularly, as they offer everything from classes to full-scale concerts throughout the year.

THEATER

Upper Keys

ICE (ISLAMORADA COOL ENTERTAINMENT)
MM 87 Bayside, Founders Park
MM 89.9 Oceanside, Coral Shores High School, Plantation Key
(305) 395-6344
keysice.com
"Stars above . . . stars onstage" is the bill for bringing great dance, music, and theater to the Upper Keys. These venues invite friends, neighbors, and visitors to enjoy wonderful performances in the Founders Park amphitheater or in the Coral Shores High School of the Performing Arts. The calendar sparkles with concert series, special events, and plays for every age and artistic taste.

Middle Keys

MARATHON COMMUNITY THEATER
MM 49.5 Oceanside, Marathon
(305) 743-0994
marathontheater.org
Providing top-notch live theatrical entertainment to locals and visitors for decades,
the Marathon Community Theater annually
stages 4 to 6 productions, such as *The Music
Man, Ravenscroft,* and *Applause!,* which each
run Thurs through Sat for a month. Productions utilize full sets and full costuming, and
actors hail from all throughout the Keys,
from Key Largo to Key West. The group also
hosts other productions, ranging from art
shows and concerts to the Lovewell Foundation's summer theater program for children.

Key West

✳RED BARN THEATRE
319 Duval St. (rear)
(305) 296-9911
redbarntheatre.com
Quaint and charming, the restored carriage
house that hosts the Red Barn Theatre has
stood in the shadows of one of Key West's
oldest houses, now the Key West Wom-
en's Club, for more than 50 years. Lovingly
restored as a professional theater in 1980,
the 88-seat structure shines with professional regional theater at its finest. And
because of its size and layout, there isn't a
bad seat in the house. The Red Barn Theatre does 5 or 6 shows each year, including original comedies, musicals, and dramas
by published writers. Its season runs from
late Nov through June. Past productions
have included plays by Key West's own, the
late Shel Silverstein. Full sets, costumes, and
orchestrated scores are featured.

TENNESSEE WILLIAMS FINE ARTS CENTER
5901 West College Rd., Stock Island
(305) 296-1520 or (305) 295-7676 (tickets)
tennesseewilliamstheatre.com
The Tennessee Williams Fine Arts Center
(TWFAC) opened in January 1980 on the
campus of Florida Keys Community College with the world premiere of Tennessee
Williams's unpublished play *Will Mr. Mer-
riweather Return from Memphis?* Named for
one of Key West's most illustrious writers, this
478-seat, air-conditioned theater features a
thrust stage extending 8 feet in front of the
curtain line, a fly system, and a state-of-the-
art lighting and sound system. The Tennessee Williams Fine Arts Center produces a full
season of dance, theater, chamber music,
and shows by nationally known performing artists. Professional touring companies,
like *Spamalot* and Pilobolus, bring a wave
of nationally and internationally recognized
artists to the Florida Keys.

WATERFRONT PLAYHOUSE
Mallory Square
(305) 294-5015
waterfrontplayhouse.org
Once the site of Porter's warehouse, Waterfront Playhouse's physical structure served
as an icehouse in the 1880s, storing blocks
of ice cut from New England ponds and
brought to Key West as ships' ballast. The
Waterfront Playhouse restored the old warehouse into the current theater, infusing the
crumbly stone walls with enduring creativity
and talent. In 2007 a major $300,000 transfor-
mation of the most public parts of the building gave the structure both a modern and
intimate feel while staying true to its historic
roots. The Waterfront Playhouse is Key West's

community theater, dedicated to expanding knowledge of dramatic works to the general public, and presents a variety of musicals, comedies, and dramas. The performance season is from Nov through Apr.

i For listings of current shows in Key West or to purchase tickets, visit keystix.com or call (305) 295-7676.

CINEMA

Upper Keys

B&B THEATRES TAVERNIER CINEMA 5
MM 92 Bayside, Tavernier
(305) 853-7003 (movie hotline) or (305) 853-7004 (office)
bbtheatres.com
This is a 5-plex theater that features first-run films with Dolby-enhanced sound and the latest technology. Matinees daily, late-night shows on weekends. Located in the Tavernier Towne Center.

Middle Keys

MARATHON COMMUNITY CINEMA
MM 50 Oceanside, Marathon
(305) 743-0288
marathontheater.org
This is no average movie theater. Owned and operated by the Marathon Community Theater, the cinema is small and intimate, although the screen is large. Seating is informally arranged in comfy barrel chairs around cocktail-style tables. A single movie is shown twice nightly. Matinees are offered on Sat and Sun. The theater is tucked behind Marathon Liquors.

Key West

CINEMA KEY WEST 6
3338 Roosevelt Blvd., Searstown Shopping Center
(305) 296-7211
regalcinemas.com
Six movies run concurrently at the Florida Keys' first multiplex cinema. All tickets for shows before 6 p.m. are discounted. Listening devices for the hearing impaired are available here as well.

✳TROPIC CINEMA
416 Eaton St.
(305) 295-9493
keywestfilm.org
The Key West Film Society formed in 1998 to bring the area the best of independent, foreign, and alternative movies. Since then Tropic Cinema has shown hundreds of films and even hosted premieres. Highlights have included the Cuban music documentary *Buena Vista Social Club*; a costumed Rocky Horror Picture Show, replete with stage show; and for the avant-garde, *The Celebration*—an ultimate in contrast: no lighting, no music, and shot on video. The purpose of the Key West Film Society and Tropic Cinema is to showcase film in Key West and be a magnet for this cutting-edge art.

MUSIC

Middle Keys

THE MIDDLE KEYS CONCERT ASSOCIATION, INC.
Marathon
marathonconcerts.com
Every year since 1969 the Middle Keys Concert Association has brought live concerts to the Florida Keys for the cultural enrichment

of our residents and visitors. Four to 6 concerts are held annually at Marathon venues, quite often San Pablo Catholic Church (MM 53.5 Oceanside). A well-balanced season of offerings includes classical and semiclassical music, encompassing voice, strings, brass, and organ. You may purchase a subscription to all concerts or buy tickets at the door. Children are admitted for free. Pick up a current brochure at the Marathon Chamber of Commerce, MM 53.5 Bayside, (305) 743-5417 or (800) 262-7284.

ART GALLERIES

Unique galleries dot the Florida Keys, often tucked amid commercial shops in a strip mall or gracing a freestanding building off the beaten track. In Key West, galleries abound along Duval Street, and you'll also find small lofts and garrets secreted off the beaten track down narrow lanes. Come along for a gallery crawl through the high spots of the Florida Keys' art scene, from Key Largo to Key West. Consult keysarts.com for even more information.

Upper Keys

BLUEWATER POTTERS
MM 102.9 Oceanside, Key Largo
(305) 453-1920
bluewaterpotters.com
High-fire stoneware and functional pottery set the theme for Bluewater Potters. Husband-and-wife owners Corky and Kim Wagner demonstrate their work right on the premises. The Wagners' inventory includes everything from spoon rests to full dinnerware and architectural pieces, with custom dinnerware a specialty. Some work is brought in by outside artists. Among the pieces offered are wine goblets and baking dishes. All glazes are oven-, microwave-, and dishwasher-safe.

THE GALLERY AT KONA KAI
MM 97.8 Bayside, Key Largo
(305) 852-7200 or (800) 365-7829
konakairesort.com
The Gallery at Kona Kai secrets away a small yet exquisite changing exhibit of fine art treasures. The gallery showcases artist from around the world as well as prominent South Florida artists such as Clyde Butcher, who is known for his hauntingly surreal black-and-white photography of the Everglades and Big Cypress National Preserve. Also featured is Gregory Sobran, a watercolorist who chronicles quintessential scenes of the Keys in a spectrum of pastel hues.

Seven "New Friends," by renowned sculptor J. Seward Johnson, greet travelers at Key West International Airport. The group stands atop the airport terminal eagerly awaiting your arrival. Johnson's other works are showcased at the Key West Museum of Art and History at the Custom House (see the Attractions chapter).

*KEY LARGO ART GALLERY
MM 103 Bayside, Key Largo
(305) 451-0052
keylargoartgallery.com
The theme of the Key Largo Art Gallery is to provide a creative haven for artists and educate the community on various art forms. The camaraderie of the group of artists housed here allows an explosion of creative talent. In 2007 one of the original "Highwaymen" was featured at the gallery. The Florida African Highwaymen were given that name in the 1950s because they traveled the roads

ARTS & CULTURE

and used their vehicles as showcases for their art, selling alongside highways. The gallery also showcases artists Carmen Soto-longo Kelley, Teresa Kelley, Elena Ortega, Jacqueline Campa, Dan Lawler, and Michael Mayer.

✳RAIN BARREL VILLAGE OF ARTISTS AND CRAFTSPEOPLE
MM 86.7 Bayside, Islamorada
(305) 852-3084
keysdirectory.com/rainbarrel
The infamous Betsy the Lobster stands to greet shoppers at the entrance to this artist colony. At 30 feet tall and 40 feet in length, she is a showstopper! The Rain Barrel Village of Artists and Craftspeople is a garden complex of creativity. The 2,000-square-foot mixed-media gallery features an array of paintings, sculptures, woodwork, and decorative glass. You'll find an eclectic assortment of art and craft creations, including whimsical ceramics and an expansive wind chime collection. There is a small cafe inside the complex that serves ready-to-go wraps, sandwiches, salads, key lime pie, and ice cream.

REDBONE ART GALLERY
MM 81 Oceanside, Islamorada
(305) 664-2002
redbone.org
The Redbone Art Gallery features a variety of saltwater and marine art and sculptures from local artists and others noted for their works related to sportfishing, such as Don Ray, Diane Peebles, James Harris, Jeanne Dobie, and C. D. Clarke. Redbone exclusively showcases the original watercolors of Chet Reneson in South Florida.

STACIE KRUPA STUDIO GALLERY OF ART
MM 82.9 Oceanside, Islamorada
(305) 9420614
staciekrupa.com
You can watch Stacie Krupa, artist-in-residence, as she creates her huge, vibrant, mixed-media works on canvas at this contemporary, SoHo-style gallery. A powerful combination of bright colors and massive images, some of which depict Florida Keys birds and fish, Krupa's expressive creations will knock your sandals off.

Lower Keys

ARTISTS IN PARADISE
MM 30.5 Bayside, 221 Key Deer Blvd., Big Pine Key
(305) 872-1828
artistsinparadise.com
Artists in Paradise is a cooperative gallery in Big Pine run by the artists from the Lower Keys Artists Network (see the listing in this chapter), who use the gallery to display their work. More than 30 artists currently show works done in a variety of media: sculpture, oil, watercolor, acrylic, pen and ink, pottery, copper, and stained glass. The gallery is open daily.

Key West

ALAN S. MALTZ GALLERY
1210 Duval St.
(305) 294-0005
alanmaltz.com
Using the mystical nature of light, Alan S. Maltz, a world-renowned fine-art photographer, is an inspiration with his haunting and magical images. When you enter his gallery and view the art on the walls, you feel as though you are not looking at a piece of

artwork hanging there but rather upon the actual scene he photographed. His pieces are large and compelling. Alan's framing technique is as unique as his talent, because he has the ability to keep his audience involved in the piece as a whole.

ART@830 GALLERY AND STUDIO
830 Caroline St.
(305) 295-9595
art830.com
The gallery owners have been on the Key West art scene since 1993. Their Art@830 showcases photography, paintings, ceramics, contemporary glass art, turned wood art, and body painting. Most of the works are by local artists, and emerging artists are featured.

✳ART SPACE KEY WEST
1102 Truman Ave.
(305) 533-0165
artspacekeywest.com
Key West artists Michael Marrero and Marky Pierson opened Art Space in 2012 to showcase new talent as well as dynamic art projects from local and national artists. The space offers monthly shows that often feature slightly subversive multimedia art. Show themes have included highly charged pop art, political posters, erotic and sensual photography, and graffiti and tattoo art.

FLORIDA KEYS COMMUNITY COLLEGE
5901 West College Rd., Stock Island
(305) 296-9081
fkcc.edu
Florida Keys Community College stages 4 art shows a year in the Library Gallery. Invitational shows are held in Oct and Feb, and the Florida Artist series is showcased in Jan

and Feb. Student work is exhibited during the month of Apr.

THE GALLERY ON GREENE
606 Greene St.
(305) 294-1669
galleryongreene.com
Among the offerings here are works by the late part-time Key West resident Jeff MacNelly (he drew the cartoon strip *Shoe*) and Henry La Cagnina, the last survivor of 12 artists brought to Key West in the 1930s by the WPA. This gallery also supports working artists. You can usually expect to find at least one artist-in-residence, bent over his or her work, in a corner of the gallery.

GINGERBREAD SQUARE GALLERY
1207 Duval St.
(305) 296-8900
gingerbreadsquaregallery.com
Billed as Key West's oldest private art gallery, established in 1974, Gingerbread Square Gallery on upper Duval features sculptures, art glass, one-person shows, and ongoing presentations of the highly acclaimed works of Key West's favorite artists. Sal Salinero, whose oils depict the treasures of the rain forest, is a featured artist.

GLASS REUNIONS
825 Duval St.
(305) 294-1720
glassreunions.com
Glass is the business here, and you can get it in almost any form or color imaginable. Lamps, vases, and mirror wall hangings all showcase the talents of the various artists. For the traditionalist, a wide selection of stained-glass art is available.

GUILD HALL GALLERY
614 Duval St.
(305) 296-6076
guildhallgallerykw.com
More than 20 local artists display their work here, presented in a vast array of media. Most of the pieces focus on island life, with a definite Bahamian and Caribbean influence thrown in. Head upstairs for more unusual, and larger, works of art. This is Key West's original artists' co-op, established in 1976.

HAITIAN ART COMPANY
1100 Truman Ave.
(305) 296-8932
haitian-art-co.com
Bold, wild colors and primitive designs mark the artistic offerings of Haiti, displayed in the multiple rooms of the Haitian Art Company. The intricate paisley-style designs often weave an image of a serpent or wild animal within the overall picture. The work of Haiti is a study of form and color not readily encountered in this country. All pieces are originals.

HANDS ON
1206 Duval St.
(305) 296-7399
handsongallery.com
The loom in the front of this attractive shop says it all. Here you will find the ever-changing, always exquisite creations of owner Ellen Steiniger. Her handwoven scarves, jackets, and shawls are as beautiful to see as they are enjoyable to wear. Shop here, too, for handcrafted earrings, bracelets, and beads to accessorize your wearable art as well as an array of other fine American-made crafts. The gallery is also home to the work of 50-plus artists, each with a unique style.

✻HARRISON GALLERY
825 White St.
(305) 294-0609
harrison-gallery.com
Sculptor Helen Harrison and her husband, Ben, a musician and author, have operated this charming gallery since 1986. Helen's spirit is discovered in a calabash, a palm frond, and a gourd. Her pieces are just glorious! In addition to Helen's own work, changing exhibitions highlight local artists. Open daily, but please ring the bell.

✻ISLAND NEEDLEWORK
527 Fleming St.
(305) 296-6091
islandneedlepoint.com
Julie Pischke is one of a handful of needlepoint designers who specialize in tropical designs. Her award-winning creations draw from the colors and textures of her home in the Florida Keys, and she offers her art on pillows, bags, belts, shoes, rugs, and footstools. Julie's bold, bright, colorful, and eclectic motifs befit their inspiration. Long after your trip has ended, a bright, handmade memento reminds you of your hot days in the sun and your cool tropical nights in paradise.

KEY WEST ART CENTER AND GALLERY
301 Front St.
(305) 294-1241
keywestartcenter.com
This nonprofit organization is devoted to encouraging local talent by giving artists a canvas for their creativity. Dues and commissions for their works keep this artistic colony thriving. Housed in a historic building that was once a grocery store near the waterfront, the Key West Art Center helps

(Q) Close-up

Art Here, Art There, Art Everywhere

The Florida Keys Council of the Arts created **Art in Public Places** in 2000 to visually maintain the character, identity, and history of our island community. This public display of creative talent charges no admission fees for events; some works are permanently mounted in or on buildings, and the pieces are appropriate for all age groups.

Walk or drive around our towns and see for yourself why so many artists draw inspiration from this "Paradise." Beginning in Key Largo, inside the Murray Nelson Government Building at MM 102 Bayside, there are various rotating art exhibits. Press onward to Plantation Key, where photographer Debra Yates's murals grace the walls of the Roth Building, located at MM 88 Bayside.

Head down to Key West and travel along Junior College Road on Stock Island, where you can locate works by Jae DeVoe, Chod Stine, and Dick Moody. Wander back into town and roam by the Key West city swimming pool to marvel at Duke Rood's wooden sculpture. Make your next stop at the end of Seminole Avenue, where the lovely floor design by J. T. Thompson is part of the Mary and John Spottswood Waterfront Park. Traverse to Wall Street in Old Town to appreciate the children's tile mural that is priceless. Then head out to the White Street Pier and gaze at the planters by Wally McGregor at the AIDS Memorial.

At Key West International Airport, check out the art on the walls and listen to the sounds being played, featuring original music recorded by local musicians. The Lower Keys Medical Center and the Freeman Justice Center also offer various artworks on display. So much art and so little time! Visit keysarts.com for more information.

the arts stay glowing in a city that fans the flames of talent.

LUCKY STREET GALLERY
540 Greene St.
(305) 294-3973
luckystreetgallery.com

Contemporary fine art of the cutting-edge variety is the focus here. Sculptures by John Martini and the works of famed Key West artists Rick Worth, Lauren McAloon, and Debra Yates are featured, as well as many others. New shows are staged often and coincide with gallery events. Check their website for an up-to-date schedule of events.

SODU GALLERY
1102 Duval St.
(305) 296-4400
sodugallery.com

An unrestricted window display showcases amazing local artists, enabling them to strut their stuff in grand style. Jewelry, acrylics, paintings, and pencil drawings, with painting on furniture, dinnerware, and fabrics, fill the shop with excitement and fun.

SOUTH POINTE GALLERY
1201 Duval St.
(305) 295-9354
authenticvintageposters.com

ARTS & CULTURE

The owner of South Pointe Gallery travels extensively in pursuit of authentic vintage posters to add to her collection. The striking works are primarily French, with a mix of American, German, and Italian. Decorating with posters is not a unique idea, but very appealing due to their bold images and less expensive prices than other art forms.

i During high season on the third Thursday of every month is Walk on White, where all the galleries and boutiques on White Street open their doors in the evenings. You'll find wine tastings, live music, and art of all kinds at venues down White Street. The evening culminates in a party at the Studios of Key West at 600 White St.

✳ **THE STUDIOS OF KEY WEST**
600 White St.
(305) 296-0458
tskw.org
This nonprofit artist colony, located in the historic Armory building (built in 1891), evolved after many talented artists could not find affordable space to house their creations. Located in the already popular, art-filled neighborhood of White Street, the Studios of Key West (TSKW) has attracted writers, painters, and poets among their eclectic virtuosos. TSKW offers workshops and lectures that are open to the public.

WYLAND GALLERIES
102 and 623 Duval St.
(305) 295-5240 and (305) 292-4998
wylandkw.com
Wyland's world-renowned, life-size whaling wall murals reflect his unshakable commitment to saving the earth's oceans and thereby its marine creatures. In 2007 Wyland painted his 95th and final "Whaling Wall" in the US at MM 99.2 in Key Largo. The mural covers 7,500 square feet and wraps completely around a building (a whaling cube). A time-lapse view can be seen at wylandfoundation.org. The Key West galleries showcase Wyland's art as well as other passionate nature-inspired artists such as Steve Barton, Michael Cheval, Stephen Muldoon, and Tracy Taylor.

SHOPPING

So here is the ultimate road map to the shops. We describe our favorite shops by category (Bookstores, Clothing & Jewelry, Home Decor, and Gift & Specialty Shops) and location within each category. Be sure to scope out the Arts & Culture chapter for descriptions of galleries selling creative works, many by local artists. And turn to our Specialty Foods, Cafes & Markets chapter to find piscatory treasures and other palate pleasers.

Many of our shops are open daily until 9 p.m., especially in Key West, but many close on Sunday. Some close on different days, so it is best to call before venturing out, as hours and days of operation can vary from season to season.

BOOKSTORES

Upper Keys

HOOKED ON BOOKS
MM 81.9 Oceanside, Islamorada
(305) 517-2602
hookedonbooksfloridakeys.com
Hooked on Books is filled to the rafters with used books and paperbacks. In addition to their extensive Florida and Florida Keys collection, Hooked on Books stocks a large selection of current fiction and nonfiction titles, both new and used. There is also a children's room with books for all ages.

Key West

✳**KEY WEST ISLAND BOOKSTORE**
513 Fleming St.
(305) 294-2904
keywestislandbooks.com
This shop sells everything from the classics to the bestsellers, along with topical nonfiction and the works of Florida Keys and Key West

writers. The store is especially supportive of Florida authors and often hosts book-signing events that generate lots of local excitement and a party atmosphere. Carl Hiaasen, James Hall, Jimmy Buffett, Philip Caputo, James Dickey, and Thomas McGuane have all signed books here. Be sure to check the rare-book room in the back.

> **i** The New Town area along N. Roosevelt Boulevard is often overlooked by shoppers enamored with the funky shops of Old Town. But this is where the locals shop. A series of strip malls or plazas—Kennedy Drive, Key Plaza, Luani Plaza, Overseas Market, Searstown—are within blocks of each other and feature the staples of everyday life, as offered by major retail chain stores Kmart, Pier One Imports, Ross, and Sears.

CLOTHING & JEWELRY

Upper Keys

*ANGELIKA
MM 81.9 Bayside, Islamorada
(305) 664-9008
angelikaclothing.com
Everything from casual clothing to beach wedding gowns can be found here. Natural fabrics and whimsical designs mark the merchandise at Angelika. Look for Angelika's great hats and handbags.

BLUE MARLIN JEWELRY
MM 81.9 Oceanside, Islamorada
(305) 664-8004 or (888) 826-4424
bluemarlinjewelry.com
Discover gold in this interesting jewelry shop. Blue Marlin sports a great selection of gold charms, depicting most of the species of our ecosystem. Especially striking are the black coral fish. Many pieces are also offered in sterling silver.

MILK AND HONEY
MM 82.2 Oceanside, Keys Plaza,
Islamorada
(305) 304-9107
milknhoneystore.com
This sweet jewelry store sells select designer pieces that will make you feel very special. Known for unique styles that are feminine and fun to wear, they also carry handbags and shearling boots to boot!

SANDAL FACTORY OUTLET
MM 102.4 Oceanside, Key Largo
(305) 453-9644
The Sandal Factory Outlet allows you to fit yourself. Pick from a copious sea of ladies' sandals—strappy, sport, and utilitarian. Men and children can be accommodated here,

too. You won't find every style in every size, but you can choose from hundreds of designs. A second location is at MM 82 Oceanside in Islamorada (305-664-9700).

*WORLD WIDE SPORTSMAN INC.
MM 81.5 Bayside, Islamorada
(305) 664-4615 or (800) 227-7776
basspro.com
Don't miss a stop at World Wide Sportsman, the massive fishing emporium that is an Islamorada must-see. World Wide showcases a 6,000-gallon saltwater aquarium that presents the creatures of our reef, including baby tarpon, bonefish, and redfish. A small art gallery upstairs features works by local artists. In addition to the other treasures, World Wide is stocked to the rafters with a wide assortment of fishing tackle (see the Outfitters section in the Fishing chapter), and a full line of men's and women's clothing is offered, including Ex Officio, Woolrich, Sportif, and Columbia.

Middle Keys

BAYSHORE CLOTHING
MM 52 Oceanside, Marathon
(305) 743-8430
bayshoreclothing.com
Bayshore caters to men's and women's tropical garment needs, a guaranteed attitude adjustment from the busy workaday world up north. The children's department beckons parents and especially grandparents with a cute selection of swimsuits, warm-weather clothing, and toys.

BLUE
MM 82.2 Oceanside, Islamorada
(305) 517-9225
blueislandstore.com

Shop here for classic linen skirts, tops, jackets, pants, and dresses that will look just as appropriate on Fifth Avenue as they do on Duval. Be sure to check out the accessories here, too. The bead jewelry is handmade, and the colors are a perfect complement to the easy-fitting, understated styles. A second location is at 718 Caroline St. (305-292-5172).

KEY BANA RESORT APPAREL
MM 53.5 Oceanside, Key Colony Beach Causeway, Key Colony Beach
(305) 289-1161
keybana.com

Ladies, you are sure to find a new swimsuit or tropical cotton item here that you can't pass up. And Key Bana has a roomful of shorts and shirts for men, too. Check out suits by Miraclesuit, Nautica, and Guess for the ladies and Beer-Can Island for the gentlemen.

KEYKER'S BOUTIQUE & GALLERY
MM 50.3 Oceanside, 67 53rd St., Marathon
(305) 743-0107
keykers.com

Keyker and other local clothing designers create custom island clothing for women and children, unusual yet flattering styles using exquisitely fine cottons. You'll find them displayed at this elegant establishment, along with interesting jewelry, accessories, craft items, and paintings.

Key West

ABACO GOLD
418 Front St.
(305) 296-0086

A honeymoon voyage to the Abaco Islands prompted owners John and Angela to dub their store Abaco Gold. The jewelry line here is exclusive—like no other in the Florida

Keys, or elsewhere for that matter. Abaco Gold specializes in unique nautical designs featuring mermaids, dolphins, and tropical themes. If you love jewelry, you'll love this store.

✳ASSORTMENT, INC.
514 Fleming St.
(305) 294-4066

This chic men's clothing store, just a few steps off Duval Street, carries the latest in men's casual fashions with a dressy flair. Handsome jackets, shirts, slacks, and shoes are tastefully displayed. Polo by Ralph Lauren, Barry Bricken, and Cole-Haan shoes are just a few of the lines you'll find here. Assortment, Inc., also offers great-looking gifts and accessories for that special guy in your life.

THE BEACH HOUSE SWIMWEAR
714 Duval St.
(305) 292-9300
thebeachhouseswimwear.com

You can spend your whole vacation in this shop just trying on bathing suits, because they have more than 4,000 from which to choose. This tiny shop with the big selection has been on Duval since 1977. At the Beach House Swimwear, you will find designer and name brands for women, men, and kids.

✳BESAME MUCHO
315 Petronia St.
(305) 294-1928
besamemucho.net

Step into this tastefully decorated shop, and you will feel as though you have stepped back in time. The shelves are filled with items that look as though they belong on a movie set, ca. 1940. Here you'll find an assortment of picture frames, desk accessories, tableware, lucky tokens, tropical cards and books, baskets, and Tahitian bath oils—in short, what the owners lovingly refer to as "essential island provisions."

BIRKENSTOCK OF OLD TOWN
612 Duval St.
(305) 294-8318 or (800) 330-2475 (orders)
birkenstore.com
With sandals being essential apparel for island life, it makes good sense for Birkenstock to have a large, full-service store right in the middle of it all. Although Birkenstocks don't come cheap, the shoes are exceptionally durable and comfortable. You can sometimes get a pretty good deal here on discontinued styles. This store also does in-house repairs.

☀COMMOTION
800 Caroline St.
(305) 292-3364
localcolorkeywest.com
Stylish island separates that are as fun to wear as they are practical to own await you here. These natural, washable linen and flax fabrics will help you keep your cool—a definite must in the Florida Keys. Best of all, unlike some island designs that look out of place outside the Tropics, these will look just as great when you get back home.

IN ONE ERA
1118 White St.
(305) 293-0208
rubylane.com/shops/in1era
This tiny shop has a large selection of delightful estate jewelry, old period costumes (great for Fantasy Fest), vintage lighting, chandeliers, and small antiques. Their inventory also includes Cuban and Key West memorabilia.

ISLE STYLE
1204 Simonton St.
(305) 292-4000
Step inside this airy boutique packed with designs from artisans all over the world, and meet an owner who is a "stylist." The stock changes frequently, so one visit may not fill your shopping bag. Also on the property is a spa where you can get a manicure and pedicure. So, you can shop till you drop, be revived, and do it all over again.

JIMMY BUFFETT'S MARGARITAVILLE STORE
500 Duval St.
(305) 296-9089 or (800) 262-6835
margaritavillestore.com
Everything here is tuned to one thing: the works of Key West's favorite son, Jimmy Buffett. All his albums are available here, along with tons of shirts, books, photos, and other Parrothead paraphernalia. Spend some time perusing the walls—they're packed with photos and memorabilia related to events in the life of the man from Margaritaville. This place is a must-stop for Buffett fans old and new.

☀KINO SANDALS
107 Fitzpatrick St.
(305) 294-5044
kinosandalfactory.com
After Roberto and Margarite Lopez emigrated from Cuba, they opened a sandal factory in Key West in 1966. Using his nickname, Kino, for the business, Roberto built a lovely Cuban-style factory that is still in operation today. Here you choose from a variety of leathers and colors for your custom sandals. Prices are extremely reasonable (typically under $15 per pair), and they make a terrific souvenir.

LILLY PULITZER
600 Front St.
(305) 295-0995
lillypulitzer.com

In 1960 a young socialite, Lilly Pulitzer, opened a juice stand in West Palm Beach. When her uniform seemed more popular than her juice, the famous "Lillys" were created. Today Lilly Pulitzer shops offer the signature piece in tropical green and hot pink, along with bright and fun prints in various other tantalizing colors. You can also find jewelry, shoes, home accents, and a clothing line for children at this chic boutique.

LILO SURF SHOP
813 N. Roosevelt Blvd.,
Kmart Shopping Center
(305) 294-1800

The Keys might not be known for surfing waters, but you can still look the part. The owner stocks everything from Reef and Rainbow sandals, T-shirts, shorts, and swimsuits to skim boards, skateboards, hats, and, of course, surfboards.

LIPPY'S HOT HATS
613 Duval St.
(305) 294-1333
lippyshothats.com

If you're heading outdoors in Key West, you'd best wear a hat. And you're sure to find a flattering one at this shop devoted entirely to headgear, including everything from canvas caps to straw boaters for both men and women.

✳LOCAL COLOR
274 Margaret St., Key West Historic
Seaport
(305) 292-3635
localcolorkeywest.com

This Margaret Street shop is where locals and tourists come to purchase the colorful, comfortable clothing that fits the Key West lifestyle. In addition to casual apparel for men and women, you'll find fun hats, handbags, and beautiful jewelry to complete your island look.

✳NEPTUNE DESIGNS
301 Duval St.
(305) 294-8131

Most of the jewelry filling this shop has an oceanic motif and is wrought in gold or silver. Leaping silver dolphins frolic with golden, gliding sea turtles on necklaces displayed on a black background. Noah's Ark figurines are also on display—tiny ships decked with all manner of wildlife.

"KW" Jewelry

Created in Key West for Key Westers and visitors, this jewelry design has made a huge hit with men, women, and kids. The design features the initials "KW" hooked together, with a braided nautical wrap signifying the tribute to Key West and the islands' connection to the sea. For those who wear such pieces, this symbol means they will always return here. A lot of stores carry these items, but to ensure you are getting the real thing, the following list is a good guide: Local Color, 276 Margaret St. (305-292-3635) and 425 Greene St. (305-296-0151); Commotion, 800 Caroline St. (305-292-3364); Lili's, 424 Greene St. (305-292-2343); or keywestbracelet.com.

RON JON SURF SHOP
503 Front St.
(305) 293-8880
ronjons.com
Four thousand four hundred square feet of the latest beachwear and accessories await you at Ron Jon Surf Shop. They carry everything you need to spend a day in the sun, from swimsuits to boogie boards and even skateboards.

THE SEAM SHOPPE
1113 Truman Ave.
(305) 296-9830
tropicalfabricsonline.com
This fabric shop offers a fabulous selection of tropical fabrics for fashion, quilting, and home decor. Patterns include fish, shells, nautical and Hawaiian themes, palm trees, and tropical foliage. You'll find quilt fabrics, batiks, and bark cloth here as well.

THE SOLE MAN
610 Duval St.
(305) 292-2505
Everyone who lives here, or visits for any length of time, winds up buying clever, glitzy, fun sandals. The Sole Man has something for every "sole," and you will end up tossing those socks in the back of your drawer or suitcase.

TIMMY TUXEDOS
812 Fleming St.
(305) 294-8897
timmytuxedos.com
In spite of what you may think about the Keys dress code of flip-flops and T-shirts, we do dress up occasionally, and Timmy's Tuxedos is the only formal attire shop in the Keys. Here you can buy all the "dress-up" garb you need, plus rent jackets and tuxedos.

They also carry beautiful Keys prints for ties and cummerbunds, to make that formal gathering tropical.

HOME DECOR

Upper Keys

THE BANYAN TREE
MM 81.2 Oceanside, Islamorada
(305) 664-3433
banyantreegarden.com
A shaded courtyard is the cool, unruffled invite greeting you at the Banyan Tree. The proprietors are a knowledgeable couple who know their stuff with an ever-changing inventory, making the Banyan Tree a find! An eclectic mix of antiques and contemporary items for home and garden abound.

*RAIN BARREL VILLAGE OF ARTISTS AND CRAFTSPEOPLE
MM 86.7 Bayside, Islamorada
(305) 852-3084
keysdirectory.com/rainbarrel
You can't miss this place with the famous sculpture of Betsy the Lobster greeting shoppers. At 30 feet tall and 40 feet long, it's a great photo opportunity. Inside is a lush, tropical hideaway housing artists and crafters who work in retail shops that are peppered beneath the gumbo-limbos and amid the bougainvillea.

SEA DRAGON
MM 82 Oceanside, Islamorada
(305) 664-0048
seadragonfurniture.com
Billing itself as "exotic island decor," Sea Dragon will help you create your own Shangri-la. The owners travel to Bali each season to make selections that help their customers create a tropical Asian look in their home.

Indonesian artwork and teak furniture with unusual pieces make this shop a must-see.

Middle Keys

*D'ASIGN SOURCE
MM 52.7 Bayside, Marathon
(305) 743-7130
dasignsource.com
At D'Asign Source, you'll find the very latest and very best in materials, fixtures, finishes, and designs for home remodeling, building, and furnishing. Even if you aren't in the market for a home makeover, make your way to D'Asign Source's megastore, with home ideas for both indoors and out. Browsing the 25,000-square-foot showroom is an inspiration.

WICKER WEB
MM 52 Oceanside, Marathon
(305) 743-3696
Across from the Marathon Airport runway, in the Southwind Building, you'll discover the Wicker Web, 3 showrooms chock-full of tropically inspired items for every room in your house. You'll find a wide selection of baskets, wall hangings, wicker items, lamps, plasticware, and bath accessories.

Key West

ARCHEO GALLERY
1208 Duval St.
(305) 294-3771
archeogallery.com
Not everyone can trek to Timbuktu, Ouagadougou, Djenne, or Paris, but at this shop you can. The owners fly halfway around the world to bring one-of-a-kind rugs, ceremonial pieces, sculptures, and artifacts to their customers. You might feel the need for a passport here!

COCKTAILS! KEY WEST
808 Duval St.
(305) 292-1190
cocktailskeywest.com
To think there is a shop that celebrates drinking but without one real bottle of spirits in sight! This distinctive atelier has all of the accent pieces to fashionably enhance bending your elbow. Hand-painted martini glasses, coasters, towels, cocktail shakers, wine holders, and the most unique of all—old doorknobs and pool balls made into wine stoppers—can be found here.

CUBA! CUBA!
814 Duval St.
(305) 295-9442
cubacubastore.com
Get a little "*Libre!*" in your life with this quaint little shop that espouses a passion for all things Cuban. Art is very much a part of the selection, as evidenced by nostalgic wood carvings depicting a typical Cuban kitchen. Cookbooks and authentic jams and marmalades line the shelves, and guitars and maracas are just begging to be played. A selection of cigars is also on display.

Duval Street is 14 blocks long and runs from the Atlantic to the Gulf of Mexico. It is known as the longest main street in the world because it goes from coast to coast.

DUCK AND DOLPHIN ANTIQUES
601 Fleming St.
(305) 295-0499
This elegant shop—reminiscent of the antiques shops we've seen in Europe—is filled with ornate furnishings and accent pieces that can only be called *trés chic*. You'll find everything from a grand piano to a

crystal chandelier. These items are in mint condition, with price tags to match.

KEY ACCENTS
804 Caroline St.
(305) 293-8555
keyaccents.net

New England in feel but Key West in style, Key Accents is like a breath of fresh air. Nicely displayed inside an old home, you will find furniture, pictures, lamps, and home accessories. The inventory is not large, but the pieces they do offer show very well.

THE RESTAURANT STORE
1111 Eaton St.
(305) 294-7994
keywestchef.com

The Restaurant Store is chock-full of kitchen and cooking gear to feed 5 or 50. You'll discover state-of-the-art utensils, pots and pans, and accessories for culinary aficionados and chefs alike. This store is nirvana for foodies.

i Monroe County (which is all of the Florida Keys) was created in 1823 and named for the fifth US president, James Monroe. Duval Street, in Key West, is named after William Pope Duval, Florida's first territorial governor, serving from April 1822 to April 1834. He was appointed by President Monroe.

STYLE KEY WEST
313 Margaret St.
(305) 292-4004
stylekeywest.com

The sweetness and enchantment of this shop are a reflection of the husband-and-wife team that owns Style Key West. The furniture pieces, accessories, and colors that grace the walls make you want to go home and replace all that you own with everything they showcase. They offer classic tropical pieces with such appeal that you can decorate your castle in the tropics or your chateau back home.

GIFT & SPECIALTY SHOPS

Upper Keys

CAPTAIN'S IMPORTS WORLD CLASS BRONZE TROPHIES
MM 99 Bayside, Key Largo
(305) 453-1800
captainsimports.com

Captain's Imports creates bronze replicas of your latest catch, including trophies, wall mounts, statues, and even fountains. Their beautiful one-of-a-kind fish trophies of all sizes and shapes are true works art. This is not a store you'll find on Main Street back home.

✴ICHTHYOPHILE
MM 82 Bayside, Islamorada
(305) 664-8960
ichthyophile.com

This unique shop with an even more unique name is sure to hook your attention. Ichthyophile (one who enjoys and studies fish) is lovingly stocked with rare, historic prints of sea life that have been preserved from books that are up to 200 years old. The owner was a backcountry guide for 13 years, and his interest led him to open this entertaining and interesting shop. Look for the Kids' Corner, with toys and books with a water or fish subject; it's a great way to interest kids in becoming anglers.

ISLAND SMOKE SHOP
MM 103.5 Bayside, Pink Plaza, Key Largo
(305) 453-4014 or (800) 680-9701
islandsmokeshop.com

With a 1,000-square-foot walk-in humidor and over 3,000 square feet of retail space, the Island Smoke Shop is one of the largest in South Florida. Showcasing a full line of cigars, lighters, and accessories, it has one of the largest selections of pipes in the area, as well as some wonderful house blends of tobacco.

KEY LIME PRODUCTS AND TROPICAL GIFTS
MM 95 Oceanside, Key Largo
(305) 853-0378
keylimeproducts.com
From tangy edibles and thirst-quenching beverages to soothing lotions and luscious bath products, Key Lime Products and Tropical Gifts offers a cornucopia of Florida Keys products. Have no fear about getting this stuff home: They ship worldwide, so you can buy full size!

LARGO CARGO
MM 103.1 Oceanside, Key Largo
(305) 451-4242 or (800) 795-8889
largocargo.com
Inside this bright blue dwelling is some pretty cool stuff for your souvenir collection. They have pirate flags and wind socks with skulls and crossbones, key lime products, tropical apparel, nautical jewelry handcrafted from silver and sea glass, metal sculptures, and the all-time favorite, a message in a bottle.

PINK JUNKTIQUE
MM 98 Oceanside, Key Largo
(305) 853-2620
You can't miss this unusual building going north on US 1. It is hot pink with giant flamingos out front. Inside is an inviting, nostalgic collection of vintage clothing, housewares,

bedding, jewelry, and collectibles. The inventory changes constantly, so it is a great place to browse and recall those "happy days" of whatever era you remember.

SHELL WORLD
MM 106 Bayside, Key Largo
(305) 451-9797 or (888) 398-6233
shellworldflkeys.com
At Shell World you'll think you've been beached with every type of shell in existence. Yes, they have your typical clam, oyster, and mussel shells, but they also carry a tremendous variety of other shells from throughout the world. In the aisles throughout the store are conch, abalone, cone, and nautilus shells, as well as wind chimes, jewelry, and flowers made from various shells.

Marathon

GOOFY GECKO, LAZY LIZARD, AND KRAZY LARRY'S LAST STORE
MM 50.3 Oceanside, in the Publix Shopping Center
(305) 289-4228
keysgiftsonline.com
This combo store, actually three stores in one rambling space, stocks unique tropical "stuff." The store meanders from room to room, chockablock with palmy treasures—furniture, rugs, pillows, items for entertaining, soaps and lotions, garden items, and even swishy, islandy clothes.

MAROONED IN MARATHON
MM 53 Bayside
(305) 743-3809
Definitely cast yourself ashore and hurry into this charming shop so you can be marooned in Marathon, too! This is a fun gift shop for the young and young at heart.

As they say to their customers, they carry "everything you want, some things you need, and many things you can't live without when you're not marooned on this tiny tropical island." They offer T-shirts, kids' stuff, Atocha jewelry, and other things you can't live without!

PIGEON KEY FOUNDATION GIFT SHOP
MM 47 Oceanside, Pigeon Key Visitor Center
(305) 743-5999
pigeonkey.net
Look for the old railway car, still sitting on the tracks of Flagler's railroad at MM 47 Oceanside. Hidden unassumingly inside is the Pigeon Key Foundation Gift Shop, a potpourri of Keys memorabilia and gift items. The gift shop, like everything on Pigeon Key, is run by a contingent of loyal volunteers, and all proceeds go to the Pigeon Key Foundation.

i Not enough space in your luggage for your shopping purchases? Several mail shops in the Keys will ship your treasures home. Visit the UPS Store in Key Largo (305-453-4877), in Marathon (305-743-2005), or in Key West (305-292-4177); Package Solution in Key Largo (305-451-5461); the Mail Spot in Key West (305-296-5333); or PakMail, Fourth Street in Key West (305-295-1491).

Lower Keys

LITTLE PALM ISLAND GIFT SHOP
MM 28.5 Oceanside, Little Torch Key
(305) 872-2524 or (800) 343-8567
littlepalmisland.com
Stop at this mainland substation of Little Palm Island and visit the gift shop. You'll find interesting glassware, sculptures, and hand-painted plates, in addition to upscale clothing and straw hats. If you go out to Little Palm Island itself, for lunch or dinner or to stay the night, don't miss the island shop. The tropical ambience will tempt you to discard your shorts and don an island caftan.

i Scan local newspapers and look for yard sales. This is a fun way to get out into the neighborhoods, up and down the Keys, and see how the natives live! The houses and streets of our vacation mecca are beautiful and charming.

Key West

*DOG 30
1025 White St.
(305) 296-4848
dogthirty.com
Florida Keys residents love their animals, and here at Dog 30 they show how much they care. The owners carry healthy dog food, homemade bakery treats, dog beds, carriers, and even catnip.

KEY WEST ALOE
416 Green St. and 419 Duval St.
(305) 293-1885 and (305) 384-7742
keywestaloe.com
Step into Key West Aloe on Front Street for a showroom of the only perfumes, skin-care products, and cosmetics to boast a "made in Key West" label. Their products are shipped throughout the world.

KEY WEST CONCH TRADERS
Clinton Square Market
(305) 296-2369 or (888) 592-6624
conchtraders.com
You can take home, mail, or order almost anything that reminds you of your visit to the

Florida Keys from this shop. Conch Traders is full of local retail vendors offering art, books, music, key lime products, jewelry, and any other items they can add to their inventory. Get home and wish you had bought that wall hanging? Call or go to their website and it can still be yours!

KEY WEST HAMMOCKS
717 Duval St.
(305) 293-0008
kwhammocks.com

A favorite local pastime is to head out to Fort Zach, set up a hammock, and read or snooze to the sounds of the ocean. Key West Hammocks has been keeping locals swinging happily for more than 10 years. They have numerous selections and they do ship, so you don't have to haul your hammock back home.

KEY WEST KITE COMPANY
408 Greene St.
(305) 296-2535

The Key West Kite Company is just waiting to make windy days wondrous with flags, banners, and flying tours. The first kite store to set up shop in all of Florida, Key West Kites offers everything from handmade to high-performance sport kites. There's a great selection of yo-yos here, too, plus juggling supplies and instruction.

KEY WEST WINERY, INC.
103 Simonton St.
(305) 292-1717 or (866) 880-1717
thekeywestwinery.com

This is wine like you've never tasted before: Not one variety is made from grapes! Most of the wines are made from fruits, such as Eleganta, a semisweet red raspberry variety. And 40 Karats, a buttery semidry white wine

that is similar to a Chardonnay, is 100 percent carrot and much more flavorful.

MILLIE'S
425 Front St.
(305) 294-6877

Want to be in the UK and Key West at the same time? Stop in at Millie's and you will have done just that. Everything British is here, from Spotted Dick Pudding to British daily newspapers to Cadbury chocolates. Why, the Queen herself greets you (in a comical depiction) at the front door!

PELICAN POOP SHOPPE
314 Simonton St.
(305) 292-9955
pelicanpoopshoppe.com

This eclectic collection of artwork includes originals from all over the Caribbean. For a small purchase or a nominal admittance fee, you can tour the private Casa Antigua gardens out back, linked forever to Ernest Hemingway by a quirky twist of fate. He completed *A Farewell to Arms* here while awaiting delivery of his new Ford back in 1928.

REEF RELIEF ENVIRONMENTAL CENTER & STORE
631 Greene St.
(305) 294-3100
reefrelief.org

You can learn about our fragile coral reef here at the Reef Relief Environmental Center. Continuous videos, displays, and free information will heighten your awareness of what you can do to protect North America's only living coral reef. Merchandise on sale includes coral reef books, educational products for both adults and children, and informational videos.

TOWELS OF KEY WEST
806 Duval St.
(305) 292-1120 or (800) 927-0316
towelsofkeywest.com

Towels in all shapes and sizes and for all budgets fill this simple store. Get the best-selling, colorful print terry robe, or immerse yourself in big, warm, oversize, colorful beach and bath towels.

Appendix

LIVING HERE

In this section we feature specific information for residents or those planning to relocate here. Topics include real estate, education, health care, and much more.

RELOCATION & VACATION RENTALS

Most snowbirds and full-time residents of the Florida Keys (except for the native-born Conchs) first rented homes, condominiums, or mobile homes while on vacation in Paradise. Rentals primarily are classified as short-term and long-term. Short-term rental agreements range from a weekend to six months; anything exceeding six months is considered a long-term rental. However, to preserve the integrity of our residential communities, the Monroe County Planning Commission has prohibited short-term rentals of 30 days or less throughout residential areas of unincorporated Monroe County. Incorporated areas such as Islamorada, Layton, Key Colony Beach, Marathon, and Key West can opt for differing regulations. Few short-term rental options are currently available in the Florida Keys, and the competition is fierce for those that are. The best advice we can offer is to work through a rental agent who knows what's legally available, and always book your accommodation early.

OVERVIEW

Owning a parcel of Paradise in the Florida Keys can be summed up in two words: very expensive. Real estate prices in the Florida Keys depend largely upon access to the water. Direct oceanfront or bayfront property garners the highest prices, followed by property on a canal with an ocean or bay view, and by property on a canal with access to the ocean or bay. Other areas, such as Ocean Reef, Duck Key, and Sunset Key, have special features that make homes desirable—such as gated security, golf courses, swimming pools, strict building covenants, and other community amenities—and owning a home there is pricey indeed.

Some relief is available for certain owners in the form of a homestead exemption. In Florida this exemption allows $25,000 of the assessed value of a house purchased

as a primary residence to be exempt from property tax. Real estate taxes in Monroe County are based on a millage rate that changes annually with the county budget and are some of the highest in the state. In addition, besides homeowner's insurance, homeowners must factor in the cost of wind storm and flood insurance to guard against our ever-threatening hurricanes.

Those of us who have chosen to live in the Florida Keys think the price of paradise is worth it. To assist you in your search for a piece of the rock, we provide you with a general overview of the communities of the Florida Keys, as well as the types of homes you'll encounter in our neighborhoods. At the end of the chapter, we include listings of real estate professionals who can assist you in finding a rental property or a home of your own. Look to our Key West section of this chapter for vacation rental and real estate information in our southernmost city.

RENTAL PROPERTIES

The Role of Real Estate Agents

Real estate agents handle most short-term rental properties. The exceptions are condominiums that act as hotels and employ on-site managers (see the Accommodations chapter) and homeowners who market rentals on their own. Because of changes in laws as indicated above, the latter choice is becoming more and more scarce.

Depending upon its size and specialty, an agency that handles rentals may list anywhere between 10 and 200-plus short-term rental options. Most large agencies employ sales associates who specialize in short-term rentals. Except for Key West, where agents handle much of the entire island, Florida Keys agents typically specialize within the region of their office (see the Real Estate Companies sections in this chapter).

Finding a rental property through an agency has its advantages. Rental agencies almost always offer descriptions and photographs of available properties and advice on the best option for your needs and desires. Most of them, in fact, maintain websites, which allow you to peruse the options at your leisure and, in most cases, actually see the property you are booking. Agents ensure that a home is clean and that its grounds are maintained.

In order to manage short-term rentals for stays of fewer than 30 days, real estate agencies and/or property owners and managers of condominium complexes must be licensed by the state of Florida. Units rented for fewer than 30 days are considered resort dwellings, and agents and/or owners and managers must therefore abide by a Florida statute that applies to hotels and restaurants. Depending upon the category of accommodation (condominium or single-family home, for instance), safety and health standards set by this statute may require fire extinguishers, electric smoke detectors in sleeping areas, mattress covers on all beds, and deadbolt locks on doors.

Seasonal Rates

In the wintertime, travelers flock to the Florida Keys seeking respite from the cold and snow. Referred to locally as "snowbirds," these visitors drive rental rates up between the months of December and April, the high season. Summertime is when diving is typically best (see the Diving & Snorkeling chapter), and it's also the time of year when residents throughout Florida head to the Keys for the relief of the ocean breezes. However, the rest of the mass market moves back home, so rents may be a bit lower than high season during the months of May through August. September through November is relatively quiet tourism-wise, because autumn is the prime season for hurricanes in the Florida Keys. During this period you'll find reduced rates, and, as long as you keep a watchful eye on the forecasts, you'll be able to enjoy uncrowded shops, attractions, and streets.

Minimum Stays

Most short-term tenants rent a home or condominium in the Florida Keys for a week to 3 or 4 months. The bulk of the short-term rental market consists of 2-week vacationers, but our islands are also popular with northern residents and retirees who retreat here for the winter. Virtually no private homes are available for rent on a daily basis.

During holidays, such as Christmas and Easter, and special events, including sport lobster season and Fantasy Fest, minimum stays range from 4 days to 2 weeks. Individual property owners establish these policies. Inquire of your rental agent or property owner/manager.

Options & Restrictions

Owners designate their rental properties as smoking or nonsmoking.

Children are generally welcome, but some condominium complexes restrict the number of children allowed in a single unit. One adults-only facility, Silver Shores, a mobile-home park in Key Largo catering to senior citizens, exists in the Florida Keys.

Condominiums typically do not allow pets, but some single-family homes and mobile-home parks do accept them. An additional security deposit or a fee (sometimes both) is often required. The fee covers the cost of spraying the home for fleas, which ensures accommodations free of pesky insects. Tending to pets outside the rental facility, however, is the owner's responsibility, and fleas can be abundant on hot and humid days.

i In the 1950s Philip Toppino built houses on Summerland Key for avid pilots. The homes sit along the airstrip, and private planes can be parked underneath the houses.

Reservations & Payment Options

Naturally, the most desirable rental properties tend to book the earliest, and many tenants book the same home for the same weeks year after year. To achieve the greatest selection of rentals, we suggest that you reserve at least 6 months to a year in advance. During holidays the demand for short-term rentals can exhaust the supply. If you plan to travel to the Florida Keys during the high season (December through April) and holidays (especially Christmas week or during Fantasy Fest), you would be wise to reserve 1 to 2 years in advance.

Payment options vary according to how far in advance you book and when you check in. Typically, an initial deposit of 10 to 25 percent of the total rental cost, made with a personal check or a credit card, will hold a unit. Some agents allow you to pay with cash or credit card upon arrival, provided that you check in during office hours, which vary from agency to agency. Ask about these specifics when you call.

Security Deposits

Your rental agreement holds you responsible for any damage to the dwelling and its contents. Security deposits provide the homeowner with added protection and a means of paying any telephone charges not billed to your credit card. As a general rule, count on supplying 50 to 75 percent of one week's rent (slightly more for a monthly rental). Security deposits on large homes with expensive furnishings can be much higher.

Cancellation Policies

Homeowners set monetary penalties for cancellations anywhere between 30 days in advance of reservations, with a nominal cancellation fee for administrative services, to 60 days in advance, with a full refund. Don't assume that an impending hurricane or other emergency beyond your control will warrant a refund of your payment. In such cases, some homeowners may be generous in providing full or partial refunds or offering credit toward accommodations at a future date—but don't bank on it. Generally, you forfeit your deposit when weather emergencies cancel your vacation plans.

Refund policies are negotiated among the tenant, real estate agency, and property owner and usually are not included in lease agreements.

REAL ESTATE: COMMUNITY PROFILES

Upper Keys

Key Largo

Key Largo is popular with divers interested in the abundant reefs within John Pennekamp Coral Reef State Park and the Florida Keys National Marine Sanctuary. And because Key Largo is within 20 miles of the mainland, property here often is in great demand by weekday commuters and South Floridians purchasing weekend retreats. In real estate terms, Key Largo generally includes the exclusive, members-only Ocean Reef subdivision at the extreme northeast edge and encompasses all land southwest to Tavernier.

Ocean Reef

A luxury subdivision in North Key Largo, Ocean Reef is a private, all-inclusive gated community of large single-family homes, condominiums, and town houses. Properties here attract buyers seeking privacy, exclusivity, and the opportunity to fish, dive, snorkel, swim, shop, and dine out without ever leaving the complex. This community has three golf courses, a marina, and other amenities open only to residents.

Tavernier

Toward the southern end of Key Largo is Tavernier, one of the Florida Keys' oldest settlements. Some Tavernier homes date from the early farming settlements at the turn of the last century. Plantation Key (its northern end also maintains a Tavernier postal designation) has a wide range of real estate opportunities, with single-family subdivisions primarily bayside. The Snake Creek Drawbridge makes Plantation Key an ideal homesite for owners of large yachts and sailboats.

Islamorada

Islamorada stretches from Plantation Key to Lower Matecumbe. Lot sizes in Islamorada typically are larger than those in other areas of the Florida Keys, a factor intended to attract builders of large, impressive homes. Upper Matecumbe Key is the heart of Islamorada, commercially developed but with homes tucked along the waterfront in quiet residential areas. Lower Matecumbe Key is Islamorada's predominantly residential island, with a bike path, tennis club, and private beach.

Layton

The late Del Layton, a Miami grocery store owner, developed tiny Layton into a subdivision in the 1950s. Later he incorporated it as the Florida Keys' smallest city. Except for several oceanfront homes, all single-family residences in Layton are on oceanside canals, with the nearby Channel 5 Bridge allowing access to the bay. Fifteen miles from Marathon and Islamorada, Layton is largely a community of retirees.

Middle Keys

Duck Key

Duck Key is composed of five islands connected by white Venetian-style bridges. A series of flow-through canals encircle each island, ensuring that nearly half the homes or lots offer canalfront dockage or openwater views. The uniquely situated islands allow direct access to both the ocean and the Gulf of Mexico. The Duck Key Property Owners Association, an active group, maintains rights-of-way and public-area plantings, has established distinctive signage, and sponsors social events throughout the year. Duck Key Club, a private swim and tennis club, is located on Center Island and also sponsors myriad social activities for its members. Residents pay a small out-of-pocket tax to employ a private security firm to supplement county services. Hawk's Cay Resort is on the first island, Indies Island, which is zoned differently from the rest. The other four islands—Center, Plantation, Harbour, and Yacht Club—are designated for single-family residential housing only. All homes must be of concrete-block-style (CBS) construction.

Grassy Key

Grassy Key, a sleepy, rural island with a few oceanfront bungalow courts and several restaurants, is distanced from Marathon by preservation lands. With no canals on Grassy Key, there is no pricing middle ground. The area has single-family homes on dry lots or waterfront estates along the Gulf of Mexico and the Atlantic. Grassy Key is now a part of incorporated Marathon.

Key Colony Beach

Incorporated in 1957, Key Colony Beach—a 285-acre peninsular finger surrounded by incorporated Marathon—developed its property with a row of condominiums directly on the Atlantic and single-family homes built on a series of canals. Key Colony Beach employs its own police and enforces its own signage and zoning ordinances. Accessed by a causeway from US 1, Key Colony Beach has a post office and a few small shops and restaurants.

Marathon

Marathon was heavily developed in the 1950s, when dredging was relatively commonplace. This area probably has more canals and waterways—and thus more canalfront properties—than any other region of Monroe County. However, with no active zoning ordinances for all these years, in some neighborhoods it is not uncommon to find a run-down mobile home situated next to an upscale canalfront dwelling. Marathon was incorporated in 1999 and now has its own mayor and city commission, as well as the ability to levy citywide property taxes. Marathon is the commercial hub of the Florida Keys, featuring supermarkets, a movie theater, Home Depot, Office Depot, Kmart, and other shops and restaurants.

Lower Keys

Big Pine Key

This rural, semi-isolated island has acres of open space and limited development potential. Home to the National Key Deer Refuge, the island is popular with many Key West and Marathon workday commuters. Big Pine Key probably offers the best value for the money in affordable housing.

Little Torch & Ramrod Keys

Little Torch Key and Ramrod Key have a rural feeling, with homes on both the Atlantic and the Gulf of Mexico as well as on dry lots.

Summerland, Cudjoe & Sugarloaf Keys

Heading closer to Key West and into the more exclusive subdivisions of Summerland, Cudjoe, and Sugarloaf Keys, you'll find luxurious properties. Summerland features a number of waterfront homes, along with a small airstrip that allows residents to park their private airplanes directly beneath their homes.

Baypoint, Shark Key, Big Coppitt & Key Haven

Shark Key is a gated community developed with strict architectural guidelines. The large open-water lots on Shark Key are beautifully landscaped, and the houses set on them typically are very expensive. Baypoint, Big Coppitt, and Key Haven are in demand for their convenient location, only minutes from Key West.

Key West

Old Town

Settled in the early to late 1800s and the early 1900s, Old Town is characterized by large wood-frame houses of distinctive architectural styles. Typically built by shipbuilders and carpenters for New England sea captains, many of these homes feature Bahamian and New England influences and high ceilings. Several historic district homes are now exquisite guesthouses (see the Accommodations chapter).

In addition to its obvious aesthetic qualities, Old Town is desirable because it is within walking distance of just about everything Key West has to offer, including shops, restaurants, nightlife, and galleries. Among the community's residents are a large number of artists and writers.

Toward the southern end of Whitehead Street and west of Duval on Petronia Street, about a block from the Ernest Hemingway Home and Museum, lies **Bahama Village.** This community now is undergoing gentrification, as home buyers purchase and renovate existing properties here.

One of Key West's more recent developments in Old Town is **Truman Annex,** where private homes, town houses, and condominiums all boast features of Key West's distinctive architecture. This self-contained development once was an extension of the island's Bahama Village section and later a portion of the Key West naval base. Truman Annex was constructed and renovated according to a unified plan reminiscent of Old Town but with more green space and winding streets. Because of the charm that this gated development exhibits, even the hubbub created by large cruise ships entering the nearby harbor does not affect its pricey real estate values. Condominiums in the Harbour Place complex of Truman Annex are almost directly on the water and run well into seven figures. Single-family homes are in the multimillion-dollar price range.

Mid Town & New Town

Stretching from White Street all the way east to Kennedy Boulevard, Mid Town boasts a mix of wood-frame and concrete-block ground-level homes built in the late 1950s and 1960s. New Town, developed a bit later, spreads out along N. Roosevelt Boulevard and is largely commercial on its perimeter.

Recently completed in the Mid Town area is **Roosevelt Annex,** a gated community of 25 single-family homes and town houses fronting the Gulf of Mexico on the former county fairgrounds along N. Roosevelt Boulevard. Billed as the last developable site in Key West with open-water views, Roosevelt Annex was constructed by the developer of Truman Annex and the Key West Golf Club.

The **Key West Golf Club community,** on Stock Island, looks a lot like Truman Annex. Here, single-family homes, town houses, and condominiums display elements of Conch-style architecture. Each residence overlooks the Florida Keys' only 18-hole public golf course, along with surrounding lakes and ponds. If you are not in the market to buy at this time, a variety of long-term rental options are available. All residents have free access to tennis courts, nature walks, several swimming pools, and, of course, golf.

Sunset Key

If you would truly like to live on a secluded island—but not too far from civilization—consider a home on Sunset Key. Formerly known as Tank Island (the navy once stored its fuel in huge tanks here), Sunset Key is just a stone's throw across the harbor from Mallory Square. About half of the island is devoted to guest cottages and a beachfront restaurant-bar operated by the **Westin Key West Resort and Marina** (see the Accommodations chapter); the rest is reserved for single-family homes. Interior building lots begin at $1.5 million. In addition to fabulous open-water sunset views, homeowners on Sunset Key enjoy such amenities as a health club, pool, tennis courts, and putting green. Their cars, however, must remain behind at the Westin parking garage on Key West; only golf carts and bicycles are permitted on Sunset Key. Regular ferry service is available from the Westin Marina.

KINDS OF PROPERTIES

Condominiums

Condominiums are scattered throughout the Upper and Middle Keys, and many home buyers find them to be a low-maintenance way to keep up a part-time residence. For full-time residents, condos commonly offer amenities not always available in a single-family home, such as swimming pools, fitness facilities, saunas, hot tubs, boat dockage, and covered parking.

During our peak tourist season (generally December through April), condominiums often are teeming with activity, affording residents the opportunity to meet renters from across the country. When the low season rolls around and occupancy typically drops to 30 percent or less at any given time, full-time residents have the facilities nearly all to themselves. If you plan to become a full-time Florida Keys resident in a condominium, be sure to check on whether the complex you have your eye on maintains an active rental program. You may not enjoy living alongside transient residents.

What you'll pay for a condo depends on the size of the unit, its location, and its view. You also need to factor monthly maintenance fees into the overall cost; these increase with unit sizes and cover maintenance of the common area, a reserve account for future major repairs, and insurance for damage by flood, wind, storm, peril, and salt air. (See the Close-up in this chapter.)

Mobile Homes

First the good news: A mobile home is the least expensive real estate you can buy in the Florida Keys. The bad news? Most vulnerable to hurricane damage, mobile homes are the first properties ordered for evacuation

Close-up

Hot—It's Not

Key Wester and famed playwright Tennessee Williams's *Cat on a Hot Tin Roof* is a slinky, sensual, artistic play and movie. In the real world of tin roofs, the title could not be further from the truth.

Thomas Jefferson was an advocate of tin roofs and used one for his home, Monticello (construction began in 1768 and ended in 1809). Prior to tin roofs, copper was imported from England until the end of the 18th century, when rolling sheet metal was developed in America. Corrugated, stiffened sheets allowed greater span over lighter framework, thus decreasing installation time and labor. In 1857 one of the first metal roofs in the South was used on the US Mint in New Orleans. In the late 19th century, patterned tin roofs were all the rage, as they are today.

The durability of these roofs proves they hold up during hurricanes. Heat from the sun reflects off the metal, and lightning discharges over the metal, thus helping to prevent the spread of fires. Long used on barns and rural outbuildings, they hold an authentic simplistic charm of another era. The resurgence of metal roofing in newer homes is on the increase due to attractive designs, the distinctive look that is more compatible with historic neighborhoods, and the fact that the metals may be recycled.

Wend the streets of Old Town in Key West on foot or trolley, cast your eyes skyward, over the delicious cakelike, gingerbread-trimmed, historic homes, and marvel at the icing of tin on the roofs of these beautiful ladies. The Tennessee Williams home on Duncan Street still sports a metal roof and is as charming today as when the famous owner was in residence in this southernmost city. Tin roofs on vintage homes are "hot" commodities in the ever-sizzling South Florida real estate market.

during severe-storm watches in the Florida Keys.

Zoning ordinances restrict mobile homes to specific communities. Often the least expensive mobile homes are those that have existed in residential subdivisions since before zoning ordinances were established. These mobile homes, which have individual septic tanks, lack the recreational and service-oriented amenities typically offered in mobile-home communities here.

Buyers who purchase property in a mobile-home community pay more but frequently enjoy a clubhouse atmosphere complete with a swimming pool, shuffleboard court, boat ramp, dockage, on-site manager, sewage treatment, and a convenience store. The price of any mobile home increases with a concrete or wood-frame addition, an elevated Florida room, built-up gravel roof, poured concrete slab, and other features.

Single-Family Homes

Dry-lot homes—those not fronting a water view or canal—are the least expensive single-family home option in the Keys. Canalfront homes generally sell for much more, with homes on the open water usually in the millions. Because many real estate purchases here are made by boaters, homes that sit closer to a bridge—providing access to both the ocean and the bay—sell more quickly.

Since 1975 the county has required that most homes be constructed of concrete block, be positioned on stilts, and have hurricane shutters. Nonconforming structures built before the 1975 ordinance took effect have been grandfathered, but if 50 percent or more of the dollar value of a nonconforming use structure is destroyed and requires rebuilding, new zoning laws and building restrictions apply.

Much of a buyer's decision to purchase a home in the Florida Keys depends upon the structure's ability to withstand a hurricane. Concrete-block-style (CBS) homes are considered more solid than those made of wood. Most are elevated on stilts to avoid potential flooding. CBS stilt homes typically cost more than ground-level CBS homes of comparable sizes. CBS homes typically command higher prices than all-wood frame structures.

A large percentage of Lower Keys homes are factory-built, wood-frame modulars. Because they are constructed under controlled circumstances and designed to withstand 135-mph winds, some homeowners believe they're stronger than wood-frame homes built on the site.

If you are considering buying a home in the Florida Keys, landscaping also may influence your decision. Some buyers prefer intricate vegetation, which requires costly irrigation, while others want low-maintenance pearock and xeriscaping (landscaping using indigenous plantings that require no irrigation).

REAL ESTATE COMPANIES

Though all Florida Keys agents share a multiple listing service (MLS) with properties available throughout Monroe County, each agency tends to specialize in its own territory. We describe some of the largest agencies for sales and rentals in the section that follows. This is not meant to be a comprehensive listing by any means. For a complete list, consult the Yellow Pages for the appropriate communities, or pick up copies of the many real estate guides available free of charge at supermarkets and other locations throughout Monroe County.

Upper Keys

AMERICAN CARIBBEAN REAL ESTATE INC.
MM 81.8 Bayside, Islamorada
(305) 664-4966
americancaribbean.com
American Caribbean handles more than 100 properties for sale or rent from Duck Key to Key Largo.

FREEWHEELER REALTY
MM 98.5 Bayside, Key Largo
(305) 852-4400 or (877) 852-4450
freewheeler-realty.com
Freewheeler deals in property management, rentals, and sales for homes, condos, villas, and efficiencies on the beach, bay, and canal. Another location is at MM 86 Bayside in Islamorada (305-664-4444 or 866-664-2075).

MARR PROPERTIES
MM 100 Bayside, Key Largo
(305) 451-4078 or (800) 277-3728
floridakeysproperties.com
Serving the Keys since 1965, this office offers sales of commercial and residential

properties and knowledge of the upper Keys real estate market.

i Driving along our residential streets, our neighborhoods look like any small town. But every once in a while you see a house or building that is completely entombed in a red and yellow circus-like tent. These are signs that the exterminators are at work! In the tropical Florida Keys, we have all sorts of critters that a can of bug spray just won't eradicate.

Middle Keys

AMERICAN CARIBBEAN REAL ESTATE INC.
MM 52 Oceanside, Marathon
(305) 743-7636 or (800) 940-7636
acresales.com
American Caribbean specializes in Middle Keys sales and rental properties from Duck Key to Key Largo.

COLDWELL BANKER SCHMITT REAL ESTATE
MM 52.5 Bayside, Marathon
(305) 743-5181 or (800) 366-5181
realestatefloridakeys.com
Sales and vacation rentals in the Middle Keys are the focus at this office of a firm that covers the real estate market from one end of the Keys to the other.

EXIT REALTY FLORIDA KEYS
MM 58, Oceanside, Marathon
(305) 743-9292
exitfloridakeys.com
Residential and commercial sales are the thrust of this company. They also offer annual and vacation rentals as well as property management services.

RE/MAX KEY TO THE KEYS
MM 49.5 Bayside, Marathon
(305) 743-2300 or (800) 743-2301
wilkinsonteam.com
Agents handle sales and rental properties from Long Key to Big Coppitt.

THE WATERFRONT SPECIALIST
MM 54 Oceanside, 80th Street Station, Marathon
(305) 743-0644 or (800) 342-6398
waterfrontspecialists.com
Despite its name, this agency can direct you to sales and rental opportunities both on and off the water.

Lower Keys

ACTION KEYS REALTY, INC.
MM 24.8 Oceanside, Summerland Key
(305) 745-1323 or (800) 874-1323
actionkeysrealty.com
In addition to residential sales throughout the Lower Keys, this agency handles vacation rentals, primarily on Summerland, Ramrod, and Little Torch Keys.

ERA LOWER KEYS REALTY
MM 30 Oceanside, Big Pine Key
(305) 872-2258 or (800) 859-7642
eralowerkeysrealty.com
This establishment deals with sales and rentals in the Lower Keys.

PRIVATE ISLANDS, HOMES & HIDEAWAYS

Picture yourself in the following locations, and soon you will know the meaning of "lost in paradise." Vacationing at its finest, these properties will leave you incredulous: You were where? On an island? Out in the middle of the ocean? On a helicopter pad? Aboard a private skiff? Only one word can sum it up: fabulous.

Upper Keys

ALLIGATOR REEF
MM 86 Bayside, Islamorada
(305) 664-2075 or (866) 664-2075
alligatorreef.net
Need 10 bedrooms, 4 kitchens, 2 heated pools, 8 bathrooms, and accommodations for 25 people? Then Alligator Reef compound is for you! With an observation deck overlooking the Atlantic Ocean, you can relax or enjoy all of the amenities on the property. Go kayaking, play Ping-Pong, swim, or swing in the hammocks. Do it all or nothing—this getaway packs a true "tropical punch."

TERRA'S KEY
MM 79.3 Oceanside, Islamorada
(305) 664-2361 or (877) 412-7339
terraskey.com
Located off Islamorada is Terra's Key (also known as Tea Table Key). This sun-drenched 7-acre private island is connected to US 1 by a causeway. Five bedrooms, 6 bathrooms, a tennis court, a heated pool with a wet bar, and inspiring vistas of the Atlantic Ocean make this a setting for a vacation you will never forget.

Middle Keys

EAST SISTER ROCK ISLAND
MM 50 Oceanside, Marathon
(305) 796-8439
floridaisland.com
Piloting your own 21-foot Carolina skiff to and from the mainland of Marathon, you travel to your island in the sun, East Sister Rock Island. Completely surrounded by a moat, the house sits on a coral reef. A 12-foot veranda swings around the 5,000-square-foot home. This a diver's and snorkeler's haven. If that isn't your bag, you can swim in the pool or a bigger "pool"—the Atlantic Ocean! If the skiff is too slow for your entrance—or exit—there is a helicopter pad on the grounds.

Key West

Despite the fact that Key West is heavily developed, with both old and new homes on generally small lots throughout the city, real estate agents report that the demand for homes far outstrips the island's supply. Also, while waterfront property is a prime attraction for home buyers throughout the rest of the Florida Keys, it is rarely found in Key West, because commercial development lines all waterfront areas. Nevertheless, real estate in the southernmost city is expensive.

The island of Key West is an incorporated city governed by local elected representatives as well as by Monroe County. Consequently, the property tax structure here includes both city and county government expenses. Key West has its own land-use plan with zoning ordinances, permitting units, density requirements, and building height and setback minimums. Within the historic district of Old Town, another layer of control and review exists. The Historical Architecture Review Commission (HARC) reviews applications for improvements and new construction. Established in 1986, HARC works to ensure the integrity of the historic district.

Key West offers a selection of styles in single-family homes, town houses, and condominiums. The island has few mobile-home parks, and the only mobile-home communities here are small and hidden away. There are also several on Stock Island.

Town houses, typically adjoining structures with a common wall, allow homeowners to own the ground beneath them. The center of the common wall is the dividing line, and party wall agreements determine who maintains responsibility in cases of repair or destruction.

If you wish to purchase beachfront housing, a condominium is without a doubt the way to go. Along the south side of Key West are several multistory beachfront condominiums with elevators, enclosed parking, pools, tennis courts, and hot tubs.

The majority of single-family homes in Key West are in areas known as Old Town, Mid Town, and New Town, and real estate agents further break two of these regions into "old" and "new" Old Town and "old" and "new" New Town. Boundaries are roughly established, with some overflow, and within all Key West areas you'll discover a diverse array of properties dating from between the early 1800s and the late 1900s.

Convenience to the water or to touristy Duval Street is not usually a factor in the cost of Key West property. Rather, prices generally depend on the size and condition of the house, its lot, and its location. The island itself is only 2 miles long by 4 miles wide, so beaches and harbors are never far away. Some home buyers seek property as far from the busy roadways and attractions as possible.

BASCOM GROOMS REAL ESTATE
1110 Truman Ave.
(305) 295-7511 or (888) 565-7150
bascomgrooms.com
In addition to residential sales, this agency handles commercial properties and vacation rentals.

BEACH CLUB BROKERS INC.
1075 Duval St., Ste. C-11
(305) 294-8433 or (800) 545-9655
kwreal.com
Specializing in the sale, purchase, and management of local and international property, Beach Club Brokers also has a separate rental division, Rent Key West Vacations (see separate listing).

CENTURY 21 ALL KEYS
1720 N. Roosevelt Blvd.
(305) 294-4200 or (800) 373-4200
c21allkeys.com
Century 21 deals with real estate sales and rentals in our southernmost city.

✳CENTURY 21 SCHWARTZ
211 Simonton St.
(305) 766-0585
Regularly featured on HGTV, these agents will work with you, whatever your home buying needs.

✳COMPASS REALTY
201 Front St., Ste. 101
(305) 292-1881 or (800) 884-7368
compass-realty.com
Compass Realty sells property throughout Key West but also focuses on the sale and rental of Truman Annex properties as well as those in the Key West Golf Club and Roosevelt Annex communities.

ISLAND GROUP REALTY
2409 N. Roosevelt Blvd., Ste. 10
(305) 295-7110 or (800 225-4277
isellkw.com
This real estate company offers any of the services you might need for relocating to the Florida Keys. If your needs are residential, commercial properties, or rentals, the sales

associates at Island Group Realty can assist with your request.

KEY WEST REALTY INC.
1109 Duval St.
(305) 294-3064
keywestrealty.com
This agency is very heavily into real estate sales in Key West.

PREFERRED PROPERTIES COASTAL REALTY, INC.
520 Southard St.
(305) 294-3040 or (800) 462-5937
realkeywest.com
This agency offers residential and commercial property sales as well as vacation rentals, investment properties, and long-term property management.

PRUDENTIAL KNIGHT & GARDNER REALTY
336 Duval St.
(305) 294-5155 or (800) 843-9276
keysrealestate.com
Prudential Knight concentrates its efforts on the purchase, sale, rent, or lease of properties and boat slips from Key West to Marathon.

RENT KEY WEST VACATIONS, INC.
1107 Truman Ave.
(305) 294-0990 or (800) 833-7368
rentkeywest.com
This agency handles rentals exclusively. Rent Key West offers extensive listings, with properties ranging from studio apartments to four-bedroom homes.

TRUMAN & COMPANY
1205 Truman Ave.
(305) 292-2244
trumanandcompany.com
This is a highly professional company with a great knowledge of the Key West and Monroe County real estate market. Most of the principals in this company are long-time residents and handle with first-hand knowledge the unique residential and commercial aspects of buying and selling property in the Florida Keys.

VACATION KEY WEST
(305) 295-9500 or (800) 595-5397
vacationkw.com
This agency will help you choose a great location for a few days or for an extended visit here in the tropics. They can place you in a historic inn, romantic hideaway, condo, or cottage.

VIVA ON DUVAL
1224 Duval St.
(305) 294-7358 or (800) 404-2802
vacationhomesofkeywest.com
Built in 1935, this gleaming white home glows in the bright Key West sun. Twelve-foot ceilings in the downstairs area open into the living room, dining room, laundry room, and kitchen. Outside the kitchen is a private pool and landscaped garden. Upstairs there are 3 bedroom suites. Once here you can walk to many shops, restaurants, and attractions.

RETIREMENT

If we are to believe Noah Webster, retirement means "withdrawing from active life." Not so in the Florida Keys. Our retirees are anything but retiring. Each year, about the time Jack Frost starts whistling up north, the influx of snowbirds to our sun-kissed islands begins, and the collective pulse of our communities quickens.

Unlike other retirement areas in Florida, our seniors usually don't keep to themselves in preplanned communities. You'll find them living in residential neighborhoods and condominiums, RV parks, and mobile-home villages. Our seniors contribute an added dimension to our communities. They form a much-needed core of volunteers for many of our public services, including the county libraries, local hospitals, and area schools.

The American Association of Retired Persons (AARP) accepts individuals age 50 and older into membership, , and some are taking the Florida Keys by storm. These prime-of-lifers have taken a career-course detour, leaving that corporate 9-to-5 (or, more likely, 9-to-9) grind to venture off the track into uncharted territory.

Regardless of age, the retirees in the Florida Keys remain youthful. Our warm, tropical climate is kind to old bones (young ones, too!). The pace of our lifestyle moves to a different drummer—well, more of a reggae beat. Some people even feel we live longer down here . . . and they're in their 90s. Our energetic retirees enjoy fishing and scuba diving, golf and tennis, boating and bridge. They are active in myriad special-interest organizations the length and breadth of the Keys. Many pursue artistic hobbies long put on the back burner while the rest of their lives simmered. Some go back to school, developing new skills and honing others.

OVERVIEW

At the heart of the retirement community in the Florida Keys are the senior citizen centers, which serve as cohesive units of companionship and support to retirees of all ages and circumstances. The centers were constructed and are maintained as a joint venture between Monroe County and the local chapters of AARP. Membership in AARP is not a prerequisite for most activities of the senior centers, but anyone age 50 or older may pick up an application to AARP at any of the centers. Because our seniors participate in activities based all throughout the Keys, we have organized this chapter by interest group, incorporating all areas of the Keys from Key Largo to Key West.

SENIOR CENTERS

BIG PINE KEY SENIOR CENTER
MM 31 Bayside, 380 Key Deer Blvd., Big Pine Key
(305) 872-3990
monroecounty-fl.gov
Not to be outdone by the other Keys centers, the seniors in the Lower Keys boogie in a bevy of activities like their compatriots up the Keys. The winter season finds them country line dancing and exercising, taking French lessons, and attending classes in hatha yoga. The center shows classic movies and hosts potlucks and bingo. The Big Pine Key Senior Center, which is right behind the Big Pine Key firehouse, is open every day for card playing and puzzle making. During the winter season the center often holds dances, playing recorded Big Band music.

KEY WEST SENIOR CENTER
1016 Georgia St., Key West
(305) 295-5165
monroecounty-fl.gov
The seniors in Key West often go their own way, we are told, so not as many organized activities emanate from this center as from others in the rest of the Keys. The seniors are active in the Key West Garden Club, the Art and Historical Society, the Maritime History Society, the Key West Yacht Club, the Power Squadron, and fraternal organizations such as Moose and Elk. Bingo and bridge are popular here, with games held in season on Tues, Thurs, and Sun.

MARATHON SENIOR CENTER
MM 48.8 Bayside, 535 33rd St., Marathon
(305) 743-3346
monroecounty-fl.gov
This lively bunch in the Middle Keys maintains a whirlwind of activities, especially during the winter season, such as bridge, crafts, weekly bingo, and regular exercise sessions. The seniors trip the light fantastic with special events, such as the Valentine Sweetheart Dance and the St. Patrick's Day party. The Marathon Senior Center has a large lending library. It also has free income tax preparation when that dreaded time rolls around. Free flu shots and blood pressure checks are available on a regular basis.

PLANTATION KEY SENIOR CENTER
88800 Overseas Highway, Oceanside, Plantation Key
(305) 852-7133
monroecounty-fl.gov
This active group of seniors in the Upper Keys has a series of fund-raisers, such as its annual rummage sale, to raise money for community organizations, including the fire department, the ambulance corps, and the local Red Cross chapter. Besides monthly meetings, this Upper Keys group enjoys bingo; members donate the money raised to Hospice. Many of the retirees in the Upper Keys are active in conservation and preservation organizations, fraternal organizations, the Florida Keys Council of the Arts, and human service groups such as Hospice and the Domestic Abuse Shelter. The center is next to the sheriff's substation.

COLLEGE COURSES

Florida Keys Community College (FKCC) offers a selection of courses of interest to seniors, but there is no tuition break for senior citizens. Check fkcc.edu for current course offerings and tuition charges. The academic year is divided into three terms: The fall class session runs Aug through Dec, the spring term is Jan to May, and summer classes are held from the beginning of May through mid-Aug. Class offerings change often, so call the college branch of your choice for a course catalog and the most recent class schedule.

FLORIDA KEYS COMMUNITY COLLEGE MAIN CAMPUS
5901 W. College Rd., Stock Island
(305) 296-9081
fkcc.edu

The main campus of Florida Keys Community College offers many more classes of interest to seniors than the other branches up the Keys. Art classes in ceramics, stained glass, jewelry making, lettering and calligraphy, drawing, wheel throwing, printmaking, photography, graphic arts, painting, and sculpture will intrigue the artistically inclined. FKCC has a beautiful swimming pool and offers classes in water aerobics and fitness swimming. Seniors can take classes as non-degree-seeking students or work toward an associate of arts or associate of science degree.

Lifelong learning doesn't necessarily mean that you must enroll in a degree program or semester-long course. FKCC also offers a variety of continuing education workshops and seminars. These classes may meet for a single session or several weeks, depending on the complexity of the subject matter.

FLORIDA KEYS COMMUNITY COLLEGE MIDDLE KEYS CAMPUS
MM 50 Oceanside, 900 Sombrero Beach Rd., Marathon
(305) 743-2133 or (305) 743-0749
fkcc.edu

The Middle Keys branch of FKCC offers general-interest classes in foreign language and computer science as well as more unusual fare, such as nature walks, tours of the Everglades, conservation classes, and photography instruction.

FLORIDA KEYS COMMUNITY COLLEGE UPPER KEYS CAMPUS
MM 89.9 Oceanside, Coral Shores High School, Tavernier
(305) 852-8007
fkcc.edu

Seniors and retirees particularly enjoy the computer classes offered at this branch of Florida Keys Community College. They also sign up for such classes as conversational Spanish, watercolor painting, beginning drawing, creative writing, and American and English literature.

PUBLIC LIBRARIES

The Monroe County libraries are popular reading-room destinations with seniors in the Keys. They all maintain ever-growing large-print collections and a wide selection of current magazines. In addition, most of the libraries have a burgeoning number of DVDs and books on tape that may be checked out. Electronic catalogs in each of the libraries list all the materials in the system. Your local library will be able to get items from other branches for you upon request.

The libraries also host special events, such as lectures and film screenings, throughout the year. The library system has a strong volunteer program as well. The Key West library maintains a well-stocked Florida History Room that provides a fascinating look back through the centuries in Key West and all of the Keys. Volumes of old photographs are housed here.

The Monroe County library system includes the following branches: Key Largo, MM 101.4 Oceanside, Tradewinds Shopping Center, (305) 451-2396; Islamorada, MM 81.5 Bayside, (305) 664-4645; Marathon, MM 48.5 Oceanside, next to Fishermen's Hospital, (305) 743-5156; Big Pine, MM 31 Bayside, 213 Key Deer Blvd., (305) 872-0992; and Key West, 700 Fleming St., (305) 292-3595. Visit monroecounty-fl.gov for more information.

SPECIAL-INTEREST ACTIVITIES

It is not uncommon here in the Florida Keys to hear a senior citizen complain, "Since I've retired, I've never been so busy in my life!" Seniors get involved in civic clubs and fraternal organizations such as the Elks, Eagles, Moose, and Shriners. They work with human service organizations such as Big Brothers/ Big Sisters, Florida Keys Children's Shelter, Domestic Abuse Shelter, and the AIDS Prevention Center. Retirees donate valuable time to the Florida Keys Council of the Arts, the American Cancer Society, and Guardian Ad Litem. And they participate in activities helping the Florida Keys themselves, such as Reef Relief, Florida Keys Wild Bird Rehabilitation Center, and Friends of the Everglades.

i Each month the Florida Keys Southernmost Car Club holds a "Show and Shine" event that allows the general public to behold dream classic autos from an era long gone, up close and personal. All makes and models, including trucks, lowriders, and chrome motorcycles, are on display. The Car Club chooses various locations throughout the Keys, so call ahead for dates and times at (305) 942-1758 or visit southernmostcarclub.com.

Contact the chamber of commerce in your area for a complete listing of special-interest organizations in the Florida Keys. Area chambers include those in Key Largo, (305) 451-4747 or (800) 822-1088; Islamorada, (305) 664-4503 or (800) 322-5397; Marathon, (305) 743-5417 or (800) 262-7284; Lower Keys, (305) 872-2411 or (800) 872-3722; and Key West, (305) 294-2587 or (800) 527-8539. Visit monroecounty-fl.gov for more information.

Garden Clubs

Some of the most popular organizations in the Florida Keys are its garden clubs, perhaps because we have so many days of glorious sunshine or because our subtropical climate fosters the growth of such exotic flowering foliage and palms.

KEY WEST GARDEN CLUB
Atlantic Boulevard and White Street at West Martello Tower, Key West
(305) 294-3210
keywestgardenclub.com
The Key West Garden Club maintains the gardens of West Martello Tower, an old Civil War fort at Higgs Beach on Atlantic Boulevard. The club meets once a month for a short business meeting followed by a presentation by a guest speaker, often a visiting horticulturist. These events are open to the general public. Twice a year the group holds a plant sale at its West Martello Tower headquarters. You can walk away with beautiful plants at bargain prices and a wealth of free gardening tips and information to boot.

MARATHON GARDEN CLUB
MM 50 Bayside, Marathon
(305) 743-4971
marathongardenclub.org

The Marathon Garden Club was organized in March 1955, and much of the lovely landscaping gracing Marathon's public areas is the work of the club. You'll notice the group's creative handiwork at the American Legion, the chamber of commerce building, the firehouse, Fishermen's Hospital, the public library, the Key Colony Causeway, along the Overseas Highway, and at Marathon High School. The group sponsors successful house and garden tours, plant and crafts fairs, and flower shows throughout the year. The Marathon Garden Club meets the third Fri of each month from Oct through May. The public is invited. The gift shop, which offers a changing selection of unusual specialty gift items, is open year-round.

Habitat for Humanity

Looking for something to do? Why not call Habitat for Humanity in the Keys and volunteer your talents. Three locations serve the community: Upper Keys, (305) 453-0050 or (305) 453-7855; Middle Keys, (305) 395-1386; and Lower Keys, (305) 872-4456. Ongoing projects include fishing tournaments, raising money for hurricane season, spelling bees, an annual gala, and a ReStore offering furniture, appliances, and building supplies in their redistribution center located at mile marker 30.5 in Big Pine Key. Visit habitatlowerkeys.org for more information.

UPPER KEYS GARDEN CLUB
MM 94 Bayside, Tavenier
upperkeysgardenclub.com

The Upper Keys Garden Club meets at various locations on the third Tues of the month from Sept through Apr. The group often hears a lecturer speak on some aspect of subtropical horticulture. They hold a Plant Ramble sale as a fund-raiser and sponsor a garden walk through lovely private gardens of the Upper Keys each year. Members support the community's landscaping needs by donating plants and labor to landscape the Coast Guard Station, Coral Shores High School, and Plantation Key Elementary School.

American Contract Bridge League

Duplicate bridge passes muster as the game of choice among those addicts of the sport. "If there's a game in town, we'll find it," says one duplicate player. The play is recognized by the National American Contract Bridge League, and you can earn Life Master's points. The games are open to all. If you don't have a partner, don't worry: The director will pair you with a partner for the day's game. A nominal fee is charged to play.

It is best to call the director before the day of play to make sure the schedule has not been changed. The groups are listed here by location.

- **Civic Club,** MM 99.5 Oceanside, Key Largo; (305) 451-9833. Play is year-round on Mon and Fri afternoons and on Tues evening.
- **Senior Center,** Harvey Government Center, 1016 Georgia St., Key West; (305) 295-5165. Play is on Tues, Thurs, and Sun afternoons.

Golf & Tennis

Two of the most popular sports among seniors are golf and tennis. See our Recreation chapter for information on facilities in the Florida Keys.

SENIOR SERVICES

AMERICAN ASSOCIATION OF RETIRED PERSONS
Upper Keys, (305) 852-7132
Middle Keys, (305) 743-4008
Big Pine Key, (305) 872-3990
Key West, (305) 295-5156
aarp.org
The nationally known American Association of Retired Persons (AARP) has local chapters in most cities. Here in the Florida Keys there are four offices from Plantation Key to Key West. Each chapter offers their own programs in areas of interest to their members. You must be at least 50 years of age to join. For a nominal fee, members can select from line dancing and computer classes to county services. Helpful folks with helpful information.

THE AMERICAN RED CROSS OF GREATER MIAMI AND THE FLORIDA KEYS
5450 McDonald Ave., Unit 11, Stock Island
(305) 296-4033
miamiredcross.org
Clara Barton founded the American Red Cross in 1881 and now there are more than 1,300 chapters nationwide. Everyone knows what this humanitarian organization means to any community, near and far. The services rendered on a local basis range from emergency relief to health and safety education and everything in between.

COMMUNITY SUPPORT SERVICES
Upper Keys, (305) 852-7125
Middle Keys, (305) 289-6016
Lower Keys/Key West, (305) 292-4408
Monroe County, which encompasses the Florida Keys, has the highest cost of living of any county in the state of Florida. Yet no adjustment is made in eligibility requirements for aid for senior citizens, who are usually managing on fixed incomes. This county agency works with seniors on a case-by-case basis as an interim assistance agency, helping solve unexpected crises that put them at temporary financial risk. The agency also aids seniors in matters of lost checks, robbery, wheelchairs, and walkers, and helps out with short-term medical needs such as prescriptions, eyeglasses, and hearing aids. This help is designed to restore the individuals to self-sufficient status or to refer them to the appropriate state or federal agencies for more long-term support. Documentation of need is required to qualify for assistance.

MONROE COUNTY EXTENSION SERVICES
1100 Simonton St., #2-260, Key West
(305) 292-4501
ifas.ufl.edu
Monroe County Extension Services, in partnership with the University of Florida, has been empowering citizens since 1987. This enormously beneficial agency creates an objective of educating the folks in their community on a variety of topics, including agriculture, the environment, lawn and garden, relationship to ocean waters, 4-H programs, and hurricane preparedness.

Close-up

Mix It Up

BINGO

The Florida Keys is not all about fishing and sunsets. If you enjoy bingo, check out the game at the **801 Club** (801 Duval, 305-293-9644) or at **La-Te-Da** (1125 Duval, 305-296-6706). Neither has a cover, and all proceeds go to charity. Bingo can also be played at the **Key West Senior Center** (305-295-5165) and at **Sons of Italy at the American Legion** (305-294-7374).

DANCING

If you like salsa, swing, or ballroom, you can dance your way up and down the Keys: **Paradise Health and Fitness in Key West,** (305) 294-4120; **Big Pine Senior Center,** (305) 872-3990; **Marathon Community Theatre** (Tropical Tappers meet for classes), (305) 743-3346; and **Theo and Ganies Dance Center** in Marathon (for training like a pro), (305) 743-0660.

WALKING

For information on the **Key Largo Hammock** nature walks, call (305) 451-1202.

QUILTING

For information on the **Quilter's Club,** call the chamber of commerce number for Key Largo, Big Pine, or Key West.

BOCCE

Bocce is a game of Italian origin similar to lawn bowling. The sport is played at **Indigenous Park,** and the season begins in October. Call (305) 297-3595 for information.

PHOTOGRAPHY

Make that a Kodak moment and join the **Upper Keys Photography Club.** The club meets monthly, with all levels of expertise welcomed. Call (305) 852-4533.

BIKING

Bike paths are plentiful in the lower Keys. Try the one at MM 17, Sugarloaf Road. You can park at the Sugarloaf Lodge, across US 1. The round-trip is approximately 15 miles. MM 19.5 on Sugarloaf Key takes you on Crane Boulevard to the bay. MM 27.8, Middle Torch and Big Torch, is just off US 1. Park on Middle Torch Road. The scenic trip is about 15.5 miles.

MONROE COUNTY IN-HOME SERVICES
Key West
(305) 292-4583
monroecounty-fl.gov
Monroe County In-Home Services networks information and referrals between the private and public sectors for family members, friends, and agencies seeking services on behalf of impaired elderly persons. The program is designed so the elderly may maintain quality of life while remaining in their homes. Participants must be at

least age 60. The information and referral telephone line is staffed by case managers from 8 a.m. to 5 p.m., Mon through Fri. They will specifically target the needed assistance and refer the caller to the resources available. Case management provides a social worker to support and help those requiring assistance.

Chore services are available for impaired seniors who can no longer accomplish the tasks themselves. These services include yard work, heavy-duty cleaning services, and small minor household repairs. Homemaking support with light housekeeping, meal planning and preparation, shopping, laundry tasks, and other essential errands assist clients in need. In-home respite aids are available to help with bathing, dressing, and other personal-care needs, providing relief for caregivers. A fee schedule assessment based on the client's income determines the cost, if any, of these services.

MONROE COUNTY SOCIAL SERVICES
monroecounty-fl.gov

The Florida Keys offers senior citizens a wide range of services through the Monroe County Social Services Agency, whose main administrative offices are in Key West. We also have listed the branch office locations in the Keys and the contact numbers of each department in the individual descriptions below. Note that services in the Middle Keys also include Big Pine Key, which ordinarily is included with the Lower Keys throughout this book. The rest of the Lower Keys are handled from the offices in Key West. Alternately, you can call the Elder Helpline

(800-273-2044) and describe your problem or need; you will be referred to the proper agency.

Monroe County Social Services office locations include: in the Upper Keys, Plantation Key Government Center Annex, MM 88.8 Bayside, Tavernier; in the Middle Keys, Marathon Government Annex, MM 50.5 Oceanside, 490 63rd St., Ste. 190, Marathon; and, in the Lower Keys, Public Service Building, Wing III, 5100 College Rd., Key West.

i Bet you didn't know . . . The official Florida state symbols are: the cracker horse (brought here 500 years ago by Spanish explorer Ponce de León), the loggerhead turtle, the alligator, the panther, the manatee, the mockingbird, the orange (and its juice), and last and the tastiest—key lime pie!

VETERANS AFFAIRS
88820 Overseas Hwy., Tavernier
(305) 453-8777
va.gov

This office is a liaison between veterans and the Veterans Administration, providing services for more than 21,000 vets in Monroe County. This office helps in locating education benefits, outpatient and hospitalization needs, insurance claims, Social Security appeals, transportation to the Miami VA, and other services. A second and third location are at 490 63rd St. in Marathon (305-289-6009) and 1200 Truman Ave. in Key West (305-295-5150).

HEALTH CARE

We have included information on health-care options, ranging from full-service hospitals and specialty care providers for patients in need of cancer or dialysis treatments to physical therapy clinics and mental health services. And don't miss the information on veterinary options. We care about Spot and Fluffy, too!

Please be reminded, however, that this is not intended to be a comprehensive listing of all possible health services. The Florida Keys and Key West are served by physicians in nearly every specialty as well as by osteopaths, chiropractors, podiatrists, dentists, and optometrists. So if, while visiting our islands, you should develop a sudden toothache from downing one too many frozen coladas or drop a contact lens somewhere in the sand, don't despair. One of our many health-care providers will be available to help you, even on short notice. Ask your hotel concierge for a referral to the appropriate specialist or consult the Yellow Pages.

And should your situation call for medical expertise that is not available in the Florida Keys, rest assured that you will still be able to receive state-of-the-art treatment in a timely manner. The University of Miami's renowned Jackson Memorial Medical Center as well as other mainland hospitals and trauma facilities are just a helicopter ride away.

OVERVIEW

This chapter lists health-care options by category in alphabetical order by location from the Upper Keys down to Key West.

ACUTE-CARE CENTERS

Upper Keys

THE GOOD HEALTH CLINIC
MM 91.5 Oceanside, Tavernier
(305) 853-1788
thegoodhealthclinic.org
This Upper Keys clinic opened for the specialized and primary care of the uninsured population. The facility offers X-rays, general orthopedic surgery, and the services of doctors in Miami who specialize in hematology, oncology, back surgery, ophthalmology, and more. Local doctors associated with the clinic include dermatologists, mental health practitioners, pediatricians, and optometrists.

✳MARINERS HOSPITAL
MM 91.5 Bayside, Tavernier
(305) 434-3000
baptisthealth.net
Mariners Hospital, established as a nine-bed physicians' clinic in 1959, today is a state-of-the-art hospital facility. Among the services provided here are 24-hour emergency care, surgery (including outpatient), respiratory therapy, pulmonary rehabilitation, cardiac rehabilitation, and radiology (including MRI,

CT scans, and mammography). Mariners maintains a sleep diagnostic center, laboratory, and pharmacy and has a hyperbaric, or decompression, chamber. The hospital has a helicopter pad for transfer of severe cases to mainland hospitals.

Mariners Hospital is a part of Baptist Health South Florida, a nonprofit health-care organization. Mariners also maintains and operates a state-of-the-art physical therapy center in a separate location at MM 100.3 Bayside, Key Largo, (305) 451-4398.

SELECT PHYSICAL THERAPY
MM 100 Bayside, Key Largo
(305) 453-0409
novacare.com
Select Physical Therapy maintains a network of therapists throughout the Florida Keys, specializing in physical, speech, and occupational therapy. Some locations also offer orthopedist, family physician, and internist referrals. A location in Key West is at 3156 Northside Dr., (305) 292-1805.

Middle Keys

FISHERMEN'S HOSPITAL
MM 48.7 Oceanside, Marathon
(305) 743-5533
fishermenshospital.com
The medical staff at Fishermen's Hospital offer care in the areas of cardiology, cardiac rehabilitation, family practice, general surgery, gynecology, oncology, internal medicine, neurology, pathology, radiology, rheumatology, and plastic/reconstructive surgery. A CT scanner, known as a helical scanner, provides three-dimensional images with extraordinary clarity. Emergency service and same-day surgery also are available.

A helicopter pad allows for emergency chopper services, and a hyperbaric emergency response team is on call for divers. Fishermen's Overnight Guest program provides testing and pre-surgery (the night prior to surgery) room and board. Also licensed to provide home health care, Fishermen's accepts most forms of insurance. Other hospital resources include a certified diabetes educator and nutritional support services. Fishermen's Hospital also offers physical therapy services at two separate locations: at MM 54, on Marathon Key, and at the Big Pine Key Plaza at MM 29.7. For information on either of these physical therapy centers, phone (305) 289-9950. This hospital is a for-profit organization.

Lower Keys

BIG PINE MEDICAL AND MINOR EMERGENCY CENTER
MM 30 Oceanside, Big Pine Key
(305) 872-3321
This emergency-care center, conveniently located on Big Pine Key, treats minor illnesses and emergencies (broken bones, cuts, insect bites, and so on). Although appointments are encouraged, walk-ins are welcome. The clinic is generally open Mon through Fri from 8 a.m. to 5 p.m. and some Sat mornings. However, hours may vary with the season and patient demand, so it is best to phone ahead.

Key West

BODY OWNERS
5450 MacDonald Ave., Stock Island
(305) 294-8866
keywestphysicaltherapy.com
The knowledgeable staff and compassionate care make this physical therapy and wellness center a popular one with patients and physicians. Everyone goes out of their way

to make sure your therapy sessions are comfortable and informative. They offer sessions for children with special needs as well.

KEY WEST URGENT CARE
1503 Government Rd. (corner of Flagler Avenue and Seventh Street)
(305) 295-7550
keywesturgentcare.com
Not feeling so hot? Need to see a doctor in a hurry? This is the place to go, no appointment necessary. Treatment for minor illnesses and injuries is available Mon through Fri, from 8 a.m. to 3 p.m., and credit cards are accepted. Some local insurance plans may also be accepted.

LOWER FLORIDA KEYS HEALTH SYSTEM
5900 Junior College Rd., Stock Island
(305) 294-5531
lkmc.com
This accredited primary-care facility is the only hospital in the Florida Keys to offer maternity services. Lower Florida Keys Health System maintains 169 beds, a 24-hour emergency room, a clinical lab, and a heliport. Added services include pediatrics, inpatient and outpatient psychotherapy, physical therapy, radiation therapy, chemotherapy, and cardiovascular and ambulatory care. The hospital offers substance-abuse assistance and comprehensive wellness programs.

MARTA A. GONZALEZ CANCER CENTER
3426 N. Roosevelt Blvd.
(305) 296-0021
21stcenturyoncology.com
This health-care treatment center provides a full spectrum of radiation therapy services to cancer patients. The center offers conventional external beam treatments and advanced services such as prostate seed implants, 3-D conformed treatment planning, intensity modulated radiation, and image-guided radiotherapy.

TRUMAN MEDICAL CENTER
540 Truman Ave.
(305) 296-4399
Truman Medical Center makes no appointments but is open 7 days a week. This walk-in clinic will see patients from 9 a.m. to 4:30 p.m. Mon through Fri, 9:30 a.m. to noon on Sat, and noon to 2 p.m. on Sun.

MOBILE MEDICAL CARE

RURAL HEALTH NETWORK OF MONROE COUNTY
Key West and Lower Keys, (305) 292-6422

Marathon and Middle Keys, (305) 289-8915

Tavernier and Upper Keys, (305) 735-4218
rhnmc.org
The Rural Health Network was established to provide primary medical care and dental services to the uninsured and underinsured residents of and visitors to Monroe County. Two fully equipped RVs travel up and down the Keys to provide medical services to folks who are uninsured and might not otherwise seek primary-care treatment. A combined effort of the Monroe County Health Department, the three Keys hospitals, the Health Foundation of South Florida, Catholic Charities of the Archdiocese of Miami, HUD, FEMA, HRSA, and the Florida Keys Area Health Education Center in conjunction with the University of Miami, this mobile medical service covers Key Largo to Key West.

The vans are equipped like doctors' offices. Each has two small examination rooms and a cab that doubles as a triage area, and is staffed by a registered nurse, a nurse practitioner, and a health educator, as well as nursing and medical students. Patients needing care beyond the scope of the Medi-Van staff may be referred to specialists and area hospitals. Appointments are available and walk-ins are welcome. The Medi-Vans charge a co-pay for their services.

HOME HEALTH SERVICES

HOSPICE OF THE FLORIDA KEYS/
VISITING NURSE ASSOCIATION
MM 92 Oceanside, Tavernier
(305) 852-7887
hospicevna.com
Hospice provides care for terminally ill patients with six months or less to live. Services are provided in private homes and nursing homes throughout the Keys by a staff of registered nurses, patient-care managers, and social workers. Certified nursing assistants tend to personal needs such as bathing, grooming, and bedding. All home-care patients must be referred to the agency by a physician. Comfort Care, which is private-duty nursing care, is also available. Hospice's purpose is to ensure patients' comfort so that the last days of their lives are quality ones.

Within this same nonprofit organization, the Visiting Nurse Association (VNA) provides more aggressive home care for patients still undergoing various treatments or who need blood tests or care for wounds. This service also is provided upon a physician's request. Both Hospice and VNA are on call 24 hours a day, 7 days a week. Medicare and Medicaid are accepted. Additional Hospice locations are at MM 50.5 Oceanside in Marathon (305-743-9048) and 1319 William St. in Key West (305-294-8812).

LIFELINE HOME HEALTH CARE
MM 53 Oceanside, Marathon
(305) 743-9817
lhcgroup.com
As the name implies, Lifeline Home Health Care provides registered nurses, home health aids, physical therapists, rehabilitation, and hospice. An RN is on call 24/7 through their call center. Lifeline Home Health Care also installs personal response (lifeline) devices. Medicare and private insurances are accepted for their services.

MEDICAL/HOSPITAL EQUIPMENT

CORAL MEDICAL HOME EQUIPMENT
MM 88 Oceanside, Islamorada
(305) 852-4393
coralmedical.com
This long-established Keys business gives customers first-rate delivery of their medical equipment needs, including 24-hour emergency service, home IV provisions, respiratory and oxygen supplies, and the usual variety of crutches, walkers, and various medical apparatuses.

ALTERNATIVE HEALTH CARE

Many of the people who reside full-time in the Florida Keys are laid-back types who were drawn to our islands by a desire to pursue a less-than-conventional lifestyle. In many cases their approach to health care is as nontraditional as their approach to life.

The Florida Keys, and Key West in particular, boast a wealth of options in the alternative health-care category. These

---

Emergency Numbers

While we sincerely hope you won't ever need to use the following telephone numbers, it is a good idea to keep this information in a convenient place.

Police, Fire, or Rescue	911
Florida Poison Information Center	(800) 282-3171
US Coast Guard Marine and Air Emergency	(305) 295-9700 or
	CG/VH channel 16
Florida Marine Patrol of the FWCC	*FMP or (800) DIAL FMP
Florida Highway Patrol	*FHP or (800) 240-0453
Monroe County Emergency Management	(305) 289-6018
Hurricane Preparedness	(800) 427-8340
Emergency Information Hotline	(800) 955-5504

---

include everything from yoga classes and massage therapy on the beach to acupuncture, homeopathic medicine, organic foods, and herbal remedies. For a complete list of alternative health-care options and practitioners throughout the Florida Keys, consult the local Yellow Pages under the following categories: Acupuncture, Health Clubs, Health and Diet Food Products, and Massage Therapists.

ISLAND DOLPHIN CARE
150 Lorelane Place, Key Largo
(305) 451-5884
islanddolphincare.org
Island Dolphin Care specializes in working with special-needs children interacting with dolphins. This not-for-profit facility provides assisted therapy to children with critical illnesses, disabilities, and special needs who come from all over the world.

VETERINARY SERVICES

Your four-legged friends and "family" sometimes need health care, too. These pet clinics cater to their needs from the top of the Keys to Key West.

Upper Keys

ANIMAL CARE CLINIC
MM 100.6 Bayside, Key Largo
(305) 453-0044
animalcareclinickeylargo.com
Boarding and grooming are small parts of the operation at Animal Care Clinic. The clinic maintains oxygen-intensive critical-care units and offers surgery, lab testing, X-rays, EKG, and ultrasound dentistry, as well as emergency on-call service, 24 hours a day, 7 days a week.

Middle Keys

*KEYS ANIMAL HOSPITAL
MM 52.5 Bayside, Marathon
(305) 743-6250
keysanimalhospital.com
This veterinary hospital has been serving Marathon since 1974. They offer 24-hour emergency service and air-conditioned boarding facilities for your pets, along with separate areas for cats, small dogs, and large dogs.

*MARATHON VETERINARY HOSPITAL
MM 52.5 Oceanside, Marathon
(305) 743-7099 or (800) 832-7694
marathonvet.com
Marathon Veterinary Hospital offers full services, including 24-hour emergency care, for dogs, cats, and all exotics. You do not have to be a client to be seen for an emergency.

Lower Keys

CRUZ ANIMAL HOSPITAL
MM 27 Bayside, Ramrod Key
(305) 872-2559
cruzanimalhospital.com
Cruz Animal Hospital offers a variety of medical services for virtually all pets, plus 24-hour emergency service. Military and senior citizen discounts are available.

DOC SYN'S VETERINARY CARE
MM 22.7 Bayside, Cudjoe Key
(305) 744-0074
keysveterinary-docsynsvetcare.com
At Doc Syn's the motto is, "We treat your pets as if they were our own." The facility offers complete medical and surgical care for dogs, cats, birds, ferrets, and reptiles. Evening hours are available.

Key West

ISLAND PAWS OF KEY WEST
(305) 859-0005
islandpawshousecalls.com
Island Paws of Key West will make the trek to you and your pet as they make veterinary house calls in the lower Keys.

Real Playboy Bunnies

Sylvilagus palustres hefneri is not the name of a *Playboy* centerfold, but it is the name of a marsh rabbit found on Big Pine Key in 1980. Hugh Hefner, founder and editor of *Playboy* magazine, funded a study that identified the species as endangered. In 2007 feral cats were killing the marsh rabbits, and Hef once again stepped in and donated funds to Stand Up For Animals to capture the cats and to ensure they would not be euthanized.

---

*LOWER KEYS ANIMAL CLINIC
1456 Kennedy Dr., Key West
(305) 294-6335
This facility treats small exotics but mostly sees cats and dogs. The staff offers regular checkups, surgery, dentistry, vaccinations, X-rays, and general medical treatment for pets.

EDUCATION & CHILD CARE

The Florida Keys and Key West are served by public and private schools, preschools, and a community college. Thanks to a visiting institute and college degree programs at the Boca Chica Naval Air Station in the Lower Keys, students can earn bachelor's, master's, and even doctoral degrees without ever leaving our islands. In addition, several institutions of higher education in Miami are within commuting distance. Also included in this chapter is a comprehensive look at the child-care scene in the Florida Keys and Key West. We explore traditional child-care services along with other handy (sometimes vacation-saving) options such as drop-in care, babysitting, sick-child and respite care, family child-care homes, and public after-school programs.

EDUCATION

Public Schools

The Monroe County School District oversees schools from Key Largo to Key West, including three high schools. Some elementary and middle schools within our county occupy the same building; other facilities are shared by middle and high schools. Stretching more than 100 miles, traversing 42 bridges, with more than 8,000 students attending 17 schools and centers in its jurisdiction, the Florida Keys is a unique and stimulating classroom setting.

The school system operates on a school year that runs from late Aug through early June. An elected board headed by an elected superintendent, who oversees five district representatives, governs our public schools. Board members serve four-year terms. School funding comes from Monroe County property taxes. For more information on Monroe County Public Schools, go to monroe.k12.fl.us.

Charter School
BIG PINE ACADEMY
MM 30.2 Oceanside, Big Pine Key
(305) 872-1266
bigpineacademy.com
This small charter school on Big Pine Key is for preschool through seventh grade. Their curriculum is designed to ensure a safe and nurturing school environment teaching basic skills that enrich and challenge children's lives and prepare them for their next grade levels.

ⓘ Promenade down to 1302 White St. in Key West to gaze at the front of the Glynn Archer Elementary School. Before you stands a beautiful explosion of flowers. In 2007 a group of citizens led by the Tropia Butterfly Foundation created this garden to attract more butterflies to our tiny island, embellishing public spaces with color and piquing the interest of schoolchildren.

EDUCATION & CHILD CARE

Private Schools

Private schools typically offer smaller student-teacher ratios and a variety of learning curricula. The following list includes private schools operating in the Florida Keys and Key West.

GRACE LUTHERAN SCHOOL
2713 Flagler Ave., Key West
(305) 296-8262
gracekw.ctsmemberconnect.net
Established in 1952 and designed for pre-kindergarten through eighth-graders, Grace Lutheran offers computers and teaches Spanish in all but pre-kindergarten classes. During "God Time," students learn about Christian ideals and how to live them.

ISLAND CHRISTIAN SCHOOL
MM 83.4 Bayside, Islamorada
(305) 664-2781
islandchristian.org
Established in 1974 by a group of parents from Island Community Church, Island Christian began with 54 students. As grade levels were added and the school became accredited, enrollment increased to 300. Island Christian today teaches pre-kindergarten through high school students in a traditional college-preparatory curriculum that incorporates the Abeka and Bob Jones Christian teachings. The school offers a full interscholastic sports program to junior and senior high school students.

KEY WEST MONTESSORI CHARTER SCHOOL
1400 United St., Key West
(305) 294-4910
keywestmontessori.com
The Key West Montessori Charter School is a nonprofit, public school teaching children in kindergarten through middle school. The school utilizes the work of Maria Montessori, who developed a method of educating children focusing on the child as the foundation for learning.

MARATHON LUTHERAN SCHOOL
MM 53.3 Bayside, 325 122nd St., Marathon
(305) 289-0700
lutheransonline.com/mlc2
A service of Martin Luther Chapel and the Lutheran Church Missouri Synod, a national Lutheran organization, Marathon Lutheran School provides education from kindergarten through sixth grade. Using the School of Tomorrow PACE program, Marathon Lutheran offers its students the opportunity to learn at their own speeds with several class levels combined. Established in 1987, the school requires students to attend weekly chapel service and take religion classes.

I Spy . . .

In 2004 two students doing a moth survey in the Key West Tropical Forest & Botanical Gardens (see the Attractions chapter) looked up in an Arjuna almond tree, *Terminalia arjuna,* the only one of its kind in the garden, and discovered a *Phyllops falcatus,* better known as the Cuban fig-eating bat or white-shouldered bat. This was an exciting discovery because these bats have only been known to exist in Cuba, Hispaniola, and on Grand Cayman. The appearance of the Cuban fig-eating bat is the first recorded in Florida and the first in the US.

MARY IMMACULATE STAR OF THE SEA
700 Truman Ave., Key West
(305) 294-1031
keywestcatholicparish.org

Mary Immaculate follows a pre-kindergarten through eighth-grade curriculum outlined by the Archdiocese of Miami, including religious instruction. The school's mission is to provide opportunities for all Lower Keys families to experience a Catholic education. Within a Christian environment, the instructors foster spiritual, academic, and social development.

MONTESSORI ISLAND SCHOOL
MM 92 Oceanside, Tavernier
(305) 852-3438

Montessori Island School offers guidance for infants and toddlers up to pre-kindergarten in a natural setting. There is no air-conditioning in the building, and the use of natural light brings the environment closer to the classroom.

TREASURE VILLAGE MONTESSORI SCHOOL
MM 86.7 Oceanside, Islamorada
(305) 852-3482
treasurevillagemontessori.com

Montessori schools across the country work on the principle of self-pacing for children. This Montessori school, established in 1996, works on the same idea of purposeful action. The school provides education for preschool through eighth grade with Montessori-certified teachers.

Additional Educational Opportunities

Residents and visitors to the Florida Keys may participate in a number of hands-on educational opportunities, such as those listed below.

MARINELAB, MARINE RESOURCES DEVELOPMENT FOUNDATION
51 Shoreland Dr., Key Largo
(305) 451-1139 or (800) 741-1139
mrdf.org

Since 1972 the nonprofit Marine Resources Development Foundation (MRDF) has offered students an in-depth introduction to the ecology of the Keys. The MRDF provides customized programs for students, who learn about sea life in the Emerald Lagoon or explore the MarineLab Undersea Laboratory. Customized programs also include scuba certification, coral reef ecology, mangrove ecology, and a trip to the Everglades.

SEACAMP
1300 Big Pine Ave., Big Pine Key
(305) 872-2331 or (877) 732-2267
seacamp.org

This scuba and marine science camp for children ages 12 through 17 has been in Big Pine Key since 1966. Children from across the world sign up for Seacamp's 18-day program to experience scuba diving, sailing, snorkeling, and sailboarding. Marine science classes teach about such subjects as exploring the seas, animal behavior, and Keys critters. Scuba certification is available.

Higher Education

FLORIDA KEYS COMMUNITY COLLEGE
5901 W. College Rd., Key West
(305) 296-9081
fkcc.edu

When Florida Keys Community College (FKCC) began operation in the fall of 1965, it became the first institution of higher education in the Florida Keys. Today FKCC offers associate of science and associate of arts degree programs in such fields as business administration, computer programming and analysis, nursing, multimedia technology, and marine environmental technology.

FKCC's performing and visual arts programs are enhanced by the college's Tennessee Williams Fine Arts Center (see the Arts & Culture chapter). Its marine environmental technology and dive programs are especially popular. In addition to its main campus on Stock Island, Florida Keys Community College also offers a limited number of classes at two other Keys locations: the Middle Keys Center at 900 Sombrero Beach Rd., MM 50, Marathon, (305) 743-2133; and the Upper Keys Center at MM 89.9, Tavernier, (305) 852-8007.

SAINT LEO COLLEGE–KEY WEST CENTER
Boca Chica Naval Air Station, Key West
(305) 293-2847
saintleo.edu
Saint Leo College offers the only regionally accredited bachelor's degree program in the Florida Keys. Located in Key West since 1975, Saint Leo is a private college that offers associate of arts and bachelor of arts degrees in business administration, criminology, human services, and/or human resource administration. Situated at the naval air station, Saint Leo College is open to all civilian and military personnel and their families in the Florida Keys. Classes are designed for the working adult.

LIBRARIES

MONROE COUNTY PUBLIC LIBRARY
Key Largo, MM 101.4 Oceanside, (305) 451-2396

Islamorada, MM 81.5 Bayside, (305) 664-4645

Marathon, MM 48.5 Oceanside, (305) 743-5156

Big Pine, MM 31 Bayside, (305) 289-6303
Key West, 700 Fleming St., (305) 292-3595
keyslibraries.org
Each library offers a free paperback exchange and ongoing book sale, with most titles less than $5. The libraries host numerous kid-friendly events and readings throughout the year. Call ahead or check the website for specifics.

CHILD CARE

The problem of finding good, competent child care is compounded here by a shortage of available providers at any cost. According to the National Association for the Education of Young Children, child care is the fourth-largest item in the family budget after food, housing, and taxes. Infant care (birth to age 1) and weekend and evening care are in particularly short supply in Monroe County, which encompasses the Keys. Day-to-day child care in the county generally falls into two categories: center-based care and family child-care homes. In this section we provide information on types of childcare programs and contacts for centers that serve the Florida Keys and Key West.

Resources

WESLEY HOUSE FAMILY SERVICES COORDINATING AGENCY
1304 Truman Ave., Key West
(305) 809-5000
wesleyhouse.org
With offices in Key West and serving all of the Florida Keys, Wesley House assists families in making the best of a difficult situation. (Wesley House is a national division agency of the United Methodist Church and a United Way of Monroe County agency.) The Wesley House

Resource & Referral Network (WHR&RN) is perhaps the most important resource in the Keys for parents looking for appropriate, quality child care. WHR&RN acts as a link between families and the child-care services they seek. It can recommend affordable child care for children up to 5 years old and after-school and summer care for children up to 12 years old. Families may access services at three locations in the Florida Keys: 175 Wrenn St., Tavernier, (305) 853-3518; 2796 Overseas Highway, Marathon, (305) 289-2675; and 1304 Truman Ave., Key West, (305) 809-5000.

WHR&RN offers other assistance in the forms of subsidized child care, scholarships, and help in obtaining legal aid, medical aid, food stamps, and other services. The network conducts classes for parents in money management, parenting skills, nutrition, and handling everyday pressures. It provides personal help for families with at-risk children, assisting them in filling out paperwork to meet eligibility requirements. Wesley House also offers transportation to and from child-care centers for children in at-risk situations. It will also provide referrals for families needing sick care or in-home nursing specialists. Some child-care centers offer drop-in care.

Baby Chicks Rental

It's hard to travel on a plane (or in a car, for that matter) and bring along cribs, strollers, high chairs, and all the gear for the little one. By calling the owner of this come-to-your-door baby equipment rental business, you can travel with just your luggage and baby! Call (305) 879-3340 or visit babychicksrental.com for more information.

Types of Programs

This section describes the center- and home-based child-care options available to parents in Monroe County.

Child-Care/Preschool Centers

The minimum state licensing requirements dictate that a child-care center must hold a valid license from the Health and Rehabilitative Services (HRS) Department of the State of Florida. The license must be posted in a conspicuous place within the center.

The center must adhere to the number of children for which it is licensed, and it must maintain the minimum staff-to-child ratio for each age level: younger than age 1, 1 teacher for every 4 children; age 1, 1 to 6; age 2, 1 to 11; age 3, 1 to 15; age 4, 1 to 20; and age 5, 1 to 25. We stress that this is the minimum ratio, which may not be sufficient to give your child the level of care you desire.

Licensing standards mandate health and safety requirements and staff training requirements. These include child abuse and neglect training, a 20-hour child-care training course, a 10-hour specialized training module, and 8 hours of in-service training annually. In addition, there must be one CPR- and first-aid-certified person on-site during business hours. Some centers are prepared to accept infants; others are not.

Some child-care centers are exempt from HRS licensing. They are accredited and monitored by religious agencies, the school board, or the military. Contact Wesley House (see listing under Resources) for a list of HRS-licensed and license-exempt child-care/preschool centers in the Florida Keys and Key West. Unfortunately, no child-care centers are open weekends or evenings in the Keys.

Aquarius Install Project

In June 2011 Teens4Oceans brought a 20-person group—composed of student representatives, parents, and dive instructors—down to Key Largo, Florida, to complete the Aquarius Install Project, installing cameras on the Aquarius Reef Base. Teens4Oceans uses these cameras as lenses into the ocean, allowing them to produce unique educational materials for students of all ages and empowering students and teens to be good stewards of the oceans through science, research, and philanthropy. Visit teens4oceans.org for more information.

Family Child-Care Homes

Family child-care is considered by the State of Florida to encompass home-based child care with five or fewer preschool-age children from more than one family unrelated to the caregiver. Any preschool children living in the home must be included in the maximum number of children allowed. The adult who provides the child care is usually referred to as a family child-care home operator.

Some counties in Florida require that family child-care homes be licensed. Monroe Country, which includes the Florida Keys, requires only registration with the Department of Health and Rehabilitative Services. Every adult in the household must be screened. Registration requires no on-site inspection of the home for minimum health, safety, and sanitation standards, however. Nor is there a requirement that the family child-care operator have CPR or first-aid training.

Military programs are exempt from this registration. They have their own accreditation procedures and are available only to family members of military personnel.

Wesley House offers and actively recruits for a 3-hour course covering basic health and safety issues to persons who wish to operate registered family child-care homes.

Public After-School Programs

Many public schools in the Florida Keys and Key West run their own after-hours programs for school-age children from 2:15 to 5:30 p.m. and also on school holidays and summer weekdays. Most schools charge for this service.

Contacts at the schools are: Key Largo Elementary School, MM 104.8, Key Largo, (305) 453-1255; Plantation Key School, 100 Lake Rd., Tavernier, (305) 853-3281; Switlik Elementary, MM 48.8 Bayside, 33rd St., Marathon, (305) 289-2490; Big Pine Key Neighborhood School, Palomino Horse Trail, Big Pine Key, (305) 872-1266; Sugarloaf Elementary/Middle School, 255 Crane Road, Sugarloaf Key, (305) 745-3282; Poinciana Elementary School, 1407 Kennedy Dr., Key West, (305) 293-1630; Sigsbee Elementary, Sigsbee Naval Base, Key West, (305) 294-1861 (military families only); Gerald Adams Elementary School, 5855 W. Junior College Rd., Key West, (305) 293-1609.

Babysitting

Personal knowledge of the person you choose to care for your child in your absence is the best of all possible worlds, but it isn't always a reality. If you are a visitor to the Florida Keys or a newly relocated resident, you may have to take a leap of faith and entrust your child to someone you do not know. Therefore, you should check references. For referrals, contact Wesley House (see listing under Resources) or ask the concierge at your hotel.

You can also contact local chambers of commerce, which often keep lists of local residents who babysit: Key Largo, (305) 451-1414 or (800) 822-1088; Islamorada, (305) 664-4503 or (800) 322-5397; Marathon, (305) 743-5417 or (800) 262-7284; Lower Keys, (305) 872-2411 or (800) 872-3722; and Key West, (305) 294-2587 or (800) 527-8539. Be sure to ask by what criteria these referrals have been checked for more insight as to who may best suit your needs.

MEDIA

Even after Henry Flagler's extension of the Florida East Coast Railroad provided Florida Keys residents access to the mainland, communications on our islands were limited. To receive local news and news outside the South Florida area, residents relied on radio broadcasts from Miami, sporadic postal service, and what was probably their most effective and timely means of dispatch: word of mouth, or what is jokingly referred to as "the Conch telegraph."

Today two dailies and a contingent of weeklies and free papers tie the Keys together. Both AM and FM radio stations are still restricted by wattage, and residents must subscribe to satellite or cable service to get television reception.

NEWSPAPERS

In addition to home delivery, our newspapers are often sold in curbside vending racks, grocery stores, pharmacies, convenience stores, and bookstores. A handful of shops carry national and international newspapers. Because the Florida Keys are considered a remote distribution site, some national newspapers, such as the *New York Times*, are sold at a higher newsstand price. A rule of thumb: Get to the newsstand early. The farther you travel from the mainland, the more quickly the out-of-town papers sell out.

Dailies

KEY WEST CITIZEN
3420 Northside Dr., Key West
(305) 292-7777
keysnews.com
In 1904 a small weekly newspaper known as the *Citizen* appeared on the newspaper scene in Key West; it was later consolidated with the 1899 *Inter-Ocean* to form the *Key West Citizen*. Cooke Communications now owns the *Key West Citizen*, along with weekly *Solares Hill* (now published in the Sunday edition of the *Citizen*), the *Free Press* community newspapers, and the Florida Keys News Service.

The *Citizen*'s editorial focus is primarily on features. *Paradise,* which appears in Thursday's edition, is a comprehensive compendium of what's currently happening in the theaters and at the clubs and galleries around town. Free copies of *Paradise* are available at newsstands, hotels, guesthouses, restaurants, and other businesses throughout Key West. The *Citizen* also publishes "The Menu," a free quarterly guide containing menus from many area restaurants.

THE MIAMI HERALD
1 Herald Plaza, Miami
(305) 350-2111 or (800) 437-2535
miamiherald.com
The largest-circulation daily newspaper in the southeastern US, this Pulitzer Prize

winner has maintained Key West correspondents for decades and now has a bureau in the southernmost city. The *Miami Herald* features crisp writing and tends to favor features over hard news, except when issues are pressing. The *Herald* is widely available throughout the Keys. The Key West location is at 619 Eaton St. (305-294-5131).

> **i** Prior to 1917 the Florida Keys were a much more peaceful place. It was in that year that the first long-distance phone connection linked the Keys to Miami.

Weeklies & Biweeklies

CONCH COLOR
314 Simonton St., Key West
(305) 294-7566
conchcolor.com
Publisher and editor Tom Oosterhoudt's *Conch Color* showcases the exciting and entertaining life in the Keys. Tom is everywhere and is invited to everything that is anything. He has taken this lifestyle and turned it into a fun and colorful photographic chronicle. This is the Keys version of *People* magazine. The paper is published weekly, covers Marathon to Key West, is free, and can be picked up at most commercial locations.

FLORIDA KEYS KEYNOTER
MM 48.6 Oceanside, Marathon
(305) 743-5551

KEY WEST KEYNOTER
2720A N. Roosevelt Blvd., Key West
(305) 296-6989
keysnet.com
The *Florida Keys Keynoter* is owned by the McClatchy Company and is considered

the *Miami Herald*'s sister newspaper. The *Keynoter* is Monroe County's second-oldest publication. With a weekly television news program and a separate Key West edition, the twice-weekly *Keynoter* offers comprehensive local coverage of the Florida Keys. Known for its in-depth coverage of the Keys' political scene, once a week the *Keynoter* also features "L' Attitudes," an arts and entertainment section that includes complete television listings for the area, special features, and upcoming Keys events. The *Keynoter* is published each Wed and Sat and is widely available in shops, newsstands, and curbside racks throughout the Keys.

THE REPORTER
MM 91.6 Oceanside, Tavernier
(305) 852-3216
keysnet.com
When the *Reporter* began in the early 1900s, the newspaper, which was based in Key Largo, was mimeographed. As the publication grew, its owners bought what was at the time a top-of-the-line printing press—a monumental event in Keys publishing, since few newspapers were actually printed in this stretch of Monroe County. *The Reporter* is published by the McClatchy Company, which also publishes the *Miami Herald* and the *Florida Keys Keynoter*. Published each Thurs, this weekly packages community news from south Miami-Dade County to Marathon and is available in stores throughout the Upper Keys.

> **i** Handy websites for visitors and locals: general information, fla-keys.com; cities: islamorada.fl.us, keywestcity.com, keycolonybeach.net, and ci.marathon.fl.us.

Hidden Talent

Everyone knows Jimmy Buffett can sing, but did you know he also wrote three books that made the *New York Times* bestseller list? Three of his books were fiction: *Tales from Margaritaville, Where is Joe Merchant?,* and *Swine Not.* His nonfiction book is titled *A Pirate Looks at Fifty.* Buffett is one of only six authors in the list's history to have number-one titles in both fiction and nonfiction. The others were Ernest Hemingway, Dr. Seuss, Mitch Albom, William Styron, and John Steinbeck. Wanna bet those five couldn't sing?

SOLARES HILL
3420 Northside Dr., Key West
(305) 294-3602
keysnews.com

Founded in 1971, the free weekly *Solares Hill* ceased its independent status in 1998 when it was acquired by the publishers of the *Key West Citizen* and the *Free Press* community newspapers. Although the newspaper's former slogan, "The straight truth plainly stated," has been replaced with the words, "The way a newspaper should be," its focus remains primarily on politics and business, along with a smattering of restaurant, theater, and book reviews. *Solares Hill* is inserted in the Sunday edition of the *Citizen* newspaper.

RADIO

Radio reception in the Florida Keys is heavily influenced by factors such as weather and distance from the transmitter. Clear skies and sunshine will optimize good reception; luckily, we have plenty of both most of the time. Some of our more popular radio stations include:

- **WEOW Today's Hits,** 92.7
- **Key-Z FM,** 93.5
- **Conch Country,** 98.7
- **Sun Classic Rock,** 99.5
- **US-1 Radio,** 104.1
- **Island,** 107.1

TELEVISION

Florida Keys residents must pay for cable television service in order to receive network channels. Our cable provider is Comcast, (866) 288-3444.

In addition to national programming, local-origination programming is offered on channels 5, 24, and 75 through 79. This public service programming includes live coverage of city commission and local political meetings, as well as real estate listings and local-interest shows on a variety of topics such as health care and fishing. Channel 5 also offers interesting and informative infomercials during the day and evening, highlighting many of the Keys attractions found in this book.

Satellite communication is an alternative to cable service. Check the Yellow Pages for companies offering satellite dishes and service.

INDEX

INDEX

INSIDERS' GUIDE®

The acclaimed travel series that has sold more than 2 million copies!

Discover: Your Travel Destination.
Your Home. Your Home-to-Be.

Albuquerque

Anchorage &
   Southcentral
   Alaska

Atlanta

Austin

Baltimore

Baton Rouge

Boulder & Rocky Mountain
   National Park

Branson & the Ozark
   Mountains

California's Wine Country

Cape Cod & the Islands

Charleston

Charlotte

Chicago

Cincinnati

Civil War Sites in
   the Eastern Theater

Civil War Sites in the South

Colorado's Mountains

Dallas & Fort Worth

Denver

El Paso

Florida Keys & Key West

Gettysburg

Glacier National Park

Great Smoky Mountains

Greater Fort Lauderdale

Greater Tampa Bay Area

Hampton Roads

Houston

Hudson River Valley

Indianapolis

Jacksonville

Kansas City

Long Island

Louisville

Madison

Maine Coast

Memphis

Myrtle Beach &
   the Grand Strand

Nashville

New Orleans

New York City

North Carolina's
   Mountains

North Carolina's
   Outer Banks

North Carolina's
   Piedmont Triad

Oklahoma City

Orange County, CA

Oregon Coast

Palm Beach County

Palm Springs

Philadelphia &
   Pennsylvania Dutch
   Country

Phoenix

Portland, Maine

Portland, Oregon

Raleigh, Durham &
   Chapel Hill

Richmond, VA

Reno and Lake Tahoe

St. Louis

San Antonio

Santa Fe

Savannah & Hilton Head

Seattle

Shreveport

South Dakota's
   Black Hills Badlands

Southwest Florida

Tucson

Tulsa

Twin Cities

Washington, D.C.

Williamsburg & Virginia's
   Historic Triangle

Yellowstone
   & Grand Teton

Yosemite

**To order call 800-243-0495
or visit www.Insiders.com**